Objective-C® FOR DUMMIES®

by Neal Goldstein

WILEY

Wiley Publishing, Inc.

Objective-C® For Dummies®

Published by
Wiley Publishing, Inc.
111 River Street
Hoboken, NJ 07030-5774

www.wiley.com

Copyright © 2009 by Wiley Publishing, Inc., Indianapolis, Indiana

Published by Wiley Publishing, Inc., Indianapolis, Indiana

Published simultaneously in Canada

For general information on our other products and services, please contact our Customer Care Department within the U.S. at 877-762-2974, outside the U.S. at 317-572-3993, or fax 317-572-4002.

For technical support, please visit www.wiley.com/techsupport.

Wiley also publishes its books in a variety of electronic formats. Some content that appears in print may not be available in electronic books.

Library of Congress Control Number: 2009935231

ISBN: 978-0-470-52275-2

Manufactured in the United States of America

10 9 8 7 6 5 4 3 2

WILEY

About the Author

Neal Goldstein is a recognized leader in making state-of-the-art and cutting-edge technologies practical for commercial and enterprise development. He was one of the first technologists to work with commercial developers at firms such as Apple Computer, Lucasfilm, and Microsoft to develop commercial applications using object-based programming technologies. He was a pioneer in moving that approach into the corporate world for developers at Liberty Mutual Insurance, USWest (now Verizon), National Car Rental, EDS, and Continental Airlines, showing them how object-oriented programming could solve enterprise-wide problems. His book (with Jeff Alger) on object-oriented development, *Developing Object-Oriented Software for the Macintosh* (Addison Wesley, 1992), introduced the idea of scenarios and patterns to developers. He was an early advocate of the Microsoft .NET framework, and successfully introduced it into many enterprises, including Charles Schwab. He was one of the earliest developers of Service Oriented Architecture (SOA), and as Senior Vice President of Advanced Technology and the Chief Architect at Charles Schwab, he built an integrated SOA solution that spanned the enterprise, from desktop PCs to servers to complex network mainframes. (He holds three patents as a result.) As one of IBM's largest customers, he introduced them to SOA at the enterprise level and encouraged them to head in that direction. He is currently leading an iPhone startup that is developing an application that will radically change how people can use iPhones to manage information.

Dedication

To my brother, Jay, who went above and beyond the call of duty to cover for me in the real world as I wandered around in Objective-C land.

To my children, Sarah and Evan, who help me understand what is really important

But most of all, to my wife Linda. With equanimity and grace she's lived with me through not just one, but two books this year. If there is ever a Nobel Prize for patience, understanding, support, and friendship, she deserves the first one.

Author's Acknowledgments

Carole Jelen, agent extraordinaire, who does an extraordinary job of taking care of business so that I can pay attention to writing.

Acquisitions Editor Kyle Looper whose understanding of programming and the issues involved in learning how to program helped make this a far better book. Project Editor Colleen Totz Diamond took over in mid stream and did an outstanding job of making this book what it is. Copy Editor Melba Hopper kept me focused on making things clear and simple. Technical reviewer Dennis Cohen added a great second pair of eyes.

Publisher's Acknowledgments

We're proud of this book; please send us your comments at http://dummies.custhelp.com. For other comments, please contact our Customer Care Department within the U.S. at 877-762-2974, outside the U.S. at 317-572-3993, or fax 317-572-4002.

Some of the people who helped bring this book to market include the following:

Acquisitions, Editorial, and Media Development

Project Editor: Colleen Totz Diamond

Acquisitions Editor: Kyle Looper

Copy Editor: Melba Hopper

Technical Editor: Dennis R. Cohen

Editorial Manager: Jodi Jensen

Media Development Assistant Project Manager: Jenny Swisher

Media Development Associate Producers: Josh Frank

Editorial Assistant: Amanda Graham

Sr. Editorial Assistant: Cherie Case

Cartoons: Rich Tennant (www.the5thwave.com)

Composition Services

Project Coordinator: Patrick Redmond

Layout and Graphics: Samantha K. Cherolis

Proofreaders: Context Editorial Svcs, John Greenough

Indexer: Valerie Haynes Perry

Special Help:

David A. Diamond, Kelly Ewing

Publishing and Editorial for Technology Dummies

    Richard Swadley, Vice President and Executive Group Publisher

    Andy Cummings, Vice President and Publisher

    Mary Bednarek, Executive Acquisitions Director

    Mary C. Corder, Editorial Director

Publishing for Consumer Dummies

    Diane Graves Steele, Vice President and Publisher

Composition Services

    Debbie Stailey, Director of Composition Services

Contents at a Glance

Table of Contents

Introduction

When the folks at Wiley Publishing approached me about writing *Objective-C For Dummies,* I thought long and hard about it. Within 480 pages, I wanted to be sure that I could explain to someone with no programming experience how to actually create useful programs.

So I started to think about what makes programming so difficult.

It isn't the concept of how programs work, which I cover easily in Part I. And it isn't really the language itself (or the instruction set — I cover that in Chapter 4). It isn't even the user interface — all that code needed to open and close windows, process menus and the mouse and user touches, draw graphics, and play audio and video (did I leave anything out?). No, while all that used to be really hard, now it's made much easier by using the frameworks available on the Mac and iPhone.

What is really hard, after you've learned the language and framework, is how you structure your program. How you actually go about taking your idea for an application and turning it into a robust Objective-C application.

Learning to use the tools is (relatively) easy; knowing how to use them to create a useful application is the real challenge.

So besides explaining the instruction set and everything else involved with coding, what I do along the way is explain the other things you need to know (things like application architecture and design). Those things that will make it possible for you, when you are done with this book, to go out and start developing your first application. Nothing less.

So instead of a book that only shows you *how* to use all the features (instructions and frameworks) available to you, I decided to write a book that shows you both *how* and *why*. I do that by having you start to develop an application in Chapter 5 (once I go over the instruction set) and add to that same application until you end up with it running on both the iPhone and Mac in Chapters 17 and 18. Granted, this application isn't the most exciting one in the world, but it gives you the opportunity to use every feature of Objective-C that you'll need to know to go out and build your own killer app. What's more, you build the application incrementally, just as a professional develops a commercial application. Occasionally, you will enter some code only to delete it later, which may seem annoying at times. However, you will get a flavor for how you'll work when you are out on your own.

And while some development will be annoying and tedious, in general it is fun. So go enjoy yourself while you're learning. I know I do.

About This Book

Objective-C For Dummies is a beginner's guide to developing applications for both the iPhone and the Mac. You don't need any programming experience to get started. I expect you to come as a blank slate, ready to be filled with useful information and new ways to do things. In some ways, the less you know, the easier it will be for you because you won't have any preconceived notions about programming.

This book distills the hundreds (or even thousands) of pages of Apple documentation, not to mention my own development experience, into only what's necessary to start you developing real applications. I'll explain not only the language, but also along the way I'll explicitly talk about object-oriented principles and how doing things in a certain way (that is, following those principles) lead to more extensible and enhanceable programs, which you will discover is the holy grail of programming.

Conventions Used in This Book

This book guides you through the process of building applications using Objective-C.

Code examples in this book appear in a monospaced font so they stand out a bit better. That means the code you'll see will look like this:

```
NSLog(@îI am an Objective-C statement.î);
```

Objective-C is based on C, which (I want to remind you) *is* case-sensitive, so please enter the code that appears in this book *exactly* as it appears in the text. I also use the standard Objective-C naming conventions — for example, class names always start with a capital letter, and the names of methods and instance variables always start with a lowercase letter.

All URLs in this book appear in a monospaced font as well:

```
www.nealgoldstein.com
```

If you're ever uncertain about anything in the code, you can always look at the source code on the CD. And from time to time, I'll provide updates for the code, and post other things you might find useful on my Web site, www.nealgoldstein.com.

Foolish Assumptions

To learn to program in Objective-C for the Mac or iPhone, you'll need a Macintosh computer with the latest version of the Mac OS on it. You will also need to download the Software Development Kit (SDK). You will have to become a registered Apple developer before you can do that. (Don't worry; I show you how to do both, and it doesn't cost a cent.)

I assume that you don't have any programming knowledge but that you have at least a passing acquaintance with some of the ideas, and more importantly, a desire to know how to program. In general, the code is easy and straightforward (the book isn't written to dazzle you with fancy coding techniques).

I also assume that you're familiar with the Mac and/or iPhone and that you are comfortable doing all the things you have to do on the Mac to run applications, including using the Finder to cruise the filesystem to see what's there.

How This Book Is Organized

Objective-C For Dummies has five main parts.

Part 1: Getting to the Starting Line

Part I introduces you to the world of application development. You find out how programs work and what you have to do to take an idea and turn it into a computer program. I explain the tools available to you and how to use them and lead you through downloading the Software Development Kit (SDK), which includes Xcode (Apple's development environment for the OS X and iPhone operating systems). You get up and running on your first application, which gives you a taste for what words like *compiling* and *building* mean. You also find out how to become a registered Apple developer, both for the Mac and the iPhone (and if you are an iPhone developer, what you are required to do in order to distribute your applications through Apple's App Store).

Part II: Speaking the Language of Objective-C

As with any other skill, you have to pay your dues, and that means understanding the instruction set of the language and how to use some of the language-like features made available to you in the frameworks. You start by building an application that you will add to as you learn more and more about Objective-C.

Think of this as getting down the vocabulary of a new language, but without the pain and all that memorization.

Part III: Walking the Objective-Oriented Walk

Once you understand the basic instruction set and the other Objective-C and framework features, it's time to put those instructions together to create a program. In this part, I focus on the right way to structure your program — what's known as the program architecture. Having the right architecture results in a program that not only works but also can be extended to add new functionality easily. And not only that, it enables you to easily track down and fix those pesky bugs that make their home in everyone's programs. I also show you how to deal with the mundane, but necessary, plumbing issues such as memory management and object initialization.

While Part II is about getting down the vocabulary, Part III is about using the vocabulary to create sentences and paragraphs and even entire books.

Part IV: Moving from Language to Application

With an architecture in place, you can now begin to add more and more functionality to your program. You start to work with data and learn some of the tricks that framework redevelopers use to make their frameworks so extensible.

Once you have your application doing what you want it to do, you need to take all that functionality and make it available to the user. So, in this part, I show you how your application fits into the user SDK-supplied frameworks that do all the user interface heavy lifting on the Mac and the iPhone. And because you design the application the right way from the start, you'll be able to plug it into the user interface with minimal effort. You just do some building of the user interface in Interface Builder (part of the SDK), add a few lines of code, and you are there. No sweat, no bother. And yes, because you did it the right way from the start, the same application code will run on both the Mac and iPhone (using the frameworks for the Mac OS and iPhone).

Part V: The Part of Tens

Part V consists of voices from the trenches. I'll also show you some tips on debugging (yes, your application will, upon occasion, have bugs) that might shorten those late, into-the-night debugging sessions that are (unfortunately) part and parcel of being a developer. While they may not always be fun, solved bugs are often a great source of conversation among developers. I'll also offer some tips about approaching application development that will lead to good health and happiness as a developer.

Icons Used in This Book

When you see this icon, you can be sure that the code on the CD applies to the current example. The CD contains the code for all projects in this book — perfect for those who don't feel like typing the code.

This icon indicates a useful pointer that you shouldn't skip.

This icon represents a friendly reminder. It describes a vital point that you should keep in mind while proceeding through a particular section of the chapter.

This icon signifies that the accompanying explanation might be informative (dare I say, interesting), but it isn't essential to understanding Objective-C application development. Feel free to skip past these tidbits if you'd like (though skipping while trying to absorb the main concepts may be tricky).

This icon alerts you to potential problems that you may encounter along the way. Read and obey these bits of experience to avoid trouble.

Part I
Getting to the Starting Line

"I wrote this horse racing software program. It analyzes my betting history and makes suggestions. Right now it's suggesting I try betting on football."

In this part . . .

So you've decided you want to learn to program. You may have a good idea for a Mac or iPhone application and realize that the first thing you need to do is find out how to program in Objective-C. And while you may have a vague idea about it, you know you're going to have to learn exactly what programming is and what's required to create an application.

In this part, I help you understand what you need to know to get started. First of all, how do applications even work? How do you translate your ideas into a computer language that tells the computer what you want it to do, and then how does it take those instructions and actually do them? What is all this complier and framework stuff, and what exactly is object-oriented programming?

You find out what makes a good application and what you can do to make yours a good one. Finally, so that you can get free development software from Apple, I take you through the process of registering as an Apple developer. I explain how you can download the Software Development Kit (SDK), and even how to build your first program.

Chapter 1

Computer Programming Exposed!

· ·

· ·

*L*ooking at it from the outside, computer programming can appear compli-cated and a bit mysterious. But once I let you in on a few of the secrets, you'll realize that when you write a computer program, whether it is a small program that's just a few lines or one that is tens or even hundreds of thou-sands of lines, you are generally doing the same thing:

1. **Getting input — from a keyboard or touch screen, or even something stored on your computer.**

   The input might be instructions to the program itself — for example, to display the Web page, `developer.apple.com`; or to print a docu-ment such as Chapter 1; or to process data like "enter your Apple ID and Password" when you log on to the Mac Dev Center (the browser is just another program); or even to process a list of credit card transactions stored on a computer.

2. **Doing something based on, or with, the input.**

   Your browser may go on the Internet and access the page correspond-ing to `developer.apple.com`; or your word-processing program may display a Print dialog and print the chapter (at least that is what mine does). Based on your input, the program may also go out and use data it has stored or even has access to over the Internet. For example, when you enter your Apple ID and Password, eventually a computer accesses a database to see if your Apple ID and Password are both valid and, if so, allows you access to the site and displays the site for you.

3. **Displaying the results of your adroitness on a monitor (or storing it away for future use).**

There is no doubt that computers are engineering marvels. But what will make you a good programmer is not your understanding of all that wizardry.

No, what will make you a good programmer is taking the time to really understand the world of the user, and what you can do with a computer to make things better. For example, when I travel I often zone out on the fact that even though it looks like monopoly money, foreign currency actually does amount to something in dollars. I could use a computer to keep track of my budget and convert foreign currency into dollars for me. Writing a program simply involves detailing the steps the computer needs to follow (in a language the computer understands — but I'll get to that). You know, something like

> subtract the amount he just spent from the amount he started with

or

> multiply the amount in foreign currency times the exchange rate.

Is it hard? No, not really. It can be pedestrian, but even more often it is fun.

Why a Computer Program Is Like a Peanut Butter and Jelly Sandwich

At its heart (yes, it does have one), computer programming is actually not that alien to most people. If you don't believe me, take the following programming test. Now, don't peek ahead for the answer. Okay?

The Never Fail Programming Test:

> Write down the recipe for making a peanut butter and jelly sandwich.

Answer:

> If what you wrote down looks anything like

```
Recipe: Peanut Butter and Jelly Sandwich
  Ingredients
    Peanut Butter
    Jelly
    2 slices of bread
  Directions
    Place the two slices of bread close to each other
    Spread peanut butter on one slice of bread
    Spread jelly on the other slice of bread
    Put one slice of bread on top of the other
```

> then you're ready to go.

While this example may seem overly simple, it generally illustrates what programming is all about. When you write a program in Objective-C, all you are doing is providing a set of instructions for the computer to follow. The preceding example is not perfect, but actually it is much closer to illustrating how Objective-C programming works than you might think. So, considering the peanut butter and jelly sandwich example, here is how you get your lunch made (if you are lucky enough to have a chef):

1. **You give your chef the recipe.**

2. **He or she gets the ingredients together and then follows the instructions on what to do with the ingredients.**

   Voilà, a peanut butter and jelly sandwich.

Figure 1-1 shows how a computer program works, using the peanut butter and jelly sandwich example.

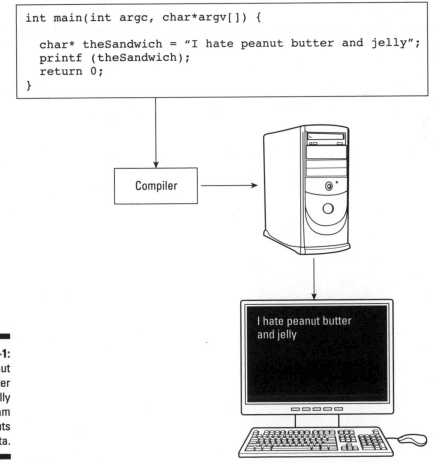

```
int main(int argc, char*argv[]) {

    char* theSandwich = "I hate peanut butter and jelly";
    printf (theSandwich);
    return 0;
}
```

Compiler

I hate peanut butter and jelly

Figure 1-1:
The peanut butter and jelly program outputs data.

This is what you do to get that output.

1. **You write instructions for the computer to follow.**

   Unfortunately, the computer can't speak English, or read for that matter, so you use something called a *compiler* to take the instructions you have written in the Objective-C language and translate it into something the computer can understand.

2. **You provide data for the computer to use.**

   In this case, you write, "I hate peanut butter and jelly," and then the computer follows the instructions you have given it on what to do with that data.

   Voilà, you see "I hate peanut butter and jelly" displayed on your computer screen.

Fundamentally, programs manipulate numbers and text, and all things considered, a computer program has only two parts: *variables* (and other structures), which "hold" data, and *instructions*, which perform operations on that data.

Examining a simple computer program

Is there really any difference between a chef reading a recipe and creating a peanut butter and jelly sandwich and a computer following some instructions to display something on a monitor? Quite frankly, no.

Here is the simple Objective-C program that displays `I hate peanut butter and jelly` on the computer screen:

```
int main(int argc, char *argv[]) {

  char* theSandwich = "I hate peanut butter and jelly";

  printf (theSandwich);
  return 0;
}
```

This program shows you how to display a line of text on your computer screen. The best way to understand programming code is to take it apart line by line:

```
int main(int argc, char *argv[]) {
```

Ignore the first line; it's not important now. It just provides your program with some information it can use. I'll explain exactly what that line means over the next few chapters.

```
char* theSandwich = "I hate peanut butter and jelly";
```

theSandwich is what is known as a *variable*. The best way to think of it for now is as a bucket that holds some kind of data (I get more precise in Chapter 4). char* tells you what kind of variable it is; in this case, theSandwich is a bunch of characters (text) known as a *string* (while technically a string is more than that, for now that description is good enough for our purposes). I hate peanut butter and jelly is the data that the variable contains.

```
printf (theSandwich);
```

printf is an instruction that tells the computer to display (this is called an *operation*) whatever data is in the theSandwich bucket.

You can also safely ignore the last two lines for the time being.

```
    return 0;
}
```

Figure 1-2 shows the similarities between the program and the recipe for making a sandwich.

Figure 1-2:
A computer program can be compared to a peanut butter and jelly sandwich recipe.

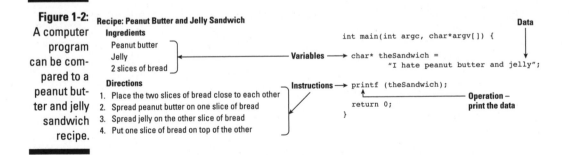

You can think of the following ingredients as variables that represent the data. For example, peanut butter is the name you give to pureed peanuts (and whatever else is in peanut butter), jelly the name you give to some fruit that's been processed and put in a jar, and so on.

```
Peanut Butter
Jelly
2 slices of bread
```

Similarly

```
Place the two slices of bread close to each other
Spread peanut butter on one slice of bread
Spread jelly on the other slice of bread
Put one slice of bread on top of the other
```

are simply instructions on how to take the ingredients and make a sandwich. Spread peanut butter on one slice of bread is the instruction. Actually, spreading the peanut butter is the operation you are performing on the pureed peanuts being referenced by the peanut butter variable.

Understanding How Computer Languages Work

While conceptually it is pretty easy to understand computer programming — all you are doing is giving it a set of instructions and some data on which to perform those instructions — one of the challenges, as I mentioned previously, is that it's not that easy to tell a computer what to do.

Computers don't speak English, although computer scientists have been working on that for years (think of trying to do that as the Computer Scientist Full Employment Act). A computer actually has its own language made up of ones and zeros. For that matter, Objective-C is not something a computer can understand either, but it is a language that can be turned into those ones and zeros by using a *compiler*. A compiler is nothing more than a program that translates Objective-C instructions into computer code.

Creating a computer program

To create a computer program using a computer language, follow these steps (see Figure 1-3):

1. **Decide what you want the computer to do.**

   You can have the computer write a line of text on the monitor or create an online multiplayer game that will take two years to complete. It really doesn't matter.

2. **Break the task you want the computer to complete into a series of modules that contain the instructions the computer follows to do what you want, and then provide the data it needs to do that.**

   The series of modules is often referred to as your *application architecture*. The data you provide to the computer can be some text, or graphics, or where the hidden treasure is, or the euro US dollar exchange rate.

3. **Run the instructions through the compiler.**

   A compiler is actually just another program, albeit one that uses your instructions as data for its instructions on how to turn Objective-C into computer code.

4. **Link the result to other precompiled modules.**

   As you will see, the code you write is a relatively small part of what makes up your program. The rest is made up of all the plumbing you need to run the program, open and close windows, and do all that user interface stuff. Fortunately, that code is provided for you in a form that is easy to attach (link) to your program. A linker program takes your code, identifies all the things it needs, collects all pieces together (from the disk), and combines them into the executable program you see in your applications or utilities folder.

5. **Store that output somewhere.**

   You usually store the output on a hard disk, but it can be anything the computer can access, like punch cards.

6. **Run the program.**

   When you want to run the program (say, the user double-clicks the program icon), the operating system (Mac OS X, for example, which is also just another program) gets the program from where it's stored and loads it into memory, and then the CPU (central processing unit) executes the instructions.

Running a computer program

Just as you don't need to be a weatherman to know which way the wind blows, you don't need to be an engineer who understands the intimate details of a computer to write a world-class application.

Most people don't find it that difficult to learn to drive a car. While you don't have to know all that stuff about internal combustion engines, fuel injection, drive trains and transmissions, you do need to know a little bit about how a car works. That means knowing about how to turn it on, make it go forward, make it go backward, make it stop (generally a very valuable piece of information), make it turn left or right, and so on.

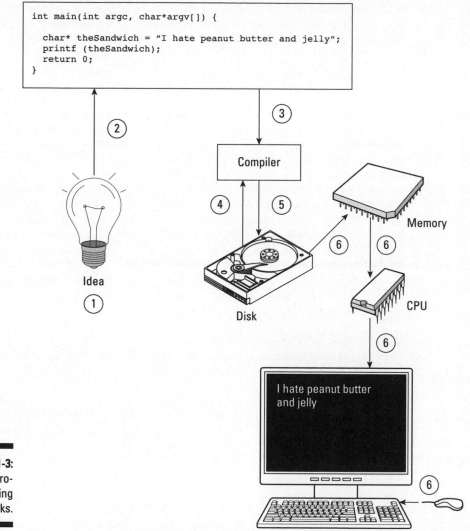

```
int main(int argc, char*argv[]) {

    char* theSandwich = "I hate peanut butter and jelly";
    printf (theSandwich);
    return 0;
}
```

Figure 1-3:
How pro-
gramming
works.

In the same way, you do need to know *a little bit* about how computers work to have what you do to write a computer program make sense.

When you run a computer program, the computer does its primary work in a part of the machine you cannot see, the CPU, which executes the program instructions that are loaded into the computer's memory. (This is a fast, temporary form of storage that is in one of those chips you see when you look inside a computer, as opposed to the hard disk which is slower and permanent storage.) It requests the data it needs from memory, processes it, and writes new data back to memory millions of times every second.

But if the data is all in memory, the CPU needs to be able to find a particular instruction or piece of data. How does it do that?

The location in memory for each instruction and each piece of data is identified by an *address,* like the mailboxes in the post office or an apartment house you see in Figure 1-4 (and notice that the first address for a mailbox in your computer is always 0). But these are very small mailboxes that can hold only one character of information at a time (not technically true, but good enough) referred to as a *byte.* So for all practical purposes (although again not technically true), you can think of the smallest division of memory as a byte, with each byte being able to be addressed on its own. The good news is that if you need more mailboxes, they are yours for the taking. So if you get more than one letter a day, the number of mailboxes assigned to you will increase to hold all the letters you need them to.

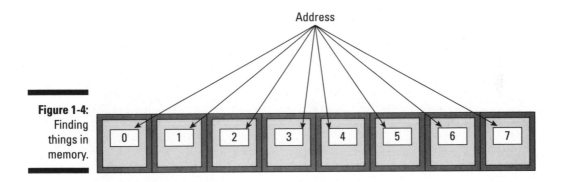

Figure 1-4: Finding things in memory.

What Is Objective-C, Anyway?

Objective-C is an object-oriented programming language, which means that it was created to support a certain style of programming. Yes, I know it is hard to believe, but even things like programming have different styles, in fact a lot of them, although the two heavyweights are object oriented and procedural. Unless you're a dyed in the wool member of a particular camp, it is really unnecessary to get into that discussion here (or probably ever). But you will, I promise, intimately understand what object-oriented programming is by the time you're done with this book, and you'll probably wonder why anyone would ever want to program in any other way.

But it takes more than a language to write a program; it takes a village. So who lives in the Objective-C village? Most object-oriented development environments consist of several parts:

✔ An object-oriented programming language

✔ A runtime environment

✔ A framework or library of objects and functions

✔ A suite of development tools

This is where, for many people, things start to cloud up. You mean I have to learn more than the language, and what is all this stuff about runtime environment and frameworks and libraries? The answer is yes; but not to worry. I'll take you slowly through each part. The following sections cover each part of the Objective-C development environment.

Understanding programming languages

When you write a program, you write it as series of *statements*. Some of these statements are about data. You may allocate areas of memory to use for data in your program, as well as describe how data is structured. Other statements are really instructions for the computer to do something.

Here is an example of an Objective-C statement that adds together b and c and assigns the result to a (and you thought you'd never use all that algebra you learned in school):

```
a = b + c;
```

Statements like these use operators (like + or -) or tell *modules* (functions or objects) to do something to, or with, the data. For now think of functions or objects as simply a packaged series of statements that perform a task. It might help to think of operators and modules as words you use to create sentences (the statements) that tell the computer what to do. Chapters 4, 5, and 6 cover operators, functions, objects, and modules in detail.

When most people want to learn how to program, they usually focus on the language. I want to program in C++, for example. Or C++ is a real dog, give me Java any day. People really do become passionate about languages, and believe me it is best to keep out of the way when an unstoppable force meets an immovable object.

What you really should keep in mind, unless computer science is your life, is that what you want to learn is how to create applications. What makes that easy or difficult is not just the language, but the application development tools available to you, as well.

Objective-C has its fans and its detractors, My advice to you is to ignore both sides and get on with your development. There are some things I really like about the language, and others I don't; but in essence, it is what it is, and it is what you'll use.

Running your program in a runtime environment

One of features of Objective-C is its runtime system. This is one of those things that gets linked into your program in Step 4 in the section "Creating a computer program." It acts as a kind of operating system (like the Mac or iPhone OS) for an individual Objective-C program. It is this runtime system that is responsible for making some of the very powerful features of Objective-C work.

Objective-C's runtime environment also makes it possible to use tools like Interface Builder (I explain Interface Builder in Chapters 17 and 18) to create user interfaces with a minimum of work (I'm all for that, and after you learn about Interface Builder, you will be, too).

Using frameworks and libraries

The framework you will use is called *Cocoa*. It came along with Objective-C when Apple acquired NeXT In 1996 (when it was called NextSTEP). I have worked in many development environments over my life, and Objective-C and Cocoa are hands down my favorite.

Cocoa allows you to write applications for Mac OS X, and a version of it allows you to write applications for the iPhone. If the operating system does the heavy lifting vis-à-vis the hardware, the framework provides all the stuff you need to make your application an application. It provides support for windows and other user-interface items as well as many of the other things that are needed in most applications. When you use Cocoa, to develop your application all you need to do is add the application's specific functionality — the content and the controls and views that enable the user to access and use that content — to the Cocoa framework.

Now, two excellent books explain the use of frameworks on the Mac and iPhone. One is *Cocoa Programming for Mac OS X For Dummies* by Erick Tejkowski. The other is *iPhone Application Development For Dummies* by Neal Goldstein (I know, a shameless plug).

Framework or library

What is the difference between a library and a framework?. A library is a set of reusable functions or data structures that are yours to use. A framework, on the other hand, has an architecture or programming model, which requires an application be designed (divided into modules) in a certain way (application architecture) to use it. I like to think that while *you use a library, a framework uses you.*

Your suite of development tools

The two main development tools you use are Xcode and Interface Builder. You'll be using Xcode throughout this book, which I explain in Chapter 2. I talk a little about Interface Builder in Chapters 17 and 18, but again, pick up copies of *iPhone Application Development For Dummies* and *Cocoa Programming for Mac OS X For Dummies* to really learn about the frameworks.

Using Xcode 3.2

You will be using the Xcode 3.2 developer tools package that was released with Mac OS X 10.6 (Snow Leopard). This is an improvement over Xcode 3.1 that was included in Leopard and I will assume that you are using both Xcode 3.2 and Mac OS X 10.6 in this book.

Using Objective-C Version 2.0

You will be learning Version 2.0 of the Objective-C language, which was released with Mac OS X 10.5, and yes, you should care. Version 2.0 has some new and very useful features such as declared properties, fast enumeration, and garbage collection, which greatly simplify memory management (unfortunately, garbage collection is not available on the iPhone). As I explain these new features, I will remind you that they are available only in Objective-C Version 2.0, which works only with Mac OS X 10.5 or later and the iPhone OS. If possible, I'll also indicate some workarounds if you need to write applications that run under earlier versions of the OS, but in general, writing applications that run under earlier versions of the OS will be up to you.

Chapter 2

Creating Your First Program

. . . .

. . . .

*I*n Chapter 1, I provide some of the background context you need to know in order to write computer programs, and I complete that discussion in Chapter 3. While there is still more you need to know in order to write *good* programs, it's time for a break. In this chapter, you get a taste of what programming is about.

But before you do that, you need to go through some administrative matters, such as downloading the Software Development Kit (SDK) that you use to write programs. But to do that, you first have to become a registered Apple Developer.

Getting Started with the Software Development Kit

Everything you need to program in Objective-C for the Mac or iPhone is included in something known as the *software development kit,* or SDK. It contains Xcode (and some tools); frameworks and libraries; and iPhone OS, Mac OS X, and Xcode documentation — in short, everything you need to develop applications for the Mac and iPhone. Once you have it installed on your computer, you are ready to begin developing that killer app you have been thinking of.

This book is designed to teach you how to use Objective-C to write both Mac OS X and iPhone applications. I try to alternate which comes first in each discussion (just to be fair). Deciding which platform you want to develop for is a decision only you can make. Fortunately, the two are not mutually exclusive when it comes to the SDK.

In order to download the SDK though, you need to register with Apple, so let's go through the process.

Registering as a Developer

Apple has two developer programs — one for Mac OS X developers and one for iPhone developers. From the tools perspective, with one exception, both are virtually the same. That one exception is that if you are registered as an iPhone developer when you download the SDK from the iPhone Dev Center, you get both the iPhone and Mac OS X frameworks and libraries and documentation (and the iPhone simulator). If you register as a Mac developer and download the SDK from the Mac Dev Center, you only get the Mac OS X frameworks and libraries and documentation.

Because you need to use the iPhone SDK in Chapter 17, I have you register as an iPhone developer. As an iPhone developer, you also have access to both the iPhone and Mac Dev centers.

1. **Point your browser to** `http://developer.apple.com/iphone`.

   This takes you to the iPhone Dev Center (see Figure 2-1). Once you are registered, the iPhone and Mac Dev Centers provide a plethora of resources for developing applications. Take some time to explore them on your own.

Apple continually updates the look and feel of its Web site, so the pages may look different when you see them, and the site's functionality may be slightly different. If there are any significant changes, please go to my Web site, `www.nealgoldstein.com`, where I provide updated screenshots and instructions.

2. **Right underneath the iPhone Dev Center banner, click Register.**

   A new page appears giving you some information about the program.

3. **Click Continue.**

   You see a page that asks you if you have an existing Apple ID or if you want to create one. See Figure 2-2.

Figure 2-1:
The iPhone
Dev Center.

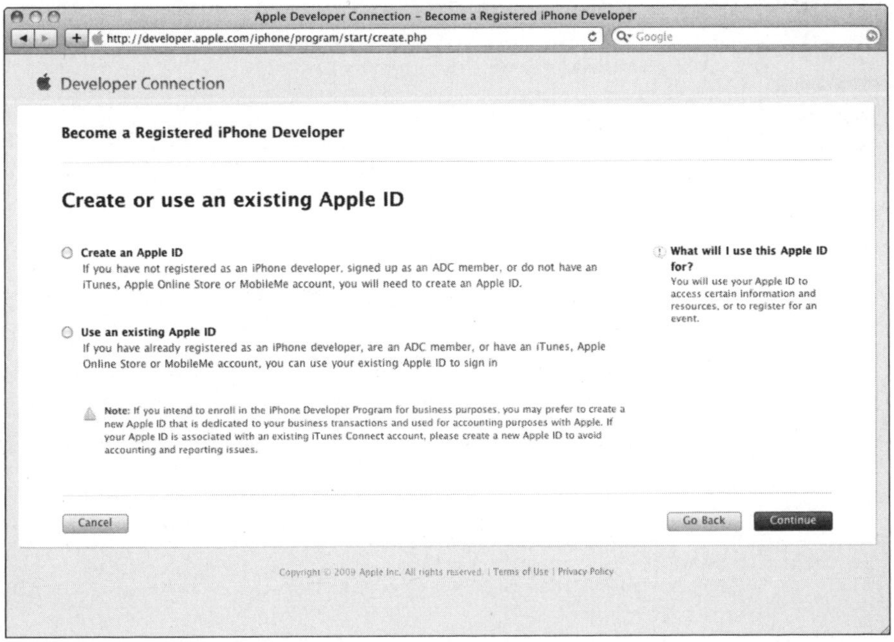

Figure: 2-2:
Create
or use an
existing
Apple ID.

If you do not have an Apple ID, you are asked to create one. After you create your Apple ID, you see a page (Figure 2-3) that asks you to complete your professional profile.

If you do have an Apple ID, you are sent to a page where you can log in. After you log in, you see the page that asks you to complete your professional profile.

4. Fill out your professional profile and then click Continue.

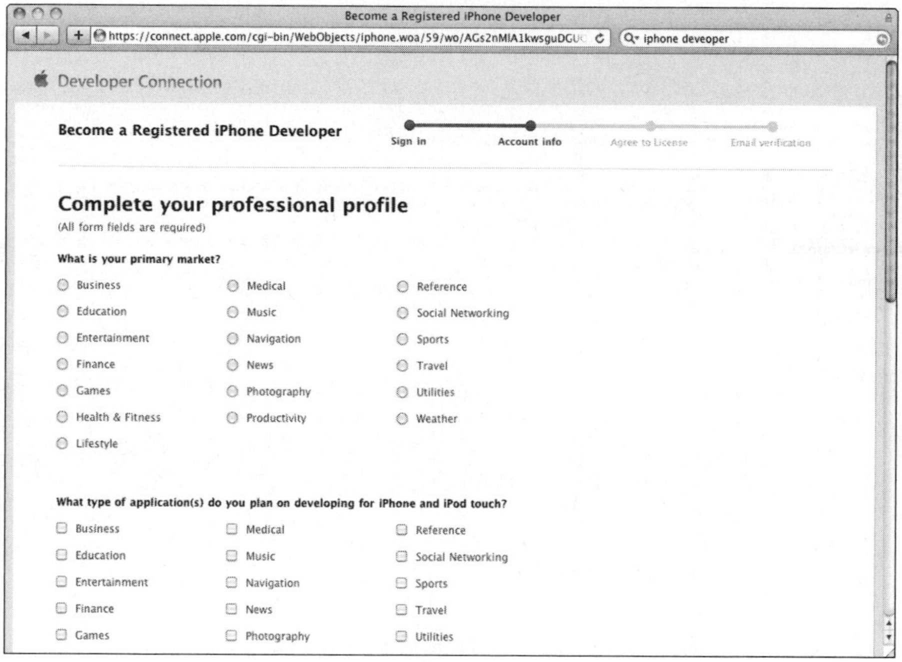

Figure 2-3: Professional Profile.

This takes you to the Registered iPhone Developer Agreement page where you need to accept the agreement.

5. Check the box and click I Agree (see Figure 2-4).

Next, you are asked to enter the verification code sent to the e-mail address you provided Apple when you set up your Apple ID (see Figure 2-5).

6. Find the e-mail and enter the verification code.

After completing the preceding steps, you are returned to the iPhone Dev Center (see Figure 2-6).

Figure 2-4:
Developer
Agreement.

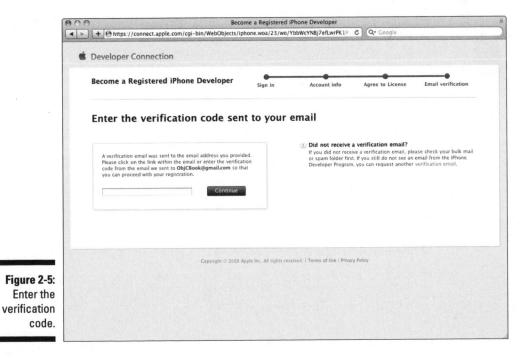

Figure 2-5:
Enter the
verification
code.

Figure 2-6:
iPhone Dev
Center.

While anyone can develop applications for the Mac without paying to join a developer program, if you want to be able to have your iPhone application actually run on an iPhone, you have to join one of the iPhone Developer programs (refer to Figure 2-6), which costs you something.

1. **Click Learn More to access a page (shown in Figure 2-7) that tells you a little about the program.**

2. **On this page, click Enroll Now (don't worry; you aren't committing to anything at this point).**

   This step accesses a page where you can find out more about each program (see Figure 2-8).

The iPhone developer program has two versions:

✔ **Standard Program ($99 per year):** For commercial developers — meaning App Store.

✔ **Enterprise Program ($299 per year):** For in-house development and distribution only.

Figure 2-7:
iPhone
Developer
Program.

Figure 2-8:
The iPhone
developer
programs.

If you want your application to run on an iPhone, even on your own iPhone for testing, you have to pay to join one of these programs. If you don't, you can run your application only on the iPhone simulator included with the iPhone SDK.

You don't need to decide right away, and you can start by becoming a registered developer (which you just did) and then joining the developer program later.

Just be aware it can take some time for you to get approved for the developer program.

If you are interested in developing for the Mac, you can make some choices about being a developer.

1. **Go back to the iPhone Dev Center page, click the Dev Centers drop-down menu and choose Mac Dev Center; you can also do that from the iPhone Developer Program page (see Figure 2-9).**

   The Mac Dev Center appears. Here you can learn about the Mac Developer Program.

2. **Choose Learn More under Join the Mac Developer Program (see Figure 2-10).**

   A new page appears giving you some information about the program. You have several options.

Figure 2-9:
Accessing
the Mac
Dev Center.

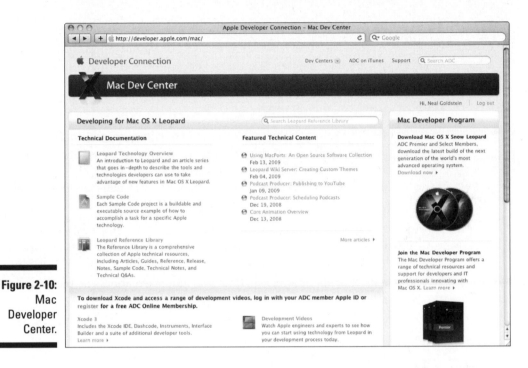

Figure 2-10:
Mac
Developer
Center.

3. Scroll down to the bottom of the page, and click compare member-ships under the Become an ADC Member.

Another window will appear where you see a comparison between the various memberships (see Figure 2-11). I did say that the SDK was free, and it is, but you can pay for additional support and privileges if you like.

There are some advantages to paying the $499 for the ADC Select membership — the hardware discount, compatibility lab, ADC on iTunes, some coding head starts, software seeding, and two free tech support calls a year. You can find out more about these advantages by clicking Join Now (again, you are not committing to anything yet).

Figure 2-11:
Mac
Developer
program
options.

	Premier Member	Select Member	Online Member	Student Member
WWDC Ticket	Included	May purchase	May purchase	May purchase
Software Seeding Program	✓ Available	✓ Available	Not available	Not available
Technical Support	8 per year	2 per year	May purchase	May purchase
Developer Forums	✓ Available	✓ Available	Not available	Not available
ADC on iTunes	✓ Available	✓ Available	Limited Access	Limited Access
Compatibility Labs	3 days per month	2 days per month	Not available	Not available
Hardware Purchase Program	10 systems per year	1 system per year	Not available	1 system (one time only)
Price	US $3499.00	US $499.00	Free	US $99.00

Downloading the SDK

Whether you are an iPhone or Mac OS developer, be sure that you are logged in to the iPhone Dev Center. It's now time to download the iPhone OS SDK. As I said, doing it this way gives you everything you need to develop on the iPhone (which you do in Chapter 17) or Mac (which you do in Chapter 18), or even both.

1. **Go back to the iPhone Dev Center and under Resources for iPhone OS 3.0, click Downloads (shown in Figure 2-12).**

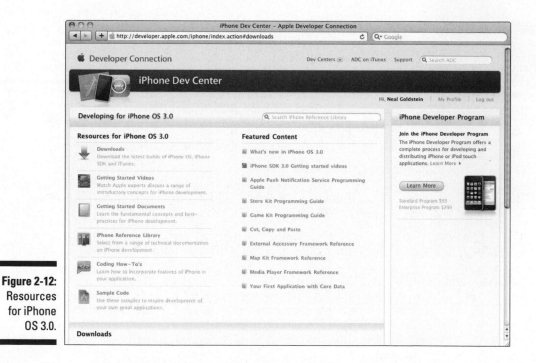

Figure 2-12:
Resources
for iPhone
OS 3.0.

This step takes you to the bottom of the page where you can choose the download you want (see Figure 2-13).

2. **Click iPhone SDK 3.0 (Snow Leopard), and the download starts (as you can see if you open Safari's Downloads window, or your browser's equivalent, as I did in Figure 2-14).**

Since the download is 1.75GB, you really need a broadband connection, or if not, a hobby to keep you busy while the SDK downloads.

Once the SDK is downloaded, the iPhone SDK window appears (see Figure 2-15).

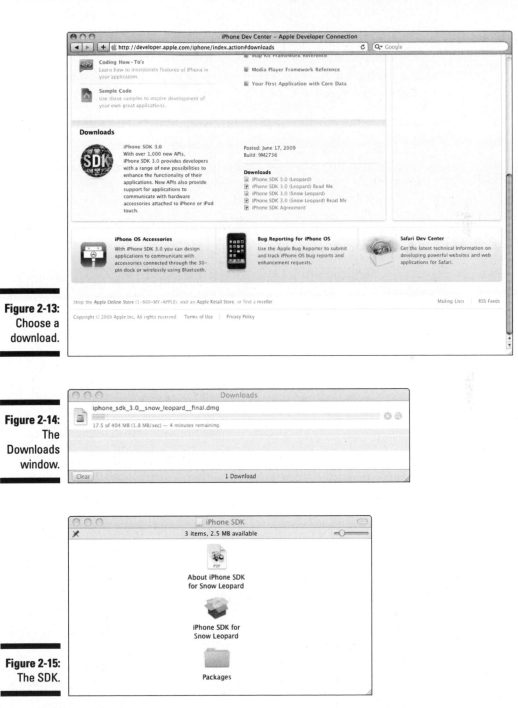

Figure 2-13:
Choose a
download.

Figure 2-14:
The
Downloads
window.

Figure 2-15:
The SDK.

3. **Double-click iPhone SDK for Snow Leopard.**

    The installer launches.

4. **Follow the instructions, and in no time, you'll have the SDK installed and ready to code.**

As I said, Apple continually updates the look and feel of its Web site, so the pages may look different when you see them, and the site's functionality may be slightly different. If there are any significant changes please go to my Web site, `www.nealgoldstein.com`, where I provide updated screenshots and instructions.

Creating Your Xcode Project

To develop a Mac OS X or iPhone application, you work on what's called an *Xcode project*. Here's how to start your foray into Xcode:

1. **Launch Xcode.**

    After you download the SDK, it's easy to launch Xcode. By default, Xcode was downloaded to /Developer/Applications, where you find and launch it.

    Since you use Xcode a lot, you can also drag the icon for the Xcode application onto the Dock, so you can launch it from there.

    When you first launch XCode, you see the welcome screen shown in Figure 2-16. It has some links you can explore on your own. You may want to leave this screen up to make it easier to get to those links, but I usually close it. If you don't want to be bothered with the welcome screen in the future, uncheck the Show at Launch checkbox.

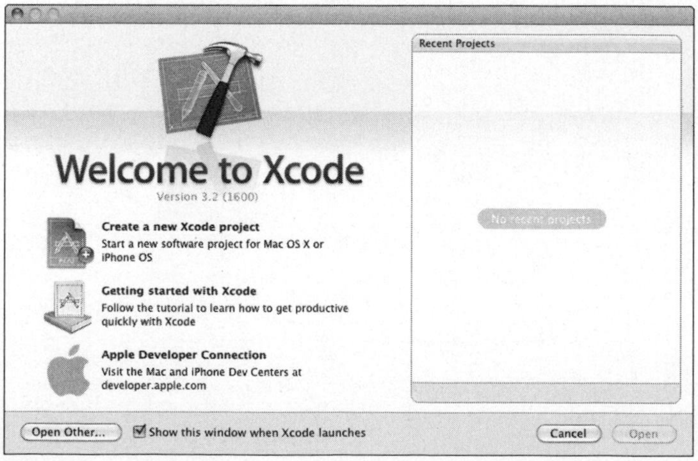

Figure 2-16: Xcode welcomes you.

Welcome to Xcode screen, Version 3.2 (1600), showing Recent Projects pane and options: Create a new Xcode project, Getting started with Xcode, Apple Developer Connection. Options at bottom: Open Other..., Show this window when Xcode launches, Cancel, Open.

If you have your iPhone connected, you may also see Figure 2-17.

2. **Start the New Project Assistant by choosing File⇨New Project from the main menu to create a new project.**

You can also just press Shift+⌘+N.

Either way, you see the New Project window, which looks something like Figure 2-18, depending on the kind of project you created previously.

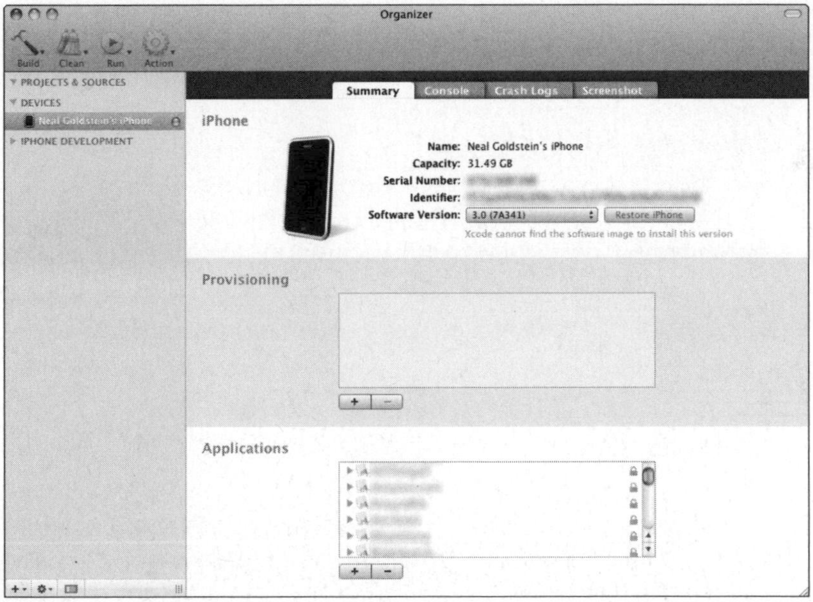

Figure 2-17:
Xcode
Organizer.

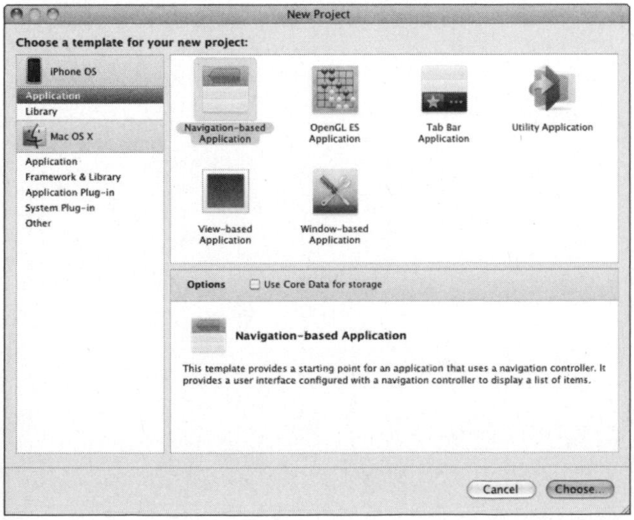

Figure 2-18:
New Project
window.

The New Project window is where you get to choose what kind of project you want to create. Note that the leftmost pane has two sections: one for the iPhone OS and the other for Mac OS X.

3. **In the New Project window, click Application under the Mac OS X heading.**

The main pane of the New Project window refreshes, revealing several choices, as shown in Figure 2-19. Each of these choices is actually a template that, when chosen, generates some code to get you started. You can then enter your own code into the template, build your application, and then generate output in the Debugger Console window (don't worry; I get to that very soon).

4. **Select Command Line Tool in the upper-right corner, as shown in Figure 2-19.**

Note that when you select a template, a brief description of the template displays underneath the main pane. Quite a few templates are available for both the iPhone and Mac OS X. You don't need any of the others until Chapters 17 and 18, but you may want to click around just to get a feel for what is available. Just be sure to click back to Application under the Mac OS X heading and select Command Line Tool when you're done exploring.

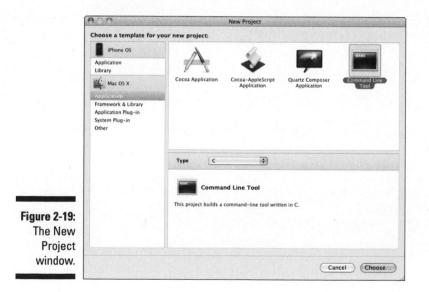

Figure 2-19: The New Project window.

5. **In the same page, select Foundation from the Type drop-down menu, as shown in Figure 2-20; then click Choose.**

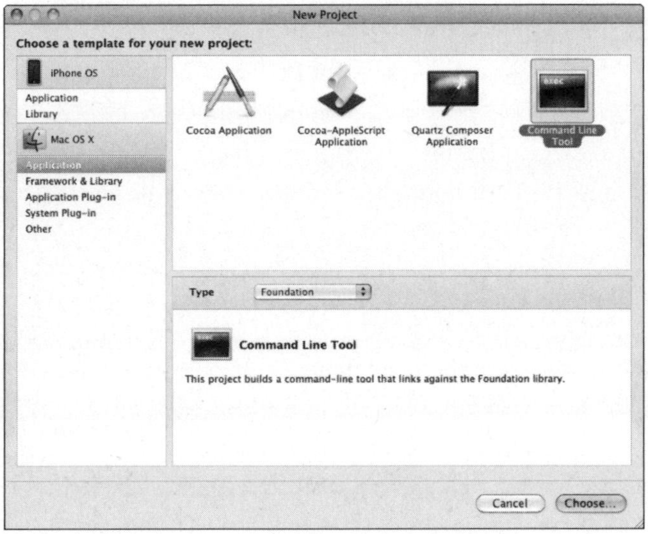

Figure 2-20:
Select
Foundation
for the
Command
Line Tool.

Xcode displays a standard save sheet (see Figure 2-21).

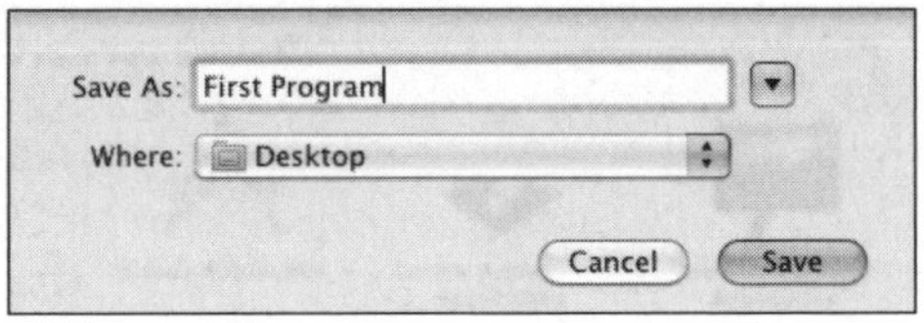

Figure 2-21:
Name the
new project.

6. **Enter a name for your new project in the Save As field. (I named my project First Program. I suggest you do the same if you're following along with me.) Then choose a Save location (the Desktop or any other folder works just fine) and click Save.**

After you click Save, Xcode creates the project and opens the Project window — which should look like what you see in Figure 2-22.

Groups & Files list   Build and Run   Info
Toolbar   Breakpoints   Tasks   Detail view

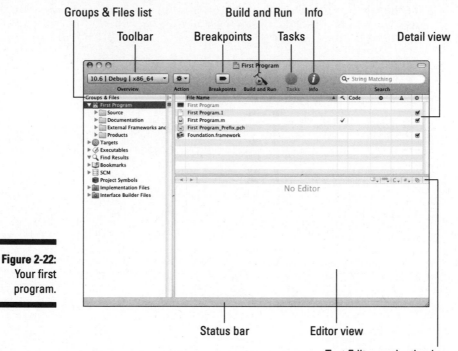

Figure 2-22:
Your first
program.

Status bar   Editor view

Text Editor navigation bar

Exploring your project

To develop an iPhone application, you have to work within the context of an Xcode project. It turns out that you do most of your work on projects using a Project window very much like the one in Figure 2-22. Notice the Project window displays the name of your project, but I just refer to it as the Project window. This is Command Central for developing your application; it displays and organizes your source files and the other resources needed to build your application.

If you refer to Figure 2-22, you see the following:

✔ **Groups & Files list:** An outline view of everything in your project including all of your project's files — source code, frameworks, graphics, as well as some settings files. You can move files and folders around and add new folders. If you select an item in the Groups & Files list, the contents of the item are displayed in the topmost pane to the right — otherwise known as the Detail view.

Notice that some of the items in the Groups & Files list are folders, whereas others are just icons. Folders have a little triangle, called a disclosure triangle, next to them. Clicking the triangle to the left of a folder expands the folder to show what's in it. Click the triangle again to hide what the folder contains. The triangle points to the right when the item is collapsed and it points down when the item is expanded.

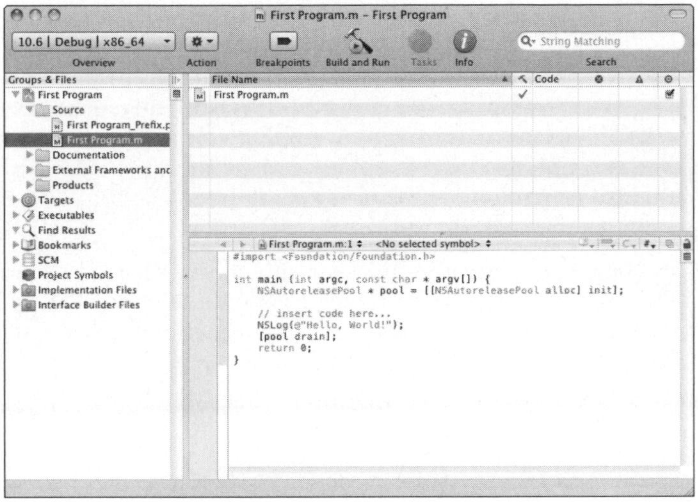

Figure 2-23:
First
Program.m.

✔ **Toolbar:** Gives you quick access to the most common Xcode commands. You can customize the toolbar to your heart's content by right-clicking it and selecting Customize Toolbar from the contextual menu that appears. You can also choose View➪Customize Toolbar.

- Pressing the Build and Run button compiles, links, and launches your application.

- The Breakpoints button turns breakpoints on and off and toggles the Build and Run button to Build and Debug. (I explain this in Chapter 8.)

- The Tasks button allows you to stop the execution of the program that you've built.

- The Info button opens a window that displays information and settings for your project.

✔ **Detail view:** Here you get detailed information about the item you selected in the Groups & Files list.

✔ **Text Editor navigation bar:** This navigation bar displays a number of shortcuts I explain later in this chapter in the section "Getting to Know the Xcode Text Editor."

✔ **Editor view:** Displays a file you selected in either the Groups & Files or Detail view. You can edit your files here, although you can also double-click a file in Groups & Files or Detail view to open the file in a separate window.

To see how Editor view works, check out Figure 2-23, where I clicked on the disclosure triangle next to the Source folder in the Groups & Files view, and then clicked on `First Program.m`. You can see the code in the Editor view.

`First Program.m` contains code generated by Xcode, based upon the Xcode template (a Foundation Command Line Tool) you selected. Once you start using Xcode to develop applications, you will find that the templates make getting started very easy for you. You can also see the code in Listing 2-1, later in the section "All that stuff in First Program.m." If you have problems understanding what all of that means (and since you are new to programming, you will), don't worry about it. I explain it all (gently) soon.

✔ **Status bar:** Look here for messages about your project. For example, when you're building your project, Xcode updates the status bar to show where you are in the process — and if the process completed successfully or not.

For now, just concentrate on the Groups & Files view.

Groups & Files view

The first item in the Groups & Files view, as you can see in Figure 2-24, is labeled `First Program`. This is the container or folder that contains all the "source" elements for your project, including source code, resource files, graphics, and a number of other pieces that remain unmentioned for the time being (but I explain those you need to know about in due course). For now, I just want you to click the disclosure triangle next to Source.

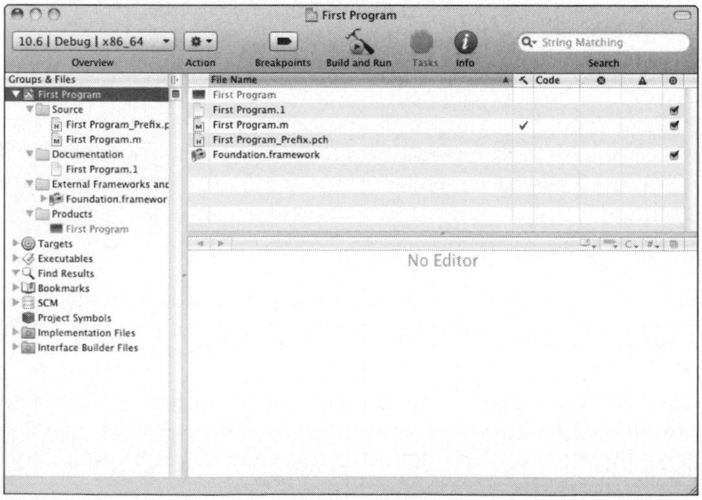

Figure 2-24: A little more Groups & Files detail.

✔ **Source** contains two files: My First Program.m and My First Program_ Prefix.pch, which are the source code for your program and something called a precompiled header, respectively. I talk about header files in Chapter 6; for now, all you need to know is that precompiling them significantly reduces the amount of time it takes to build your program.

Xcode uses the .m extension to indicate a file that holds Objective-C code and will be processed by the Objective-C compiler. (Filenames ending in .c are handled by the C compiler, and .cpp files are the province of the C++ compiler — yes, you actually get all of those with Xcode as well.)

✔ **External Frameworks and Libraries** are code libraries that contain a good deal of what you would normally have to write yourself to create a functioning program — including things you need to display text in the Debugger Console. (I know, you don't know what that is, but I explain that in the next section "Building and Running Your Application.") By choosing the Foundation Command Line Tool template, you let Xcode know that it should add the Foundation.framework to your project, since it expects that you need what's in the Foundation framework in a Foundation Command Line Tool.

Note: You use only this framework for now. Later, you use other frameworks when you start building iPhone OS and Mac OS X applications.

✔ **Products** is the *compiled application*. It contains First Program. At the moment, this file is listed in red because the file cannot be found (which makes sense, since you haven't compiled the project yet).

A file's name in red lets you know that Xcode can't find the underlying physical file.

If you happen to open the First Program folder on your Mac, you won't see the "folders" that appear in the Xcode window. That's because those folders are simply "logical" groupings that help organize and find what you're looking for; this list of files can grow to be pretty large, even in a moderate-size project.

When you have numerous files, creating subgroups within the Classes group and/or Resources group, or even new groups, helps you find things. You create subgroups (or even new groups) by choosing New Project⇨New Group. You then can select a file and drag it to a new group or subgroup. I show you that in more detail in Chapter 6.

Building and Running Your Application

It's really exciting to see what you get when you build and run a project that you created using a template from the New Project window (but then again, I'm easily entertained). Building and running a project is relatively simple:

On the left side of the toolbar, the selection in the Overview drop-down menu is "10.6 | Debug | x86_64" (or whatever the current Mac OS X release is). This menu lets you choose the active software development kit (SDK), and a number of other options for the program you are going to build. This is what you will use in this book until you get to Chapter 17.

It tells the compiler to build a debug version for the computer you are developing on (x86_64 is a 64-bit Intel processor) using Mac OS X 10.6 (Snow Leopard). You can also build for other platforms. The only thing you might want to experiment with is changing from debug to release, which gives you a smaller footprint but doesn't include some of the debug information useful during development.

You can see this illustrated in Figure 2-25.

Figure 2-25:
Overview
options.

Now for the main event — I'll explain how to build and then run this program.

1. **Select the Build and Run button in the Project window toolbar.**

   You can also press ⌘+Return or choose Build⇨Build and Run (Run) from the main menu to build and run the application. The status bar in the Project window tells you all about build progress, build errors such as compiler errors, or warnings — and (oh, yeah) whether the build was successful. Figure 2-26 shows that this is a successful build.

2. **Open the Xcode Debugger Console by choosing Run⇨Console or pressing Shift+⌘+R, which displays your program's output. You can see the Debugger Console in Figure 2-27.**

   And there are your results in Figure 2-28.

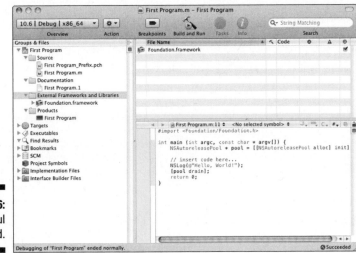

Figure 2-26:
A successful
build.

Run

Run	⌥⌘↵
Run – Breakpoints Off	⌥⌘R
Debug – Breakpoints On	⌥⌘Y
Run with Performance Tool	▶
Stop	⇧⌘↵
Attach to Process	▶
Debugger	⇧⌘Y
Mini Debugger	^⌘\
Console	⇧⌘R
Clear Console	^⌥⌘R
Show	▶
Debugger Display	▶
Variables View	▶
Activate Breakpoints	^⌘\
Stop on Objective-C Exceptions	
Manage Breakpoints	▶
Fix	
Pause	⌥⌘P
Step Into	⇧⌘I
Step Over	⇧⌘O
Step Out	⇧⌘T
Next Thread	^⌥⌘↑
Previous Thread	^⌥⌘↓
Sync with Debugger	
✓ Stop on Debugger()/DebugStr()	
Enable Guard Malloc	

Figure 2-27:
Show the
Debugger
Console.

Now that you have your first working program, I'm ready to explain to you
how it all happened.

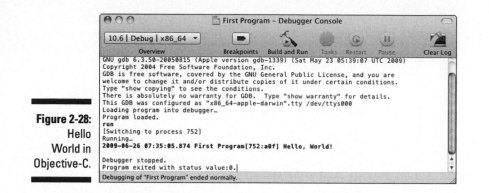

Figure 2-28:
Hello
World in
Objective-C.

All that stuff in First Program.m

The Objective-C code you just built and ran is shown in Listing 2-1. It displayed "Hello World" on the Debugger Console and connected you with generations of C programmers who have created and run this as their first application. Over the next few chapters, I dissect each and very element in this program, but for now, the real point is to get you comfortable with Xcode and the compiler, although I point out a few highlights.

Listing 2-1: Your First Program

```
#import <Foundation/Foundation.h>

int main (int argc, const char * argv[]) {
  NSAutoreleasePool * pool = [[NSAutoreleasePool alloc]
          init];

  // insert code here...
  NSLog(@"Hello, World!");
  [pool drain];
  return 0;
}
```

The first line you see tells the compiler to include the Foundation.h header file of the Foundation framework.

```
#import <Foundation/Foundation.h>
```

The Foundation framework provides plumbing features such as data storage, text and strings, dates and times, object creation, disposal persistence, and common Internet protocols — none of which you have a clue about at this point. But rest assured that you will not only understand but also appreciate them by the time you are done with this book. The Foundation framework provides commonly used functionality that is not part of the Objective-C language that you use hand-in-hand with Objective-C when you code your application. After all, it makes sense not to have to redo all of the common things that programmers need (like display text in the Debugger Console) in every program.

The way a program accesses the framework is through *headers*, and I explain those mechanics in Chapter 6.

The next line in the listing begins the `main` function:

```
int main (int argc, const char * argv[])
```

As I explain in Chapter 1, a *function* is a collection of instructions all neatly packaged together to perform a task. `main` is the mother of all functions and is the place where all Objective-C programs start their execution — the instructions contained within `main` are always the first ones to be executed in Objective-C programs. All Objective-C programs have one. When you start to work with the frameworks, however, you really won't be aware of this because all of the startup stuff is handled within the framework. But for now, this is where you start.

The word `main` is followed in the code by

```
(int argc, const char * argv[])
```

These are function arguments, which I cover in Chapters 5 and 7. Ignore them for now.

Before `main`, you also see another symbol, `int`. A function can return data to its caller. For example, the function `howOldAreYou` returns the age as an `int`, which, as you discover in Chapter 4, is the Objective-C official term for a whole number.

Right after the function arguments, you can find the body of the `main` function enclosed in curly braces (`{}`). What the function does when it is executed is contained within these braces. The first *statement* (a line of Objective-C code that terminates with a semicolon)

```
NSAutoreleasePool * pool =
                       [[NSAutoreleasePool alloc] init];
```

as well as

```
[pool drain];
```

have to do with memory allocation and management, which you don't need to know about until Chapter 13.

Just a reminder about statements. In some cases (like the first of the two preceding ones), you see statements on two lines in the book. I have to do that in order to fit the code on the book page. The code appears on one line in the Editor and you should generally use one line for statements unless they become too long to see all the complete line in the Project window.

Now, explore the statement

```
NSLog(@"Hello, World!");
```

All it does is display (or print, if you like) "Hello World" on the Debugger Console. To start with, NSLog is a function, just like main. Inside of it is a *string* (a variable that stores more than a single non-numerical character is known as a *string*).

```
@"Hello, World!"
```

The @ sign before the quotation mark tells the compiler that this is not a C string. It is actually a Cocoa object called an NSString that has a number of features, including the ability to covert a "numeric" string (like "42") to its numeric value (42) that you can use in a computation and to compare itself to another string. I explain more about this object later, but you use it now as an introduction to how you use strings in Objective-C.

NSLog is really used to log an error message, not as an application's output function. That's why the output is to the Debugger Console. But because Debugger Console is so convenient, you use it to display the program's output until you put on a user interface in Chapters 17 and 18 (and lots of people, me included, use it during development as a way to output program information that is not part of the user interface).

As you saw, what is displayed in the Debugger Console when you build and run your program is:

```
2009-06-26 07:35:05.874 First Program[752:a0f] Hello,
          World!
```

`2009-06-26 07:35:05.874 First Program[752:a0f]` is a time stamp and process id that tells you when and from where the output string originated. It's not important here, and I won't include it when I show you output — that means from now on, I show the preceding output as

```
Hello, World!
```

As I explain various features of Objective-C, you use this NSLog quite a bit to see for yourself how things work, and I expect you will become rather fond of it. It is, as I mentioned earlier, part of the Foundation framework, which was automatically included when you used the Foundation Command Line Tool template. If you don't believe me, try leaving it out and see what happens.

The last line of the program is the `return` statement that ends the execution of `main` and finishes the program:

```
return (0);
```

The zero value returned says that our program completed successfully (remember earlier I explained that functions can return data; here is example). As you see in Chapter 5, this is the way `return` statements work in Objective-C.

Congratulations, again! You've just written, compiled, run, and deconstructed your first Objective-C program.

Customizing Xcode to Your Liking

Xcode has options galore, many of which won't make any sense until you have quite a bit of programming experience, but a few are worth thinking about now. So let's go through how you can set preferences in Xcode.

1. **With Xcode open, choose Xcode⇨Preferences from the main menu.**

2. **Click Debugging in the toolbar, as shown in Figure 2-29.**

   The Xcode Preferences window refreshes to show the various preferences.

3. **Select the On Start drop-down menu and choose Show Console, as I did in Figure 2-29. Then click Apply.**

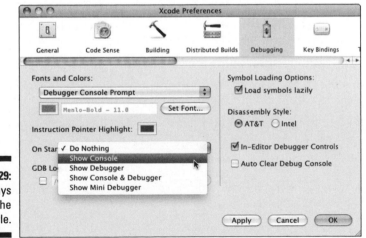

Figure 2-29:
Always show the console.

This step automatically opens the Debugger Console after you build your application. This means you won't have to open Debugger Console to see your application's output.

4. **Click Building in the toolbar, as shown in Figure 2-29.**

5. **Select the Open during builds drop-down menu and choose Always (right now it is set to Never) as I did in Figure 2-30. Then click Apply.**

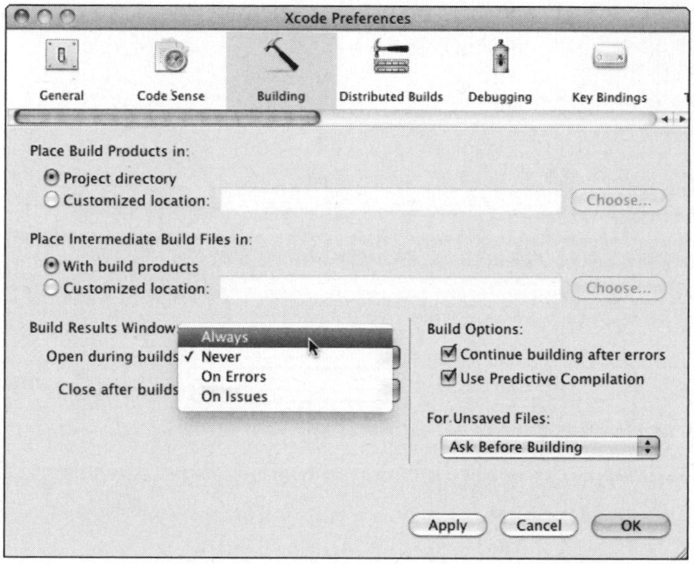

Figure 2-30:
Show
the Build
Results
window.

This opens the Build Results window and keeps it open. You might not like this, but some people find it is easier to find and fix errors this way. I explain this more in Chapter 8.

6. **Click Documentation in the toolbar, as shown in Figure 2-31.**

7. **Click the Check for and install updates automatically checkbox, and the press Check and Install Now.**

This ensures that the documentation remains up to date (this also allows you to load and access other documentation).

8. **Click OK to close the Xcode Preferences window.**

Now click the Build and Run button in the toolbar to build your application with the new preferences. You see the results in Figure 2-32.

You can also set the tab width and other formatting options in Indentation. I set mine to 2 so that I can display more on a page. The default is 4.

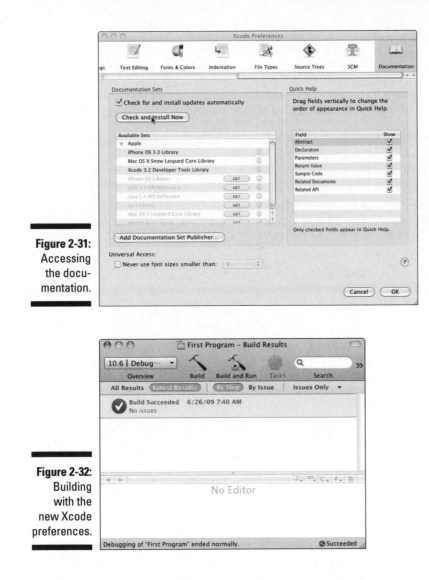

Figure 2-31:
Accessing
the docu-
mentation.

Figure 2-32:
Building
with the
new Xcode
preferences.

Getting to Know the Xcode Text Editor

The main tool you use to write code for an iPhone or Mac OS application is the Xcode Text Editor. The Text Editor has a lot of great features, such as these:

✓ **Code Sense:** As you type code, you can have the Editor help out by inserting text that completes the name of whatever Xcode thinks you're going to enter.

Using Code Sense can be really useful, especially if you are like me and forget exactly what the arguments are for a function. When Code Sense is active (it is by default), Xcode uses the text you typed, as well as the context within which you typed it, to provide suggestions for completing what it thinks you're *going to* type. You can accept suggestions by pressing Tab or Return. You may also display a list of completions by pressing Escape.

Try typing NSL in the Editor view and see what happens.

✔ **Code Folding:** With code folding, you can collapse code that you're not working on and display only the code that requires your attention. You do this by clicking in the column to the left of the code you want to hide.

✔ **The Text Editor navigation bar (see Figure 2-22):** This navigation bar contains a number of shortcuts. These are shown in Figure 2-33. I explain more about them as you use them.

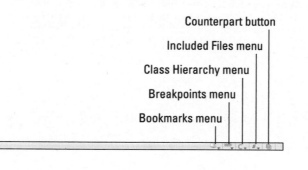

Counterpart button

Included Files menu

Class Hierarchy menu

Breakpoints menu

Bookmarks menu

Figure 2-33:
The Text
Editor
navigation
bar.

- **Bookmarks menu.** You create a bookmark by choosing Edit⇨Add to Bookmarks.

- **Breakpoints menu.** Lists the breakpoints in the current file — I cover breakpoints in Chapter 8.

- **Class Hierarchy menu.** I explain class hierarchies in Chapter 10.

- **Included Files menu.** Lists both the files included by the current file and the files that include the current file.

- **Counterpart button.** This allows you to switch between header and implementation files. You discover why this is so useful in Chapter 6.

✔ **Launching a file in a separate window:** Double-click the filename in the Groups & Files list to launch the file in a new window. This enables you folks with big monitors, or multiple monitors, to look at more than one file at a time.

If you have any questions about what something does, just position the mouse pointer above the button, and a tooltip explains it.

If you have never programmed before, some of this information may not make sense right away. But it makes sense as you do more coding while going through this book. I suggest you come back to this section and the next two sections as you go through Chapter 6.

Accessing Documentation

Like many developers, you may find yourself wanting to dig deeper when it comes to a particular bit of code. That's when you really appreciate Xcode's Quick Help, header file access, documentation window, Help menu, and Find tools. With these tools, you can quickly access the documentation for a particular class, method, or property.

For example, what if you had a burning desire to learn more about NSLog?

Quick Help

Quick Help is an unobtrusive window that provides the documentation for a single symbol. It pops up inline, although you can use Quick Help as a symbol inspector (which stays open) by moving the window after it opens. You can also customize the display in Documentation preferences in Xcode preferences.

To get Quick Help for a symbol, double-click the symbol in the Text Editor (in this case, NSLog; see Figure 2-34).

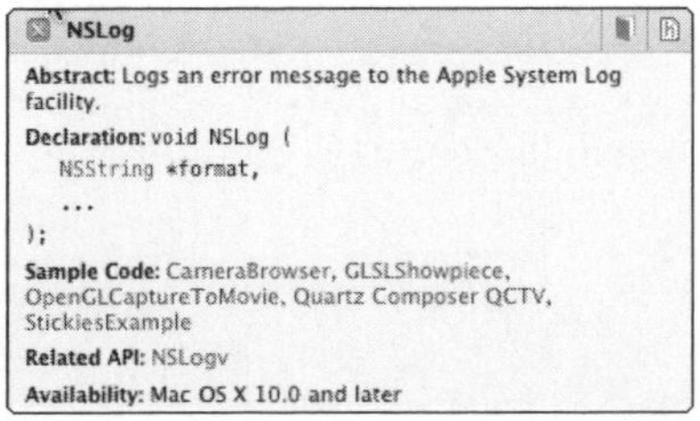

Figure 2-34:
Getting
quick help.

> **NSLog**
>
> **Abstract:** Logs an error message to the Apple System Log facility.
> **Declaration:** void NSLog (
>   NSString *format,
>   ...
>);
> **Sample Code:** CameraBrowser, GLSLShowpiece, OpenGLCaptureToMovie, Quartz Composer QCTV, StickiesExample
> **Related API:** NSLogv
> **Availability:** Mac OS X 10.0 and later

The header file for a symbol

Headers are a big deal in code because they're the place where you find the class declaration, which includes all of its instance variables and method declarations — you learn about classes and headers in Chapter 6). To get the header file for a symbol, press ⌘ and double-click the symbol in the Text Editor (for example, see Figure 2-35, where I pressed ⌘ and then double-clicked NSLog). This works for you classes as well.

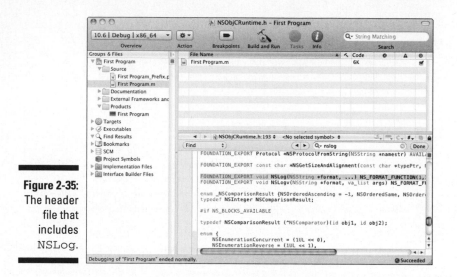

Figure 2-35: The header file that includes NSLog.

Documentation window

The documentation window lets you browse and search items that are part of the ADC Reference Library as well as any third-party documentation you have installed.

You access the documentation by pressing ⌘+Option+double-clicking a symbol to get access to an API reference that provides information about the symbol. This enables you to get the documentation about a method to find out more about it, or the methods and properties in a framework class. In Figure 2-36, I pressed ⌘+Option and double-clicked NSLog.

Using the documentation window, you can browse and search the developer documentation — the API references, guides, and article collections about particular tools or technologies — installed on your computer.

Help menu

The Help menu search field also lets you search Xcode documentation as well as open the documentation window and Quick Help.

You can also right-click on a symbol and get a pop-up menu that gives you similar options to what you see in the Help menu. This is shown in Figure 2-37.

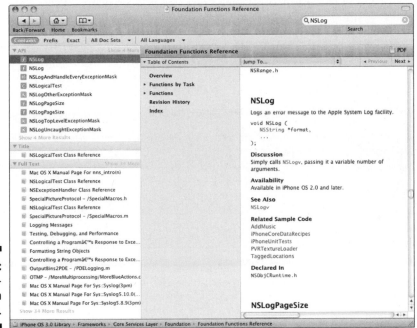

Figure 2-36:
The docu-
mentation
window.

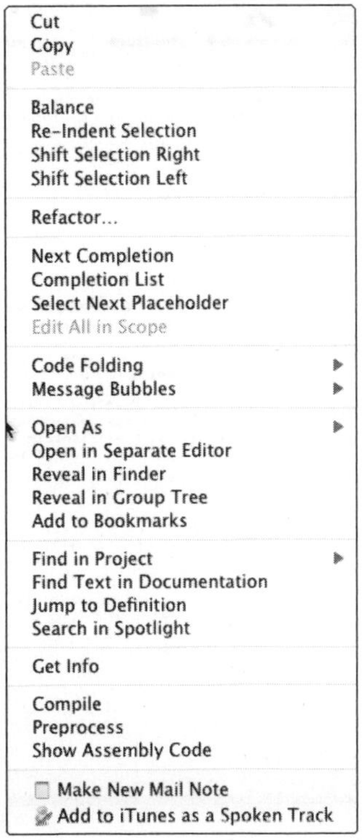

Figure 2-37:
Right-click
NSLog.

Find

Xcode can also help you find things in your own project. The submenu accessed by choosing Edit⇨Find provides several options for finding text in your own project. Choosing Edit⇨Find⇨Find or ⌘+F searches in the file in the Editor window. It opens a Find toolbar to help you navigate.

You can also use Find to go through your whole project by choosing Edit⇨ Find⇨Find in Project or by pressing ⌘+Shift+F. I pressed ⌘+Shift+F, which opened the window shown in Figure 2-38. I typed NSLog, and then in the drop-down menu, I selected In Project.

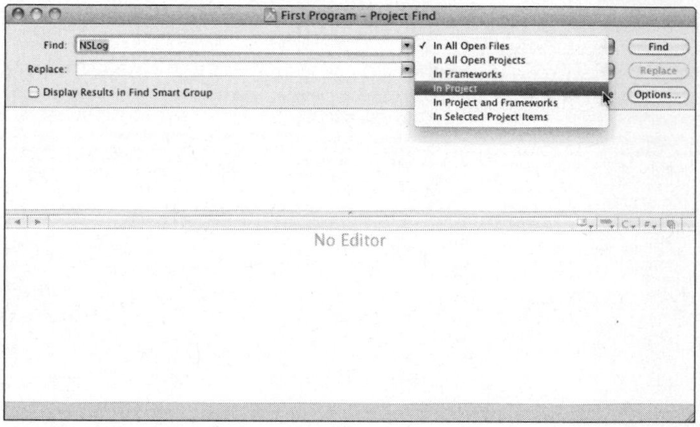

Figure 2-38:
Project Find.

Press Find to see the results shown in Figure 2-39. I selected NSLog @"("Hello, World!"); in the top pane, and the file it's in opened in the bottom pane.

If you've had some programming experience, you also may realize that there are a lot of options as far as the compiler is concerned. You have a great deal of control over the warnings the compiler gives you, as well as the option to turn warnings into errors so they don't slip by you (it happens to the best of us). So take a look at Figure 2-40. If you select First Program in the Files & Groups list, and then click the blue info button on the toolbar you bring up a window that has project information. If you select the Build tab and scroll all the way down (as I did in Figure 2-40) to GCC 4.2 - Warnings, you can customize those warnings to you heart's content. (You may have to click on the disclosure triangle for GCC 4.2 – Warnings.) You can even tell Xcode to always treat warnings as errors by checking the Treat Warnings as Errors checkbox. The configuration drop-down menu allows you to do this for Debug, Release, or All Configurations.

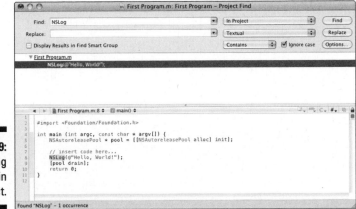

Figure 2-39:
Finding
NSLog in
your project.

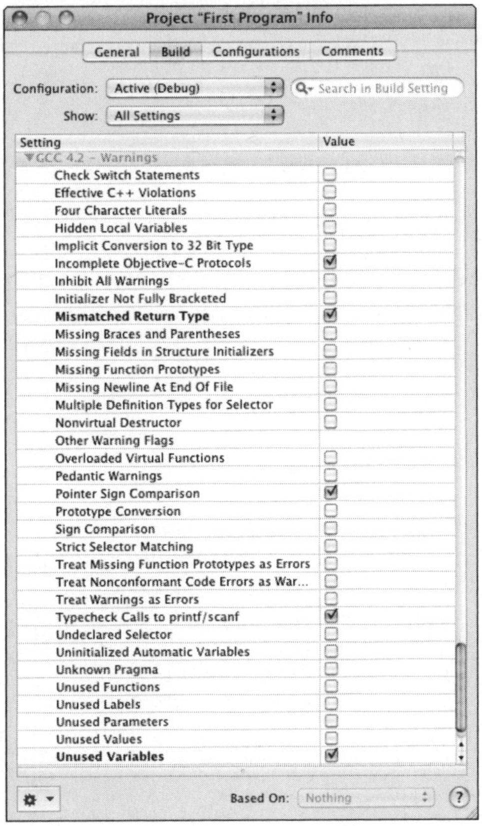

Figure 2-40:
Build con-
figuration.

On the CD

The CD that accompanies this book has a folder for each chapter starting with Chapter 4. Each of these folders has another folder that contains the Xcode project that provides the starting point for each chapter — labeled (cleverly enough) Chapter *XX* Start Here.

That same chapter folder has a folder that contains the final version of the project for each chapter labeled Example *XX* (except for Chapters 4 and 8, where a final version isn't applicable) or, in those chapters with more than one exercise, you see the exercises are labeled Example *XX* A, Example *XX* B, and so on. I explain what is in each of the folders in the appropriate chapter.

If you want to work with anything on the CD, you have to drag it onto your desktop (or into any other folder) to be able to build the project.

Working with the Examples

My experience both personally and in teaching is that the more you type — that is, the more code you actually write — the more you learn, and the faster you learn it.

You work on a single application starting in Chapter 5 that finally ends up as an application for both the iPhone and Max OS X. This application illustrates all of the things you need to know to program in Objective-C. I help you build it step by step; much like a developer creates a "real" application. At times, you enter some code only to delete it later. Go with the flow. There is a method behind all of this, one that has been developed to get you going as quickly as possible and know as much as you need to, without being overwhelmed. More important, you see not only how to do something, but also why you should do it that way.

The best way to work through this book is to complete Chapter 4, and then follow along with me and add to that project as you go from chapter to chapter (and create the new project along the way). If you are not the linear sort, or you want a fresh, up-to-date copy of the project, you can always use the Start Here copy on the CD for each chapter. I do think adding to what you have already done is better and more in tune with how you (and other developers) really work — often two steps forward and a quarter step back.

Finally, experiment as much as you can. Don't always take my word for it; test things out, see what happens when you change something, and play with it until you really understand how something works. That's how I learned Objective-C, and I'm sure it will work for you as well.

Chapter 3

The Object in Objective-C

*I*n Chapter 2, you get your first taste of programming (all right, enough with the food), and over the next 15 chapters, I show you everything you need to know to write computer programs. While you may think that's pretty cool, you shouldn't be satisfied with that alone. Your goal shouldn't be to simply be able to write programs using Objective-C; your goal should be to write *good* programs using Objective-C.

So what makes a good program? Well, a blinding flash of the obvious answer is one that meets the needs of the user. While that is true, it is only part of the answer. What also makes a program good is how easy it is to make changes to it.

I want to use the example I give you in Chapter 1 — a computer program that tracks my expense when I travel. It keeps track of my budget and converts foreign currency charges into dollars.

As I develop this program, I am going to have to make changes to it for three reasons.

> ✔ **I'll want to add new functionality.** For example, starting out, the program will work with cash and credit card transactions. I'll get that up and running, and then eventually I'll want to be able to add ATM transactions, and also track my hotel and plane reservations. I will want to be able to do this without having to completely rewrite the program. In fact, I would like to be able to add a new feature without changing anything at all in the existing program and have that feature transparently incorporated into the program. The term for this is *extensible*, and that means adding functionality to an existing program or module.

> ✔ **I'll want to improve or change functionality.** To start with I'm willing to enter the exchange rate by hand. Eventually, I'll want the program to go out and find the current exchange rate for me. Again, I want to be able to do this without having to make any changes in the program except to code the new functionality. The term for this is *enhanceable*. And that means changing the way existing functionality works.
>
> ✔ **I'll want to fix bugs.** Hard to believe, but there will be bugs. I want to be able to fix them, without breaking something else.

One of the problems with changing things is that often a little change in one part of your program can have disastrous impact on the rest of it. Most of us have had a similar experience when upgrading a program or the OS version. I remember a fellow programmer once lamenting, "but I only changed one line of code," after making changes to a program and then putting it into production (without taking it through the entire testing process) — only to have it take down an entire mainframe complex.

To minimize the side effects of "only changing one line of code" requires that you divide your programs into *modules* so that a change you make in one module won't have an impact on the rest of your code. I refer to this as *transparency*.

A *module* is simply a self-contained, or independent, unit that can be combined with other units to get the job done. Modules are the solution to a rather knotty problem — even a simple program can run into hundreds of lines of instructions, and you need a way to break them into parts to make them understandable. But more importantly, you want to use modules because they make programs easier to modify, which, as you saw, you invariably need to do.

Not All Modules Are Created Equal

The idea of dividing your program into modules is as old as programming itself, and you know how old that is. The programming style or *paradigm* I mention in Chapter 1 dictates the way you do that.

You need to be concerned with two paradigms at this point, although with more experience you'll probably explore others.

Functions (or things like that), and groups of functions, have historically been the basis of modularization. This way of dividing things up into modules is used in the programming style or paradigm known as *procedural programming*. Going back to the example I started with — a program that helped me track my expenses — you will find functions like *spend dollars* or *charge foreign currency*, which will operate on *transaction* and *budget data*.

In the last few years, however, the procedural paradigm has pretty much been supplanted, at least for commercial applications, by *object-oriented programming*. In Objective-C (and other object-oriented languages) objects (and as you will see, their corresponding classes) are the way a program is divided up. In an object-oriented program, you will find *transaction objects* and *budget objects*.

For years, the arguments raged about which was the better way, procedural or object oriented, with each side pointing out the limitations in the other's approach. This is not the place to relive it. It will serve no value because a) for all practical purposes the debate has been settled in favor of object-oriented programming for commercial applications (except for a few fanatics), and b) because you are learning Objective-C, which is an object-oriented language. You experience for yourself the differences in Chapters 5 and 6.

But to give you some perspective, you can think of objects in an *object-oriented program* as working as a team necessary to reach a goal. Functions in a *procedural program* are more like the command and control structure of a large corporation (think GM) or the army. Which is more flexible?

So let's get on with understanding objects.

Understanding How Objects Behave

An object-oriented program consists of a network of interconnected objects, essentially modules that call upon each other to solve a part of the puzzle. The objects work like a team. Each object has a specific role to play in the overall design of the program and is able to communicate with other objects. Objects communicate requests to other objects to do something using *messages*.

Object-oriented programmers (including yours truly) think about objects as actors and talk about them that way. Objects have responsibilities. You *ask* them to do things, they *decide* what to do, and they *behave* in a certain way. You do this even with objects like sandwiches. You could, for example, tell a sandwich in an object-oriented program to go cut itself in half (ouch!), or tell a shape to draw itself.

It's this resemblance to real things that gives objects much of their power and appeal. You can use them not only to represent things in the real world — a person, an airplane reservation, a credit card transaction — but also to represent things in a computer, such as a window, button, or slider.

Inventing Objective-C

Brad Cox (a computer scientist among other things) invented Objective-C in the early 1980s. He took SmallTalk — one of the favorite object-oriented programming languages at the time — and used it as a basis to add extensions to the (non–object-oriented) standard ANSI C language to make it object-oriented.

ANSI C is the standard published by the American National Standards Institute (ANSI) for the C programming language. Having a standard means that there are no if, ands, or buts about what an instruction does — and it does the same thing no matter what computer, operating system, or compiler you are using.

Objective-C got its big break when it was chosen for the NextSTEP development environment, which eventually became the development system you use today on the Mac to develop applications for the Mac and iPhone.

But what gives object-oriented programming its power is that the way objects are defined and the way they interact with each other make it relatively easy to accomplish the goals of extensibility and enhanceability — that is, achieve the transparency that is the hallmark of a good program. This is accomplished using two features in object-oriented programming languages.

- ✔ *Encapsulation* **is about celebrating your object's ignorance about how things work in the objects they use.** My wife has no idea how a computer works, but can effectively browse the Internet, create documents, and receive and send e-mail. Most people who can successfully drive cars have no idea of how the engine works. I'll refer to this as the I-Don't-Care-And-Please-Don't-Tell-Me approach.

    Encapsulation makes it possible for me to change how an object carries out its responsibilities or behaves (enhanceability) and to add new responsibilities to an object (extensibility) without having to disturb the existing code that uses those objects. One of the primary things that objects encapsulate is their data, and while this probably evokes a big yawn now, you will realize why this is important in Chapter 5. It also makes it possible, as you will see in Chapter 11, to even transparently add new objects.

- ✔ *Polymorphism* **is about cultivating more of the same.** When I get dressed in the morning, I throw on a pair of jeans and a black T-shirt. For me at least, one black T-shirt is as good as another, whether it comes from Niemen Marcus or Costco. Your objects shouldn't have to care about how one object is different from another as long as the object does what the requesting object needs it to do. I'll refer to this as the More-Of-The-Same approach.

    This feature in object-oriented languages makes it possible to add new objects of the same type, and have your program handle them without making any changes to the code that uses them. For example, I can create a program that processes cash and credit card transactions, and then sometime later I can add an ATM transaction and have the program process that new kind of transaction without having to make any changes to the processing logic.

With respect to all the new ideas I have thrown at you, this is usually the hardest concept for most people to grasp right away (the name polymorphism doesn't help), although everyone gets it after seeing it in action. I give you a good example later in this chapter and cover it extensively in Chapter 11. I promise you that once you use it in your program, you'll wonder why you thought it was so hard in the first place.

Seeing the Concepts in Action

Reading about concepts can keep me entertained for only a short time, a very short time, before I need some concrete examples. I want to tell you a story about how encapsulation and polymorphism became real for me.

Encapsulation

I lived (briefly) in Minneapolis, Minnesota, where it can be not just cold, but *really* cold. During that time, I invented a device (in my head at least) called the uPhone — which was a handheld device (it looked something like Figure 3-1) that enabled me to start my car and turn on the heater before I left the house in the morning.

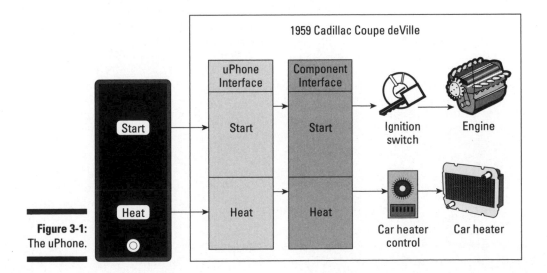

Figure 3-1: The uPhone.

I happily used my uPhone until one day my mechanic found a new heater for me that worked much more quickly and used a lot less gas. I was a bit concerned, but he told me not to worry; it was plug-compatible with my old heater — it had the same controls; all he had to do was just plug it in. Surprisingly (to me not to him), when he installed it, my uPhone application still worked in the same way. You can see that in Figure 3-2.

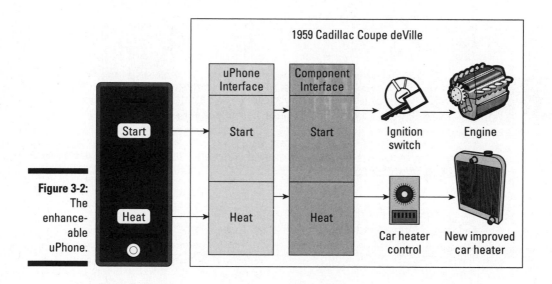

Figure 3-2: The enhance-able uPhone.

The reason that worked, as you can see in Figure 3-2, was because my application (including the uPhone, uPhone Interface, and Component Interface) knew nothing about heaters. All the application really cared about was the heater switch (car heater control). As long as that stayed the same, every-thing worked. Had I not used the uPhone and Component Interfaces, but had instead modified the heater so the uPhone actually interacted with the heater components, I would have had a more difficult job on my hands.

To make your programs enhanceable, you want to depend on the imple-mentation details as little as possible. As I mentioned previously, the pro-gramming term for this I-Don't-Care-And-Please-Don't-Tell-Me approach is *encapsulation*.

What you are doing is hiding *how* things are being done from *what* is being done. In a program, that means hiding the internal mechanisms and data struc-tures of a software component behind a defined interface in such a way that users of the component (other pieces of software) only need to know what the component does and do not have to make themselves dependent on the details of how the component does what it promises to do. This means the following:

✔ The internal mechanisms of a module can be improved without having to make any changes in any of the modules that use it.

✔ The component is protected from user meddling (like me trying to rewire a heater).

✔ Things are less complex because the interdependencies between modules have been reduced as much as possible.

This is the way modules, or objects, should work in an object-oriented program. You want the objects to limit their knowledge of other objects to what those objects can do — like turn on and off. That way, if you change something, you don't have to go digging through a zillion lines of code to figure out if there is any code in your program that is depending on something being done a particular way and then changing that dependent code to work with the new way it will be done. Ignorance is bliss, for the programmer that is.

Polymorphism

After my device worked so well for me, my wife decided she wanted one, too. The problem is she had a different kind of car with a different heater control, and my old component interface wouldn't work. Well, this time I did have to make some changes, but all I had to do was change the Component Interface to the heater. I kept the uPhone Interface the same, which also meant no changes to the uPhone, as shown in Figure 3-3.

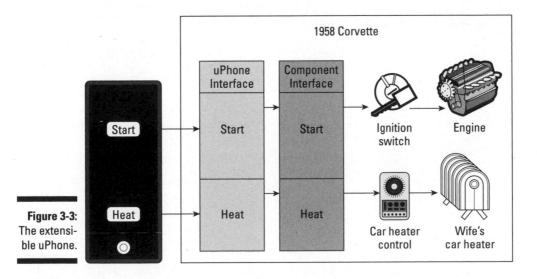

Figure 3-3: The extensible uPhone.

What you are looking for is a situation in which the requestor doesn't even care who receives the message, as long as it can get what it wants.

So the uPhone doesn't care whether it is sending the heat message to a 1959 Cadillac, or a 1958 corvette, or even an SSC Ultimate Aero TT, as long as it can respond to the message.

This capability of different objects to respond, each in its own way, to identical messages is called *polymorphism*.

While encapsulation allows you to ignore how things are done, polymorphism allows you to escape the specific details of differences between objects that do the same thing in different ways. In the real world, if you can drive a Chevy, you can drive a Caddy or any other car, as long as the controls are more or less the same. It is not that a 1959 Cadillac and a 1958 Corvette are the same; if they were what would be the point? What is important is that they are different, but you can go about using them in the same way.

I used to travel a lot and rent lots of cars. Can you image if I had to spend two hours being trained every time I rented a different car? In a program, different objects might perform the same methods in different ways — if I spend cash, a cash transaction object will subtract that amount from my budget. If I use my credit card, a credit card transaction will first have to convert the amount in foreign currency that I charged to dollars and then subtract it from the budget.

Reusable Code

When people talk about object-oriented programming, they tend to talk about two things. The first is all that cool encapsulation and polymorphism stuff, which makes it easy to modify programs. Then they talk about reuse, and that you can create reusable objects that save time and money. Years ago there was always talk about object stores where you could buy objects that would do what you needed them to do.

Will this book teach you how to write reusable code? Well, it depends on what you mean by *reusable*. If you really think about it, when you enhance or extend your program, what you are doing is *reusing* the existing code to create essentially a "new" program. And in that respect, the answer is yes.

As you will see, the best models for reusability are found in the frameworks you'll use to develop applications for the iPhone and Mac. You reuse the frameworks by adding your own application functionality to the framework that already includes the code that can display windows and controls and menus — the whole kit and caboodle of the user interface, and then some.

I'll explain some of the things that the framework designers did to make reusing their frameworks as easy as it is. You'll find that when you use those same principles and techniques in your programs, you will have taken a giant step forward in enabling the kind of reusability you need to make your programs enhanceable and extensible.

Part II
Speaking the Language of Objective-C

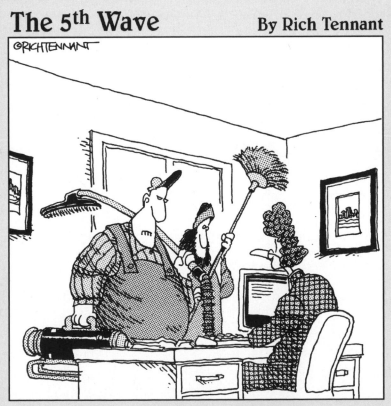

The 5th Wave   By Rich Tennant

"We're here to clean the code."

In this part . . .

Now that you have the tools downloaded, it's time to start programming. I help you do that in this part by first covering most of the Objective-C instruction set, which you'll need to get started. Think of the instruction set as the words that Objective-C understands, along with some rules about how you are allowed to combine them into sentences.

I also show you the language features that will enable you to create industrial-strength applications. This is what will make your application suitable for commercial distribution. I also get you up to speed using some prepackaged functionality (frameworks) that help make your programming tasks easier.

You get the rundown on the vocabulary of a new language, but as you will find out, it's a lot easier than learning to speak Sanskrit, for example.

Chapter 4

Language and Programming Basics

A s I mention in Chapter 3, Objective-C is a set of extensions to standard ANSI C. This means that at some point (that is, this chapter), you'll have to sit down and learn the basics of the C instruction set, along with some less than inspiring examples and detailed explanations on the basics of the language — kind of like learning your alphabet. I know all this can be tedious and excruciatingly boring, although when you're just starting out there's no other way (we all have to pay our dues at some point). But once you are done with this chapter, you will switch to learning Objective-C by developing a "real world" application, which I promise is (for the most part) much more interesting. So hang in there.

It All Comes Down to Your Statements

At the end of the day, it's all about the instructions you give the computer. Those instructions are called *statements*. You can easily recognize a statement because it ends with a semicolon, as shown here:

```
NSLog(@"This is a statement");
```

There are a number of different kinds of statements. In this chapter, I show you two of them:

- ✔ *Declarations* of a variable allow space for data. They look something like this:

```
int aNumber;
```

  Declarations are used to allocate areas in memory where you can store data.

- ✔ *Instructions*, or "do this, please." They usually look like the following:

```
a= b + c;
NSLog(@"Yo Stella");
```

  Instructions can consist of the following:

  - *Operators*, which are symbols that represent operations. For example the +, shown in the preceding example, is an arithmetic operation. I cover operators in this chapter.

  - *Functions*, which are groups of statements. `NSLog` and `printf` and `main` are examples of a function. I cover functions in Chapter 5.

  - *Objects*, which group together methods (similar to a function) and data. I cover objects in Chapter 6.

There are also other kinds of statements. One kind you'll be using describes how data is structured (see Chapter 5 for more on data structures). Another kind of statement has to do with the language itself, such as `typedef`, which I cover in Chapter 5. There are also control statements, such as the `if` statement, which I will start explaining later in this chapter in the section "Making Logical Decisions in Your Code." I'll finish that explanation, along with loops, in Chapter 9.

Your program will also have other lines of code. These lines will consist of things like compiler directives such as

```
@implementation
```

as well as preprocessor directives (the preprocessor is used by the compiler before compilation to expand macros, which are brief abbreviations for longer constructs) such as

```
#include
```

I will explain compiler and preprocessor directives as you need to use them.

Computer languages are really like all other languages in that they have *syntax* and *semantics*. Since the compiler will be happy to give you *syntax errors*, and some things you will read will use the term *semantics*, I'll explain what each means.

Syntax

Syntax refers to the ways symbols may be combined to create well-formed statements in a given language. Think of all the grammar you had to learn in school, and you have a good idea of what syntax is. Syntax errors are what the compiler gives you when it can't understand the code you have written.

Semantics

But even though your code may be syntactically (grammatically) correct, it still may be meaningless. For example, Noam Chomsky's

Colorless green ideas sleep furiously

is syntactically correct but has no meaning (at least to most of us). *Semantics* is about meaning, and it describes the behavior of a computer when executing a program in the language. It describes what you get as the result of an operation:

```
a = b + c;
```

For example, a = b + c means that the value of b is added to the value of c, without modifying either of their values, and the result is assigned to a. The previous value for a is gone and replaced with the new value. (I bet you never thought high school algebra would come in this handy.)

Semantics also describes the results of a series of operations or statements as well. For example, a function named computeZimbabweanValue (I explain what functions are in Chapter 5) computes the number of Zimbabwean dollars you can get for one U.S. dollar at the current exchange rate.

You have semantic errors when the program doesn't do what you expect it to do.

Understanding How Variables Work

The memory in a computer is organized in *bytes*. A byte is the minimum amount of memory that you can address. A byte can store a relatively small amount of data — one single character or a small integer (generally an integer between 0 and 255). But the computer actually groups bytes together to create and manipulate more complex data, such as integers and floating point numbers.

Variables are nothing more than convenient names to refer to a specific piece of data, such as a number, that is stored in memory.

In order to use a variable in Objective-C, you must first *declare* it by specifying which *data type* you want it to be and give it a name — called an *identifier* — and, optionally, an initial value. Here is an Objective-C statement (that is, a line of code) where the type of the variable is specified, along with a name and an initial value:

```
int anInteger = 42;
```

Data types

When you ask for some memory to store data, the compiler has to know what kind of data you want to store. The compiler needs to know that in order to determine how much memory you need and how that variable can be used (how to do math with it is one example). The kind of data you are requesting memory for is called a *data type*, and this concept will become important because not only can you use what are known as *built-in* types, which I explain in this section, but you can also create your own types, which I explain in Chapters 5 and 6.

While the minimum amount of memory that your computer can manage is one byte, the data types you will be working with will range from that one byte up to eight bytes (or more for your own types or some of the types defined in the frameworks you will be using).

Table 4-1 shows the basic data types.

Table 4-1	Basic Data Types		
Type	*What It Is*	*Example*	*Size*
Char	A character	N or g	1 byte
Int	An integer — a whole number	42, -42, 1234	4 bytes
Float	Single precision floating point number	1.99999	4 bytes
Double	Double precision floating point number	1.9999999999	8 bytes

Figure 4-1 illustrates an example of the amount of memory allocated to a char and an int, respectively.

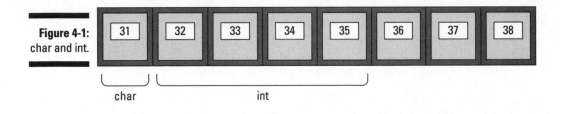

Figure 4-1: char and int.

There is also a number of variations on the int, which are shown in Table 4-2.

Table 4-2	Additional Types Based on int		
Type	**What It Is**	**Example**	**Size**
short	A short integer	42, -42 1234	2 bytes
long	A double short	42, -42, 1234	4 bytes
long long	A double long	1.99999	8 bytes

There are also types like BOOL, void, and id, which I explain as you need to use them.

With the exception of both the float and the double, each of the types can be *signed* or *unsigned* (this has to do with binary arithmetic and is beyond the scope of this book). If you don't specify *signed* or *unsigned,* the compiler will assume signed.

int is often the default if you don't specify a type. For example, you can use signed and unsigned to mean a signed int and unsigned int, respectively.

Note that

```
signed anInteger = 42;
```

is the same as

```
int anInteger = 42;
```

If it's a kind of int, the largest value a data type can hold depends on its size and whether it is signed or unsigned, as shown in Table 4-3.

Table 4-3	Signed and Unsigned Data Types
Size	Range
1 byte	signed: -128 to 127
	unsigned: 0 to 255
2 bytes	signed: -32768 to 32767
	unsigned: 0 to 65535
4 bytes	signed: -2147483648 to 2147483647
	unsigned: 0 to 4294967295
8 bytes	signed -9,223,372,036,854,775,808 to +9,223,372,036,854,775,807
	unsigned 0 to18,446,744,073,709,551,615

For floating point numbers, such as float or double, you should think instead in terms of *significant digits*. For a float, the number of significant digits is 7 or 8, and for a double, the number of significant digits is 15 or 16.

Identifier

As I said, when you declare a variable in Objective-C, not only do you specify the data type, but you also give it a name — called an *identifier* — that you can use to refer to the variable. Consider the declaration I started with:

```
int anInteger = 42;
```

In this case, the name or identifier is anInteger. I can then use anInteger whenever I want to refer to the variable.

You do have to follow some rules when it comes to the identifier.

- ✓ **Use only letters from the alphabet.** For your purposes, even though there are other choices, name your identifiers using one or more of the 26 letters of the alphabet.

- ✓ **Use uppercase to help readability.** Start by using lowercase, but, as I did with anInteger, if it helps readability and describes the variable better, use uppercase inside the name. Be sure to give your variables a name that describes them so that your code is more readable.

✔ **Avoid using words used by Apple or Objective-C.** Also be aware that names cannot match any of the words used by Apple (in the frameworks) or Objective-C. I include a list of reserved words at the end of this chapter, but don't worry, if you make a mistake, the compiler will let you know. Naming is generally not one of the major challenges in programming (easy for me to say), and after a while, you get the hang of it.

✔ **Pay attention to upper- and lowercase.** And, oh yes, this is very important: The Objective-C language is a *case-sensitive* language. That means an identifier written in uppercase letters is not equivalent to another one with the same name but written in lowercase letters. Thus, for example, the Neal variable is not the same as the NEAL variable or the neaL variable. These are three different variable identifiers.

Initialization

In a declaration, not only do you specify a type and a name, but you also *may* specify an initial value — as in the declaration

```
int anInteger = 42;
```

Take a look at the equal sign; it's not what you may think. Most people learn the equal sign by, oh, about first grade, but the equal sign here is a little more than that. In fact, the equal sign is an *operator*, more specifically the *assignment operator*. It is an instruction that tells the computer to set that portion of memory that I am calling anInteger to the value of 42.

Specifying an initial value is called *initialization*, and it's not required. For example,

```
int anInteger;
```

works just fine. Memory will be reserved, but you can't count on what the value will be. Of course, sometimes you don't care, such as when you are going to use that variable to hold the result of a subsequent operation.

I could also declare two variables by doing the following:

```
int anInteger1, anInteger2;
```

In this case, I reserved space for two ints: anInteger1, and anInteger2.

Finally, note the semicolon at the end of the statement. A semicolon is required at the end of every statement. Since an *instruction* can span multiple lines, the semicolon is the way to tell the compiler that you are done with your instruction.

To summarize, the *declaration* I have been explaining is a request for memory to hold a data type of int that I can refer to using the name anInteger, which has an initial value of 42, as illustrated in Figure 4-2. The memory location 32 is for illustrative purposes only. But I will return and use this example again when I discuss pointers later in this chapter in the section "Accessing Data with Pointers."

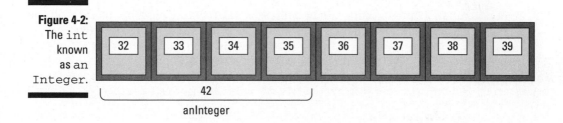

Figure 4-2:
The int known as an Integer.

Giving Instructions with Operators

Operators perform operations on (do things to) data, which enables you to actually do something with those pesky variables. As I explain in Chapter 1, operators are one of the basic building blocks that you'll work with.

In this chapter, I cover the operators you'll need to use. Quite a few operators are available to you, but if you made it through grammar school, most of them will be familiar.

Really learning how operators (and everything else) work in Objective-C

Before you start coding, I want to help you understand the best way to go through this chapter and the rest of the book. Entering the code is not meant to be a typing exercise. As you enter each line, you should be thinking about what will happen as a result of that line of code being executed. Then after you build the project, you should look to see if you were correct in your expectation. If you were, great; then continue. If not, you should reread the explanation until you are sure you understand it. In most of this chapter (with a few exceptions), this issue won't be a problem. There will be times, however, when the results of executing your code are not so obvious, or you may not be sure you completely understood what you just read. I encourage you (I'll actually do a bit of nagging as well) to write code that uses what I am explaining, even if I do not have you do it in a formal exercise, to make sure you understand it.

In fact, one of the themes running through this book is code, code, code. My experience both personally and in teaching is that the more you type (that is, the more code you actually write), the more you learn and the faster you learn it. (I know I have said this before, but just in case you thought I wasn't serious about it, I'll say it again.)

Using arithmetic operators

Using the lowly (or lovely, depending on your perspective) int, let's look at the various operations you can perform.

In Chapter 2, you created a project called My First Program. You can continue to use that project in this chapter, or you can copy it (onto your desktop, for example) from the CD that accompanies this book. You can find it in the Chapter 4 Start Here folder in the Chapter 4 folder.

To use that project to start writing code, follow these steps:

1. **Go to the Xcode Project Window and in the Groups & Files pane, click the triangle next to Source to expand the folder.**

2. **From the Source folder, select** My First Program.m **— the main function**.

   The contents of the file appear in the main display pane of the Xcode editor.

3. **Look for the following lines of code:**

```
#import <Foundation/Foundation.h>

int main (int argc, const char * argv[]) {
  NSAutoreleasePool * pool = [[NSAutoreleasePool
                                    alloc] init];

  // insert code here...
  NSLog(@"Hello, World!");
  [pool drain];
  return 0;
}
```

In some cases in the book, you'll see statements on two lines. I have to do that in order to fit the code on the page; you should use only one line where you can. This is especially important for strings, which will give you an error if they are on two lines, unless you tell the compiler that's what you want to do. I'll show you a way to have a single string span multiple lines in the section "Using Constants."

4. **Delete everything with a strikethrough (you won't need the memory management features).**

```
#import <Foundation/Foundation.h>

int main (int argc, const char * argv[]) {
  NSAutoreleasePool * pool = [[NSAutoreleasePool
       alloc] init];

  // insert code here...
  NSLog(@"Hello, World!");
  [pool drain];
  return 0;
}
```

Your editor window should look like Figure 4-3.

I will be using this format for the balance of this chapter. So when I tell you to start with an *empty main function*, this is what I mean.

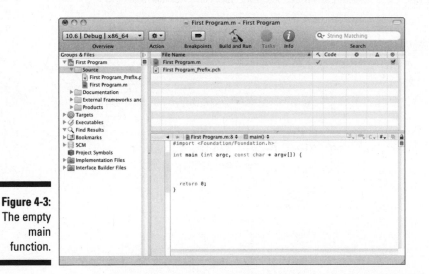

Figure 4-3:
The empty main function.

5. **Type the following lines of code after the first brace, and before the** `return 0;` **statement:**

```
int a;
int b;
int c;

a = 1;
b = 2;
c=a+b;
```

```
NSLog (@" a + b = %i", c);
NSLog (@" a + b = %i",a + b);
NSLog (@" a still = %i", a);
NSLog (@" b still = %i", b);
```

When you're done typing, your code should look exactly like Figure 4-4.

Remember, I said that variables should be descriptive, except sometimes, and this is one of those times. You'll also use single letter variables like *i* and *n* in things like loops (I cover loops in Chapter 9).

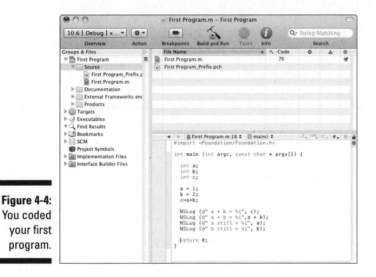

Figure 4-4:
You coded
your first
program.

As I said, the point of these exercises is to make sure that you understand what I am explaining. As you enter the code, you should be thinking about what the results of each line of code will be, and then build the program and use the output to confirm your understanding. To do that, I want to review what you just did:

1. You declared three variables, a, b, and c (they are not initialized, so you don't know what their value is).

   ```
   int a;
   int b;
   int c;
   ```

2. You assigned values to a and b.

   ```
   a = 1;
   b = 2;
   ```

As I mentioned earlier, assignment is an operator that tells the computer to set the area of memory represented by a to 1 and the area represented by b to 2.

3. You added a and b and then assigned (placed) the result in c.

```
c=a+b;
```

In doing that, you just used another arithmetic operator, the *addition operator* (the assignment operator was the first one). There are five arithmetic operators, as shown in the following list:

- +: Addition
- –: Subtraction
- *: Multiplication
- /: Division
- %: Modulo

In a programming language, a + b is an *expression*. An expression is a combination of variables, operators (and functions and messages, which I explain in Chapters 5 and 6, respectively) that can have a value. Computing that value is called *evaluating* the expression.

Although perhaps not obvious, a number like 42 or a variable like a are also considered expressions because both have a value.

In the statement c=a+b, there are no spaces between the c and the +, or any of the other identifiers or operators. Generally, spaces are not needed if the compiler can tell what you mean (although feel free to use them for readability, as I will). In this case, the compiler can recognize the operators, so spaces are not necessary.

4. You displayed the results.

```
NSLog (@" a + b = %i", c);
```

NSLog enables you to display in the Debugger Console (see Chapter 2 for more on displaying in the Debugger Console).

In the NSString (again, refer to Chapter 2 if this is unfamiliar), you use a % character as a placeholder for a value, and the character that follows it indicates the kind of value it is. This is called a *string format specifier*. So, in the expression

```
(@" a + b = %i", c)
```

%i is a string format specifier, and it says replace me with the value of what you see after the closing ", in this case c, and display c as an integer (i). As you can see, you follow the string you want to display with a comma, and then a list of what you want replaced in the same order as they are specified in the string.

The string format specifiers supported are the format specifiers defined for the ANSI C function `printf()` plus `%@` for any object. Here are some of the string format specifiers:

- `%i`: Signed 32-bit integer (`int`)

- `%u`: Unsigned 32-bit integer (`unsigned int`)

- `%f`: 64-bit floating-point number (`double`)

You can find all the string format specifiers by entering `string format specifiers` in the Search ADC field on the Mac or iPhone Dev Center Web sites, and then selecting the document String Programming Guide for Cocoa: String Format Specifiers.

5. You did a computation in the `NSLog` function and displayed the results.

```
NSLog (@" a + b = %i",a + b);
```

Even though you did a computation in the `NSLog` function, `a + b`, the value of the variables used as *operands* or *arguments* (such as `a` and `b`) did not change when using the arithmetic operators you have been using. To ensure you understood that, you displayed `a` and `b` to make sure they were both still the same.

```
NSLog (@" a still = %i", a);
NSLog (@" b still = %i", b);
```

This is a good example of what you should do to make sure you understand how something works — display the result of a line of code. In this case, you want to make sure you understand what does happen to the variables `a` and `b` after the expression `(@" a + b = %i",a + b)` is evaluated.

There are, however, as you will see shortly, operators that do change the value of their operands, and I will be sure to point them out when you get to them.

With that review finished, you are ready to build and run the application. To do that, just select the Build and Run button in the Project Window toolbar. The status bar in the Project Window tells you all about build progress, build errors such as compiler errors, or warnings — and (oh, yeah) whether the build was successful.

Your results should look like Figure 4-5. If you changed your Xcode preferences in Chapter 2, the Debugger Console will open automatically. Otherwise, you will have to open it yourself by selecting Run⇨Console or pressing Shift+⌘+R.

Now that you have gone through coding your first real program, I want to show you some things about the other arithmetic operators.

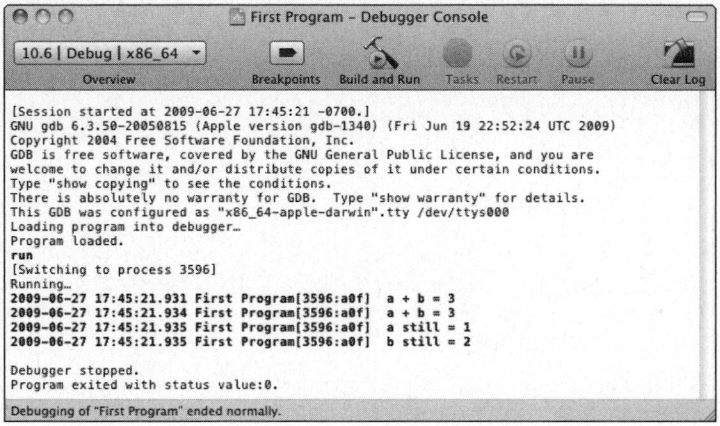

Figure 4-5:
The
Debugger
Console
after build-
ing your
program.

Start with an empty `main` function (delete the code you typed) and do the
following:

1. **Type the following lines of code between the first curly brace and the**
   `return 0;` **statement:**

```
int a;
int b;
int c;

a = 2;
b = 3;

c = a % b;
NSLog (@" a %% b = %i", c);
c = b % a;
NSLog (@" b %% a = %i", c);
c = a % a;
NSLog (@" a %% a = %i", c);
c = a + b;
NSLog (@" a + b = %i", c);
c = b + a;
NSLog (@" b + a = %i", c);
c = a - b;
NSLog (@" a - b = %i", c);
c = b - a;
NSLog (@" b - a = %i", c);
c = a * b;
NSLog (@" a * b = %i", c);
c = a * b + 5 ;
NSLog (@" a * b + 5 = %i", c);
c = a * (b + 5);
NSLog (@" a * (b + 5) = %i", c);
c = (a * b) + 5;
NSLog (@" (a * b) + 5 = %i", c);
```

```
c = b * a;
NSLog (@" b * a = %i", c);
c = a / b;
NSLog (@" a / b = %i", c);
c = b / a;
NSLog (@" b / a = %i", c);
```

Writing code to make sure you understand the arithmetic operators should be old hat to you by now, and perhaps a little boring; you may be thinking, "This is arithmetic!" Well, that's true, but some things are not so obvious when you do arithmetic on the computer. Take a look at some of the code you just entered where the result of its execution may surprise you.

For example, an operator you probably haven't used that much (if ever) is % — the *modulus operator.* It is not what it appears to be, a percentage calculation. The result of the % operator is the remainder from the integer division of the first operand by the second (if the value of the second operand is zero, the behavior of % is undefined).

```
c = a % b;
NSLog (@" a %% b = %i", c);
```

results in

```
a % b = 2
```

and

```
c = b % a;
NSLog (@" b %% a = %i", c);
```

results in

```
b % a = 1
```

and finally

```
c = a % a;
NSLog (@" a %% a = %i", c);
```

results in

```
a % a = 0
```

So, as you can see, a divided by b, which is 2 divided by 3, gives you a remainder of 2. Similarly, 3 % 2 gives you a remainder of 1. However, 3 divided by 3 has no remainder, so the modulus is 0. Try a few other values for a and b and compile the code to see what happens.

The modulus operator can come in handy at times (you can use it to tell whether a number is even or odd, or whether it's a multiple of another number, for example), but it only works with integers. Notice that the NSLog statement that displays the results has two %s. That's because the % is also a control character, as you just saw (it tells the NSLog function that what follows is formatting information), so if you want to display an %, you have to use %%.

Look at the following statements :

```
c = a + b;
NSLog (@" a + b = %i", c);
c = b + a;
NSLog (@" b + a = %i", c);
c = a * b;
c = b * a;
NSLog (@" b * a = %i", c);
```

As you would expect, the order of operands using the arithmetic operators + and * doesn't matter, although when you are programming, it's generally better not to make too many assumptions.

Next, take a look at the following:

```
a * b + 5 = 11
a * (b + 5) = 16
(a * b) + 5 = 11
```

If parentheses were a challenge for you in high school, here's a chance to redeem yourself. Parentheses, as used in the preceding code, determine the order in which operations are performed. In Objective-C, * and / take precedence over + and –, which means that the compiler, unless directed otherwise, will generate code that does multiplication and division before it does the addition and subtraction. That's why a * b (or 2*3) then + 5 = 11. By using parentheses, you can force the addition to be performed first: a * (b + 5) = 2 * (3 + 5) equals 16.

2. Select the Build and Run button in the Project Window toolbar to build and run the application.

From now on, I'll just ask you to do this, although you can always press ⌘+Return, or choose Build⇨Build and Run from the main menu if you would like.

Your results in the Debugger Console should look like

```
a % b = 2
b % a = 1
a % a = 0
a + b = 5
b + a = 5
a - b = -1
b - a = 1
a * b = 6
a * b + 5  = 11
a * (b + 5) = 16
(a * b) + 5 = 11
```

```
b * a = 6
a / b = 0
b / a = 1
```

Where you may have gotten unexpected results is when you predicted a / b and b / a. Here's what you found:

```
a / b = 0;
b / a = 1;
```

Why does 2 divided by 3 equal 0, much less 3 divided by 2 equal only 1? As I said earlier, ints are whole numbers. If you want a decimal, you need to declare it that way, and that is what floats are about.

Back to variables — floats

Floats and doubles are the types you will use if you want to see decimal places in the results of your arithmetic calculations.

1. **Delete the previous example and type the following into your project:**

```
float a;
float b;
float c;

a = 2;
b = 3;

NSLog (@" a + b = %i", a + b);
NSLog (@" a - b = %i", a - b);
NSLog (@" b - a = %i", b - a);
NSLog (@" a * b = %i", a * b);
NSLog (@" a * b + 5 = %i", a * b + 5);
NSLog (@" a / b = %i", a / b);
NSLog (@" b / a = %i", b / a);
```

I'm going to save you some typing by just doing the computation in the function as I showed you earlier.

2. **Select the Build and Run button in the Project Window toolbar to build and run the application.**

You should see the following results in the Debugger Console:

```
a + b = 1606416408
a - b = 8542208
b - a = 8546304
a * b = 8542208
a * b + 5 = 8546304
a / b = 8542208
b / a = 8546304
```

Were you surprised? You got this result because I didn't have you change how the results were to be formatted in the NSLog statement (remember the String Format Specifiers in the first example). In the code you just entered, you are specifying that the result is an int (see the %i shown in bold in the following line):

```
NSLog (@" a * b + 5 = %i", a * b + 5);
```

The computer, just following your instructions, does what it is supposed to do with the int. I had you do this because this is a common error, and a source of great confusion for many beginning programmers (see also some discussion of it in Chapter 18 in the debugging tip to create a "paper" trail).

Also notice the compiler warning in Figure 4-6. This warning might be useful if you realized you actually meant to use a variable and didn't. Here it was just sloppiness on my part (actually I wanted to make the point).

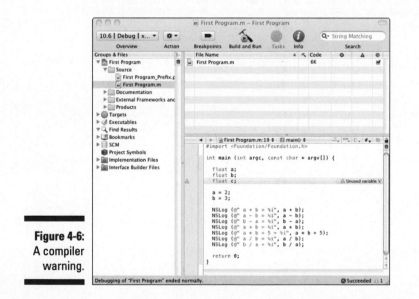

Figure 4-6:
A compiler
warning.

In order to get the results of your calculation to display correctly, and to get rid of that annoying compiler warning, please do the following:

1. **Delete the previous example and this time type the following:**

```
float a;
float b;
//float c;

a = 2;
b = 3;
```

```
NSLog (@" a + b = %f", a + b);
NSLog (@" a - b = %f", a - b);
NSLog (@" b - a = %f", b - a );
NSLog (@" a * b = %f", a * b);
NSLog (@" a * b + 5 = %f", a * b + 5);
NSLog (@" a / b = %f", a / b);
NSLog (@" b / a = %f", b / a);
```

The String Format Specifier `%f` in an `NSLog` function tells the function to display a `double` — that is more or less the standard on the Mac for a floating point. The difference is a `float` that will have only 7 or 8 significant digits, whereas a `double` will have 15 or 16.

Although you won't see comments in the examples I will be taking you through (because I'll be describing what is happening in detail in the text), it is important that you use them in your own code. In order to have the compiler treat something as a comment, you use two forward slashes.

```
//float c;
```

Anything to the right of a `//` is a comment, even if it is on the same line as an instruction or declaration or anything else (it also turns green in Xcode).

```
double a = 4.2; //This is treated as a comment
```

You can also comment out large blocks by starting with `/*` and ending the block with `*/`. Be careful; these blocks can't be nested. If you try to compile the following code, the `even more stuff` line will not be treated as a comment. Go try that on your own. You'll see that `even more stuff` will not turn green, and you'll get a compiler error when you build it.

```
/* some stuff
/* some more stuff */
even more stuff */
```

Extensively commenting your code is critical. Use real explanations about what something does, as well as why you wrote the code the way you did. What and why you did something may not be obvious, not only to someone else who reads your code, but even to you a few days later.

2. **Select the Build and Run button in the Project Window toolbar to build and run the application.**

   You should see the following results in the Debugger Console:

```
a + b = 5.000000
a - b = -1.000000
b - a = 1.000000
a * b = 6.000000
a * b + 5 = 11.000000
a / b = 0.666667
b / a = 1.500000
```

This time you get what you expect.

Floating point numbers can be expressed in the following ways:

```
double a = 4.2;
double b = 4.2e1;
double c = 4.2e-1;
```

The following code will display a, b, and c:

```
NSLog (@" a = %f, b = %f, c = %f",a , b, c);
```

What you get is

```
a = 4.200000, b = 42.000000, c = 0.420000
```

If you want to specify the significant digits you want displayed, all you have to use are a decimal point and a number between the % and the f — %.2f, as in the following:

```
NSLog (@"a = %.2f, b = %.2f, c = %.2f",a ,b, c);
```

This displays

```
a = 4.20, b = 42.00, c = 0.42
```

Bitwise operators

On the computer, your data is actually stored as ones and zeros, which corresponds to something called a bit. In fact, the basic computations you do are in something called *binary arithmetic*.

I'm going to leave binary arithmetic as an exercise for the reader. While I find it fascinating, you probably don't, and it is not usually necessary for most programmers to know. If you need to learn it, learn it when you need to; that's what I always say.

If you do understand it, however, several operators are available to you that work on the bit level. Table 4-4 describes these bitwise operators.

Table 4-4	Bitwise Operators
Operator	*What It Does*
&	Bitwise AND
|	Bitwise Inclusive OR
^	Bitwise Exclusive OR

Operator	What It Does
~	Unary complement (bit inversion)
<<	Shift Left
>>	Shift Right

Compound assignment operators

I love this feature. It enables you to compute and assign a value to a variable. Table 4-5 describes the compound assignment operators.

Table 4-5	Compound Assignment Operators
Operator	**What It Does**
+=	Addition
-=	Subtraction
*=	Multiplication
/=	Division
%=	Modulo
&=	Bitwise AND
|=	Bitwise Inclusive OR
^=	Bitwise Exclusive OR
<<=	Shift Left
>>=	Shift Right

To make sure you understand how the compound assignment operators work, you should code a few examples.

1. **Start with an empty main function and enter the following code:**

```
int a;
int b;
//float c;

a = 2;
b = 3;

NSLog (@" a += b = %i", a += b);
NSLog (@" a now = %i", a );
a = 2;
```

```
NSLog (@" a -= b = %i", a -= b);
a = 2;
NSLog (@" a *= b = %i", a *= b);
a = 2;
NSLog (@" b /= a = %i", b /= a);
b = 3;
NSLog (@" b %%= a = %i", b %= a);
b = 3;
NSLog (@" a *= b + 2 = %i", a *= b + 2);
```

I previously made the point that the arithmetic operators did not affect the value of its operands. The compound assignment operators do change the value of the first operand, however (assignment in the operator name does give you a hint). You use a compound assignment operator to modify the value of a variable by performing an operation on the value currently stored in that variable. For example,

```
a += b
```

says that you want to take the value of b, add it to a, and store the result in a. This is the equivalent to

```
a = a + b;
```

The results here are what you would expect, but I want to call your attention to the last statement.

```
NSLog (@" a *= b + 2 = %i", a *= b + 2);
```

The compound assignment treats whatever is on the right side of the assignment operator as if it were in parenthesis. That means that a *= b + 2 is equivalent to a = a * (b + 2) and not a = a * b + 2.

2. **Select the Build and Run button in the Project Window to build and run the application.**

   You should see the following in the Debugger Console:

```
a += b = 5
a now = 5
a -= b = -1
a *= b = 6
b /= a = 1
b %= a = 1
a *= b + 2 = 10
```

Anything to avoid typing, that's my motto. As you saw, there are also a set of compound assignment operators that allow you to use the bitwise operators.

Increment and decrement operators

These operators are also some of my favorites because they provide another way to avoid typing. They are called the *increment operator* (++) and the *decrement operator* (--). They increase or reduce by 1 the value stored in a variable. They are equivalent to +=1 and to -=1, respectively. They can be a little tricky to use, however.

When used on a pointer, the increment and decrement operators increment and decrement a pointer by the size of the object being referenced.

To discover the increment and decrement operator subtleties that are important for you to understand, you should code the following example. Before you look at the output, see if you can predict what it will be.

1. **Start with an empty main function and enter the following code:**

```
int a;
int b;

a = 2;
b = 3;
NSLog (@" a++ = %i", a++);
NSLog (@" a now = %i", a );
a = 2;
NSLog (@" ++a = %i", ++a);
NSLog (@" a now = %i", a );
a = 2;
NSLog (@" a-- = %i", a--);
NSLog (@" a now = %i", a );
a = 2;
NSLog (@" --a = %i", --a);
NSLog (@" a now = %i", a );
```

There is a difference depending on whether you put the ++ before or after the variable. Where you place the operator determines when the operation is performed. Sometimes you don't care, but in other situations, when the operation is performed may be important.

When it is a *suffix*, as in a++, the value stored in a is increased *after* the expression a++ = %i is evaluated. When the ++ is a *prefix*, as in ++a, the value of a is increased *before* the expression ++a = %i is evaluated. Notice the difference:

```
NSLog (@" a++ = %i", a++);
```

In this case, the a replaces the %i in the string and displays 2. After that, a is incremented

```
NSLog (@" a now = %i", a );
```

And as you will see, it becomes 3.

In this next series of statements, a is assigned back to 2, but in this case, a is incremented before it replaces the %i in the string, and as a result displays 3.

```
a = 2;
NSLog (@" ++a = %i", ++a);
```

As I said, sometimes when the operation occurs doesn't matter, but when it does, it really does.

2. **Select the Build and Run button in the Project Window toolbar to build and run the application.**

   The output in the Debugger Console should look like the following (remember, after every operator, you reset a to 2):

```
a++ = 2
a now = 3
++a = 3
a now = 3
a-- = 2
a now = 1
--a = 1
a now = 1
```

Comma operator

The comma operator (,) allows you to use two or more expressions where only one expression is expected. It evaluates the first operand (usually an expression) and then discards the results. It then evaluates the second operand and returns that value. Obviously, the only time you'll want to use this is when the evaluation of the first operand changes something in the second operand.

For example, the code

```
int a;
int b;

a = (b = 3, b + 2);

NSLog (@" a = (b = 3, b + 2) = %i", a);
NSLog (@" b = %i", b);
```

produces the output

```
a = (b = 3, b + 2) = 5
b = 3
```

The comma operator, in the expression (b = 3, b + 2) will first evaluate b = 3, resulting in the value of b becoming 3. The second operand is then evaluated, adding 2 to b, which results in the comma operator returning 5. Finally a is assigned that result, or 5. So, at the end, variable a will contain the value 5, whereas variable b will contain value 3.

Cast operator

The cast operator (()) enables you to convert one type to another.

```
int i;
float f = 42.9;
i = (int)f;
```

The previous code converts the float number 42.9 to an integer value (42); the remainder is lost. Here, the typecast operator was (int).

As you'll see, this is something you will become familiar with when you start working with objects and classes (for example, you'll use it to tell Objective-C what the argument types are in messages you send to objects).

Sizeof operator

If you are curious about how much memory variables really use (and don't necessarily distrust me, but like to prove things for yourself), you can use the sizeof operator to determine sizes.

You can discover for yourself how much memory a variable uses by doing the following:

1. **Start with an empty main function and enter the following code.**

   As I have been saying, in some cases in the book, you'll see statements on two lines. I have to do that in order to fit the code on the page; you should use only one line where you can. This is especially important for strings, which will give you an error if they are on two lines, unless you tell the compiler that's what you want to do. This is especially relevant in the following code. As I said, I'll show you a way to have a single string on multiple lines in the section "Using Constants."

   ```
   NSLog(@" A char = %i bytes", sizeof(char));
   NSLog(@" An unsigned char = %i bytes",
                                   sizeof(unsigned char));
   NSLog(@" A short = %i bytes", sizeof(short));
   NSLog(@" An unsigned short =
                   %i bytes", sizeof(unsigned short));
   NSLog(@" An int = %i bytes", sizeof(int));
   ```

```
NSLog(@" An unsigned int =
                    %i bytes", sizeof(unsigned int));
NSLog(@" A long = %i bytes", sizeof(long));
NSLog(@" An unsigned long =
                    %i bytes", sizeof(unsigned long));
NSLog(@" A long long = %i bytes", sizeof(long long));
NSLog(@" An unsigned long long = %i bytes",
                        sizeof(unsigned long long));
NSLog(@" A float = %i bytes", sizeof(float));
NSLog(@" A double = %i bytes", sizeof(double));
//There is no unsigned float or double
```

 2. **Select the Build and Run button in the Project Window toolbar to build and run the application.**

 You will soon find the following in the Debugger Console:

```
A char = 1 bytes
An unsigned char = 1 bytes
A short = 2 bytes
An unsigned short = 2 bytes
An int = 4 bytes
An unsigned int = 4 bytes
A long = 4 bytes
An unsigned long = 4 bytes
A long long = 8 bytes
An unsigned long long = 8 bytes
A float = 4 bytes
A double = 8 bytes
```

If you aren't deadly bored by now, all the more power to you. I am pretty much done with the real boring part (at least as compared to the more interesting things you'll learn starting in the next chapter), so hang in there.

It's time to move on to the last two operators you'll need to know before you get going on a real application in Chapter 5 — the logical and relational operators. This upcoming section also includes a brief discussion of the if statement, which allows you to make some logical decisions in your code. (I will cover a few more ways to make decisions in your code in Chapter 9.) Now is when things start to get interesting — well, at least I think so.

Making Logical Decisions in Your Code

When you are programming, you may need to make some decisions within your code. If the user just pressed a button, does that mean I should play Pink Floyd's "The Wall" or a selection from Barry Manilow's greatest hits? A number of control structures are available that enable you to make these kinds of decisions. In this section, I cover one, the if statement. (I cover the balance in Chapter 9; it's amazing how far you can actually get without ever making a decision.)

In general, control structures use *relational* and *equality operators* to compare variables. The result is a Boolean value that is either YES or NO, or true or false. To start, I will explain what a Boolean type is.

Boolean types

A *Boolean type* is a variable whose value is either true or false. In Objective-C you are lucky; you actually have two Boolean types. Objective-C provides a type, BOOL, which can have the values YES and NO (corresponding to true and false, respectively). In C, there is a Boolean data type, bool, which can take on the values true and false. (You would normally use the Objective-C version when writing Objective-C code.) Unfortunately, they do not always behave the same way. (There is also an historic Mac OS type Boolean that you shouldn't use.)

The BOOL type in Objective-C is actually a typedef (you'll learn about typedefs in Chapter 5).

```
typedef signed char BOOL;
```

And since the type of BOOL is actually char, it does not behave in the same way as a bool in C (I'll leave exactly why as an exercise for the reader).

Keep in mind that sometimes programmers will actually assign a value to the BOOL, and that can get you into trouble. To avoid that problem, assign only YES or NO to an Objective-C BOOL.

Several operators return a Boolean type, and I'll give you a list of them shortly. Of course, determining if something is true or false is kind of point-less, unless you can do something based on that information, and that is where the if statement cones into play.

Take a look at how if statements, logical and equality operators, and Boolean types work to allow you to implement logic into your program:

1. **Start with an empty main function and enter the following code:**

```
int a = 5;
int b = 6;

if (a == b) NSLog(@" a is equal to b");
if (a != b) NSLog(@" a is not equal to b");
if (a > b) NSLog(@" a is greater than b");
if (a < b) NSLog(@" a is less than b");
if (a >= b)
        NSLog(@" a is greater than or equal to b");
if (a <= b) NSLog(@" a is less than or equal to b");
```

```
if (!(a == b)) NSLog(@ " a is NOT (equal to b)");
if ((a == b) || (a =-- b)) NSLog(@" a is equal to b,
                                  or a is equal to --b");
if ((a <= b) && (a < ++ b)) NSLog(@" a is less than or
                  equal to b, and a is less than ++b");

if (a == b) NSLog(@" a is equal to b");

if (a == b) {
  NSLog(@" a equal to b");
}
else {
  NSLog (@" a is not equal to b");
}

BOOL z = (a == b);
if (!z) NSLog(@" a is NOT (equal to b)");
BOOL y = (a > b);
if (y != YES) NSLog(@" a is NOT (greater than b)");
```

2. **Select the Build and Run button in the Project Window toolbar to build and run the application.**

   You'll see the following in the Debugger Console:

```
a is not equal to b
a is less than b
a is less than or equal to b
a is NOT (equal to b)
a is equal to b, or a is equal to --b
a is less than or equal to b, and a is less than ++b
a is not equal to b
a is not equal to b
a is NOT (equal to b)
a is NOT (greater than b)
```

   Now go through it in detail:

   The first line of code

```
if (a == b) NSLog(@" a is equal to b");
```

   simply says, if a is equal to b, then execute the NSLog statement. If not, do nothing. Which is what happened — nothing. (Remember, (== is the equality operator, — the two equal signs are not misprints.)

   The if keyword is used to execute a statement or block (I explain what a block is momentarily) only if a condition is true. Its form is

```
if (condition) statement
```

`condition` is an expression that is evaluated. If the result of the valuation is true, `statement` is executed. If it is false, `statement` is ignored, and the program chugs merrily along.

The next statement

```
if (a != b) NSLog(@" a is not equal to b");
```

says if a is not equal to b (!= is the not equal operator), execute the NSLog function, which is what happens as you can see:

```
a is not equal to b
```

The code continues chugging along exercising each relational and logical operator in turn until something else interesting pops up.

```
if (a == b) NSLog(@" a is equal to b");
else NSLog (@" a is not equal to b");
```

Previously, if evaluation of a compare were false, the execution bypassed the next statement and continued. In this case, the else says, if it's not true, do this instead. In this example, the code in one of those two statements will be executed based on the compare.

```
if (condition) statement1; else statement2;
```

The `if else` structures can be concatenated as well. For example:

```
if (x > 0) doThis;
else if (x < 0) doThat;
else takeABreak;
```

As you can imagine, these can get pretty complicated, and I will show you in Chapter 9 a way to get the same result using other, more obvious means.

Then you see the `if else` statements looking a little different.

```
if (a == b) {
  NSLog(@" a equal to b");
}
else {
  NSLog (@" a is not equal to b");
}
```

In this case, you can see that the NSLog statement is in braces, which defines a *block*. A block is a group of statements enclosed in braces: { }:

```
{ statement1; statement2; statement3; }
```

If you want to execute only one statement as the result of the `if` or `else`, you don't *need* a block. But you can choose to use a block, as you just saw. A block is required, however, whenever you want to execute more than one statement as a result of an `if` or `else`.

Finally, the lines of code

```
BOOL z = (a == b);
if (!z) NSLog(@" a is NOT (equal to b)");
BOOL y = (a > b);
if (y != YES) NSLog(@" a is NOT (greater than b)");
```

show us that the result of a compare can be assigned to a Boolean variable.

In this case, z is a BOOL, to which you assign the result of the comparison (a == b). You then use that result (remember, it is either YES or NO) in the if statement (!z).

I'll leave it as an exercise for the reader to study the results of these operations. Admittedly, they do make more sense in context, and you will have an opportunity to use them later in the book.

Pay real attention to the equality operator — *two* equal signs. It is all too easy to use only one by mistake. If you do, rather than make a compare, you do an assignment.

Relational and equality operators

In the section on Boolean types, you used a number of operators that enabled you to compare two expressions. They allowed you to determine, for example, if two expressions were equal, or if one was greater than the other. When you use one of these operators, the result is the Boolean value, as you saw in the previous section.

You used the following relational and equality operators, described in Table 4-6, in the preceding examples.

Table 4-6	Relational and Equality Operators
Operator.	*What It Does*
==	Equal to
!=	Not equal to
>	Greater than
<	Less than
>=	Greater than or equal to
<=	Less than or equal to

Logical operators

Logical operators are similar to the relational operators in that they return Boolean values. In this case, instead of comparing two *expressions*, you are comparing the results of two *comparisons* (except for the NOT operator). Table 4-7 describes the logical operators.

Table 4-7	Logical Operators
Operator	*What It Does*
!	NOT
&&	Logical AND
||	Logical OR

! (NOT) evaluates a single expression and returns the opposite Boolean value. For example, !(a < b) returns back NO if a is less than b, and YES if a is greater than or equal to b.

&& (logical AND) evaluates two expressions and returns YES when both expressions result in YES. For example, (a < b) && (a < c) returns YES when a is less than both b *and* c. Otherwise, it returns NO.

|| (logical OR) evaluates two expressions and returns YES when either one or both expressions result in YES. For example, (a < b) && (a < c) returns YES when X is less than either b *or* c. It returns NO when a is greater than or equal to both b and c.

Conditional operator

The conditional operator (?) evaluates an expression and enables you to do one thing if an expression is true, and another if it is false.

```
condition ? result1 : result2;
```

If condition is true, the expression will execute result1; if it is not true, the expression will execute result2.

For example:

```
int a = 5;
int b = 6;
```

```
(a == b) ? NSLog(@" a is equal to b"):
                         NSLog(@" a is not equal to b") ;
(a != b) ? NSLog(@" a is NOT equal to b"):
                         NSLog(@" a is equal to b");
```

If you were to build this code, you would find

```
a is not equal to b
a is NOT equal to b
```

Looks familiar, doesn't it?

Accessing Data with Pointers

As I explained earlier, memory in your computer can be imagined as a series of mailboxes, each one the smallest size (a byte) that a computer manages. These mailboxes are numbered sequentially, so to get the next address, you add 1 to the current address. Things are located in memory by these addresses.

For example, take the following declaration:

```
int anInteger = 42;
```

Assume that `anInteger` (with the value 42) is located at *memory address* 32, as shown earlier in Figure 4-2. In other words, memory address 32, which I have named `anInteger`, contains the value 42. With me so far?

Until now, variable names have held some kind of value, an `int` or `float` for example, as you just saw with `anInteger`. But they also can hold a pointer, which is an address in memory.

Now look at this declaration:

```
int *anIntPointer = &anInteger
```

The first part of that declaration declares a variable named `anIntPointer`. The * tells the compiler that this type is a *pointer to an int*, rather than an *int*. The & (reference) operator tells the compiler you want the `intPointer` initialized with the *address* of `anInteger`, the variable you declared earlier. In other words, `intPointer` will have the memory address of `anInteger`. Since I told you that the memory address `anInteger` was located at 32, `anIntPointer` will hold the value 32.

Think about it this way. The address of Apple Computer's main building is Apple Computer, Inc. 1 Infinite Loop Cupertino, CA 95014. `anIntPointer` corresponds to that address, while `anInteger` corresponds to the building itself.

To go from the pointer `anIntPointer`, which contains the address of `anInteger`, to the actual value of `anInteger`, you use the dereference operator (*) — this is called differencing a pointer.

```
#import <Foundation/Foundation.h>

int main (int argc, const char * argv[]) {

  int anInteger = 42;
  int *anIntPointer = &anInteger;

  NSLog (@"anInteger = %i", anInteger);
  NSLog (@"*anIntPointer = %i",  *anIntPointer);

  return 0;
}
```

This results in

```
anInteger = 42
*anIntPointer = 42
```

As you can see, dereferencing the pointer (`*anIntPointer`) allows you to access the value store in the address of `anInteger`.

There is also another operator that can be used to deference a pointer. The arrow operator (->) is used only with pointers to objects (as well as `structs`). I'll show you how to use the arrow operator, as well as explain more about pointers, in Chapter 5.

You will use pointers extensively when you start working with objects, and it will become a lot clearer as you work with pointers in this context. As you'll find, it won't be particularly difficult to get the hang of it.

But if you were to study C, you would find that pointers are a significant part of the language, and you would learn something called *pointer arithmetic.* This, in part, comes from C's roots as a system programming language. Most of you will never need to do pointer arithmetic, but just in case, you're not on your own. *C For Dummies* by Dan Gookin (Wiley) can offer some insight.

Using Constants

Constants, as you might expect, are expressions that have a fixed value. You had some experience with them when you did the following:

```
int a = 5;
a = 5;
```

When you do code a = 5, you are using a *literal*.

Literals are not just numbers, however. The following expression is called a string literal.

```
@"Hello World";
```

You have used string literals quite a bit already, and you will continue to use them throughout the rest of this book. But what if you want to include a double quote (") in the string literal itself? (There is also a problem with *special characters* such as newline or tab, which you won't be using). To include a double quote, all you have to do is place a backslash (\) in front of the " (or any other special character) you want to use. For example:

> \' will display as a single quote (')

> \" will display as a double quote (")

> \\ will display as a backslash (\)

As I have been warning you (more than once), string literals need to be on a single line of code. However, you can extend string literals to more than a single line of code by putting a backslash sign (\) at the end of each unfinished line.

```
@"string expressed on \
two lines"
```

You can express any character using its numerical ASCII code by writing a backslash character (\) followed by the ASCII code as an octal (for example, \23 or \40) or hexadecimal number (for example, \x20 or \x4A).

The problem with literals, however, is that tracking down and changing their values can be very difficult. There are other kinds of constants that provide a better way to include a constant in your programs.

Declared constants (const)

With the `const` prefix, you can declare constants of a specific type in the same way as you do with a variable:

```
const int aConstInt = 42;
const float aConstFloat = 42.00;
```

Here, `aConstInt` and `aConstFloat` are two typed constants. They are treated just like regular variables except that their values cannot be modified after they have been declared and initialized (obviously, you have to initialize them).

Defined constants (#define)

Defined constants are a better solution to your need for certainty, although they are best placed in a single file where you can easily find all of them. But since I haven't explained how to use more than one file in your program, (although it is coming up in Chapter 6), I'll just go through the mechanics of creating them.

`#define` allows you to define names for the constants you use:

```
#define identifier value
```

For example, you can define two new constants: `aDefineInt` and `aDefine Float` by doing the following:

```
#define aDefineInt 42
#define aDefineFloat 42.00
```

Once you have defined `aDefineInt` and `aDefineFloat`, you can use them throughout your code like you would a literal or declared constant.

`#define` is a preprocessor directive of the kind I mentioned at the start of this chapter in the section "It All Comes Down to Your Statements." Whenever the preprocessor encounters `#defines` (`aDefineInt` and `aDefineFloat`, for example), it replace them with the values you specified (`42` and `42.00`, respectively).

The `#define` is not an Objective-C statement, so it doesn't need a semicolon. If you put one in, it becomes part of the `#define`.

Let's write some code where you will use constants, float declarations, and the backslash escape code (that will allow you to define a string on two lines).

1. **Start with an empty main function and enter the following code:**

```
#define aDefineInt 42
#define aDefineFloat 42.00
#define aDefineFloat2 .4200e2
#define aDefineFloat3 4200.00e-2

  const int aConstInt = 42;
  const float aConstFloat = 42.00;
  const float aConstFloat2 = .42000e2;
  const float aConstFloat3 =4200.00e-2;


  NSLog(@" aDefineInt = %i",aDefineInt);
  NSLog(@" aDefineFloat = %.2f",aDefineFloat);
  NSLog(@" aDefineFloat2 = %.2f",aDefineFloat2);
  NSLog(@" aDefineFloat3 = %.2f",aDefineFloat3);

  NSLog(@" aConstInt = %i",aConstInt);
  NSLog(@" aConstFloat = %.2f",aConstFloat);
  NSLog(@" aConstFloat2 = %.2f",aConstFloat2);
  NSLog(@" aConstFloat3 = %.2f",aConstFloat3);

  NSLog(@" A \"\\backslash with double quotes\" \
on two lines");
```

2. **Select the Build and Run button in the Project Window toolbar to build and run the application.**

You should see the following in the Debugger Console:

```
aDefineInt = 42
aDefineFloat = 42.00
aDefineFloat2 = 42.00
aDefineFloat3 = 42.00
aConstInt = 42
aConstFloat = 42.00
aConstFloat2 = 42.00
aConstFloat3 = 42.00
A "\backslash with double quotes" on two lines
```

Knowing the Objective-C Reserved Words

As I mentioned, your names or identifiers cannot match any keyword of the Objective-C language. Some of those reserved keywords are as follows:

asm	do	inline	sizeof
auto	double	int	static
bool	else	long	struct
BOOL	enum	new	switch
break	extern	nil	true
case	false	Nil	typedef
char	float	NO	union
Class	for	register	unsigned
Class	goto	return	void
const	id	SEL	volatile
continue	if	short	wchar_t while
default	IMP	signed	
			YES

The best way to tell if a name or identifier you want to use is a reserved word is if it changes color in the editor. If it does, it is either a keyword or is being used somewhere in your program.

In addition, prefixes are used extensively. Cocoa prefixes all its function, constant, and type names with "NS." So don't prefix any of your own variables or function names with NS — doing so can cause a great deal of confusion. At a minimum, the reader will assume it is a Cocoa function, as opposed to being your code. At worst, the name is already being used, and you'll get a compiler error. (Actually, I'm not sure which is worse.)

Congratulations

Congratulations! You've gotten through the most tedious part of learning a computer language.

Some of the things I didn't cover in this chapter are certain kinds of control structures, like `switch` statements, and things called loops, which allow you to repeat a block of statements while a condition is true or until a condition is met. I will show you those, I promise, when you are going to need to use them in Chapter 9.

Chapter 5

Functions and Data Structures

· ·

· ·

As I mention in Chapter 1, learning to program in Objective-C involves more than the instruction set and data types you learned about in the last chapter. In fact, you've received a considerable amount of the instruction set covered by now. So it's time to get on with the more interesting aspects of the language, the ones you'll need to know to create the kinds of applications you are probably interested in.

One of the most important features of Objective-C is its support for object-oriented programming. While Objective-C is about objects, before I take you there in Chapter 6, I am going to introduce you to two features of C that are important to understand along the way — data structures and functions. Data structures and functions are a fundamental part of the language, and understanding them will make it easier for you to understand what objects are really about.

Thinking about an Application

In Chapter 1, I mention that when I travel, I often zone out on that fact that even though it looks like monopoly money, foreign currency actually does amount to something in dollars. I said it would be helpful if I could use a computer to let me know when I charged something on a credit card in a foreign currency, how much that was in dollars. It would also be helpful if I could use that same program to generally keep track of my spending (I do tend to get carried away when I am on vacation) against a budget I set at the beginning of a trip. While this is not the most exciting application (a classic understatement if I've ever made one), it is actually perfect for my purposes — to teach you how to develop applications using Objective-C. It will enable me to explain all of the Objective-C you'll need to know to write *any* kind of application — even a cool game or something that uses audio and video. (Of course, you'll still have to learn the *specifics* of how to use the graphics and sound on the Mac or iPhone.)

The application you are about to start developing will help me manage my budget when I travel by allowing me to track my spending in dollars. This will enable me to avoid the rather embarrassing situation of ending up with only three dollars and four days left to go in Venice.

Of course, doing this is something you really don't even need a computer to do; a computer just makes it easier and faster (and provides the example application I need to teach you Objective-C). In fact, my father, who was an accountant, did the same thing I'm planning to do using a pencil and paper whenever he and my mom went to Europe. I'll use what he did as a basis for how my application needs to work.

To manage his budget, he would use the form you see in Figure 5-1. Whenever he changed dollars into euros, he put that amount in the dollars column and subtracted it from the balance. Whenever he charged something on a credit card, he took the amount in foreign currency, multiplied it times the exchange rate to get the dollar amount, and then subtracted that amount from the dollar balance. (He was an accountant after all.)

Date	Amount in euros	Exchange rate	Amount in dollars	Balance in dollars

Figure 5-1:
Tracking
your
expenses.

Fortunately, today with my laptop or iPhone, I am free to harness the power of hundreds if not thousands of dollars worth of modern computer technology to do the same thing my dad did with pencil and paper.

At this point, you have actually learned enough Objective-C to begin creating the *model* for this application (also sometimes called the *content engine*). The model is part of a design pattern known as Model-View-Controller (MVC) that you will use to develop applications using the Cocoa framework. The model contains the application-specific logic for your application — in this case, how to track expenses and apply them to a budget. I explain MVC in detail in Chapter 11.

For the majority of this book, I will be showing you how to use what you have already learned about Objective-C, and the additional features that make it so powerful (objects, for example) to add more and more functionality to the model. Then in Chapters 17 and 18, you'll create simple user interfaces for the iPhone and Mac and see how easily it all fits together.

Enough discussion — time to code!

1. **Launch Xcode.**

   I'll be having you create a new project here. You can do that, or you can skip Steps 2 through 6 and start with the project in the Chapter 5 Start Here folder, which is in the Chapter 5 folder on the CD (you'll have to move it to your desktop).

   Remember: If you want to work with anything on the CD, you must drag it onto your desktop (or into any other folder) to be able to build the project.

2. **Start the New Project Assistant by Choosing File⇨New Project from the main menu to create a new project.**

3. **In the New Project window, click Application under the Mac OS X heading.**

4. **Select Command Line Tool from the choices displayed and then select Foundation from the Type drop-down menu; then click Choose.**

   Xcode will then display a standard save sheet.

5. **Enter the name** `Vacation Budget` **in the Save As field, choose a Save location (the Desktop works just fine), and then click Save.**

   After you click Save, Xcode creates the project and opens the project window — which should look like Figure 5-2.

   You'll work in the `Vacation Budget.m` file for the balance of this chapter.

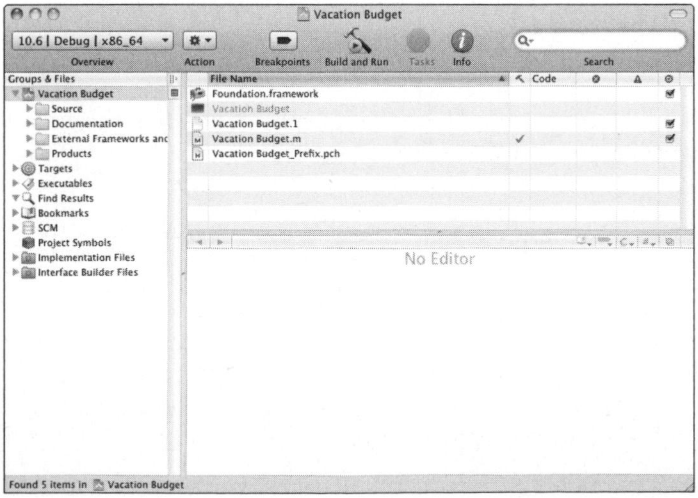

Figure 5-2:
The
Vacation
Budget
project.

6. **Start with an empty** `main` **function.**

   I cover this in Chapter 4. You will need to delete all of the statements in `main` except for `return 0;` so that you end up with a `main` function that looks like:

   ```
   #import <Foundation/Foundation.h>

   int main (int argc, const char * argv[]) {

      return 0;
   }
   ```

7. **Add the code in bold between the first brace and the** `return 0` **statement.**

   Just a reminder about statements. In some cases (like the following one), you'll see statements on two lines in the book. I have to do that in order to fit the code on the page; you should simply use one line where you can.

   ```
   #import <Foundation/Foundation.h>

   int main (int argc, const char * argv[]) {

      float  exchangeRate = 1.2500;
      double budget = 1000.00;
      double euroTransaction;

      budget -= 100;

      NSLog(@"Converting 100 US dollars into euros leaves
                                    $%.2f", budget);
      euroTransaction = 100*exchangeRate;
      budget -= euroTransaction;
      NSLog(@"Charging 100 euros leaves $%.2f", budget);

      return 0;
   }
   ```

8. **Leave Overview menu on the left side of the toolbar, and make sure the selection is "10.6 | Debug | x86_64".**

   I explained this in Chapter 2.

9. **Select the Build and Run button in the Project Window toolbar.**

   In Chapter 4, I gave you other options — press ⌘+Return or choose Build⇨Build and Run (from the main menu to build and run the application. In this chapter, and from now on, I'll only tell you to select the button, but feel free to do it anyway.

10. **If necessary, open the Xcode Console, which displays your program's output, by selecting Run⇨Console or by pressing Shift+⌘+R.**

Your output should look like the following. (*Note:* I removed the time stamp and process id that tells you when and where the output string originated, and I'll do that for the balance of this chapter and book.)

```
Converting 100 US dollars into euros leaves $900.00
Charging 100 euros leaves $775.00
```

This code is pretty simple. For a cash transaction — that is, when I am converting my dollars into euros, or actually paying in dollars — you simply subtract 100 from the budget using the compound assignment subtraction operator to simulate a straight foreign exchange transaction.

```
budget -= 100;
```

For a charge transaction. you convert the number of euros you are charging into dollars and store that amount as a euroTransaction.

```
euroTransaction = 100*exchangeRate;
```

Then you subtract that amount from the budget to simulate a charge transaction.

```
budget -= euroTransaction;
```

You can find the completed project on the CD in the Example 5A folder, which is in the Chapter 5 folder.

Defining and Declaring Data Structures

The budget-tracking system covered in the preceding section shows you how to write a program that does something more or less useful. In this section, I cover *data structures,* which are data elements grouped together under one name, and show you how to use them in your program.

You can declare the built-in data types as variables. But what about those situations when the data you need to work with, or on, is really more than one variable — it is a logical collection of variables that hang out together because they have some relationship to each other. For example, the data I used in the preceding example are all related to each other and provide the data needed for this whole idea of budgeting.

```
float   exchangeRate;
double budget;
double euroTransaction;
```

Another example is an address book, where you would want all of the information about a person grouped in a single entity. You can easily do that using a data structure (`struct`). Data structures are defined in Objective-C using the following syntax:

```
struct structName {

  type member1Name;
  type member2Name;
  ...
};
```

A `struct` tells the compiler that this is a data structure. `structName` is a name for the *structure type* — when you define a `struct`, you are actually defining a new data type that can be used just like the built-in types such as `int` and `double`. Within the braces { } is a list of the variables that are included in this `struct`, which are called *members*, each one specified with a type and a valid identifier as its name. And, yes, structures can have other structures as members, although a structure can't be a member of itself.

Variables included in a `struct` are called *members*.

Just as I would with any other variable, I have to declare a `struct` when I use it.

```
struct structName structVariable1, structVariable2 ... ;
```

When you *declare* a structure, the compiler reserves enough memory to hold the data, just as it does for the built-in types (for example, 4 bytes for an `int`), although here the compiler has to figure out how much to reserve by adding up all the requirements for each of the types that will be in the structure.

In the preceding example, `structVariable1` and `structVariable2` are the variables' names (identifiers) for the structures I declared. Since I have two declarations, memory is reserved for each. (As I mention in Chapter 4, you can declare more than one variable of the same type in one statement.)

What you are going to do now is group `exchangeRate`, `budget`, and `euroTransaction` into a `struct` named `budget` and then use the `budget` struct in your program.

If you have been following along with me, I'll be extending what you just did in the first example. If you would like to start from a clean copy of the project from where you left off, you can use the project found in the Example 5A folder found in the Chapter 5 folder.

1. **Return to your project and add the following code in bold, right after the first line** `#import <Foundation/Foundation.h>` to `Vacation Budget.m`.

```
#import <Foundation/Foundation.h>

struct budget {
  float   exchangeRate;
  double budget;
  double euroTransaction;
};
```

This code defines the `struct budget` that contains the three variables I referred to earlier, `exchangeRate`, `budget`, and `euroTransaction`.

2. **Delete the code you previously entered in the `main` function and enter the code (in bold) as shown here:**

```
#import <Foundation/Foundation.h>

struct budget {
  float exchangeRate;
  double budget;
  double euroTransaction;
};

int main (int argc, const char * argv[]) {

  struct budget vacationBudget;

  vacationBudget.exchangeRate = 1.2500;
  vacationBudget.budget = 1000.00;

  vacationBudget.budget -= 100;
  NSLog(@"Converting 100 US dollars into euros leaves
                     $%.2f", vacationBudget.budget);
  vacationBudget.euroTransaction =
                     100*vacationBudget.exchangeRate;
  vacationBudget.budget -=
                     vacationBudget.euroTransaction;
  NSLog(@"Charging 100 euros leaves $%.2f",
                          vacationBudget.budget);

  return 0;
}
```

3. **Select the Build and Run button in the Project Window toolbar to build and run the application.**

Your output in the Debugger Console should look like this:

```
Converting 100 US dollars into euros leaves $900.00
Charging 100 euros leaves $775.00
```

You can find the completed project on the CD in the Example 5B folder, which is in the Chapter 5 folder.

The code in the preceding numbered list is not all that different from the program you coded in the section "Thinking About an Application," with a couple of exceptions.

You define a `struct` that you named `budget` (you did that outside the `main` function, which makes the definition usable by any function in the file Vacation Budget.m, as you will see). You then declare a `struct budget` (which allocates some memory for its variables), named `europe`, just as you would declare any other variable.

As you can see, Objective-C treats this data structure (or `struct`) exactly as it does its built-in types. Or at least, almost the same, since the type is `struct budget`, as opposed to simply `budget`. (I'll show you how you can omit the `struct` next).

It is important to understand the difference between the *structure type name*, and a *variable* of this (structure) type. You can declare as many variables (for example, `europe` and even `england`) as you like of this structure type (`struct budget`), just as you can `int`s, `float`s, `double`s, and so on.

Once you have declared the variable of that structure type, you can operate directly on its members. To do that, you use the dot operator, a (.), inserted between the structure type variable's name (identifier) and the member name. For example:

```
vacationBudget.budget = 1000.00;
vacationBudget.budget -= 100;
```

Using Defined Data Types

When you define a `struct`, you are creating a new data type, but it can be a bit awkward to use. Every time I use it I have to use

```
struct budget someBudget;
```

Since I hate having to type more than absolutely necessary, I'm going to show you a way to avoid using `struct` in a declaration. This also makes a `struct` look more like a built-in data type. All you need to do is use the keyword `typedef` (this is another example of a statement in Objective-C that describes how data is structured).

```
typedef type typeName;
```

Here `type` is a built-in type, or one you created using a `struct` (`struct budget,` for example), and `typeName` is the name for the new type you are defining. For example:

```
typedef struct budget budget;
```

You can also create a new type name for a built-in type.

```
typedef int theTypeAlsoKnownAsInt;
```

You could then use that type name instead of `int` in the following:

```
theTypeAlsoKnownAsInt anInt;
```

To define the `budget` `typedef` in my program, all you have to do is add one line of code (in bold).

```
struct budget {
 float  exchangeRate;
 double budget;
 double euroTransaction;
 };

 typedef struct budget budget;
```

Now you can use the new type — `budget` — just like any of the built-in types (no `struct` required). For example:

```
   budget vacationBudget;
```

To make things even easier, there is a way to *define a struct and a typedef* in one fell swoop. This is then followed by the declaration of the variable of that type.

```
typedef struct {
  float  exchangeRate;
  double budget;
  double euroTransaction;
} budget;

struct budget vacationBudget;
```

This is more consistent with the way you need to think about classes and objects, and the way I'll have you do it in your program.

You need to be aware of the two-step process I explained first, because you may see it done that way in some of the framework header files. It enables you to *define a struct, and declare a variable of that type* in one fell swoop, which is then followed by the `typedef`:

```
struct budget {
  float   exchangeRate;
  double budget;
  double euroTransaction;
} vacationBudget;

typedef struct budget budget;
```

`typedef` does not actually create different types — it only creates a new name for whatever you specify. As far as the compiler is concerned, when it sees `budget`, it just understands `budget` to be `struct budget`.

As you will see, you will no longer have to use `struct` when you declare a variable of type `budget`. And just as before, with `struct budget`, when you declare a variable as type `budget`, you are reserving memory for it.

1. **Delete what you entered previously so that `Vacation Budget.m` looks like this:**

```
#import <Foundation/Foundation.h>

int main (int argc, const char * argv[]) {


  return 0;
}
```

2. **Add the following code in bold, right after the first line,** `#import <Foundation/Foundation.h>`:

```
#import <Foundation/Foundation.h>

typedef struct {
  float   exchangeRate;
  double budget;
  double euroTransaction;
} budget;
```

This defines the `struct budget` that contains the three variables I referred to earlier: `exchangeRate`, `budget`, and `euroTransaction`. It also does the necessary `typedef`.

3. **Enter the rest of the code shown in bold.**

```
#import <Foundation/Foundation.h>

typedef struct {
  float exchangeRate;
  double budget;
```

```
    double euroTransaction;
} budget;

int main (int argc, const char * argv[]) {

  budget vacationBudget;

  vacationBudget.exchangeRate = 1.2500;
  vacationBudget.budget = 1000.00;

  vacationBudget.budget -= 100;
  NSLog(@"Converting 100 US dollars into euros leaves
                         $%.2f", vacationBudget.budget);
  vacationBudget.euroTransaction =
                    100*vacationBudget.exchangeRate;
  vacationBudget.budget -=
                       vacationBudget.euroTransaction;
  NSLog(@"Charging 100 euros leaves $%.2f",
                           vacationBudget.budget);

  return 0;
}
```

4. Select the Build and Run button in the Project Window toolbar to build and run the application.

Your output in the Xcode Debugger Console should look like this:

```
Converting 100 US dollars into euros leaves $900.00
Charging 100 euros leaves $775.00
```

You can find the completed project on the CD in the Example 5C folder, which is in the Chapter 5 folder.

Writing Functions

In this section, you collect together the statements previously coded in `main` that display the results of a transaction into functions that do the same thing. One of the advantages of using a module like a function is that once you check that this set of statements works, you don't have to worry about that function anymore.

The set of statements called a *function* has a *name*, and you can *call* that set of statements by this name to have its code executed. This concept of using functions is as fundamental to programming as any of the instructions in Chapter 4. So fundamental, in fact, you can never hide from functions — it is in a function, `main`, after all, where you have been doing all your work so far.

The main function is required in your program because when you run your application, main is where execution of the code will start.

Take a look at an example of main again:

```
int main (int argc, const char * argv[]) {

    NSLog(@"Hello, World!");

    return 0;
}
```

You see a return type (int), a name (main), some arguments inside parentheses, and then some instructions inside braces ({}). This structure is the basic structure of a function. Now you will see how to create your very own function. I'll explain the main function a bit more in Chapter 7.

For now, you'll modify the program you just wrote to use functions. You start by adding code to main, something that is old hat to you by now, and then you move the code you wrote into a function.

If you have been following along with me, I'll be extending what you just did in the previous example. If you would like to start from a clean copy of the project where you left off, you can use the project found in the Example 5C folder, which is in the Chapter 5 folder.

1. **Start with the code you already have and add the following code in bold, right after the line** } budget.

```
    typedef struct {
    float exchangeRate;
    double budget;
    double euroTransaction;
} budget;

    budget vacationBudget;
```

You've now declared the variable vacationBudget outside of the main function, and in a way that makes it accessible to other functions, such as the ones you are about to create. I explain why you need to do this, which is known as *variable scoping*, in the next section.

2. **You now add some functions. Right after the line**

```
budget vacationBudget;
```

add the following lines of code:

```
void spendDollars (double dollars) {

    vacationBudget.budget -= dollars;
}
```

```
void chargeEuros (double euros) {

  vacationBudget.euroTransaction =
                 euros*vacationBudget.exchangeRate;
  vacationBudget.budget -=
                 vacationBudget.euroTransaction;
}
```

You probably noticed that all you did was move the line of code

```
vacationBudget.budget -= dollars;
```

from main to the new function spendDollars, and the lines of code

```
vacationBudget.euroTransaction =
               euros*vacationBudget.exchangeRate;
vacationBudget.budget -=
               vacationBudget.euroTransaction;
```

from main to the new function chargeEuros.

3. **In the** main **function, delete the commented code with the strikethrough, and add the code in bold.**

```
//budget vacationBudget;

  vacationBudget.exchangeRate = 1.2500;
  vacationBudget.budget = 1000.00;
  double numberDollars = 100;
  double numberEuros = 100;

//vacationBudget.budget -= 100;
  spendDollars(numberDollars);
//NSLog(@"Converting 100 US dollars into euros leaves
                    $%.2f", vacationBudget.budget);
  NSLog(@"Converting %.2f US dollars into euros leaves
        $%.2f", numberDollars, vacationBudget.budget);
//vacationBudget.euroTransaction =
                    100*vacationBudget.exchangeRate;
//vacationBudget.budget =
                    vacationBudget.euroTransaction;
  chargeEuros(numberEuros);
//NSLog(@"Charging 100 euros leaves $%.2f",
                              vacationBudget.budget);
  NSLog(@"Charging  %.2f euros leaves $%.2f",
                numberEuros, vacationBudget.budget);
```

As you can see, you deleted the line of code

```
budget vacationBudget;
```

because you declared it in Step 2.

You declared two new variables:

```
double numberDollars = 100;
double numberEuros = 100;
```

These represent individual *transactions* (and there will be more, of course), and I'll use these variables as the function arguments.

You replaced the code

```
vacationBudget.budget -= 100;
```

with

```
spendDollars(numberDollars);
```

which calls the function `spendDollars`, passing it the number of dollars (`numberDollars`) I just spent, as an argument.

And, similarly, you replaced the code

```
vacationBudget.euroTransaction =
                    100 *vacationBudget.exchangeRate;
vacationBudget.budget -=
                    vacationBudget.euroTransaction;
```

with

```
chargeEuros(numberEuros);
```

which calls the function `chargeEuros` to update my budget to take into account what I just charged on my credit card in euros.

You also replaced the two `NSLog` statements

```
NSLog(@"Converting 100 US dollars into euros leaves
                    $%.2f", vacationBudget.budget);
NSLog(@"Charging 100 euros leaves $%.2f",
                    vacationBudget.budget);
```

with

```
NSLog(@"Converting %.2f US dollars into euros leaves
        $%.2f", numberDollars, vacationBudget.budget);
NSLog(@"Charging  %.2f euros leaves $%.2f",
        numberEuros, vacationBudget.budget);
```

to display the variable that contains the amount being spent.

Your code should look like Listing 5-1.

Listing 5-1: Moving Instructions into Functions

```
#import <Foundation/Foundation.h>

typedef  struct {
  float   exchangeRate;
  double budget;
  double euroTransaction;
} budget;

  budget vacationBudget;


void spendDollars (double dollars) {

  vacationBudget.budget -= dollars;
}

void chargeEuros (double euros) {

  vacationBudget.euroTransaction =
                    euros*vacationBudget.exchangeRate;
  vacationBudget.budget -= vacationBudget.euroTransaction;
}

int main (int argc, const char * argv[]) {

  vacationBudget.exchangeRate = 1.2500;
  vacationBudget.budget = 1000.00;
  double numberDollars = 100;
  double numberEuros = 100;

  spendDollars(numberDollars);
  NSLog(@"Converting %.2f US dollars into euros leaves
        $%.2f", numberDollars, vacationBudget.budget);
  chargeEuros(numberEuros);
  NSLog(@"Charging  %.2f euros leaves $%.2f", numberEuros,
                                vacationBudget.budget);

  return 0;
}
```

4. **Select the Build and Run button in the Project Window toolbar to build and run the application.**

Your output in the Debugger Console should look like this:

```
Converting 100 US dollars into euros leaves $900.00
Charging 100 euros leaves $775.00
```

You can find the completed project on the CD in the Example 5D folder, which is in the Chapter 5 folder.

What you have done here is simply to move things around. You haven't changed functionality.

At this point, the amount of code is trivial, so why you would want to move code into functions may not be compellingly obvious. But humor me; one of the universal laws of programming is that things can get very complex very quickly, and functions (as modules), as I explain in Chapter 3, will make your life easier.

Now, take a moment to examine what you did here.

When you entered the lines of code

```
void spendDollars (double dollars) {

   vacationBudget.budget -= dollars;
}
```

You *declared* a function spendDollars.

Notice that all you actually did to create the function body was cut and paste the original code that was in the main function into the new function body. You did something called *factoring* your code. You changed the way things are organized in your program without changing its (observable) behavior. As you develop applications, you'll find yourself doing that a lot in order to improve code readability, simplify code structure, make it consistent with the principles of object-oriented programming that improve maintainability and extensibility, and so on.

To be more precise, which is important when working with computers, a function looks like this:

```
returnType functionName(functionArgument1, ...) {

   statements;
   return expression;
}
```

Let me explain what each of the pieces are.

✔ *returnType* is the data type of the data returned by the function. Every function *can* return something when it is finished. The function might return something like the cost of one euro in U.S. dollars or a status indicator, such as 0, that tells you the function successfully completed what you asked it to do. In fact, that's what you have been doing when you end your programs with return 0 in main.

The return value is optional. If you want to declare a function that does not return a value, as you did in the function `spendDollars`, use the data type of `void`. If you leave out the return type, the compiler will assume the return type is `int`, and annoy you with warnings.

✔ *functionName* is the, well, name of the function; it is how you will *call* it. This is what you did when you replaced the lines of code

```
vacationBudget.budget -= 100;
```

with

```
spendDollars(numberDollars);;
```

This is known as *calling* the function. You told the compiler you want to execute the lines of code you gathered under the function name `spend-Dollars`.

✔ *functionArgument* (as many as needed or none) are enclosed in the parentheses after the function name. These can be built-in types or even your own data types. Each argument consists of a data type specifier followed by an identifier, like all of the variable declarations you did in Chapter 4. This allows you to pass data to the function when it is called. The arguments, if there are more than one, are separated by commas.

The arguments, like the return value, are optional. The function declaration

```
void spendDollars (double dollars) {
```

has one argument. If there were no arguments, you could declare it as

```
void spendNoDollars (void) {
```

or

```
void spendNoDollars () {
```

You could simply leave out the `void` in the argument list, and the compiler, when there are no arguments, assumes void. (As opposed to when you leave out the return type, in which case the compiler assumes an `int`.)

Just as you have been doing in the `main` function, you could have also declared variables inside the functions you code. These are called *local variables*.

```
float aLocalVaraible = 1.2643;
```

When you declare a local variable and the function is called, memory is allocated for that variable and initialized if necessary.

For example, in Step 7 in the section "Thinking about an Application," you declared the following local variables in `main`:

```
float    exchangeRate = 1.2500;
double budget = 1000.00;
double euroTransaction;
```

Execution begins at the open brace and continues through to the return statement. If the return type is `void`, the return statement is optional. If it isn't present, execution returns to the calling function at the closing brace.

Always remember that the format for calling a function includes specifying its name and enclosing its arguments between parentheses. Even if there are no arguments, you need the parentheses anyway. For that reason, the call to `spendNoDollars` is

```
spendNoDollars();
```

This is how the compiler knows that this call is a call to a function and not the identifier of a variable or some other statement. The following call would generate admonishments from the compiler:

```
spendNoDollars;
```

All the various parts of a function are illustrated in Figure 5-3.

Return Type   Function Name   Function arguments

```
void doSomethingForMe (int useThis, float useThisToo) {

function body

}
```

Figure 5-3: The parts of a function.

Getting back to `spendDollars`: You created a new function with one argument and no return type. Also notice the general format for the name is lowercase.

In `main`, you call the function `spendDollars` with the variable `numberDollars` (which is a `double`) as the argument. This corresponds to the `double dollars` argument in the `spendDollars` function declaration.

At the point at which the function is called from within `main`, the control is lost by main and passed to the function `spendDollars`.

The argument is treated exactly the same way that other local variable declarations are treated. That is, when you call the function

```
void spendDollars (double dollars) {

  vacationBudget.budget -= dollars;
}
```

you are actually declaring a local variable `double dollars` that is initialized when the function is called with the value that you passed in as the argument. The only difference between `double dollars` and something like

```
float numberDollars = 100;
```

is that the variable `dollars` sits in the declaration, separated by commas, rather than in the body of the function.

You need to understand another thing. When you call the function

```
spendDollars(numberDollars);
```

the `dollars` function argument is a *copy* of numberDollars.

If you modify `dollars` in the `spendDollars` function, it will not affect `numberDollars` in `main`. That is because when a function is called, the arguments are *copies* of the variables you use as the arguments.

Within the function `spendDollars`, you could also further assign these arguments to local variables if you wanted to; but in this function, you just use the argument to subtract the amount from the budget.

The closing brace, }, terminates the function `spendDollars`, and returns the control back to the function that called it in the first place (in this case, `main`), and the program continues chugging along from the same point at which it made the function call.

You also can have a `return` statement in the function. For example, if you want to also return the value of the euro charge transaction back to `main`, you can declare and implement the function in this way:

```
double returnDollarsSpent (double euros) {

  vacationBudget.euroTransaction =
                    euros*vacationBudget.exchangeRate;
  vacationBudget.budget -= vacationBudget.euroTransaction;
  return vacationBudget.euroTransaction;
}
```

And the statement

```
return vacationBudget.euroTransaction;
```

will return control back to `main`. You can see the relationship between how a similar function is called and its various parts in Figure 5-4.

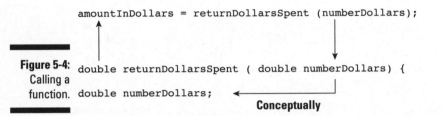

Figure 5-4: Calling a function.

At this point, go back to `main` and look at it again.

```
int main (int argc, const char * argv[])
```

`main` is nothing more than a function with two arguments — `int argc` and `const char * argv[]` — that returns an `int`. (*Note:* The second argument is an array, which I explain in Chapter 7.)

Scope of variables

While I haven't gotten into classes and encapsulation yet (which I explain a little in Chapter 3), you do need to realize that variables are not accessible from every nook and cranny in your program. In the preceding examples, variables are accessible only within the function in which they are declared (that is, within the braces). This is also referred to as *scoped* to the function.

There is actually a little more to it than that. There can be braces (which define a block) within a function, in which case variables are scoped within that code block. A code block is a group of statements grouped together in a block enclosed in braces: { }, as shown here.

```
{ statement1;
  statement2;
  statement3; }
```

(You see examples of blocks in Chapter 4, where I explain `if` statements, and you see a lot more of them in Chapter 9, where I explain more about loops and control structures.)

That means that earlier in the main function

```
int main (int argc, const char * argv[]) {

budget vacationBudget;
```

the variable budget was accessible only to instructions within the main function.

So if you move the code in main

```
vacationBudget.budget -= dollars
```

into the function spendDollars , you won't have access to vacationBudget. budget any longer.

You may want to try this yourself.

In order to be able to access vacationBudget from any function, you have to make it *global*, by moving *both* its definition (the struct statement) and subsequent declaration (budget vacationBudget;) to the *file scope* (that is, in the file but not within any particular function). That's what happened when you did the following:

```
#import <Foundation/Foundation.h>

typedef struct {
  float exchangeRate;
  double budget;
  double euroTransaction;
} budget;

budget vacationBudget;
```

Well, in general, this does violate some of the basic ideas of encapsulation I mention in Chapter 3. That being said, there are a few limited occasions when you do need variables accessible to all functions, although this is really not one of them. In Chapter 6, using objects allow me to get rid of this global reference.

Actually, the issues of scoping, especially global scoping are more complex than this. Fortunately, global scoping is something you won't have to be too concerned about until your programs become very complex, and you can learn about it at your leisure.

Variable scoping is all nicely illustrated in Figure 5-5.

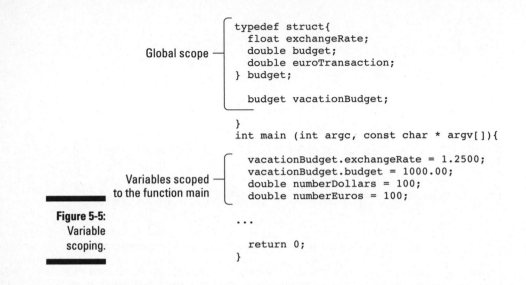

Figure 5-5:
Variable
scoping.

Unions

Unions allow the same portion of memory to be accessed using different variable names and as (potentially) different types. I'll explain a little about them since you may come across them in other people's code, but I won't get into the topic too deeply since you are not likely to use them yourself.

While a `union` looks a lot like a `struct`, it is very different.

```
union theBudget {
  double budget;
  long long amountIWantToSpend;
} europeUnion;
```

Both `budget` and `amountIWantToSpend` *occupy the same physical space in memory*. This is illustrated in Figure 5-6. Its size is one of the largest elements in the declaration. Since both of them are referring to the same location in memory, the modification of one is the same as modifying both — you cannot store different values in them independent of each other. Using unions in this way is of value when you need to conserve space.

Here is something else you might see:

```
struct theBudget {
  double budget;
  union {
    double euros;
    double pounds;
  };
};
```

Using a `union` enables you to access the same variable using two different names. While this is an amusing novelty, it actually violates some of the basic principles of encapsulation that I discussed in Chapter 3.

Once again, I remind you that in a `union`, the members euros and pounds occupy the same physical space. This means that modifying the value of one is identical to modifying the value of the other.

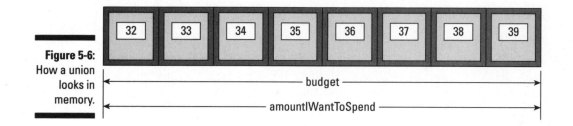

Figure 5-6:
How a union looks in memory.

Enumerations (enum)

Enumerations allow you to create new data types in a similar way you did earlier with the `struct`.

```
typedef enum {
   value1,
   value2,
   value3,
} enumerationName;
```

For example, you could create a new type of variable called `currency` to store the various currencies you might use in your program with the following declaration:

```
typedef enum {dollar, euro, pound} currency;
```

The "mechanics" of an `enum` actually work the same was as a `struct`, so the alternative ways of defining and declaring a `struct` apply to an `enum` as well.

Enumerations are actually `int`s. If you don't specify it, the integer value of the first value (`dollar`) will be 0. If you display the value of `dollar`, you get 0, the value of the `euro` will be 1, and the `pound` will be 2. You can also specify an integer value for any of the constant values that your enumerated type can take. If the constant value that follows it is not given an integer value, it is assigned the value of the previous one plus 1. For example:

```
typedef enum {dollar=1, euro, pound} currency;
```

In this case, `dollar` will be 1, `euro` 2, and `pound` 3.

The possible values that variables of this new type `currency` may take are the new constant values included within braces. For example, once the currency enumeration is declared the following works:

```
currency aCurrency = dollar;
aCurrency = pound;
```

Declaring Function Prototypes

Up until now, you have had to *define* your functions (provide the code for the function) before they were called. You may have wondered about the order I had you enter code, or even experimented with the order and found yourself chastised by the compiler.

With a *function prototype,* you inform the compiler that it will eventually see a definition of the function — so trust me, and let me use it before you get to it. As a result, the compiler will let you use it before it is defined, but if you double-cross the compiler, it won't be a happy camper, and neither will you.

To create a function prototype, all you do is this:

```
void spendDollars (double dollars);
```

Doing so means that you can move the implementation of `spendDollars` to after `main`. The value of this will become obvious in the next chapter.

If you have been following along with me, I'll be extending what you just did in the previous example. If you would like to start from a clean copy of the project where you left off, you can use the project found in the Example 5D folder, which is in the Chapter 5 folder.

   1. **Start with the code you already have and add the function prototypes in bold and move the function definitions for spendDollars and chargeEuros to after main as I have in Listing 5-2.**

Listing 5-2: Function Prototypes

```
#import <Foundation/Foundation.h>

typedef struct {
  float    exchangeRate;
  double budget;
  double euroTransaction;
} budget;
```

```
budget vacationBudget;

void spendDollars (double dollars);
void chargeEuros (double euros);

int main (int argc, const char * argv[]) {

  vacationBudget.exchangeRate = 1.2500;
  vacationBudget.budget = 1000.00;
  double numberDollars = 100;
  double numberEuros = 100;

  spendDollars(numberDollars);
  NSLog(@"Converting %.2f US dollars into euros leaves
          $%.2f", numberDollars, vacationBudget.budget);
  chargeEuros(numberEuros);
  NSLog(@"Charging %.2f euros leaves $%.2f", numberEuros,
          vacationBudget.budget);

  return 0;
}

void spendDollars (double dollars) {

  vacationBudget.budget -= dollars;
}

void chargeEuros (double euros) {

  vacationBudget.euroTransaction =
                      euros*vacationBudget.exchangeRate;
  vacationBudget.budget -= vacationBudget.euroTransaction;
}
```

   2. Select the Build and Run button in the Project Window toolbar to build and run the application.

Your output in the Debugger Console should look like this:

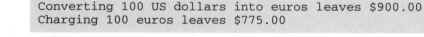

```
Converting 100 US dollars into euros leaves $900.00
Charging 100 euros leaves $775.00
```

You can find the completed project on the CD in the Example 5E folder, which is in the Chapter 5 folder.

Extending the Functionality of a Program

Since I am flying all the way to Europe from San Francisco, I decided that I might as well visit London. To me there's nothing like a spring shower with the wind blowing hard enough to make the rain go sideways. But before I go, I am going to have to make some additions to my program.

Obviously, the first thing that I will need to do is create a new `budget` for my trip to England. Doing that is pretty easy.

```
budget vacationBudgetEngland;
```

I'll also change the name of the old `budget`, `vacationBudget`, to `vacationBudgetEurope` to make things clearer. You can see that in Listing 5-3.

The problem I face, though, is how do I update the `vacationBudget England` variable? Right now, with a single `budget`, I updated the `vacation Budget` from each of the functions. But if I have two budgets, `vacationBudget Europe` and `vacationBudgetEngland`, I need a way to let the function know which budget it should update.

One way would be to have a set of functions for each country. I could create `spendDollarsInEurope` and `spendDollarsInEngland` functions (and corresponding `chargeForeignCurrencyEurope` and `chargeForeign-CurrencyEngland` functions that would convert euros and pounds into dollars ,respectively), and each one them would update the corresponding `budget`. For example:

```
void spendDollarsInEurope (double dollars) {
   vacationBudgetEurope.budget -= dollars;
}

void spendDollarsInEngland (double dollars) {
   vacationBudgetEngland.budget -= dollars;
}
```

Somehow this doesn't work for me. Adding new functions for each country I want to visit would not only be a lot of work, but also it seems like a waste, since, as you can see, they all are basically the same function — just operating on a different `budget`.

And as you could image, adding more countries would require coding and testing new functions and would quickly get out of hand. Remember, you want to make your programs easy to extend and enhance.

The alternative, which is the more sane approach, would be to pass to the function the `budget` variable it should operate on as an additional argument. So if I am spending dollars in Europe, I pass in the `vacationBudgetEurope`. If I am spending dollars in England, I pass in the `vacationBudgetEngland`. (I would also need to declare

That way the functions would operate on the right data.

The mechanics of doing that are not quite that straightforward. While, as I said earlier, I can pass a `struct` as an argument to a function, that is not going to get me what I want. For example, if I changed the `spendDollars` function to take a `budget` as an argument.

```
void spendDollars (budget theBudget, double dollars) {
  theBudget.budget -= dollars;
}
```

And I called it and then displayed the results (`numberDollarsInEuroland` is a new variable I declared that is initialized with the amount of a dollar transaction in Europe)

```
spendDollars(vacationBudgetEurope,
                      numberDollarsInEuroland);
NSLog(@"Converting %.2f US dollars into euros leaves
               $%.2f", numberDollarsInEuroland,
                  vacationBudgetEurope.budget);
```

I would find:

```
Converting 100.00 US dollars into euros leaves $1000.00
```

Whoops! This is because, as I also said earlier, when you pass in a variable as an argument in a function, it is *copied*. In order for a function to modify a member in a `budget` variable, you have to use a pointer to the `budget` variable as the argument. The function could then operate on the member (variable) directly.

To do that, I will change the `spendDollars` function to take a pointer to a `budget` as an argument and use that pointer to access and modify a member.

```
void spendDollars (budget *theBudget, double dollars) {
  theBudget->budget -= dollars;
}
```

I could then call it and display the results:

```
spendDollars(&vacationBudgetEurope,
                         numberDollarsInEuroland);
NSLog(@"Converting %.2f US dollars into euros leaves
                    $%.2f", numberDollarsInEuroland,
                    vacationBudgetEurope.budget);
```

The results will be

```
Converting 100.00 US dollars into euros leaves $900.00
```

Although I cover pointers in Chapter 4, I didn't really explain how to use them in this way, so I'll do that now.

Think of `vacationBudgetEurope` as a safety deposit box full of money. Up until now, the function withdrew money at will. When I use a pointer, instead of passing it the box, the function is passed the address of the box. That is what the `&vacationBudgetEurope` is in the function call.

```
spendDollars(&vacationBudgetEurope,
                         numberDollarsInEuroland);
```

`&vacationBudgetEurope` is the address of the `vacationBudgetEurope` variable.

Then in the `spendDollars` function itself, instead of taking money out of the box directly, the function first finds the box using the address. That is accomplished in the `spendDollars` using the arrow operator. The arrow operator tells the compiler I want to operate on the contents of an address.

```
void spendDollars(budget* theBudget, double dollars) {

   theBudget->budget -= dollars;
}
```

The arrow operator is a dereference operator that is used with pointers to `structs` (and to objects as well) with members that allow you to access a member of an object to which you have a reference (address). What you are doing is called *dereferencing* a pointer.

While for `structs` and objects, the arrow is commonly used, I could also have accessed the `budget` variable in the way I show you in Chapter 4:

```
(*theBudget).budget -= dollars;
```

Passing on the pointer to the appropriate `budget` makes adding a trip to England pretty straightforward. I need to declare and initialize the variables necessary for my new England excursion.

```
budget vacationBudgetEngland;
  vacationBudgetEngland.exchangeRate = 1.5000;
  vacationBudgetEngland.budget = 2000.00;
  double numberDollarsInPoundland = 100;
  double numberPounds = 100;
```

And I need to xxxx the code to simulate the transactions.

```
spendDollars(&vacationBudgetEngland,
        numberDollarsInPoundland);
NSLog(@"Converting %.2f US dollars into pounds
        leaves $%.2f", numberDollarsInPoundland,
        vacationBudgetEngland.budget);
chargeForeignCurrency(&vacationBudgetEngland,
        numberPounds);
NSLog(@"Charging %.2f pounds leaves $%.2f",
        numberPounds, vacationBudgetEngland.budget);
```

I also need to change the `spendDollars` and `chargeForeignCurrency` functions as I just described, to use the pointer to the `vacationBudget-Europe` and `vacationBudgetEngland` variables.

```
void spendDollars(budget* theBudget, double dollars) {

  theBudget-> budget -= dollars;
}

void chargeForeignCurrency(budget* theBudget, double
        foreignCurrency) {

  theBudget->exchangeTransaction =
        foreignCurrency*theBudget->exchangeRate;
  theBudget->budget -= theBudget->exchangeTransaction;
}
```

I'll also change a few names, from `vacationBudget` to `europeVacation-Budget` as I mentioned, and the `struct` member name from `euroTransac-tion` to `transaction`. That, of course, requires changing the code that used those names as well.

Well, it's back to work. In Listing 5-3, I bolded the changes.

If you have been following along with me, I'll be extending what you just did in the previous example. If you would like to start from a clean copy of the project where you left off, you can use the project found in the Example 5E folder, which is in the Chapter 5 folder.

1. In the `main` function, delete the commented code with the strikethrough and add the code in bold in Listing 5-3.

Listing 5-3: Adding More Functionality

```
#import <Foundation/Foundation.h>

typedef struct {
  float exchangeRate;
  double budget;
//double euroTransaction;
  double exchangeTransaction;
} budget;

//budget vacationBudget;
budget vacationBudgetEurope;
budget vacationBudgetEngland;

//void spendDollars (double dollars);
//void chargeEuros (double euros);
void spendDollars(budget* theBudget, double dollars);
void chargeForeignCurrency(budget* theBudget,
                                 double foreignCurrency);

int main (int argc, const char * argv[]) {

//vacationBudget.exchangeRate = 1.2500;
  vacationBudgetEurope.exchangeRate = 1.2500;
//vacationBudget.budget = 1000.00;
  vacationBudgetEurope.budget = 1000.00;
//double numberDollars = 100;
  double numberDollarsInEuroland = 100;
  double numberEuros = 100;

  vacationBudgetEngland.exchangeRate = 1.5000;
  vacationBudgetEngland.budget = 2000.00;
  double numberDollarsInPoundland = 100;
  double numberPounds = 100;


//spendDollars(numberDollars);
  spendDollars(&vacationBudgetEurope,
                             numberDollarsInEuroland);
//NSLog(@"Converting %.2f US dollars into euros leaves
         $%.2f", numberDollars, vacationBudget.budget);
  NSLog(@"Converting %.2f US dollars into euros leaves
                     $%.2f", numberDollarsInEuroland,
                     vacationBudgetEurope.budget);
//chargeEuros(numberEuros);
```

```
  chargeForeignCurrency (&vacationBudgetEurope,
                                    numberEuros);
//NSLog(@"Charging  %.2f euros leaves $%.2f", numberEuros,
        vacationBudget.budget);

  NSLog(@"Charging %.2f euros leaves $%.2f", numberEuros,
                          vacationBudgetEurope.budget);
  spendDollars(&vacationBudgetEngland,
                          numberDollarsInPoundland);
  NSLog(@"Converting %.2f US dollars into pounds leaves
                    $%.2f", numberDollarsInPoundland,
                          vacationBudgetEngland.budget);
  chargeForeignCurrency(&vacationBudgetEngland,
                                    numberPounds);
  NSLog(@"Charging %.2f pounds leaves $%.2f",
            numberPounds, vacationBudgetEngland.budget);


  return 0;

}
//void spendDollars (double dollars) {

//   vacationBudget.budget -= dollars;
//}

void spendDollars(budget* theBudget, double dollars) {

  theBudget->budget -= dollars;
}



//void chargeEuros (double euros) {

//   vacationBudget.euroTransaction = euros*vacationBudget.
        exchangeRate;
//   vacationBudget.budget -= vacationBudget.
        euroTransaction;
//}

void chargeForeignCurrency(budget* theBudget, double
        foreignCurrency) {

  theBudget->exchangeTransaction =
        foreignCurrency*theBudget->exchangeRate;
  theBudget->budget -= theBudget ->exchangeTransaction;
}
```

Your output in the Debugger Console should look like this:

```
Converting 100.00 US dollars into euros leaves $900.00
Charging 100.00 euros leaves $775.00
Converting 100.00 US dollars into pounds leaves $1900.00
Charging 100.00 pounds leaves $1750.00
```

You can find the completed project on the CD in the Example 5F folder, which is in the Chapter 5 folder.

Thinking about Extensibility and Enhanceability

While making the changes you just made does make it easier to add new countries (all you need to do is declare another `budget` for New Zealand, for example, and call the `spendDollars` and `chargeForeignCurrency` as needed). This approach is fraught with danger.

For example, one problem with this kind of module design is that data itself is accessible to all functions, and an errant function could think it was updating `vacationBudgetEngland` and because of a typing or copy-and-paste error (easily done on my part), it could end up updating `vacationBudgetEurope` instead.

Perhaps you think this is one of those theoretical issues that won't usually happen if you're doing your job right. Well, when I was doing the code for this example, I actually did that.

But more importantly, if you ever wanted to change the `struct`, you would have to go out and find all the functions that used it and change them. For example, what if you decided you wanted to change the `budget` member so it continued to hold the starting budget, and you wanted to add a new variable `whatsLeft` to let me know what my remaining balance was? In this program, that's not a problem, since there are only two functions to change. But in a more complex program, there could be functions all over the place that are using `budget` that I would have to find and change.

In addition, this program is not very extensible. If you wanted to have a different kind of budget for New Zealand, for example, one where I tracked my wool purchases, you would either have add that to all the countries you visited, even though you didn't use it anywhere except New Zealand. Or you would have to create a special `struct` for New Zealand and rewrite the `spendDollars` and `spendForeignCurrency` to use the new `struct`. If you then needed to go back to make a change to the original struct for any reason, you would have to remember to change both structs, and all the functions that used them.

Changes like this happen all the time, since, as you can see so far, factoring (or moving things around) and adding functionality is a way of life in the programming biz.

Objects (and classes) provide the solution to both of these problems.

The first problem, the global accessibility of data and the global impact of modifying the structure of the data, is solved by packaging data with functions that own them into something called an *object*. Objects allow you to implement encapsulation — as I explained in Chapter 3. This is the world of Objective-C's object-oriented extensions to C, and you'll be exploring objects in Chapter 6.

Using objects also can help with the second problem. In Chapter 3, I explain polymorphism, which enables me to add new "more of the same" functionality to my program without impacting the existing code. In Chapter 10, I show you how Objective-C makes that possible using a mechanism called inheritance.

Chapter 6

Adding a Little More Class to Your Program

*T*his chapter covers objects and classes and messages, and the difference between a program based on functions and global data and one based on objects. I show you quite a bit about the mechanics of using objects and classes in your program.

I also introduce you to some basic ideas about encapsulation. Encapsulation involves more than simply hiding instance variables behind the object's wall, as you'll see as you read this chapter and the rest of this book.

I also explain and illustrate some of the advantages of using objects, but to be frank, I only scratch the surface when it comes to that. As you continue through this book, I'll illustrate, and you'll discover on your own, many more.

Grasping Objects and Their Classes

In Chapter 5, I showed you what you would have to do to make your program easier to extend. You created two functions, spendDollars: and charge-ForeignCurrnecy:, that used a pointer to a budget variable. You could then pass in the pointer to europeBudget or englandBudget depending on where you were (Europe or England), and the function would operate on the data for that country.

The program architecture you created looked like the following (I'm going to omit the function implementation for the time being):

```
typedef struct {

  float exchangeRate;
  double budget;
  double exchangeTransaction;
} budget;

void spendDollars (budget *theBudget, double dollars);
void chargeForeignCurrency (budget *theBudget,
                                    double foreignCurrency);
```

The problem with that, as I pointed out, is that if I wanted to change the struct, I would have to go out and find all the functions that used it and change them. While in a program this small that would be simple (there are only two functions after all), in a more complex program, there could be functions all over the place that were using the budget struct.

This is one of the problems that object-oriented programming solves through *encapsulation*.

Moving from Functions and Global Data to Objects and Classes

As you might guess, object-oriented programs are built around *objects* — no surprises here. An object packages together data with the particular operations that can use or affect that data. A class that provided the same functionality as the budget struct and the functions that used it would look like this:

```
@interface

Budget : NSObject {

  float   exchangeRate;
  double budget;
  double exchangeTransaction;
}

- (void) spendDollars: (double) dollars ;
- (void) chargeForeignCurrency: (double) foreignCurrency;

@end
```

If you look carefully, you can see that I have taken (for the most part) the elements in the budget struct and the function prototypes and moved them into a *class* called Budget (ignore some of the details such as @interface and @end).

A class definition is like a structure definition in that it defines the data elements (which are called *instance variables*) that become part of every instance. But a class expands the idea of a data structure — containing both data and functions instead of just data. Functions, however, become *methods* that both specify and implement the behavior of a class.

This class definition is a template for an *object*; it declares the instance variables that become part of every object of that class and the methods that all objects of the class can use.

Whereas a *class* is a structure that represents an object's type — just like a struct did in the Chapter 5, an *object* is something that exists in a computer's memory. An object is an instantiation (big computer science word here) of a class. In more down to earth terms, a class is a type (just as a budget or an int is), and an object is like a variable.

When I use the word *class,* I am talking about code that you write, and when I use the word *object,* I am talking about behavior at runtime.

In Chapter 5, you declared a struct of type budget and then declared two variables of the type budget.

```
budget vacationBudgetEurope;
budget vacationBudgetEngland;
```

When you use a class, you do something similar.

```
Budget *europeBudget = [Budget new];
Budget *englandBudget = [Budget new];
```

Each instance of a class (object) has memory allocated for its own set of instance variables, which store values particular to the instance.

When you create an object from a class, you are essentially creating a struct out there in memory land that holds its instance variables. But while every object has its own instance variables, all objects of that class share a single set of methods. How a method knows which object's instance variables to use is an interesting story, and one I'll tell you shortly.

Operations (or functions) are known as the object's *methods*; the data they affect are its *instance variables*. In essence, an object bundles a data structure (instance variables) and a group of functions (methods) into a self-contained programming unit. You then ask an object to do something for you, such as subtract the amount you just spent from your budget, by sending it a *message*.

When an object receives a message, it then executes the code in the appropriate method.

This encapsulation solves the problem of the widespread impact that changing a data structure may have. Only an object's methods that are packaged with the data can access or modify that data, although an object can, and often does, make its data available to other objects through its methods.

While on the surface, it may appear that I am just changing some terminology — methods for functions, instance variables for struct members, and messages for function calls — essentially, this is a very different approach.

One more thing — in Objective-C, classes have two parts:

- An *interface* that *declares* the methods and instance variables of the class and names its superclass (don't worry, I'll explain all that).
- An *implementation* that actually *defines* the class — the code that implements its methods.

These two parts are almost always split between two files (although there can be more), but to make things easier, I'll postpone doing that until later, in the section "Spreading the Wealth across Files."

Creating the Interface

You'll begin your journey through object-oriented wonderland with the interface. The interface in the object-oriented world is the public commitment to the behavior you can count on from an object.

I want to start with a new project. Chapter 2 explains how to do this in detail, so if you need more information, refer to that chapter.

1. **Launch Xcode.**

   I'll be having you create a new project here. You can do that or you can skip Steps 2 through 6 and start with the project in the Chapter 6 Start Here folder, in the Chapter 6 folder on the CD.

2. **Start the New Project Assistant by Choosing File⇨New Project from the main menu to create a new project.**

3. **In the New Project window, click Application under the Mac OS X heading.**

4. **Select Command Line Tool from the choices displayed and then Select Foundation from the Type drop-down menu. Then click Choose.**

Xcode will display a standard save sheet.

5. **Enter the name** `Budget Object` **in the Save As field, choose a Save location (the Desktop works just fine), and then click Save.**

   After you click Save, Xcode creates the project and opens the project window. For more information on the project window, see Chapter 2.

6. **Start with an empty** `main` **function.**

   I covered this in Chapter 4. You will need to delete all of the statements in `main` except for `return 0;` so that you end up with a `main` function that looks like this:

```
#import <Foundation/Foundation.h>

int main (int argc, const char * argv[]) {

   return 0;
}
```

Declaring the class interface

The purpose of the class interface is to give users of a class the information they need to work with the class. The declaration of a class interface begins with the compiler directive `@interface` and ends with the directive `@end`. (All Objective-C compiler directives begin with @.)

```
@interface ClassName : ItsSuperclass {
   instance variable declarations
}
method declarations
@end
```

In the interface, you specify:

✔ The class's name and _superclass_.

```
@interface ClassName : ItsSuperclass {
```

A class can be based on another class called its superclass, and it inherits all of the methods and instance variables of that class. I'll explain all about inheritance in Chapter 10. For now just follow along.

✔ The class's _instance variables_. Instance variables correspond to the members (variable declarations) in a struct.

✔ The class's _methods_. Methods correspond to the function prototypes discussed in Chapter 5.

For example, here is the interface for the Budget class:

```
@interface Budget : NSObject  {

  float   exchangeRate;
  double  budget;
  double  exchangeTransaction;
}

- (void)  createBudget: (double) aBudget
             withExchangeRate: (float) anExchangeRate;
- (void)  spendDollars: (double) dollars ;
- (void)  chargeForeignCurrency: (double) foreignCurrency;
@end
```

By convention, class names begin with an uppercase letter (such as Budget); the names' instance variables and methods typically begin with a lowercase letter (such as exchangeRate: and spendDollars:).

There are four parts to the interface, and I'll have you enter them in the empty main file over the next four sections. The parts appear in this order:

1. The @interface compiler directive and first line

2. The instance variables

3. The methods

4. The @end compiler directive

Enter the @interface compiler directive and first line

Enter the following code right after the first line, #import <Foundation/ Foundation.h> and before main:

```
@interface Budget : NSObject {
```

@interface tells the compiler that you are declaring a new class.

Budget : NSObject declares the new class name and links it to its superclass.

In this case, Budget is both the name of the class and the name of the new type. This is exactly the same (well, close) as declaring the struct (see Chapter 5).

: NSObject on the @interface line tells the compiler that the Budget class is an extension of the NSObject class. As I explained, Budget will inherit all of the methods and instance variables of NSObject. This means that for all practical purposes, even though you don't see them in your class declaration, Budget includes all of the instance variables and all of the methods that are in NSObject.

Since Budget inherits from NSObject, it has all the functionality an Objective-C object needs at runtime.

Enter the instance variables

After starting to declare a new class, you tell the compiler about the various pieces of data — the instance variables and methods.

Type the following lines of code on the line after @interface Budget : NSObject {:

```
float    exchangeRate;
double budget;
double exchangeTransaction;
}
```

exchangeRate, budget, and exchangeTransaction are the *instance variables* for objects of class Budget.

The reason they are called instance variables is that when you create an object of class Budget, you are creating an *instance* of the class, which means that for each class object you create, you allocate some amount of memory for its variables (just as you do for the struct) — instance variables are often shortened to *ivars*. Notice the instance variables correspond to the ones used in the struct:

- ✔ exchangeRate is the current, well, exchange rate — the number of dollars it will cost me to get one euro, or one pound, for example.
- ✔ budget holds the amount of dollars I have left to spend in a given country.
- ✔ exchangeTransaction is the amount in U.S. dollars of a foreign currency transaction.

Objective-C is case-sensitive. Budget and budget are not the same thing — Budget is a class, and budget is a variable.

Since you declared budget, exchangeRate, and exchangeTransaction in the class definition, every time a Budget object is created, it includes these three instance variables. So every object of class Budget has its own budget, exchangeRate, and exchangeTransaction. The closing brace tells the compiler you're done specifying the instance variables for Budget.

Enter the methods

Type the following lines of code on the line after the brace (}):

```
- (void) createBudget: (double) aBudget
              withExchangeRate: (float) anExchangeRate;
- (void) spendDollars: (double) dollars ;
- (void) chargeForeignCurrency: (double) foreignCurrency;
```

In Objective-C, these lines of code are called *method declarations*. They make public the behavior that the Budget has implemented — that is, this is what the object of class Budget can do.

Method declarations are functionally similar to the function prototypes you declared in the last chapter, although they look a lot different. So let me explain methods.

I'll start with spendDollars: (I'll get to createBudget:: soon).

```
- (void) spendDollars: (double) dollars;
```

The leading dash signals that this is the declaration for an Objective-C method. That's one way you can distinguish a method declaration from a function prototype, which has no leading dash.

Following the dash is the return type for the method, enclosed in parentheses. Methods can return the same types as functions, including standard types (int, float, and char), as well as references to other objects (an object reference is similar to the pointer to the struct that you used in Chapter 5).

spendDollars: is a method that takes a single argument of type double. Notice that instead of the parentheses used in a function to indicate arguments, methods use a :. Also notice that the colon is part of the method name, as you saw when I referred to the spendDollars: earlier.

Another difference between a function and method declaration is that in a method declaration, both the *return type* and the *argument type* are enclosed in parentheses. This is the standard syntax for casting one type to a another (you can refer to Chapter 4 where I explain the cast operator, if you like).

While this method doesn't return a value, it could, just like any function does, and in the same way:

```
return someValue;
```

For all practical purposes, chargeForeignCurrency is the same.

```
- (void) chargeForeignCurrency: (double) foreignCurrency;
```

Finally, you've come to the mind-numbing part — `createBudget::`

```
- (void) createBudget: (double) aBudget
           withExchangeRate: (float) anExchangeRate;
```

`createBudget::` is a method that initializes the values — the `budget` and `exchangeRate` — for an object that is the budget for a particular country. In Chapter 5, you did that in `main` by assigning those values to the members in the `budget` struct. For example:

```
vacationBudgetEurope.exchangeRate = 1.2500;
vacationBudgetEurope.budget = 1000.00;
...
vacationBudgetEngland.exchangeRate = 1.5000;
vacationBudgetEngland.budget = 2000.00;
```

But because (as I explain later in this chapter in the section "Scoping instance variables") you don't have access to the instance variables in a `Budget` object (repeat "encapsulation" three times and click your heels), you need to create a method to assign initial values to the instance variables. Initialization is an important part of Objective-C, and I explain it in detail in Chapter 12.

While you might be able to guess that the method takes two arguments, the syntax of the declaration is probably not something you are familiar with (talk about a classic understatement).

```
- (void) createBudget: (double) aBudget
           withExchangeRate: (float) anExchangeRate;
```

When there's more than one argument, the arguments are declared within the method name after the colon. What makes it interesting is that the additional arguments after the first have a name. In fact, the real method name is `createBudget:withExchangeRate:`.

While this may appear to be confusing, operationally it is no different than a function. For example, inside of your methods, you access the arguments using the identifier, just as you did in the functions you used in Chapter 5. In this case, the identifiers are `aBudget` and `anExchangeRate`.

Argument names are one of the major differences between a method and a function.

Argument names make it easier to understand the messages in your code. `createBudget:withExchangeRate:` does have a nice ring to it. When you create your own methods, name them in the same way I just did — making them closer to sentences. This way of naming methods makes it much easier to match arguments with what they are used for. This solves one of the problems that you can run across when using functions in your code — you can't tell, when reading the code, what each of the arguments in a function call is for without looking at the function.

This does take some getting used to, but once you do, you will like it a lot.

If a method takes an argument, it has one or more colons, corresponding to the number of arguments. If it takes no arguments, it has no colons. If you are not going to specify the full name, you add the number of colons corresponding to the number of arguments to the name. For example, `createBudget::` indicates it takes two arguments.

Since `createBudget::` won't be returning anything, I used `void` to indicate that there's no return value.

Enter the @end compiler directive

Type `@end`.

This tells the compiler that you have finished the interface declaration.

The interface is done! It's the complete interface for the `Budget` class. Now, anyone using this object knows that this class has three methods that can create a new budget, spend dollars, and charge something in a foreign currency. While he or she could also see that there are three instance variables, that should be of no concern unless he or she is going to modify that class.

Scoping instance variables

As you saw in Chapter 5, instance variables are scoped to (accessible within) the code block they're in. This can be a function, a code block within a function, or, in this case, a class. It is this built-in scoping mechanism that allows an object to hide its data. But to provide flexibility, when it comes to a class (here come the Objective-C extensions to C again), you can actually explicitly set the scope to three different levels through the use of a compiler directive:

- ✔ `@private`: The instance variable is accessible only within the class that declares it.

- ✔ `@protected`: The instance variable is accessible within the class that declares it and within classes that inherit it. This is the default if you don't specify anything.

- ✔ `@public`: The instance variable is accessible everywhere.

    Don't use `@public`! If you do — go directly to jail, do not pass Go, and do not collect $200. If you have to ask why, reread the first part of this chapter, the last part of the previous chapter, and Chapter 3

There is actually another level, @package: On 64-bit machines, an instance variable acts like @public inside the framework that defines the class, but @private outside. I mention it because you may see it in some of the Cocoa header files, but it's beyond the scope of this book.

What you have just done implements one of the fundamental concepts in object-oriented programming — encapsulation. Data and functions are now both members of the object. You no longer use sets of global variables or structs that you pass from one function to another as arguments. Instead, you use objects that have their own data *and* functions as members.

Now that you have the interface done, it's time to write the code that makes this class actually do something.

The Implementation — Coding the Methods

The @interface , which I discuss in the preceding section, defines a class's public interface. This is where another developer (or even you) can go to understand the class's capabilities and behavior. But it's here in the implementation that the real work is described and done.

Just as with the interface, I am going to break the implementation down into a number of steps and explain what you are doing as you go along. Here are the steps:

1. The implementation compiler directive

2. Define the createBudget: method

3. Define the rest of the methods

4. Enter the @end compiler directive

The implementation compiler directive

Type the following line of code after the @end statement into Budget Object.m and before main.

```
@implementation Budget
```

@implementation (like @interface) is a compiler directive that says you're about to present the code that implements a class. The name of the class appears after @implementation. Here is where you code the definitions of the individual methods. (Here, order is unimportant — the methods don't have to appear in the same order as they do in the @interface.)

In fact, you can add methods in an @implementation that have not been declared in the @interface. In other languages, these might be considered private methods. Not so in Objective-C, which doesn't have private methods — those you add to the implementation that are not in the interface are still accessible to other objects.

Defining the createBudget: method

Type the following lines of code after the @implementation Budget:

```
- (void) createBudget: (double) aBudget
            withExchangeRate: (float) anExchangeRate {
  exchangeRate = anExchangeRate;
  budget = aBudget;
}
```

This is your brand-spanking new initialization function. The first line of the definition of createBudget:: looks a lot like the declaration in the @interface section (one would hope), except that instead of a semicolon at the end, you find a brace. Notice that you have an argument named aBudget and an instance variable budget. If you had named that argument budget, the compiler would have needed to decide which one you meant when you tried to access the budget variable. You will find that the compiler will tell you in no uncertain terms that it was going to hide the instance variable from your method code. I mutilated my beautiful code to illustrate that in Figure 6-1.

You want to use a name like aBudget in the method declaration because it tells the reader exactly what the argument is for. In general though, as you will see, I don't want the user to know that this is initializing an instance variable. I'll explain why, and more about encapsulation, in Chapter 14 when I explain properties.

The body of the method, as you would expect, contains these instructions:

```
exchangeRate = anExchangeRate;
budget = aBudget;
```

As I explained earlier, in the program you coded in Chapter 5, you did this initialization in main.

```
vacationBudgetEurope.exchangeRate = 1.2500;
vacationBudgetEurope.budget = 1000.00;
vacationBudgetEngland.exchangeRate = 1.5000;
vacationBudgetEngland.budget = 2000.00;
```

Figure 6-1:
The
compiler's
revenge.

But now that you are an official object-oriented programmer, you don't want
to assign the value to the variables in this way for a couple of reasons. First,
you made those instance variables protected (by default), so you can't
access them. But even if you could, you wouldn't want to because it violates
the principle of encapsulation.

Defining the rest of the methods

Enter the following lines of code after the `createBudget::` method:

```
- (void) spendDollars: (double) dollars {

  budget -= dollars;
  NSLog(@"Converting %.2f US dollars into foreign currency
                          leaves $%.2f", dollars, budget);
}

- (void) chargeForeignCurrency: (double)
                                    foreignCurrency {

  exchangeTransaction = foreignCurrency*exchangeRate;
  budget -= exchangeTransaction;
  NSLog(@"Charging %.2f in foreign currency leaves $%.2f",
                          foreignCurrency, budget);
}
```

Both of these methods are almost identical to the previous functions you used. I have also moved the NSLog statements from main into the methods because it enables me to track the methods as they are invoked.

You are not using these NSLog statements for any other reason than to be able to follow what is going on in the program, so don't get too concerned with what is being displayed. I'll add a real user interface in Chapters 17 and 18.

Entering the @end compiler directive

Type @end.

The last line of code, @end, tells the compiler that you have finished the implementation.

Exploring the Program Logic

Now that you have declared your objects, it's about time to do something with them. Although it seems as though I've been working backwards, which is true, it's time to get to the real meat (or tofu, if you prefer) of the program. Just remember, I have been working backwards because in programming, and in life, and in cooking (and in painting) most of the work is in the preparation. Once you have everything ready, then execution should be easy, and as you will see, it is.

Note: You are still working in the Budget Object.m file. If you need to, scroll down to find the main function. It should look like the following:

```
#import <Foundation/Foundation.h>

int main (int argc, const char * argv[]) {

   return 0;
}
```

Coding the functionality in the main function

I'll now take you through coding the main function. I'll break this down into a series of steps.

1. Declaring the local variables

2. Instantiating an object

3. Sending messages to your objects

4. Adding the code for England

Declaring the local variables

The first thing you do in your program is declare some local variables, just as you did in Chapter 5.

Type the following lines of code into main after the first brace, and before the `return 0;` statement:

```
double numberDollarsInEuroland = 100;
double numberEuros = 100;
double numberDollarsInPoundland = 100;
double numberPounds = 100;
```

Instantiating an object

The next thing you do is instantiate an object.

Type the following line of code after the variables you just declared:

```
Budget   *europeBudget = [Budget new];
```

Congratulations! You have instantiated (created) your first object, and you have sent it a message.

To create a new object, you send the `new` message to the class you are interested in. Messaging is an important part of working with objects in Objective-C, and it is very different than the function calls that you have been working with.

To start with, the syntax of sending a message is

```
[receiver message : arguments];
```

The receiver of a message can be either an *object* or a *class*. One of the more interesting features of Objective-C is that you can send messages to a class. If you haven't done object-oriented programming before, sending messages to a class probably means nothing to you. But if are coming from something like C++, it is very interesting. Class methods enable you to implement behavior that is not object-specific, but applicable to an entire class.

The methods defined for an object are called instance methods, and the ones defined for a class are called class methods. While I will be mentioning class methods in this book, you won't be using them. I'll only be referring to them when it is important to distinguish them from instance methods and where you really need to know about them — in Chapter 13, for example.

The line of code you entered

```
Budget *europeBudget = [Budget new];
```

sends the new message to the Budget class. The new method (inherited from NSObject) does two things, in this order.

1. Allocates memory for the object to hold its instance variables.

2. Sends the new object an init message.

    The default init method will (more or less) initialize its instance variables to 0. This works fine for the time being. Initialization, as boring as it sounds, is, however, a very important part of working with objects. In Chapters 12 and 13, I'll go into detail about initialization and show you how to write a proper init method for your objects.

At runtime, a class object for each class is created — one that knows how to build new objects belonging to the class.

What is important here is that what is returned is a *pointer* to the memory that has been allocated to hold this object's instance variables. This is similar to what you did in Chapter 5, where you created a pointer to each of the budget structs you declared. I explain more about memory allocation in Chapter 13. (If you are a little fuzzy on pointers, refer to Chapter 4.)

Sending messages to your objects

Enter the following line of code after Budget *europeBudget = [Budget new];

```
[europeBudget createBudget:
              1000.00 withExchangeRate:1.2500];
[europeBudget spendDollars:numberDollarsInEuroland];
[europeBudget chargeForeignCurrency:numberEuros];
```

You have sent three messages to the europeBudget *object* you just instantiated. Take a look at the first message:

```
[europeBudget  createBudget:1000.00
                        withExchangeRate:1.2500];
```

Using the europeBudget pointer to the object, you are sending it the createBudget:: message with 1000.00 and 1.2500 as arguments. As I explained, the net result is the same as the initialization of the members in the structs that you did in the main function.

Instead, you use this method to initialize the object with a budget and an exchange rate. As you'll see, the initialization I've done here is pretty rudimentary, especially compared to what you'll be doing in a few chapters, but it gets the job done for now.

After initialization, the next message you send to the europeBudget object tells it how much you just spent in dollars (it has an argument numberDollarsInEuroland just as the function did).

```
[europeBudget spendDollars:numberDollarsInEuroland];
```

And the third message reports a credit card transaction.

```
[europeBudget chargeForeignCurrency:numberEuros];
```

The question that occurred to me when I first learned about object-oriented programming was how did the europeBudget method code (of which there is only a single copy) get to the object's *ivars* (instance variables), which are sitting some place in memory?

The answer is very clever. When you send a message in Objective-C, a hidden argument called self, a pointer to the object's instance variables, is passed to the receiving object. For example, in the code

```
[europeBudget spendDollars:numberDollarsInEuroland];
```

the method passes europeBudget as its self argument. While the code you wrote in the method chargeForeignCurrency: looks like

```
NSLog(@"Converting %.2f US dollars into foreign currency
                    leaves $%.2f", dollars, budget);
```

what the compiler is really doing is modifying your code so that it conceptually looks like this:

```
NSLog(@"Converting %.2f US dollars into foreign currency
            leaves $%.2f", dollars, self->budget);
```

This should look familiar. This is what you did in Chapter 5 to access the struct members. The -> is the arrow operator. It is used only with pointers to objects (as well as structs). See Chapter 4 to refresh your memory about pointers.

As you create objects, you get a new pointer for each one, and when you send a message to a particular object, the pointer associated with that object becomes the self argument.

Adding the code for England

First you need to create the `Budget` object for England. (I wouldn't fancy being in England with no money to spend after all.) Then you will be able to send it message as well.

Type the following line of code, before the `return 0;` statement, to finish `main`.

```
Budget   *englandBudget = [Budget new];


[englandBudget  createBudget:2000.00
                            withExchangeRate:1.5000];
[englandBudget spendDollars:numberDollarsInPoundland];
[englandBudget chargeForeignCurrency:numberPounds];
```

You just done wrote a program that implements one of the fundamental concepts in object-oriented programming — encapsulation. The data and the operations on that data are now encapsulated within the budget object.

You no longer use sets of global variables or `struct`s that you pass from one function to another as arguments. Instead, you have objects that have their own data and functions embedded as members. (I know that I have said this before, but it is worth repeating.)

Building and running the application

To build and run the application, select the Build and Run button in the Project Window toolbar .

Your output in the Debug Console should look like the following:

```
Converting 100.00 US dollars into foreign currency leaves
        $900.00
Charging 100.00 in foreign currency leaves $775.00
Converting 100.00 US dollars into foreign currency leaves
        $1900.00
Charging 100.00 in foreign currency leaves $1750.00
```

You can find the completed project on the CD in the Example 6 A folder which can be found in the Chapter 6 folder.

Extending the program

In Chapter 4 I raised two concerns about being able to extend my program. The first one, the vulnerability you face when all of your functions have access to all the data, and are dependent on that data's structure, is mostly solved by encapsulating the data in an object. The data becomes an internal implementation detail; all the users of that data outside the object know about is the behavior it can expect from an object.

But what if another object needs to know the amount left in your budget for England, for example? This requires that you add a method that provides that information. Notice I said information, not the instance variable. It becomes the responsibility of an object to supply the budget information to any object that needs it. It does not mean, however, that there has to be an instance variable that holds that information. That makes it possible to change how you represent that data, and also makes it possible to change what instance variables you choose for the object. In the previous chapter, I brought up the problems that I would run into if I wanted to change the `struct` that the functions used. Making that change now, using classes and objects in the way you should, would have no impact on the objects that were using that information!

So while its internal data structure is part of the class interface, in reality, an object's functionality should be defined only by its methods. As a user of a class, you shouldn't count on a one-to-one correspondence between a method that returns some data and an instance variable. Some methods might return information not stored in instance variables, and some instance variables might have data that will never see the light of day outside the object.

This allows your classes to evolve over time (remember Chapter 3, where I spoke about the inevitability of change). As long as messages are the way you interact with a class, changes to the instance variables really don't affect its interface and the other objects that use this class — and that's the point.

But what about my second concern — what if I want a new kind of budget or want to tailor my `Budget` object to New Zealand to keep track of my sheep purchases? Do I have to take the old object, copy and paste it, and add the new features — thus creating a new object that I have to maintain in parallel with the existing `Budget` object?

As you might expect, the answer is, "Of course not!" But to find out exactly how to do that, you'll have to wait until Chapter 10 when I talk about inheritance.

In addition, there is even more you will do to make your program even more extensible, which you'll discover in Chapter 11.

Spreading the Wealth across Files

So far, everything you have done has been added to a single source file. You started out with My FirstProgram.m and then moved to Budget.m. While this works for what you have been doing thus far, it won't scale when you start to develop your own applications. As your program gets larger, scrolling through a single file becomes more difficult. (There are also other issues beyond the scope of this book that you need not be concerned about for a while.) But there is a well thought out solution for that problem that just about everyone uses.

When I write even the simplest programs for the iPhone or Mac, I divide things up into multiple files.

As you've seen, the source code for Objective-C classes is divided into two parts. One part is the interface, which provides the public view of the class. The `@interface` contains all the information necessary for someone to use the class.

The other part of a class's source is the implementation. The `@implementation` contains the method definitions.

Because of the natural split in the definition of a class into interface and implementation, a class's code is often split into two files along the same lines. One part holds the interface components: the `@interface` directive for the class and any `enum`, `constants`, `#defines`, and so on. Because of Objective-C's C heritage, this typically goes into a header file, which has the same name as the class with an .h at the end. For example, the class `Budget` header file will be called `Budget.h`.

All the implementation details, such as the `@implementation` directive for the class, definitions of global variables, the method definitions (implementations), and so on go into a file with the same name as the class and with an .m at the end. Budget.m will be the implementation file for your class.

I'll start by having you create a new folder in the Groups & Files pane to hold the new files. These folders (called Groups by Xcode) provide a way to organize the source files in your project. (For example, you can make one group for your user interface classes and another for your model classes to make your project easier to navigate.) When you set up groups, Xcode doesn't actually move any files or create any directories on your hard drive. The group relationship is just a lovely fantasy maintained by Xcode.

After that, you'll create the files themselves.

If you have been following along with me, I'll be extending what you just did in the previous example. If you would like to start with a clean copy of the project where you left off, you can use the project found in the Example 6A folder, which is in the Chapter 6 folder.

 1. **Select the Budget Object project icon and then choose Project⇨New Group (see Figure 6-2).**

Figure 6-2:
Creating a new folder.

You'll get a brand-spanking new folder named New Group, already selected and waiting for you to type in the name you want.

2. Type the name `Classes`, **as I did in Figure 6-3.**

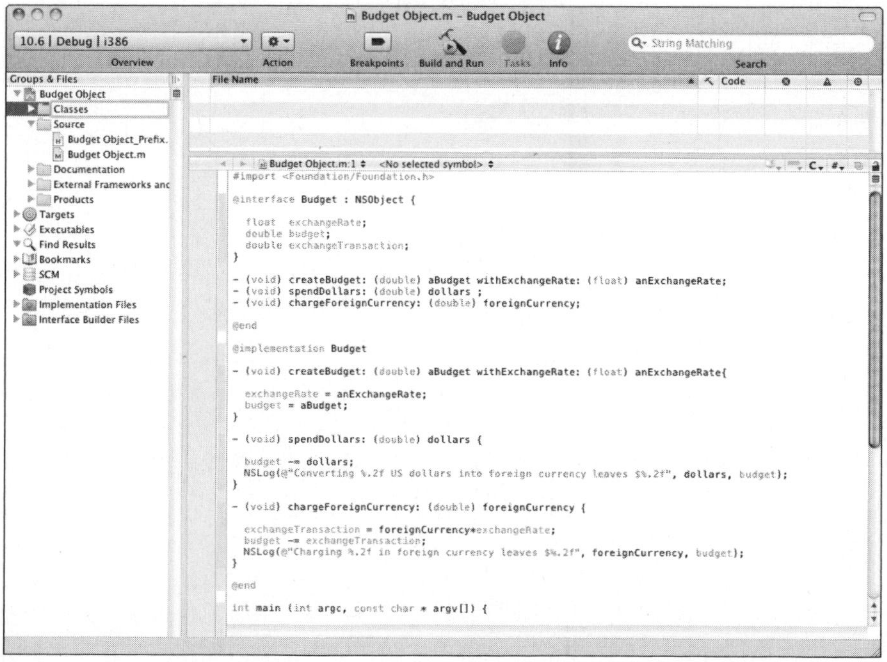

Figure 6-3:
A new classes folder.

3. **Select File⇨New File from the main menu (or press ⌘+n) to get the New File dialog.**

   Make sure the Classes folder is still selected; Xcode puts new files into the selected folder.

4. **In the leftmost column of the dialog, first select Cocoa under Mac OS X, select the Objective-C class template in the top right pane as I did in Figure 6-4, and then click Next.**

   You can specify this new class's superclass. Make sure NSObject is selected in the drop-down menu.

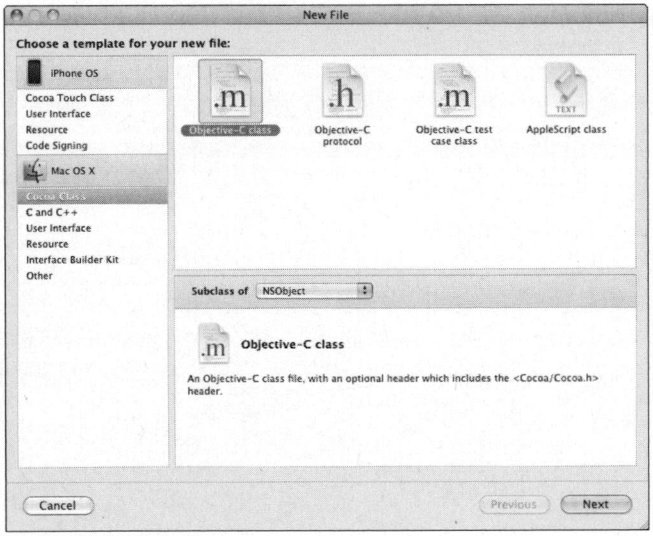

Figure 6-4:
A Cocoa
class
template.

You'll see a new dialog asking for some more information.

5. **Enter Budget.m in the File Name field and make sure the checkbox to have Xcode create Budget.h. is checked, as I did in Figure 6-5, and then click Finish.**

   Xcode will then add the files to the project as you can see in Figure 6-6 (I deleted the comments at the start of the file that Xcode automatically puts in there). Once you've created the files, you can select or double-click them in the list to edit them. Xcode also includes some standard code, depending on the template, such as empty `@interface` and `@implementations` for you to fill in as well as `#import <Cocoa/Cocoa.h>`.

What's going on here? So far in this book, you've used `#import <Foundation/Foundation.h>` because that was what was in the Foundation Command Line Tool template you used when you created the project. But when you start creating .m and .h files, Xcode assumes that you will be using Cocoa (either for a Mac OS X or iPhone OS application), so it includes Cocoa header files, which brings in the Foundation headers as well.

At this point, you have the files you need to separate out the `Budget` interface (into `Budget.h`) and implementation (into Budget.m), as you can see in Figure 6-6.

I find it useful at this point to double-click Budget Object.m to open it in a new window.

6. **Select the interface code in Budget Object.m, as shown in Figure 6-6.**

7. **Make sure that Budget.h is open in the Editor view, as you can see in Figure 6-6, and select everything except the #import <Cocoa/Cocoa.h> as shown in the figure.**

8. **Cut the interface (don't worry, you can always undo it if it doesn't work) from Budget Object.m and paste it into the Budget.h file, as shown in Figure 6-7.**

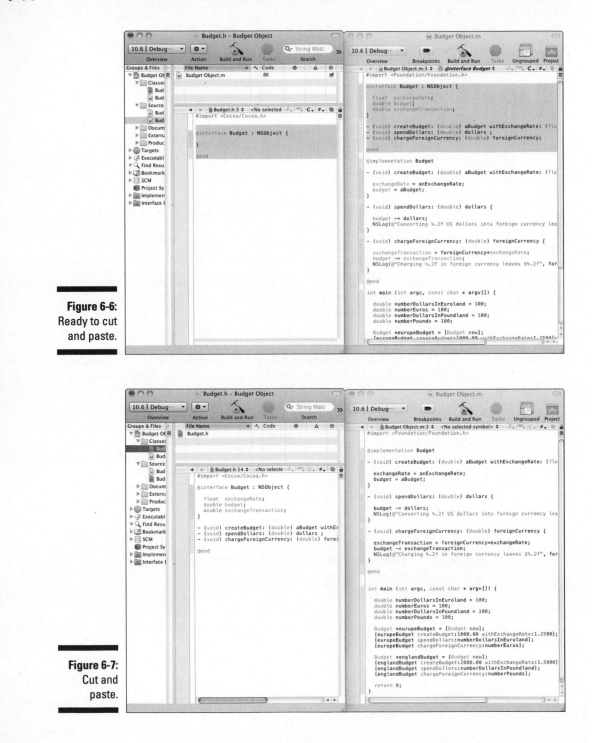

Figure 6-6:
Ready to cut
and paste.

Figure 6-7:
Cut and
paste.

9. **Select the implementation code in Budget Object.m, as I have in Figure 6-8.**

10. **Select Budget.m in the Groups & Files view so that you can see it in the Editor view, as I have in Figure 6-8, and select everything except the #import "Budget.h" as I have in Figure 6-8.**

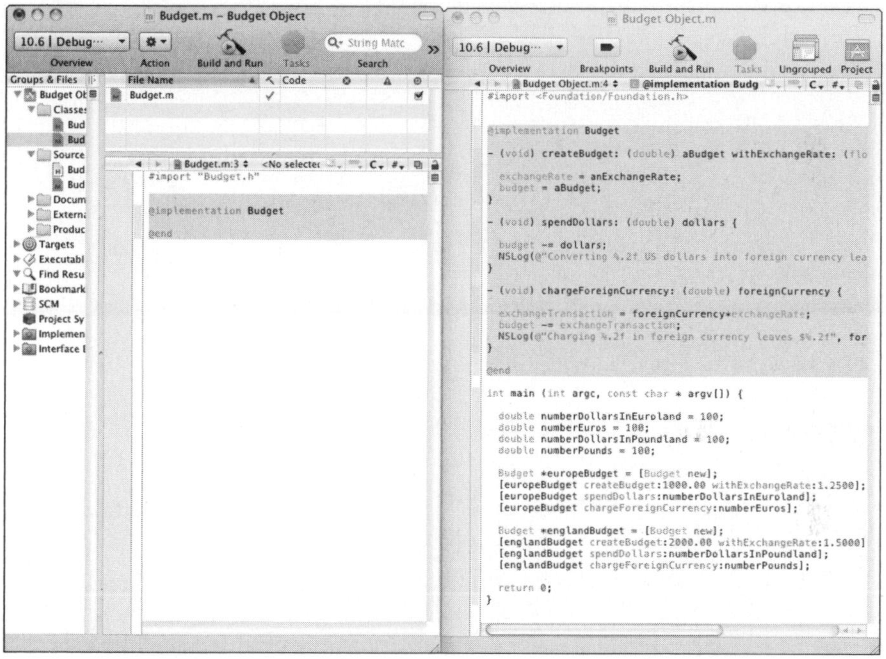

Figure 6-8: Ready to cut and paste.

11. **Cut the implementation code in the Budget.m file and paste it into the Budget.m file.**

12. **Add a line of code to the Budget Object.m file, as shown in Figure 6-9.**

```
#import Budget.h
```

This imports the header file for the class, which makes the classes and methods accessible from `main`. This is standard procedure, which you'll end up doing in virtually every project you create. The compiler needs to know what is in the interface of any classes you refer to from `main` (or any of your other classes). So to keep the compiler happy, you add the `#import Budget.h` statement. Try commenting it out and see how the compiler responds.

Figure 6-9:
Include the
new header
file.

13. Select the Build and Run button in the Project Window toolbar to build and run the application.

You should get a successful build, as I did in Figure 6-10.

Figure 6-10:
Success!

If you look on the text editor navigation bar (at the top of the Editor view), you'll see a Lock button on the far right of the bar. (I explain the text editor navigation bar in Chapter 2.) Immediately to the left of that is the Counterpart button that looks like two pages overlapping. Clicking that button will switch you from the header, or interface file, to the implementation file, and vice versa. Right under the lock is a button that lets you split the editor view. That enables you to look at the interface and implementation files at the same time, or even the code for two different methods in the same or different classes. If you have any questions about what something does, just position the mouse pointer above the button and a tooltip will explain it.

You can find the completed project on the CD in the Example 6B folder, which is in the Chapter 6 folder.

Knowing the Naming Conventions

It is helpful to have some idea about how to name things in order to avoid having the compiler scream at you. Here are some areas you need to pay attention to:

✔ The names of files that contain Objective-C source code have the .m extension. Files that declare class and category (a category is used to extend a class; I explain that in Chapter 16) interfaces or that declare protocols (I explain that in Chapter 16 as well) have the .h extension typical of header files.

✔ Class, category, and protocol names generally begin with an uppercase letter; the names of methods and instance variables typically begin with a lowercase letter. The names of variables that hold instances also typically begin with lowercase letters.

✔ In Objective-C, identical names that serve different purposes are allowed.

  • A class can declare methods with the same names as methods in other classes.

  • A class can declare instance variables with the same names as variables in other classes.

  • An instance method can have the same name as a class method.

  • A method can have the same name as an instance variable.

  • Method names beginning with "_", a single underscore character, are reserved for use by Apple.

✔ However, class names are in the same name space as global variables and defined types. A program can't have a defined type with the same name as a class.

Using id and nil

As part of its extensions to C, Objective-C adds two built-in types that you will be using.

id is a generic type that's used to refer to any kind of object regardless of class — id is defined as a pointer to an object data structure. All objects, regardless of their instance variables or methods, are of type id. You will be using id when I explain protocols in Chapter 16. For now, just keep this in mind.

Similarly, the keyword nil is defined as a null object, an id with a value of 0. You'll be using it starting in Chapter 7.

id, nil, and the other basic types of Objective-C are defined in the header file objc/objc.h.

Chapter 7

Objects Objects Everywhere

. . . .

In This Chapter

▶ Turning numbers into objects

▶ Working with mutable arrays

▶ Using each object in an array in a message

▶ Getting to know C arrays

. . . .

*N*ow that you know how to create classes and send messages to your objects, I want to expand your ideas about what you can do with objects. So far, what you have done is send messages from main to the objects you created. What you will soon find out is that your objects will be sending messages to other objects to assist them in carrying out their responsibilities as well. You'll also discover that you don't have to write all of the objects you need to use in your program. The frameworks I mentioned in Chapter 1 supply many of them for you. So you'll not only be creating your own objects, but also using the objects in Cocoa's Foundation classes that provide some of the "utility" functionality you need.

In this chapter, I'll introduce you to two of those objects. The first is NSNumber, one of the hundred or so classes in the Foundation Framework. All of the data types I explained in Chapter 4, signed or unsigned char, short int, int, long int, long long int, float, double, and BOOL, can be represented using the NSNumber class.

The second will be NSMutable arrays. Arrays are what you will use to manage lists of objects. While right now there are not that many objects to manage, as you develop your application, you'll begin to see how useful they can be. In this chapter, I'll show you how to take the NSNumber objects you create and manage them using an NSMutableArray.

Replacing Numbers with Objects

As you learn more about object-oriented programming and the Cocoa frameworks, you'll discover that virtually everything you'll work with will be an object. Many of these objects are things you would expect to be objects, such as windows and controls and the like, but some of them may surprise you.

One striking example of this is NSNumber, which enables you to represent the built-in numerical data types as objects.

While some of the reasons framework designers think it is important to use things like NSNumber objects are based upon technical computer science issues that are beyond the scope of this book, others are eminently practical. You'll discover that later in this chapter when I introduce you to arrays, and in Chapter 15 when I explain about property lists and data storage.

Up until now, you have been using a variable of type double to represent a transaction — the amount in dollars you are converting into a foreign currency when you send the spendDollars: message.

```
double numberEuros = 100;
double numberPounds = 100;
```

In the spendDollars:, method you use the dollars argument, which is also a double.

```
- (void) spendDollars: (double) dollars {

budget -= dollars;
NSLog(@"Converting %.2f US dollars into foreign currency
        leaves $%.2f", dollars, budget);
}
```

To start with, I am going to show you how you could use an NSNumber object instead of a double as an argument in the spendDollars: method. As I said, NSNumber objects allow you to create objects out of the basic number types you work with in Chapter 4 — int, long, float, double, and so on.

I am going to do this only for spendDollars: message and its arguments. This is actually only an intermediate step in evolving this program to one that uses the full-blown transaction objects in Chapter 11.

You start by creating an NSNumber object.

In Chapter 5, you create the Budget object by sending it a new message like so:

```
Budget *europeBudget = [Budget new];
```

As I said earlier, the new message actually does two things. First, it allocates memory for your object, and then it calls the default init method, which initializes everything to 0. While that works for your `Budget` object, it won't work for the `NSNumber` object because you want to initialize the `NSNumber` object with a value.

So to create an `NSNumber` object, you separate out the `new` and `init` messages.

```
NSNumber *europeDollarTransaction =
                [[NSNumber alloc] initWithDouble:100.00];
```

So, as you can see, instead of sending the `new` message to the `NSNumber` class, you are first sending it an `alloc` message.

```
[NSNumber alloc]
```

This message, just as `new` does, returns a pointer to the new `NSNumber` object, and then using that pointer, sends the `initWithDouble:` message.

```
[[NSNumber alloc] initWithDouble:100.00];
```

The preceding code returns an `NSNumber` object initialized to contain the value (the 100.00 as a `double`) you used as the argument in the `initWith-Double:` message.

There are a number of initialization methods that allow you to create `NSNumber` objects from other types.

```
initWithChar: (char) value;
initWithInt: (int) value;
initWithFloat: (float) value;
initWithBool: (BOOL) value;
```

While you create an `NSNumber` object by initializing it with a certain type, part of the power of `NSNumber` is that it is not limited by the type it is initialized with. For example, to get the numeric value as a `double` (which you'll need to use in the `spendDollars:` method), you can send the `NSNumber` object the message

```
[dollars doubleValue]
```

But `NSNumber` can also return its value converted into almost any of the built-in types such as `char`, `int`, `BOOL`, or even an `NSString` (to refresh your memory, this is what you have been using in the `NSLog` statements to display something on the Debug Console).

You could also have created an `NSNumber` using something called a *factory method*.

```
NSNumber *europeChargeTransaction =
                        [NSNumber numberWithDouble:100.00];
```

This enables you to skip the new and init messages and let the class do it for you. However, that method has some memory management implications that are covered in Chapter 13.

Revisiting the documentation

I can't possibly go through all the possibilities of every class with you, and that is why in Chapter 2 I show you how to access the documentation. Until now you haven't used the documentation all that much since what you were doing didn't involve the Cocoa classes that you find in the documentation. But all of that has now changed, and now is a good time to review how to access the documentation for the various classes you will be using.

In Figure 7-1, I typed NSNumber into the Search field of the Help menu, and selected Search in the Documentation window.

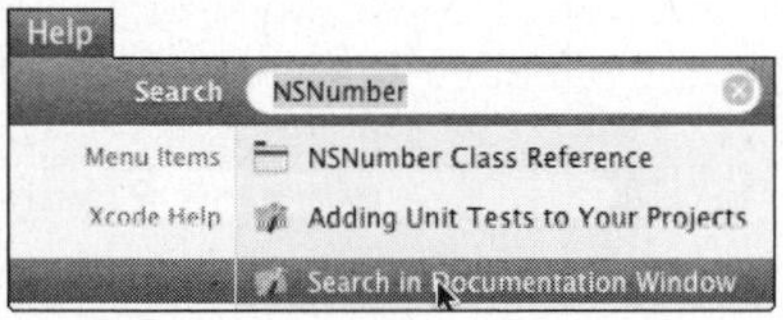

Figure 7-1:
Accessing
documenta-
tion.

Help
Search	NSNumber
Menu Items	NSNumber Class Reference
Xcode Help	Adding Unit Tests to Your Projects
Search in Documentation Window

This brings up the NSNumber Class Reference in the Documentation window. I clicked the disclosure triangle next to Instance Methods, as you can see in Figure 7-2, which displays a number of methods to create NSNumbers from quite a few types of classes.

For example:

```
initWithChar: (char) value;
initWithInt: (int) value;
initWithFloat: (float) value;
initWithBool: (BOOL) value;
```

As you become more comfortable with coding in Objective-C and using the framework objects, you'll find yourself exploring the APIs just to see what else a class can do.

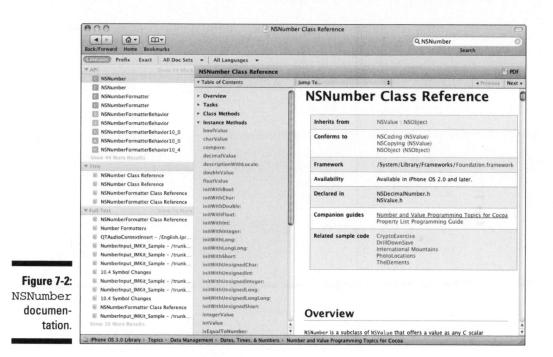

Figure 7-2:
NSNumber
documen-
tation.

Using an NSNumber as an argument

While I'm not going to have you do any coding, I'd like to go though how you could use an NSNumber object instead of a double as an argument in the spendDollars: method, because it does illustrate some important things about using an NSNumber object. To replace the double with an NSNumber, you do the following:

1. **Modify the spendDollars: method in the Budget class to take an NSNumber object as an argument instead of a double as it does currently.**

2. **Modify main to create NSNumber objects and send the new and improved spendDollars: message (the one that has an NSNumber as the argument) to the Budget objects.**

Modifying Budget

To modify the Budget class, you need to do a couple of things.

First, you must replace the method declaration in the header with a new one that takes an NSNumber as an argument.

```
//- void) spendDollars: (double) dollars;
- (void) spendDollars: (NSNumber*) dollars;
```

Of course, you also have to change the method implementation.

```
//(void) spendDollars: (double) dollars {

//  budget -= dollars;
//  NSLog(@"Converting %.2f US dollars into foreign
      currency leaves $%.2f", dollars, budget);
//}

- (void) spendDollars: (NSNumber*) dollars {

  budget -= [dollars doubleValue];
  NSLog(@"Converting %.2f US dollars into foreign
                  currency leaves $%.2f",
                  [dollars doubleValue], budget);
}
```

You deleted the previous implementation of spendDollars: and replaced it with one that has an NSNumber as an argument. But now, instead of simply subtracting the dollars amount from budget as you did previously

```
budget -= dollars;
```

you send the doubleValue message to the NSNumber object to get its value as a double.

```
budget -= [dollars doubleValue];
```

You also changed the NSLog statement in same way, sending the message, doubleValue, to the NSNumber object to get the value as a double returned.

```
NSLog(@"Converting %.2f US dollars into foreign
  currency leaves $%.2f",[dollars doubleValue], budget);
```

As you work through the example, think about why you are deleting some code, and what the code you are adding does.

Modifying main

In order to implement the new spendDollars: method, you need to make some changes to main. You start by deleting the variable, numberDollarsInEuroland you were using to represent the dollar transactions. You replace it with an NSNumber object, which you created using alloc and init and initialized with the same amounts that you used to initialize the variables you just deleted.

```
//double numberDollarsInEuroland = 100;
NSNumber *europeDollarTransaction =
                [[NSNumber alloc] initWithDouble:100.00];
```

You then delete the old spendDollars: message and replace it with the new one that uses the NSNumber argument.

```
//[europeBudget spendDollars:numberDollarsInEuroland];
[europeBudget spendDollars:europeDollarTransaction];
```

Taking Advantage of Array Objects

While using a number as an object is an interesting exercise in using objects (that is, replacing a double with an NSNumber), it doesn't really buy you anything. But it turns out that there is a similar use for an NSNumber object that can help you as you develop your program.

As you examine the program you have developed so far, you'll realize that as you add more and more transactions, the code is going to get a bit unwieldy.

Currently, for every transaction I create, I have to code a spendDollars: statement. For example, for every transaction where I spend dollars in Europe I need:

```
[europeBudget spendDollars:numberDollarsInEuroland];
```

For example, if I want to process 50 transactions, I will end up with

```
[europeBudget spendDollars:numberDollarsInEuroland1];
...
```

```
[europeBudget spendDollars:numberDollarsInEuroland50];
```

This is not a pretty picture.

Of course, this is not a problem unique to this application. In most applications, you'll find you need a way to be able to deal with large numbers of objects.

Often you may not even know how many transactions there are going to be. For example, you may be getting the transactions from a database, or from a list of previously stored instructions, or user actions may determine how many transactions you will have — the user adds address book entries, for example, or enters transactions as they occur (bingo!).

But even if you did know how many transactions you were going to have, a long series of messages simply makes your program too confusing, prone to error, and hard to extend.

Since this is a common problem, there is a widely available solution — container classes.

Container classes

In object-oriented programming, a container class is a class that is capable of storing other objects. In Cocoa, there are several kinds available, and I'll be explaining the two most widely used. One is a *dictionary*, which I cover in Chapter 15, and the other is an *array*, which you'll use in this chapter. You'll also continue to use this array in Chapter 9 and beyond, and in no time (or at least by the end of this book), using arrays will become second nature to you.

There are two kinds of arrays available to you in Cocoa. The first is an NSMutableArray, which allows you to add objects to the area as needed — that is, the amount of memory allocated to the class is dynamically adjusted as you add more objects.

Of course, you aren't really storing the object in an array any more than you stored an NSNumber object in the europeDollarTransaction1 variable when you created it.

```
NSNumber *europeDollarTransaction =
                 [[NSNumber alloc] initWithDouble:100.00];
```

In both cases, you are storing a pointer to the object.

The second kind of array is an NSArray, which allows you to store a fixed number of objects, which are specified when you initialize the array. Since in this case you need the dynamic aspect of an NSMutbaleArray, I'll start my explanation there. I explain NSArrays later in this chapter, and you actually use an NSArray in Chapter 15.

NSMutableArray arrays (I'll just call them arrays from now on when what I have to say applies to both NSArray and NSMutableArray) are ordered collections that can contain any sort of object. The collection does not have to be made up of the same objects. So you could have a number of Budget objects, for example, or Xyz objects mixed in, but they must be objects. One of the reasons for introducing you to NSNumbers, besides showing you how an object can use other objects, is that when you convert your transactions into NSNumbers, you make it possible to store them in an array.

As I've said, arrays can hold only objects. But sometimes you may, for example, want to put a placeholder in a mutable array and later replace it with the "real" object. You can use an `NSNull` object for this placeholder role.

The first step in being able to eliminate all of those `spendDollar:` messages is to create an `NSMutableArray` of the `NSNumber` objects I will be using in the `spendDollars:` message.

```
NSMutableArray *europeTransactions =
            [[NSMutableArray alloc] initWithCapacity:1];
```

This allocates and initializes the mutable array. When you create a mutable array, you have to estimate the maximum size, which helps optimization. This is just a formality, and whatever you put here does not limit the eventual size. I use 1 to illustrate that; even though I specify 1, I can actually add 2 elements (or more) to the array.

To make things simpler, for the time being, I'm just going to create an array for the `spendDollars:` transactions in Europe. You see why in Chapter 9.

After I create a mutable array, I can start to add objects to it.

```
[europeTransactions addObject:europeDollarTransaction];
```

When you add an object to an Objective-C array, the object isn't copied, but rather receives a `retain` message before it's added to the array. When an array is deallocated, each element is sent a `release` message. While you may have no idea what `retain` and `release` are (especially since I haven't covered them yet), you will when you learn about memory management in Chapter 13.

Technically (computer science–wise) what makes a collection an array is that you access its elements using an index, and that index can be determined at runtime. You get an individual element from an array by sending the array the `objectAtIndex:` message, which returns back the array element you requested. For example

```
[europeBudget spendDollars:
    [[europeTransactions objectAtIndex:0] doubleValue]];
```

returns back the first element in the `europeTransactions` array (remember the first element is 0) as a `double`. (I send the `NSNumber` the `doubleValue` message so that I can continue to use the `spendDollars:` method as is — with the argument type of a `double`.)

In your program, the index you will use is the relative position in the array, which starts at 0.

Depending on what you are doing with the array or how you are using it (arrays are very useful), `objectAtIndex:` will be one of the main array methods that you use (although you won't be using it in this chapter — you'll see why shortly).

The other method you will use is `count`, which gives you the number of elements in the array.

Arrays have some other methods you might find useful, such as sorting the array, comparing two arrays, and creating a new array that contains the objects in an existing array. In addition, mutable arrays have methods that include inserting an object at a particular index, replacing an object, and removing an object.

But one of the most powerful things you can do with an array is to use each of the elements in an array as an argument in a message — which means you won't have to code a `spendDollars:` message for each transaction. You can even send messages to all objects in the array, which will knock your socks off when you discover what you can do with that in Chapter 10.

Tiptoeing through an array

Objective-C 2.0 provides a language feature that allows you to enumerate over the contents of a collection. This is called *fast enumeration,* and it became available in Mac OS X 10.5 (Leopard) with version 2.0 of Objective-C. As I've mentioned, this book is based on that Mac OS 10.6 — and OS 3.0 on the iPhone. (If you need to program for OS X 10.4, you will need to use an `NSEnumerator`, which I'll leave as an exercise for the reader.) Enumeration uses the `for in` feature (a variation on a `for` loop, which I explain in Chapter 9).

What enumeration effectively does is sequentially march though an array, starting at the first element and returning each element for you to do "something with." The "something with" you will want to do in this case is use that element as an argument in the `spendDollars:` message.

For example, this code marches through the array and sends the `spendDollars:` message using each element in the array (an `NSNumber` "transaction"), eliminating the need for a `spendDollars:` message statement for transaction.

```
for (NSNumber *aTransaction in europeTransactions) {
    [europeBudget spendDollars:[aTransaction doubleValue]];
}
```

Here's the way this works:

1. **Take each entry** (for) **in the array** (in europeTransactions) **and copy it into the variable that you've declared** (NSNumber * aTransaction).

2. **Use it as an argument in the** spendDollars: **message** ([europeBudget spendDollars: aTransaction]).

3. **Continue until you run out of entries in the array.**

The identifier aTransaction can be any name you choose. NSNumber is the type of the object in the array (or it can be id, although I won't get into that here).

You may also have noticed that [europeBudget spendDollars: aTransaction] is enclosed in braces. The braces signify a block. (Blocks are described in Chapter 4.)

To be more formal (I just put on a tie to write this), the construct you just used is called for in, and it looks like

```
for ( Type aVariable in expression ) { statements }
```

or

```
Type aVariable;
for ( aVariable in expression ) { statements }
```

where you fill in what is italicized. There is one catch, however — you are not permitted to change any of the elements during the iteration, which means you can go through the array more than once without worry.

The for in loop is just one example of a control statement, the rest of which I explain in Chapter 9.

Adding mutable arrays

If you have been following along with me, I extend what you did in Chapter 6. If you would like to start with a clean copy of the project from where you left off, you can use the project found in the Chapter 7 Start Here folder, which is in the Chapter 7 folder.

1. **In the Groups & Files list (on the left side of the project window), click the triangles next to the Classes and Source folders to expand them, as shown in Figure 7-3.**

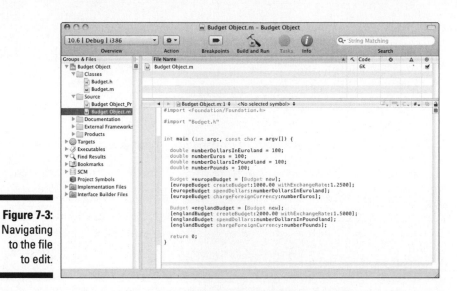

Figure 7-3:
Navigating
to the file
to edit.

2. **In the Source folder, click Budget Object.m, as shown in Figure 7-3, and you see that file ready for editing.**

   In this example, you'll be working only in main in the Budget Object.m file.

   This is the way you navigate to the file you want to edit.

3. **Delete the code with the strikethrough and then add the code in bold, as shown in Listing 7-1.**

Listing 7-1: main in Budget Object.m

```
#import <Foundation/Foundation.h>
#import "Budget.h"

int main (int argc, const char * argv[]) {

//double numberDollarsInEuroland = 100;
  double numberEuros = 100;
  double numberDollarsInPoundland = 100;
  double numberPounds = 100;

  NSNumber *europeDollarTransaction = [[NSNumber alloc]
          initWithDouble:100.00];
  NSNumber *europeDollarTransaction2 = [[NSNumber alloc]
          initWithDouble:200.00];

  NSMutableArray *europeTransactions = [
            [NSMutableArrwwwwwwwwway alloc]
          initWithCapacity:1];
  [europeTransactions addObject:europeDollarTransaction];
```

```
[europeTransactions addObject:europeDollarTransaction2];

Budget *europeBudget = [Budget new];
[europeBudget createBudget:1000.00
        withExchangeRate:1.2500];
//[europeBudget spendDollars:numberDollarsInEuroland];
for (NSNumber *aTransaction in europeTransactions) {
  [europeBudget spendDollars:
                            [aTransaction doubleValue]];
}
[europeBudget chargeForeignCurrency:numberEuros];

Budget *englandBudget = [Budget new];
[englandBudget createBudget:2000.00
        withExchangeRate:1.5000];
[englandBudget spendDollars:numberDollarsInPoundland];
[englandBudget chargeForeignCurrency:numberPounds];

return 0;
}
```

 4. **Select the Build and Run button in the Project Window toolbar to build and run the application.**

Your output in the Debugger Console should look like this:

```
Converting 100.00 US dollars into foreign currency leaves
        $900.00
Converting 200.00 US dollars into foreign currency leaves
        $700.00
Charging 100.00 in foreign currency leaves $575.00
Converting 100.00 US dollars into foreign currency leaves
        $1900.00
Charging 100.00 in foreign currency leaves $1750.00
```

Let me explain what you did here. First, you added

```
NSMutableArray *europeTransactions = [[NSMutableArray
                            alloc] initWithCapacity:1];
```

This allocates and initializes the mutable array for you. As I said, when you create a mutable array, you have to estimate the maximum size, which helps optimization. This is just a formality, and whatever you put here does not limit the eventual size.

To make it (a little) more interesting, you created two NSNumber objects

```
NSNumber *europeDollarTransaction =
                [[NSNumber alloc] initWithDouble:100.00];
NSNumber *europeDollarTransaction2 =
                [[NSNumber alloc] initWithDouble:200.00];
```

and added both to the array

```
[europeTransactions addObject:europeDollarTransaction];
[europeTransactions addObject:europeDollarTransaction2];
```

The next thing you should notice is that you deleted

```
[europeBudget spendDollars:numberDollarsInEuroland];
```

Instead you going to go through the array and send a spendDollars: message for each object.

```
for (NSNumber *aTransaction in europeTransactions) {
  [europeBudget spendDollars:[aTransaction doubleValue]];
}
```

As I explained, this takes each entry (for) in the array (in europeTransactions) and copies it into the variable that you have declared (NSNumber * aTransaction). You then get the value as a double ([aTransaction doubleValue]) and use it as an argument in the spendDollars: message until you run out of entries in the array. (aTransaction can be any name you choose.) NSNumber is the type of the object in the array (or it can be id).

You can find the completed project on the CD in the Example 7 folder, which is in the Chapter 7 folder.

What you have accomplished here is that no matter how many cash transactions you create for Europe, you'll only need one spendDollars: message. While that's pretty good, you ain't seen nothing yet. In Chapter 10, I show you how to extend that so that you need only one spend message for every transaction (both cash and change and any other transaction you can come up with) statement for all the countries you visit.

As you may have noticed, I'm not quite out of the woods yet. I still have to declare a variable for each NSNumber object I'm adding to the array. While this will disappear when you add the user interface in Chapters 17 and 18, it still is annoying. I show you how to eliminate all those variable declarations in Chapter 9.

Working with fixed arrays

Actually, NSMutableArray is a subclass (I explain that in Chapter 10) of NSArray, which manages a static array — once you have created it, you cannot add objects to it or remove objects from it. For example, if you create an array with a single NSNumber to represent a transaction, later you can't add to it another `NSNumber` object that represents another transaction. While only allowing a single transaction may be good for your budget, it's not very flexible.

`NSArray`s give you less overhead at a cost of less flexibility. So if you don't need to be able to add and remove objects, `NSArray`s are the preferred choice. I show you when that makes sense, and how to use an `NSArray` in Chapter 15. If you want to use an `NSArray` (and I suggest you experiment on your own), you have to initialize it with the objects you want in it when you create it.

So instead of

```
NSMutableArray *europeTransactions =
            [[NSMutableArray alloc] initWithCapacity:1];
  [europeTransactions addObject:europeDollarTransaction];
```

you would do the following:

```
NSArray *europeTransactions =
        [[NSArray alloc] initWithObjects:
        [[NSNumber alloc] initWithDouble:100.00],
        nil];
```

Even though I added only one object to the fixed array, `initWithObjects:` allows you to initialize the array with as many objects as you want, separating them with commas and terminating the list with `nil` as you can see.

 As with a mutable array, when you add an object to an `NSArray`, the object isn't copied, but rather receives a `retain` message before it is added to the array. When an array is deallocated, each element is sent a `release` message.

Using C Arrays

Arrays are also a part of the C language. Although most of the time you'll use array objects, you'll also find uses for C arrays, not to mention seeing them used in Apple documentation and code samples.

Arrays in C store elements just as an `NSArray` does (although they must be of the same type), and you can think about them as an ordered list as well.

That means, for example, that you can store five values of type `int` in an array without having to declare five different variables, each one with a different identifier.

To declare an array, use

```
double europeTransactionsArray [2];
```

Now you have an array with enough room for two doubles, effectively similar to the NSMutableArray you created earlier; but this one is of fixed size, just like an NSArray. It is really just like having a set of the same variable types, one right after another.

To access a specific element of the array, use

```
europeTransactionsArray[0] = 100.00;
```

This places 100.00 in the first element in an array (again, element 1 is at index 0).

You can also initialize arrays when you create them. For example

```
double europeTransactionsArray [2] = {100.00, 200.00};
```

creates a two-element array of doubles. You can access an element in the arrays as though it is a normal variable by doing the following:

```
transaction1 = europeTransactionsArray[0];
```

Expanding to multidimensional arrays

One useful aspect of arrays is multidimensional arrays. For example

```
int twoDArray[3][3] = {{1,2,3}, {4,5,6}, {7,8,9}};
```

declares and initializes an array that has two dimensions, like a tic-tac-toe board. You can make three-dimensional arrays, and even more.

While there are no multidimensional array objects, in Objective C you could have an array of arrays that accomplish the same thing. Arrays of arrays are used extensively in Mac and iPhone programming, and you can find them used in some of the samples on their respective Dev Center sites.

The following code shows a two-dimensional array in C, and the way to simulate that two-dimensional array in Objective-C. No applause — I'll leave you to figure this out on your own.

```
int main() {

  int twoDArray[3][3] = {{1,2,3}, {4,5,6}, {7,8,9}};
  NSLog (@"twoDArray[2][2] is %i", twoDArray[2][2]);

  NSArray *array1 = [[NSArray alloc] initWithObjects:
                    [[NSNumber alloc] initWithInt:1],
                    [[NSNumber alloc] initWithInt:2],
                    [[NSNumber alloc] initWithInt:3],
                    nil];
  NSArray *array2 = [[NSArray alloc] initWithObjects:
                    [[NSNumber alloc] initWithInt:4],
                    [[NSNumber alloc] initWithInt:5],
                    [[NSNumber alloc] initWithInt:6],
                    nil];

  NSArray *array3 = [[NSArray alloc] initWithObjects:
                    [[NSNumber alloc] initWithInt:7],
                    [[NSNumber alloc] initWithInt:8],
                    [[NSNumber alloc] initWithInt:9],
                    nil];

  NSArray *arrayOfArrays = [[NSArray alloc]
          initWithObjects:
                    array1, array2, array3,  nil];
  NSLog (@"NSArray of NSArrays equivalent is
          %i", [[[arrayOfArrays objectAtIndex:2]
          objectAtIndex:2] intValue]);
}
```

The results is

```
twoDArray[2][2] is 9
NSArray of NSArrays equivalent is 9
```

Finishing up with the main function

Arrays can be passed as a parameter in C. In order to accept arrays as parameters, the only thing that you have to do when declaring the function is to specify that its argument is an array by using its identifier and a pair of void brackets []. For example, the function

```
void someFunction (int arg[])
```

accepts a parameter that is an array of ints.

Now that you understand arrays, I can finally explain the argument list in the `main` function.

```
int main (int argc, const char * argv[]) {
```

The name of the variable `argc` stands for *argument count* and contains the number of arguments passed to the program. The name of the variable `argv` stands for *argument vector* and is a one-dimensional array of strings (that's what a `char*` is in C (but since you won't be using them, I won't be going any further into C strings in this book).

This finally (and thankfully) closes the chapter on `main`.

Chapter 8

Using the Debugger

*N*ow that things have gotten a little more interesting, so will the errors.

Let's face it. There are always going to be errors. No matter how good you are, how much experience you have, how careful you are, or even how smart you are, they are a programming fact of life.

You'll come up against three kinds of errors. Each one has a unique personality and associated techniques for finding and correcting. Here is a list of the three types you'll come up against:

- ✔ Syntax errors
- ✔ Runtime errors
- ✔ Logic errors

The last two types, runtime and logic errors, are what are commonly referred to as "bugs."

Identifying the Usual Suspects

While there is no exercise for this chapter, you can follow along with me if you like by using the project in the Chapter 8 Start Here folder in the Chapter 8 folder on the CD. Or you can use the project you use at the end of Chapter 7.

Catching syntax errors

As I mentioned earlier in this book, compilers take your source code and turn it into something the computer understands. For that process to go smoothly, the source code you give the compiler has to be something it understands. All of the operations and framework functionality I cover in Chapter 4 and continue to cover have to be coded in a certain way, and the compiler expects that you follow those rules (syntax). When you don't, it gets visibly annoyed. So when you type New instead of new, or the subtler [Budget new} instead of [Budget new], the compiler suddenly has no idea what you're talking about and generates a syntax error. In Figure 8-1, you can see what happens when I forget the semicolon after double number Pounds = 100.

Figure 8-1:
Syntax error.

It's generally better to ignore the subsequent errors after the first syntax error because they may be (and frequently are) a consequence of that first error. You can see that in Figure 8-1. In this case, because of the first error, europe DollarTransaction is never declared, and you get a subsequent syntax error to that effect.

If you have set your Xcode preferences to keep the Build Results window open, as I suggest you do in Chapter 2, you'll see the results of your compile in that window in Figure 8-2 (clicking the ! 2 in the lower-right corner of the Project window opens the Build Results window). If you click an error in the top pane, the error message bubble animates so that you can find it in the lower pane. In addition, double-clicking the error message in the top pane opens a new window and animates the error message in that window as well.

You may have noticed that my Editor window is now displaying line numbers. I did that by choosing Xcode⇨Preferences (as you do in Chapter 2), selecting Text Editing in the toolbar, and then checking the Show line numbers box. I explain why in the section "Using the Static Analyzer," later in this chapter.

Figure 8-2:
Build
Results
window.

Fortunately, syntax errors are the most obvious of errors out there — when you have one, your program won't compile, much less run, until the error is fixed. Many of the syntax errors are a result of typographical errors like those I just mentioned. Others occur when you try to pass the wrong argument type to a message or function. You can see an example in Figure 8-3 when I try to pass in a string instead of a double to the initWithDouble: method.

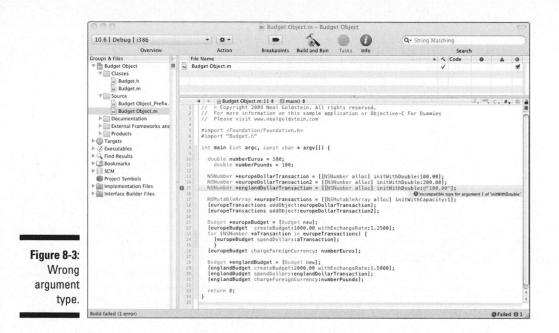

Figure 8-3:
Wrong
argument
type.

Crashing with runtime errors

Runtime errors cause your program to stop executing — this is commonly known as a "crash." You are probably familiar with that happening to programs you are using, and it's quite annoying. But it's a little different when it happens to a program you have written. You can see the result of that in Figure 8-4 for a Foundation Command Line Tool, although when you are running on the Mac as an application or on the iPhone simulator, or the iPhone itself, you'll get other kinds of messages. Don't worry; while a message may not tell you why, the fact that it is a runtime error is usually obvious.

Figure 8-4:
Runtime
error.

Runtime errors can be created all sorts of ways. However, you can rule out one way; at least it wasn't a syntax error (although it could be a warning you ignored). There might have been data that you hadn't expected (a division-by-zero error, for example), or maybe you tried to send a message to a method that didn't exist, or there was a problem with an argument you used in a message. Sometimes you even get some build warnings for these errors; sometimes you're blindsided by a crash. At other times, instead of crashing, the program may "hang" and become incommunicado.

Dealing with logic errors

When a program doesn't do what it is supposed to, people tend to blame the problem on the computer. "The computer gave me the wrong answer." Well, computers are actually blameless creatures; they do what they are told to do, and they do that with a vengeance. If you were to tell a computer to go jump off a cliff, it would. It does exactly, and I mean exactly, what you tell it to do — over and over and over again. When you have a logic error, the problem is not that the computer didn't do what you told it to; the problem is that it did. You just told it to do the wrong thing. Another possibility is that you may have forgotten to tell it to do something, like initialize an object for example. In Figure 8-5, everything looks fine — not a compiler error in sight (ignore the highlighted line for a second).

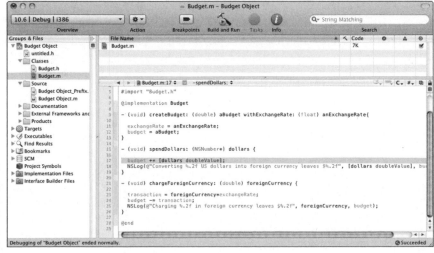

Figure 8-5:
My own
money
machine.

The problem is the output looks a little screwy:

```
Converting 100.00 US dollars into foreign currency leaves
        $1100.00
Converting 200.00 US dollars into foreign currency leaves
        $1300.00
Charging 100.00 in foreign currency leaves $1175.00
Converting 100.00 US dollars into foreign currency leaves
        $2100.00
Charging 100.00 in foreign currency leaves $1950.00
```

Think about this. I start with my $1,000 budget for Europe, and when I convert $100 (U.S. dollars) into foreign currency, I am left with $1,100. While this is a nice trick if you can do it, I doubt that is what really happened. (Somehow I don't think I have invented a perpetual balance increasing machine.)

Looking at the code that computes the balance (highlighted in Figure 8-5 and in bold here)

```
- (void) spendDollars: (NSNumber*) dollars {
  budget += [dollars doubleValue];
  NSLog(@"Converting %.2f US dollars into foreign currency
        leaves $%.2f",[dollars doubleValue], budget);
}
```

you can see that instead of subtracting the transaction amount from the balance (–=), I add it instead (+=). Wishful thinking I suppose, but regardless of the cause, what I have here is a logic error.

There is also another type of error that more or less falls into the logic error category — "typos." This is when you send the wrong message to an object, or use the wrong instance variable, because the names are very similar and you simply mistype the message name or variable.

Because of the similarity of names, the error can be pretty hard to spot because the code, at first glance, seems "right."

All three of these errors, syntax, runtime, and logic, are the bane of a programmer's existence. But get used to it. Like death and taxes, they are something you can never escape. But what you can do is learn to deal with and dispatch them as quickly and efficiently as possible. To do that, you'll call upon one of the Xcode tools that come with the SDK — the Debugger. While the Debugger is no help with syntax errors, it is a veritable star when it comes to runtime errors and your trusty assistant when you need to hunt down logic errors.

Using the Debugger

In Figure 8-6, I deliberately created a situation that gives me a runtime error. (Intentionally creating a runtime error may seem a bit bizarre, but this is for teaching purposes.)

As you can see from the highlighted code, I am going to divide by zero. If I had done something like i/0, I would have gotten a compiler warning (which I could choose to ignore for teaching purposes). In this case, I fooled the compiler (it's generally not a good idea to try and fool the compiler; it really has your best interests at heart). So the compiler thinks everything is fine, but at runtime, the processor is chugging along, executing its instructions, only to result in the unexpected exit you see in Figure 8-7.

How can the Debugger help me determine the source of a runtime error like this one? The next section gives you the details.

Figure 8-6:
About to
divide by
zero.

You can also see that in Xcode's Editor view in Figure 8-8, the offending instruction is highlighted and there is an arrow (you'll see it as red in Xcode) pointing to the line in the Editor view. The Editor view has also changed, and the Xcode debugger controllers are available to you in the Editor view.

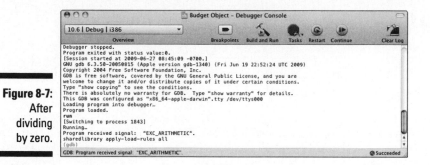

Figure 8-7:
After
dividing
by zero.

Step into method or function call

Step over method or function call   Step out of method or function

Continue execution   Show Debugger

Activate/Deactivate Breakpoints   Show Console

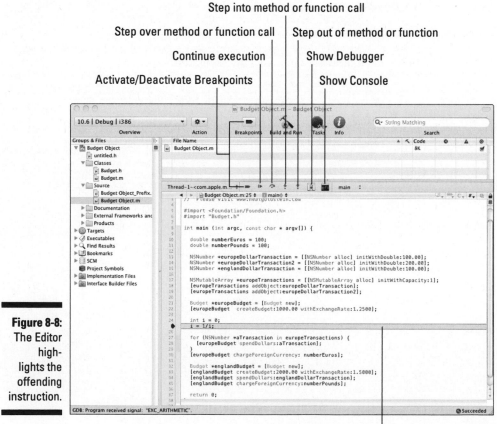

Figure 8-8:
The Editor
high-
lights the
offending
instruction.

Method or function where the error occurred

I explain most of these controls in the section "Using Breakpoints," later in this chapter. For now, click the Show Debugger control as I did in Figure 8-9.

If you have any questions about what something does, just position the mouse pointer above the icon and a tooltip explains it.

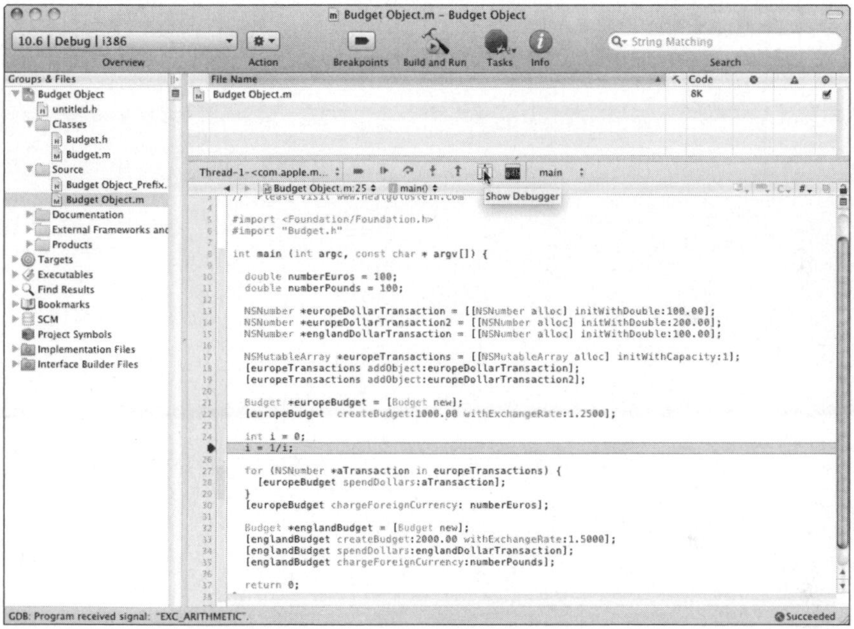

Figure 8-9:
Selecting
the
Debugger.

When you do that, you'll see the Debugger window in Figure 8-10.

In the upper-left pane, you can see the *stack* — a trace of the objects and methods that got you to where you are now.

In this case, you are in `main`, which is where you started.

Stacks *can* be very useful in complex applications. They can help you understand the path you took to get where you are. If you are tracking down a logic error, for example, seeing the path of messages from one object to another can be really helpful, especially if you didn't expect the program to execute in that order.

Looking again at the Debugger window in Figure 8-10, you can see the bottom pane shows the source code and also highlights the instruction that caused the problem. In the top-right pane, you can see the program's variables. (I show you how that can be useful in the section "Using Breakpoints.")

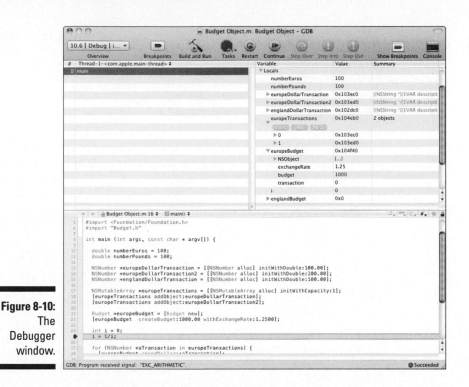

Figure 8-10:
The
Debugger
window.

Your window may not look exactly like mine. You have a number of ways to customize the look of the Debugger window. If you choose Run➪Debugger Display from the main menu, you can change the way information is displayed. I am using it as it came from the factory.

Examine the top-right pane in the Debugger window. There you'll see a list of the program's variables. I clicked the disclosure triangle next to Locals as well as the ones next to europeTransactions and europeBudget. These are what are known as *local* variables. These are the variables declared in methods and functions (like main). In the next section, I also show you some instance variables.

As you debug a program error, the Variables pane is useful in a number of ways:

   ✔ **Checking values:** Since, in this case, I have a runtime error and the Debugger has pointed out the offending instruction, and since the offending instruction involves dividing by the variable i, it doesn't take a rocket scientist to figure out that perhaps you need to look at the value of that variable. In this case, you can see in the Variable list that the value is 0. At this point, I have at least tracked down the *immediate* cause of the problem — division by zero.

I say immediate cause because in some cases, although not here, I might wonder how it got set to 0. (I'll show you how to watch the value of a variable in the next section where I explain how to set a breakpoint. But for now, just know that using a breakpoint can stop the execution of your program at any point, and you can look back and see how you got to that point.)

✔ **Checking objects:** Certain logic errors you may encounter are the result of what some people call a "feature" and others call a "design error" in Objective-C. Objective-C allows you to send a message to a `nil` object *without* generating a runtime error.

As you can see in Figure 8-10, you have variables that contain pointers to objects. I clicked the disclosure triangles next to `europeTransactions` and `europeBudget`.

`europeTransactions`, which is my transaction array, not only has a correct looking pointer, it has two entries corresponding to the values for the `europeDollarTransaction` and `europeDollarTransaction2` objects I created.

In addition, you can see `europeBudget`, which I created before my runtime error is there, and messages to it were working fine. You can also see the value for `englandBudget` is 0x0.

If I were to send a message to `englandBudget`, it would go into the aether. So, when things don't happen the way I expect, one of the things I'm going to check is whether any of the object references I am using has 0x0 as its value.

This can actually happen easily. You can forget to assign the object you created to a variable, or as you see in Chapter 17, you can forget to make a connection in Interface Builder.

But what about logic errors? In fact, the Debugger can help there as well.

One of the ways to figure out why something happened is to be able to see what is going on in your program before you wander down a particular path to oblivion (which can help you figure out runtime errors as well). For that, the Debugger provides you with the ability to set breakpoints, which is the subject of the next section.

Using Breakpoints

A *breakpoint* is an instruction to the Debugger to pause execution at that instruction and wait for further instructions (no pun intended). If you have a logic error, a breakpoint can help by allowing you to step your way through your code (refer to the earlier section "Dealing with logic errors"). By setting breakpoints at various places in my program, you can step through its execution, at the instruction level, to see exactly what it is doing. You can also examine the variables the program is setting and using, which allows me to determine whether that is where the problem lies.

Returning to the logic error introduced in Figure 8-5, I'm going to set a breakpoint at the entry of the method I think is causing the problem, spend Dollars:, to see if I can figure out what is going on. In Figure 8-10, I've set a breakpoint simply by clicking in the far-left column of the Editor window.

Take a look at Figure 8-11. Notice that the Build and Run button in the toolbar has changed to Build and Debug. In addition, the Breakpoint button to its left has inverted. This lets you know you have a breakpoint set. If you click that button, it temporarily turns off those breakpoints (if you think you fixed something and want to see how your program runs without all those pesky breakpoints) and change the Build and Debug button back to Build and Run.

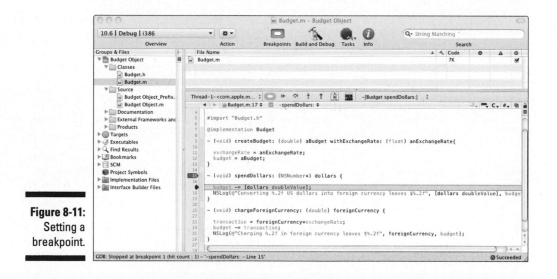

Figure 8-11:
Setting a
breakpoint.

When I build and run the program again (as you can see in the Editor window in Figure 8-12), the program has stopped executing right at the breakpoint I set.

You can see the same source code view in the Debugger window that you see in the Editor window. You can also see in the stack pane on the left that you went from main to [Budget spendDollars;]. In the variables pane, you can see I clicked the disclosure triangle next to the self variable, under Arguments. Arguments are the variables passed in as the method arguments. Under self are the object's instance variables. (I want to remind you, as I explain in Chapter 6, that self is the "hidden" argument in every message and is a pointer to the object's instance variables.) You can see the `exchangeRate` is 1.25, as it should be, and `budget` is 1000 as you would expect before the first transaction. You can also see the `dollars` argument, which is the `NSNumber` object I created. If there were any local variables, you would have also seen them as you did in Figure 8-10.

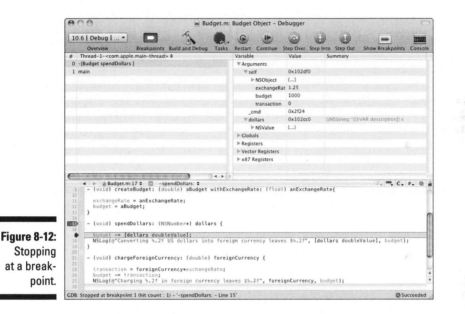

Figure 8-12:
Stopping
at a break-
point.

If I want to see how the budget variable gets changed (which is the result of the logic error), I can do two things. First, I can execute the program instruction by instruction, simply by clicking the Step Into button on the Debugger window toolbar. I can keep on clicking that Step Into button at every instruction until I get to where I want to be (which, by the way, can be a long and winding road).

In this case, I execute `budget += [dollars doubleValue];` and then go on to the next instruction, as you can see in Figure 8-13. `budget` has been changed to 1100, and the computer did exactly what I told it to do, which was to add instead of subtract the transaction amount.

I also have another option. I can set a watch point on that variable. You can do that only if your program is not executing, however. So when the program stops executing at the breakpoint I just set, for example, I get the opportunity to set a watch point. I select the variable `budget` in the Variable list in the Debugger window, and then as you can see in Figure 8-14, I can select Watch Variable from the Variable list shortcut menu, or I could select Run➪Variables View➪Watch Variable. (You also see a magnifying glass next to the variable, which you can't see in Figure 8-14.)

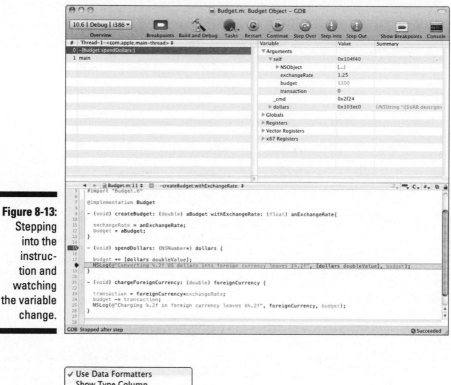

Figure 8-13: Stepping into the instruction and watching the variable change.

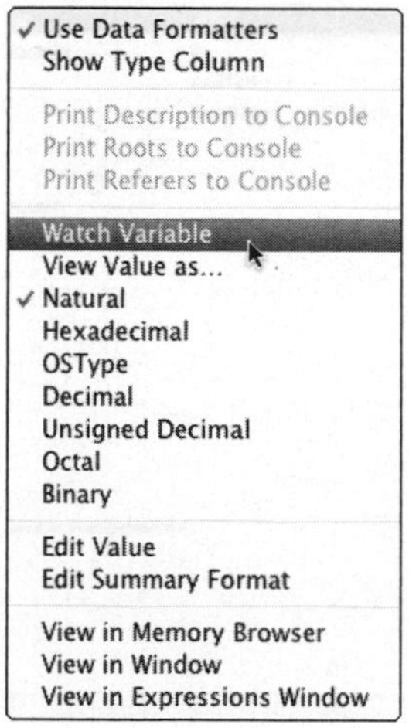

Figure 8-14: Watching a variable.

The Debugger watches that variable's value for you, and when it changes, alert you that it changed (see Figure 8-15).

You can also remove the breakpoint and let the program continue to execute (by clicking Continue on the Debugger window toolbar). The next time that variable changes, Debugger displays another alert for that value change.

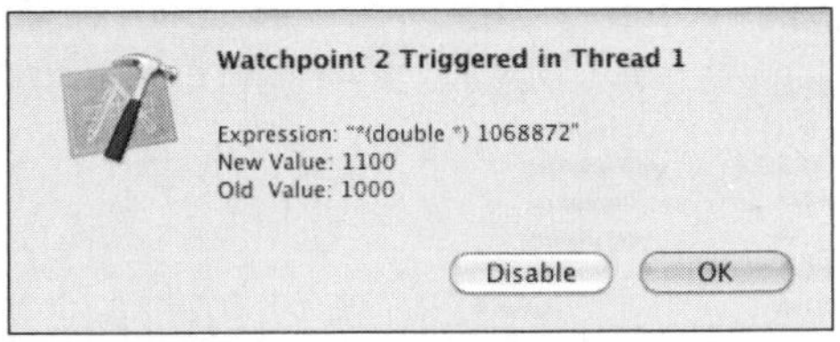

Figure 8-15:
Debugger
alerts
you that
the value
changes.

Watchpoint 2 Triggered in Thread 1

Expression: "*(double *) 1068872"
New Value: 1100
Old Value: 1000

(Disable) (OK)

The Debugger window gives you a number of other options for making your way through your program in addition to Step Into. For example, you could try one of the following:

✔ **Step Over** gives you the opportunity to skip over an instruction.

✔ **Step Out** takes you out of the current method.

✔ **Continue** tells the program to continue its execution.

✔ **Restart** restarts the program. (You were hoping, maybe, that if you tried it again it would work?)

To get rid of the breakpoint, simply drag it off to the side. You can also right-click the breakpoint and choose Remove Breakpoint from the shortcut menu that appears.

Using the Static Analyzer

Xcode has a new Build and Analyze feature (the Static Analyzer) that analyzes your code.

The results show up like warnings and errors, with explanations of where and what the issue is. You can also see the flow of control of the (potential) problem. I say potential because the Static Analyzer can give you false positives.

In Figure 8-16, I chose Build and Analyze from the Build menu (Build⇨Build and Analyze).

The results, as shown in the Build Results window (Figure 8-17), show a number of potential problems — all of them associated with potential memory leaks.

Notice that the results refer to line numbers. This is why I turned line numbers on in my Xcode preferences.

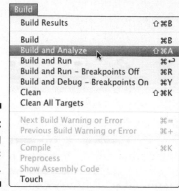

Figure 8-16:
Running
the Static
Analyzer.

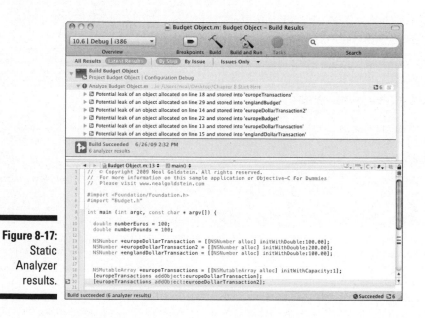

Figure 8-17:
Static
Analyzer
results.

Note: Because I explain memory leaks in Chapter 13, I'll explain the Static Analyzer in that chapter.

Chapter 9

Using Control Statements and Loops

- -

In This Chapter

▶ Understanding how control statements and loops work

▶ Knowing when to use — and not use — `switch` statements

▶ Getting a handle on loop statements

▶ Building your application

▶ Using jump statements

- -

In Chapter 7, I introduce you to `NSMutableArrays` to help you manage lists of objects. You see how you can use an array of objects and then iterate through the array, passing each object as an argument in a message. In Chapter 7, you use an array for only one transaction type, `spendDollars:` using one country's budget, `europeBudget`. If you want to extend that to `chargeForeignCurrency:`, you will need another array. And if you want to extend that to use `englandBudget`, you will need to add two additional arrays — one each for the `spendDollars:` and `chargeForeignCurrency:` messages.

This may seem pretty awkward, and it is. To manage my objects, what I really want is a single array that I can iterate through, one that holds all of the different transaction types for all of the countries I will be visiting.

And that's what you will be doing in this and the next chapter.

Along the way, I'll also complete your knowledge of the C functionality that is part of Objective-C — showing you how to use loops and control statements to determine the execution sequence of instructions.

Creating Transaction Objects

In order to start the journey to a single array that manages all of my transactions for all of the countries I visit, I want to review how the program works currently.

I start by creating a dollar transaction for Europe

```
NSNumber *europeDollarTransaction =
                [[NSNumber alloc] initWithDouble:100.00];
```

and then add it to the `europeTransactions` array. Currently, this array really can hold only dollar transactions, and Europe transactions to boot, because when I iterate through the array, I send the `spendDollars:` message to the `europeBudget`.

```
for (NSNumber * aTransaction in europeTransactions) {
   [europeBudget spendDollars:[aTransaction doubleValue]];
}
```

The way this `for in` statement is coded poses two problems:

- ✔ I need to know what kind of transaction is in the array so I can send the `Budget` object the right message. Currently, as I iterate through the array, I know these are dollar transactions, and I send the `spendDollars:` message. To use an array to process credit card transactions, I will have to create a new array and then send `europeBudget` the `chargeForeignCurrency:` message like so:

  ```
  for (NSNumber * aTransaction in
                      europeCreditTransactions) {
     [europeBudget chargeForeignCurrency:
                        [aTransaction doubleValue]];
  }
  ```

- ✔ I need to know what `Budget` to send the message to. As I iterate through the array, since I know these are dollar transactions for Europe, I send the `spendDollars:` message to the `europeBudget:` object. To use an array to process England transactions, I must create a new array and then send `englandBudget` the `spendDollars:` message like so:

  ```
  for (NSNumber * aTransaction in englandTransactions) {
     [englandBudget spendDollars:
                          [aTransaction doubleValue]];
  }
  ```

As you can see, this can be quite problematic. I need an array for each transaction type and each country. This would require a bit of coding whenever I decided to add a new transaction or go to another country.

Not a rosy future is it? Kind of makes you want to stay home.

Managing all those objects

This particular situation is not unique — managing a list of similar objects is the kind of thing you'll need to do in many of your applications.

As you'll see, using the features available in an object-oriented programming language such as Objective-C will allow you to manage all of these objects in a single array. To do that, you'll use inheritance to create different *types* of transaction objects (you haven't seen this yet, but you will in the next chapter) and take advantage of polymorphism — one of the ways to create extensible programs that I speak about in Chapter 3.

But before I do that, I want to show you an interim "solution" to the multiplying array problem using a C control statement called the *switch statement,* or switch. This solution will still require an array for each country, but you will be able to store both cash and credit card transactions in the same array.

In order to do that, you'll need to extend your NSNumber-based transaction object to store the kind of transaction it is (dollar or credit card). Then I'll show you how to use a switch statement in main to determine which "spend" message (spendDollars: or chargeForeignCurrency:) should be sent to the Budget and for what amount, based on the kind of transaction it is.

Adding the Transaction class

I'll start by having you change the current NSNumber-based Transaction object from a wrapper (an object that is there mostly to turn something into an object) into a real transaction object with its own instance variables and methods.

If you have been following along with me, I'll be extending what you do in Chapter 7. If you would like to start with a clean copy of the project from where you left off, you can use the project found in the Chapter 9 Start Here folder, which is in the Chapter 9 folder.

I'll have you start by adding a new file to your project. (I explain how to do this in more detail in Chapter 6.)

1. **Select the Classes folder in the Groups & Files list.**

   This tells Xcode to place the new file in the Classes folder.

2. **Select File⇨New File from the main menu (or press ⌘+n) to get the New File dialog.**

3. **In the leftmost column of the dialog, first select Cocoa under Mac OS X; then select the Objective-C class template in the top-right pane. Make sure NSObject is selected in the subclass of the drop-down menu.**

   You'll see a new screen asking for some more information.

4. **Enter** Transaction.m **in the File Name field and make sure the checkbox to have Xcode create Transaction.h. is checked and then click Finish.**

This is a good time to read Chapter 2 (the section "Getting to Know the Xcode Text Editor"). Many of the features I explain are now more relevant to you, especially the Counterpart button that switches you from the header, or inter-face file (.h), to the implementation file (.m), and vice versa.

I find it useful at this point to double-click Transaction.h to open it in a new window.

To add the new Transaction class, you do three things:

1. Add the Transaction class interface.

2. Add the Transaction class implementation.

3. Update the Budget class.

Adding the Transaction class interface

Navigate to the Transaction.h file and add the code in bold as shown in Listing 9-1. (I deleted, and will continue to delete, the comments inserted by Xcode at the beginning of the .h and .m files it creates — feel free to keep yours if you like.)

Listing 9-1: The New Transaction Class Interface

```
#import <Cocoa/Cocoa.h>

typedef enum {cash, charge} transactionType;

@interface Transaction : NSObject {

  transactionType type;
  double amount;
}

- (void) createTransaction: (double) theAmount
                    ofType: (transactionType) aType;
- (double) returnAmount;
- (transactionType) returnType;
@end
```

This Transaction class does what you need it to do — it stores both an amount and its type. To do that you did the following:

1. In order to know what kind of transaction it is, you created a new type, transactionType, by using a typedef (I explain typedefs in Chapter 5, so if you are a bit vague about what I am doing, you can refer to that chapter) and an instance variable type. You'll use *cash* for the dollar transaction and *charge* for the credit card ones.

```
typedef enum {cash, charge} transactionType;
transactionType type;
```

2. You added an instance variable `amount`, which is the value of the transaction.

3. You declared three new methods:

```
- (void) createTransaction: (double) theAmount
                    ofType: (transactionType) aType;
- (double) returnAmount;
- (transactionType) returnType;
```

The first method simply initializes the object with a type and amount. (I explain more about initialization in Chapter 12.) The second and third methods return the amount of the transaction and type of transaction (cash or charge), respectively. As you probably know by now, you shouldn't access an object's instance variables directly, and these two methods allow `main` to get the data it needs. In Chapter 14, I show you a way to have Objective-C create these kinds of methods for you (using declared properties).

Adding the Transaction class implementation

Now that you have the class interface defined, you'll need to implement it.

In the Transaction.m file, add the code in bold as shown in Listing 9-2.

Listing 9-2: The New Transaction Class Implementation

```
#import "Transaction.h"

@implementation Transaction
- (void) createTransaction: (double) theAmount ofType:
          (transactionType) aType{

  type = aType;
  amount = theAmount;
}

- (double) returnAmount{

  return amount;
}

- (transactionType) returnType {

  return type;
};

@end
```

This implements the methods I declared in the interface.

Now that I have created the transaction object that has an amount and know what kind of transaction it is, I can put both cash and charge transactions in the same array and use a switch statement to ensure that the right message is sent to the Budget object.

Using switch Statements

A switch statement is a kind of *control statement*. Control statements are used to determine what to do when a certain condition arises. I introduce one of those, the if statement, in Chapter 4. Later in this chapter in the section "Taking the Leap: Jump Statements," I will introduce you to the balance of those C statements. While these kinds of statements can be useful in object-oriented programming, you need to be especially careful about how you use them.

For now however, you'll work with the switch statement.

I want to review the code you will add that will implement the switch statement.

```
switch ([aTransaction returnType]) {
  case cash:
    [europeBudget spendDollars:
                        [aTransaction returnAmount]];
    break;
  case charge:
    [europeBudget chargeForeignCurrency:
                        [aTransaction returnAmount]];
    break;
  default:
    break;
  }
}
```

Let me explain how this works.

A switch statement is a type of control statement that allows the value of a variable or expression to control the flow of program execution. In this case, you are using the transactionType.

As you can see in Listing 9-3, for a transactionType cash (remember, you declared transactionType and the values it can take on in the typedef in Listing 9-1), you send the spendDollars: message to the europeBudget object with the amount returned back to you by the returnAmount method as the argument.

Similarly, for a `transactionType` charge, you send the `chargeForeign-Currency:` message to the `europeBudget` object.

The general form of a `switch` statement is as follows:

```
switch (expression) {
   case constant1:
   Statement(s) to execute for case 1;
   break;
case constant2:
   Statement(s) to execute for case 2;
   break;
 .
 .
 .
default:
   Default statement(s);
}
```

Here is the sequence:

1. Evaluate `expression`.

2. If `expression` is equal to `constant1`

   a. Execute `Statement(s) to execute for case 1` until it reaches a `break` statement.

   b. Execute the `break` statement, which causes a jump to the end of the `switch` structure.

3. If `expression` is not equal to `constant1`, see if `expression` is equal to `constant2`. If it is

   a. Execute `Statement(s) to execute for case 2` until it reaches a `break` statement.

   b. Execute the `break` statement, which causes a jump to the end of the `switch` structure.

4. If `expression` does not match any of the constants (you can include as many case labels as values you want to check), the program will execute `Default statement(s)` if there is a `default` (which is optional).

In this case, the expression used by the `switch` statement is the `transactionType` (the constant used to "do the switch") returned by the `returnType` method. `transactionType` is the `enum` you defined in Transaction.h (in Listing 9-1).

```
typedef enum {cash, charge} transactionType;
```

If the transaction type returned is `cash`, the `switch` statement executes the instructions under the `cash` case:

```
case cash:
  [europeBudget spendDollars:[aTransaction returnAmount]];
  break;
```

The `break` statement causes execution to transfer to the end of the `switch` structure. But since the `switch` statement is in the array enumerator block

```
for (Transaction * aTransaction in transactions) {
```

the next `Transaction` object in the array is fetched, and the `switch` statement is executed again. This goes on until all of the `Transaction` objects in the `transactions` array are processed.

As you can see, the `switch` statement uses *labels* (`case cash:`, for example). A label is made of a valid identifier followed by a colon (:). This is why you need the `break` statement. If there are no `break`s, all the statements following the label (`case cash:`) will be executed until the end of the `switch` block or a break `statement` is reached.

This is actually a feature, since you can do something like the following:

```
typedef enum {cash, charge, atm} transactionType;
switch ([aTransaction returnType]) {
  case atm:
  case cash:
    [europeBudget spendDollars:
                              [aTransaction returnAmount]];
    break;
  case charge:
    [europeBudget chargeForeignCurrency:
                              [aTransaction returnAmount]];
    break;
  default:
    break;
  }
}
```

In this case, I decided I want a new `transactionType` of atm, but (for the time being at least) I want to treat it in the same way as `transactionType` of `cash`. This `switch` structure would end up executing the same block of code for both `cash` and `atm` and a different block for `charge`.

There is nothing special about a `switch` statement — actually, it performs in the same way as several `if` and `else` instructions.

```
if ([aTransaction returnType] == cash) {
  [europeBudget spendDollars:[aTransaction returnAmount]];
}
else {
  if ([aTransaction returnType] == charge) {
  [europeBudget chargeForeignCurrency:
                            [aTransaction returnAmount]];
  }
  else {
     //equivalent of default
    }
}
```

If you don't want default behavior, then you could even use a series of `if` statements, as shown here:

```
if ([aTransaction returnType] == cash) {
  [europeBudget spendDollars:[aTransaction returnAmount]];
  }
if ([aTransaction returnType] == charge) {
  [europeBudget chargeForeignCurrency:
                            [aTransaction returnAmount]];
  }
```

The `switch` statement is really useful when there are many conditions and when using the `if else` construct becomes too complicated to figure out or follow.

Is there a way to simplify all of this? Yes, and in fact object-oriented programming deals specifically with making this kind of complex logic uncomplicated. I'll show you that in the next chapter.

You can use a `switch` only to compare an expression to a constant. If you need to compare an expression to something other than a constant, you are stuck with the `if else` construct.

Now that you have your `Transaction` class and your `switch` statement, you'll need to create some `Transactions` and add them to the array to test it.

You could, for example, code the following:

```
aTransaction1 = [Transaction new];
[aTransaction1 createTransaction: n*100 ofType: cash];
[transactions addObject:aTransaction1];
...

aTransactionn = [Transaction new];
[aTransactionn createTransaction: n*100 ofType: credit];
[transactions addObject:aTransactionn];
```

This is what you've been doing until now, and you could copy and paste to create more transactions to test the functionality that you are building. In the next section, however, I show you an easier way to create transactions using loop statements.

Using Loop Statements to Repeat Instructions

Loop statements allow you to have the same set of instructions repeated over and over and over again — at least until some criterion is met. You actually do that in Chapter 8 using the enumerator `for in` statement. In this chapter, I expand upon that. Loops are the kind of things you'll continue to use as you learn more about Objective-C and programming in general.

Remember, using loops here is only a convenience in your program to create transactions. In the real world (and in Chapters 17 and 18), you allow the users to enter transactions through a user interface. But even so, loops, as you will find out, are fundamental to programming — so fundamental you'll find them in most computer languages.

So it's time to learn more about loops. You'll use three kinds of loops:

- ✔ The `for` loop
- ✔ The `while` loop
- ✔ The `do while` loop

The for loop

In Chapter 7, I introduce you to loops with the `for in` loop, which enables you to take each entry in an array and do something with it until you run out of entries in the array.

```
for (NSNumber * aTransaction in europeTransactions) {
    [europeBudget spendDollars: aTransaction];
}
```

The `for in` loop is a special case of something more general called a *for loop*.

A very simple `for` loop looks like this:

```
for (int i = 1; i <  4; i++) {

   NSLog(@"i = %i", i );
}
```

This will result in

```
i = 1
i = 2
i = 3
```

The `for` loop repeats a set of statements for a specific number of times. In the example, you have only one statement:

```
NSLog(@"i = %i", i );
```

But there can be as many as you want.

`for` loops use a variable as a counter to determine how many times to repeat the loop. In this case, the counter is `i`.

The easiest way to think of the `for` loop is that when it reaches the brace at the end, it jumps back up to the beginning of the loop, which checks the condition again and decides whether to repeat the block one more time or stop repeating it and move on to the next statement after the block.

The execution flow for a `for` loop is as follows:

1. The counter is initialized (only once).

   ```
   int i = 1
   ```

2. The counter is evaluated. If it is `true`, execution within the block continues; otherwise, the loop ends, and the next statement after theblock is executed.

   ```
   i <  4
   ```

3. The loop statement(s) that appear in a block enclosed in braces, { }, or a single statement are executed.

   ```
   NSLog(@"i = %i", i );
   ```

4. The counter is incremented.

   ```
   i++
   ```

5. Steps 2 through 4 are repeated until the condition for terminating the loop is met. When It Is, execution continues with the next statement after the `for` loop statements.

You'll be adding the following `for` loop to your program to add some transactions to the array you just created.

```
Transaction *aTransaction ;
for (int n = 1; n <  2; n++) {
  aTransaction = [Transaction new];
  [aTransaction createTransaction:n*100 ofType:cash];
  [transactions addObject:aTransaction];
}
```

Can you determine how many times this loop will be executed?

That's right, once. You are creating one transaction of `transactionType` `cash` for 100 (`n*100`) and adding it to the area.

While normally you wouldn't use a loop to execute a statement only once, I use it here because it's simple enough that you can really see how the counter is evaluated and how the condition is met.

Again putting on my tie, the formal description is

```
for ( counter; condition; update counter) {
  Statement(s) to execute while the condition is true
}
```

As you can see, three sections follow the first parenthesis, each terminated by a semicolon.

- ✔ **Counter.** The counter can be declared here, or you can use some other variable you've already declared and initialized. In this case, it is declared and initialized:

  ```
  int n = 1
  ```

- ✔ **Condition.** The condition is some expression that returns YES or NO and contains one of the logical or relational operators explained in Chapter 4 (you know, like ==, < , or | |, and so on). The statements in the loop will be executed as long as the condition remains YES. In this case, it is as long as *n* is less than 2.

  ```
  n < 2
  ```

- ✔ **Expression to update counter.** The update counter can be any expression — ++n or even n + a where a is a variable that may be updated in the code block. In this case, the counter is incremented by 1 each time through the loop.

  ```
  n++
  ```

---

for or for in?

for loops are used when you know what the number of iterations is going to be. Since [europeTransactions count] determines how many times you need to iterate through the array, you could have used a for loop instead of using the for in array iterator in Chapter 7.

The iterator you used was

```
for (NSNumber * aTransaction
    in europeTransactions) {
   [europeBudget spendDollars:
    aTransaction];
}
```

To accomplish the same thing with a for loop, you use array's count method, which tells you the number of elements it has. (As I mention in Chapter 7, this is one of the key methods you will be using.)

```
for (int n = 1; n <=
    [europeTransactions
    count]; n++) {

    [europeBudget
    spendDollars:

    [europeTransactions
    objectAtIndex:n]];
}
```

The iterator is just faster and more convenient than coding your own for loop.

The initialization and increase fields are optional, but the semicolon must still be there. For example, for (; n<10 ;) specifies no initialization and no increase because the variable was initialized previously and you were incrementing it in one of the Statement(s) to execute while the condition is true.

You can also use the comma operator (,) to specify some pretty complex initialization and counter update. For example:

```
for (int n = 0, y = 10; n <= y; ++n, y-=2) {
...
}
```

The while loop

The for loop is typically used when the number of iterations is known before entering the loop, whereas the while and do while loops repeat until a certain condition is met.

To add transactions to your array using a `while` loop, you code the following:

```
int n =1;
while (n < 3) {
    aTransaction = [Transaction new];
    [aTransaction createTransaction:n*100 ofType:charge];
    [transactions addObject:aTransaction];
    n++;
}
```

A `while` loop is similar to a `for` loop. As you can see, all you have to do to turn a `for` loop into a `while` loop is the following:

1. Here's what the counter initialization and declaration before the loop looks like:

   ```
   int n;
   ```

2. Increment the counter in the code block.

   ```
   n++;
   ```

The formal `while` loop is

```
while ( condition ) { Statement(s) to execute while the
              condition is true }
```

The sequence is as follows:

1. Condition is evaluated. If it is true, execution within the block continues; otherwise, the loop ends and the next statement after the block is executed.

2. The `Statement(s) to execute while the condition is true` block is executed — it can be either a single statement or a block enclosed in braces { }.

3. The loop goes back to Step 1.

Notice that the `Statement(s) to execute while the condition is true` might never be executed.

Obviously, the value of the condition will have to change for the loop to end. In this case, you are changing the value of the condition in the loop, so this acts, for all practical purposes, like a `for` loop. In general, however, you will more likely test an outside condition in the `while` loop. For example, you might repeatedly update the position of a ball in a maze as a user is moving his or her iPhone. `while` loops are used when you don't know precisely how many times the loop needs to repeat.

The do while loop

The do while loop works the same way as the while loop with one exception. The condition is evaluated *after* the execution of code to execute
while the condition is true instead of before, meaning that there will
always be at least one execution of Statement(s) to execute while
the condition is true even if the condition is never fulfilled.

```
do {
   aTransaction = [Transaction new];
   [aTransaction createTransaction: n*100 ofType:
                                        charge];
   [transactions addObject:aTransaction];
   n++;
} while (n <= 3);
```

The do while loop is usually used when the condition determines the end
of the loop is a result of actions taken within the loop. For example, you could
use a do while to prompt the user to enter data; the user could then either
enter some data or press return or do something else to terminate the loop.

The formal do while loop is

```
do { Statement(s) to execute while the condition is true }
         while ( condition );
```

The sequence is as follows:

1. Statement(s) to execute while the condition is true is
   executed.

2. Condition is evaluated. If it is true, the loop goes back to Step 1.

You wouldn't want to use a do while loop if there were a possibility that
you might not want to execute the code at all. In this example, if an array
could be empty, you wouldn't want to use a do while loop to iterate
through it.

Keep in mind that you must include a trailing semicolon after the do while
loop in the preceding example, but the other loops should not be terminated
with a semicolon, adding to the confusion.

While the preceding code is a pretty lame example of a do while loop —
you'll never use it in this way — the example does illustrate the mechanics of
using a do while loop.

Adding Loops to Your Program

To add the `switch` statement and loops to `main` in the Budget.h file, delete the code with the strikethrough and add the code in bold as shown in Listing 9-3.

Listing 9-3: Adding switch Statements and Loops to the main Function

```
#import <Foundation/Foundation.h>
#import "Budget.h"
#import "Transaction.h"

int main (int argc, const char * argv[]) {

//double numberEuros = 100;
  double numberDollarsInPoundland = 100;
  double numberPounds = 100;

//NSNumber *europeDollarTransaction = [[NSNumber alloc]
         initWithDouble:100.00];
//NSNumber *europeDollarTransaction2 = [[NSNumber alloc]
         initWithDouble:200.00];

//NSMutableArray *europeTransactions = [[NSMutableArray
         alloc] initWithCapacity:1];
//[europeTransactions addObject:europeDollarTransaction];
//[europeTransactions
         addObject:europeDollarTransaction2];

  NSMutableArray *transactions =
  [[NSMutableArray alloc] initWithCapacity:10];
  Transaction *aTransaction ;
  for (int n = 1; n <  2; n++) {
    aTransaction = [Transaction new];
    [aTransaction createTransaction:n*100 ofType:cash];
    [transactions addObject:aTransaction];
  }

  int n =1;
  while (n < 3) {
    aTransaction = [Transaction new];
    [aTransaction createTransaction:n*100 ofType:charge];
    [transactions addObject:aTransaction];
    n++;
  }

  do {
```

```
        aTransaction = [Transaction new];
        [aTransaction createTransaction:n*100 ofType:charge];
        [transactions addObject:aTransaction];
        n++;
    } while (n <= 3);

    Budget *europeBudget = [Budget new];
    [europeBudget createBudget:1000.00
                                withExchangeRate:1.2500];

    //for (NSNumber *aTransaction in europeTransactions) {
    for (Transaction * aTransaction in transactions) {
    //[europeBudget spendDollars:[aTransaction oubleValue]];

        switch ([aTransaction returnType]) {
        case cash:
            [europeBudget spendDollars:
                                [aTransaction returnAmount]];
            break;
        case charge:
            [europeBudget chargeForeignCurrency:
                                [aTransaction returnAmount]];
            break;
        default:
            break;
        }
    }
    //  [europeBudget chargeForeignCurrency:numberEuros];

    Budget *englandBudget = [Budget new];
    [englandBudget createBudget:2000.00
            withExchangeRate:1.5000];
    [englandBudget spendDollars:numberDollarsInPoundland];
    [englandBudget chargeForeignCurrency:numberPounds];

    return 0;
}
```

Here are the steps you took to add the switch statement and loops:

1. So that the compiler knows what a Transaction is, you added

   ```
   #import "Transaction.h"
   ```

2. You deleted the following line of code because you don't need it any
   more. (You no longer need to set the number of euros. You'll do that
   when you create the Transaction.)

   ```
   double numberEuros = 100;
   ```

3. You deleted the old NSNumber transactions and the old europe Transactions array.

```
NSNumber *europeDollarTransaction =
            [[NSNumber alloc] initWithDouble:100.00];
NSNumber *europeDollarTransaction2 =
            [[NSNumber alloc] initWithDouble:200.00];

NSMutableArray *europeTransactions = [[NSMutableArray
        alloc] initWithCapacity:1];
[europeTransactions addObject:
                            europeDollarTransaction];
[europeTransactions addObject:
                            europeDollarTransaction2];
```

4. You declared the transactions array (notice you changed the initial specification of the number of entries from 1 to 10) and created and added the transactions in three different kinds of loops. You cleverly used the counter (n) to vary the transaction amount (n*100).

```
NSMutableArray *transactions =
[[NSMutableArray alloc] initWithCapacity:10];
Transaction *aTransaction ;
for (int n = 1; n <  2; n++) {
  aTransaction = [Transaction new];
  [aTransaction createTransaction:
                    n*100 ofType:cash];
  [transactions addObject:aTransaction];
}

int n =1;
while (n < 3) {
  aTransaction = [Transaction new];
  [aTransaction createTransaction:
                    n*100 ofType:charge];
  [transactions addObject:aTransaction];
  n++;
}

do {
  aTransaction = [Transaction new];
  [aTransaction createTransaction:
                    n*100 ofType:charge];
  [transactions addObject:aTransaction];
  n++;
} while (n <= 3);
```

Changing the name prepares you for Chapter 10 where you manage all transactions in a single array, regardless of transaction type or destination — which will significantly reduce the complexity of the program. You created a transaction array with the new transactions.

5. You changed the type in the enumerator from NSNumber to Transaction to reflect the new object type that is now in the array.

6. You replaced

```
[europeBudget spendDollars:aTransaction];
```

with the new switch structure

```
switch ([aTransaction returnType]) {
  case cash:
    [europeBudget spendDollars:
                      [aTransaction returnAmount]];
    break;
  case charge:
    [europeBudget chargeForeignCurrency:
                      [aTransaction returnAmount]];
    break;
  default:
    break;
}
```

7. You deleted the following lines of code because you don't need them any more (the chargeForeignCurrency is now in the switch statement).

```
//[europeBudget chargeForeignCurrency:numberEuros];
```

Building the New Application

So that you can admire all the work you've done, it is time to build the application.

Select the Build and Run button in the Project Window toolbar to build and run the application.

You should see the following in the Debugger Console.

```
Converting 100.00 US dollars into foreign currency leaves
          $900.00
Charging 100.00 in foreign currency leaves $775.00
Charging 200.00 in foreign currency leaves $525.00
Charging 300.00 in foreign currency leaves $150.00
Converting 100.00 US dollars into foreign currency leaves
          $1900.00
Charging 100.00 in foreign currency leaves $1750.00
```

You can find the completed project on the CD in the Example 9 folder, which is in the Chapter 9 folder.

Taking the Leap: Jump Statements

To finish your tour of C coding, I've provided the rest of the control statements that are available in Objective-C. You'll use a few of them, such as break (which you used in switch statements) and return in your code. You'll use the rest occasionally (with the exception of the goto statement, which you will/should never use).

- ✔ break. Using break, you can leave a loop even if the condition for its end is not fulfilled. It can be used to end an infinite loop or to force it to end before its natural end. Recall that this is how you terminate instruction execution once it starts executing instructions for a given case.

- ✔ continue. The continue statement causes the program to skip the rest of the loop in the current iteration and jump to the start of the next iteration.

- ✔ return. The return statement ends a method or function. You used a return statement in main, as well as in your methods. It is included here to remind you that you can include a return statement anywhere in a method or function, bypassing any subsequent instructions in the function (as well as being able to depart in the middle of a loop) to return control back to the caller.

- ✔ goto. The goto statement allows you to make an absolute jump to another point in the program. It is considered evil incarnate by virtually all object-oriented programmers, and more than a few procedural ones. As an object-oriented applications programmer, you should never use it.

- ✔ exit. The exit statement terminates your program with an exit code. Its prototype is

```
void exit (int exitcode);
```

exit is used by some operating systems and may be used by calling programs. By convention, an exit code of 0 means that the program finished normally, and any other value means that some error or unexpected results happened.

Knowing the Problems with switch Statements

While I have achieved my goal of creating a single array of transaction objects for a given country, I still have a way to go if I want to make it possible to have a single array that handles all transaction types for all countries.

For example, if I were to add a country and a `returnCountry:` method to the transaction, I'd have to add an additional `switch` structure within each existing `case` in order to use the right `budget` object — makes my head hurt to think about it. And as you can see, my program would become much more complicated as I add more transactions and countries. While this is only one place in this program (so far) that I need to use that kind of logic, in a real program, you could find it all over the place.

```objc
for (Transaction * aTransaction in transactions) {
    switch ([aTransaction returnType]) {
      case cash:
        switch ([aTransaction returnCountry]) {
          case Europe:
            [europeBudget spendDollars:
                            [aTransaction returnAmount]];
            break;
          case England:
            [englandBudget spendDollars:
                            [aTransaction returnAmount]];
            break;
        }
        break;
      case charge:
        switch ([aTransaction returnCountry]) {
          case Europe:
            [europeBudget chargeForeignCurrency:
                            [aTransaction returnAmount]];
            break;
          case England:
            [englandBudget chargeForeignCurrency:
                            [aTransaction returnAmount]];
            break;
        }
        break;
      default:
        break;
    }
}
```

You can get a much more elegant solution than the `switch` statement by taking advantage of inheritance and polymorphism. I cover both in Chapter 10.

Part III
Walking the Object-Oriented Walk

The 5th Wave   By Rich Tennant

SOFTWARE DOCUMENT PUBLISHERS

"They're moving on to the memory management section. That should daze and confuse them enough for us to finish changing the tire."

In this part . . .

You've mastered the instruction set and language features that you need, and now you're ready to start building a real object-oriented program — one whose code you wouldn't be embarrassed to show to your developer friends.

In this part, you focus on what is known as the program architecture. Think of it as analogous to the way an architect designs a building to meet the needs of its occupants. In this case, however, you create something that not only works but also can be extended to easily add new functionality.

I also show you the fundamental application functionality that every program needs to implement — memory management and object initialization.

Chapter 10

Basic Inheritance

*I*n Chapter 9, you create a `Transaction` object and use a `switch` state-ment to manage more than one kind of transaction in a single array. The problem with that approach is that the `switch` statements can rapidly get very complicated, and a program with `switch` statements scattered through-out becomes difficult to extend and enhance.

Quite frankly, this kind of complex control structure is characteristic of the procedural program paradigm that I speak of in Chapter 3. Object-oriented programming and Objective-C do not "improve" this control structure as much as eliminate it as much as possible. The way this is done is by using one of those Objective-C's extensions to C — *inheritance* to take advantage of *polymorphism* (which I explain in Chapter 3). As you find out as I lead you through implementing an inheritance-based class structure in this chapter, this greatly simplifies things, and you end up with a program that is a great deal easier to understand and extend (the two actually go hand in hand).

Once you get into the rhythm of thinking this way, programming and making changes becomes more fun and less dreary. You introduce fewer bugs as you add functionality to your program, and your coding becomes completely focused on the new functionality instead of having to go back through everything you have done to see if you are about to break something that now works just fine.

Replacing a Control Structure With Polymorphism

Right now you iterate through an array, and your logic in `main` (the `switch` statement) decides whether to send the `sendDollars:` or chargeForeignCurrency: message to a `Budget` for that kind of transaction, passing the transaction as an argument.

```
for (Transaction * aTransaction in transactions) {
 switch ([aTransaction returnType]) {
  case cash:
    [europeBudget spendDollars:
                      [aTransaction returnAmount]];
    break;
  case charge:
    [europeBudget chargeForeignCurrency:
                      [aTransaction returnAmount]];
    break;
  default:
    break;
  }
}
```

In the object-oriented universe, you have two kinds of transaction objects — cash and credit card. Both kinds respond to a `spend` message, and every transaction has a pointer to the budget it is associated with. You iterate through the array and send the `spend` message to each transaction. If it is a cash transaction in Europe, for example, it has a reference to the `europe Budget` object and sends `europeBudget` object the `spendDollars:` message. If it is a credit card transaction in England, it sends the `charge ForeignCurrency:` message to `englandBudget`. No fuss, no bother, and no control structure. This means you have one array that holds every transaction for every country you visit — much better. This enables you to that entire `switch` structure with

```
for (Transaction*  aTransaction in transactions) {
  [aTransaction spend];
}
```

If you want a new transaction, all you need to do it code it up and add it to the array, and if wanted to visit a new country all you have do is create a budget for that country and attach it to the transactions that occurred in that country.

You can see that illustrated in Figure 10-1.

Let's start with what a transaction object looks like:

You need two instance variables

```
Budget *budget;
double  amount;
```

You need two methods

```
- (void) createTransaction: (double) theAmount
                       forBudget: (Budget*) aBudget;
- (void) spend;
```

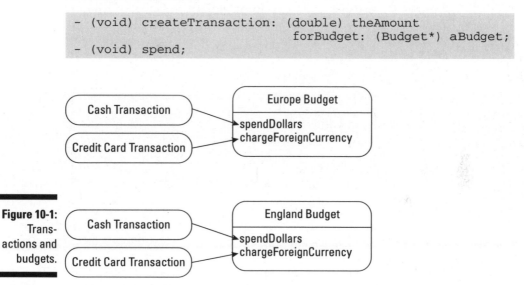

Figure 10-1:
Trans-
actions and
budgets.

As you can see, besides an initialization method, you have a method named spend. You also have an instance variable, budget, which enables the Transaction object to send a message to its budget; and another instance variable, amount, which holds the amount of this transaction. Because every type of transaction has a spend method, you can enumerate through the array and send each object a spend message, and each object, depending on its type, turns around and sends the right message to its budget.

So far both cash and credit card transactions look the same; the only difference is in the implementation of spend.

The cash transaction implements spend as

```
- (void) spend {

  [budget spendDollars:amount];
  }
```

The credit card looks like

```
- (void) spend {

  [budget chargeForeignCurrency:amount];
  }
```

This ability for different objects to respond to the same message each in its own way is an example of polymorphism, which I cover in Chapter 3, and is one of the cornerstones of enhanceable and extensible programs.

How inheritance works

You may notice a bit of a problem here. You got rid of the complicated `switch`, but now you have to maintain all those transactions. If want to make a change or add to generic transaction functionality, you have you go back and modify both the cash and credit card transactions. In Chapter 5, when I discuss adding a separate `struct` for New Zealand to track wool purchase, I say specifically that this is something you wanted to avoid (you may want to refer to Chapter 5).

What I say at the end of Chapter 5 is still true, but fortunately, I don't have to worry about maintaining a host of similar classes. Objective-C, like other object-oriented programming languages, permits you to base a new class definition on a class already defined. The base class is called a *superclass*; the new class is its *subclass*. The subclass is defined only by its extension to its superclass; everything else remains the same. All I need to do is create a transaction base superclass that encapsulates what is the same between a cash and credit card transaction, and then create cash and credit card transaction subclasses that implement the differences.

The terms *superclass* and *subclass* can be confusing. When most people think of *super*, they thing of something with more functionality, not less. In some languages, the term used is *base class*, which I think does a better job of conveying meaning. But it is what it is, so keep this in mind.

In Figure 10-2, you see an example of a *class diagram* that uses the UML (Unified Modeling Language) notation (the superclass and subclass arrows and terms are not part of the notation; they are there to illustrate the hierarchy of the Transaction classes in the program) — one often used by programmers to describe their classes. The name of the class is at the top of the box, the middle section describes the instance variables, and the bottom box shows you the methods of that (sub) class.

Figure 10-2 shows that both `CashTransaction` and `CreditCard Tranaction` classes are subclasses of `Transaction`. Each inherits all of the methods and all of the instance variables of it superclass.

Every class but `NSObject` (the root of all your classes, as I explain in Chapter 5) can thus be seen as another stop on the road to increasing specialization. As you add subclasses, you are adding to the cumulative total of what's inherited. The `CashTransaction` class defines only what is needed to turn a `Transaction` into a `CashTransaction`.

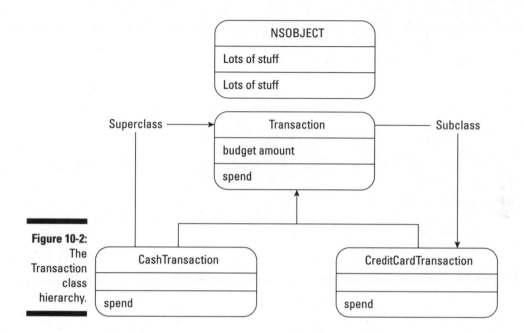

Class definitions are cumulative; each new class that you define *inherits* methods and instance variables of all of its base classes. I do not have to include the fact I am going to "re-implement" spend in the interfaces for CashTransaction and CreditCardTransaction. All I have to do is implement spend in the @implementation.

Incidentally, if you think about it, inheritance also implements a kind of encapsulation. You can extend the behavior of an existing object without impacting the existing code that already works — remember, it's all about enhanceability and extensibility.

In Objective-C, every class has only one superclass but can have an unlimited number of subclasses. In some languages, however, a class can have multiple superclasses. This is known as *multiple inheritance*. While Objective-C does not support multiple inheritance, it does provide some features not found in those languages that enable you to get many of the benefits of multiple inheritance, without the accompanying disadvantages. These include categories and protocols, both of which I cover in Chapter 16.

The new class is not a copy of the methods and instance variables of its root class, which contains all of the methods and instance variables of its root class and so on. The new class is an *extension*.

Knowing what inheritance enables you to do

Inheritance allows you to do a number of things that make your programs more extensible and enhanceable. In a subclass, you can make three kinds of changes to what you inherit from a superclass. Think of this section as describing the mechanics of creating a subclass.

- ✔ **You can add new methods and instance variables.** Although you haven't done that yet, this is the one of the most common reasons for defining a subclass in general.

- ✔ **You can refine or extend the behavior of a method.** You do this by adding a new version of the same method, while still continuing to use the code in the old method. To add a new version you implement a new method with the same name as one that's inherited. The new version *overrides* the inherited version. In the body of the new method, you send a message to execute the inherited version. I illustrate this later in this chapter, in Listing 10-6, and explain it in Step 3 following the listing (and again when I explain initialization in Chapter 12). Implementing a new method with the same name as one that's inherited is referred to as *overriding* a method.

- ✔ **You can change the behavior of a method you inherit.** You do this by replacing an existing method with a new version. This is done by overriding the old method. In this case, however, you do not send a message to execute the inherited version. The old implementation is still used for the class that defined it and other classes that inherit it, although classes that inherit from the new class use your implementation. Changing behavior is not unusual, although it does make your code harder to follow. If you find yourself frequently overriding a method to completely change its behavior, you should question your design.

Even though you may override a method in a class, subclasses of the class still do have access to the original. For obvious reasons, this is generally not a good idea, and again should have you questioning your design.

Although a subclass can override inherited methods, it can't override inherited instance variables. If you try to declare a new one with the same name as an inherited one, the compiler complains.

Using inheritance effectively

Given the preceding possibilities, here are some ways you can use inheritance in your programs:

- **Create a protocol.** You are actually creating a protocol with the `Transaction` class. A protocol in this sense is a list of method(s) that subclasses are expected to implement. The superclass might have empty versions of the methods (as `Transaction` does), or it might implement partial versions that you use in the subclass methods. In either case, the superclass's declaration (its list of methods) defines a protocol that all its subclasses must follow.

  When different classes implement similarly named methods, a program is better able to make use of polymorphism (see the discussion of More-Of-The-Same) in Chapter 3. Actually one of the things I really like about Objective-C is that it provides additional ways to do this, as you see when I explain delegation in Chapter 16. Both inheritance and delegation are extensively used in Cocoa.

  This use of inheritance is exemplified by the concept of an *abstract* class — often called an *abstract superclass* (or *abstract base class*). This is a class designed to have classes inherit from it. An abstract class brings together the methods and instance variables that are to be used by subclasses. In doing that, abstract classes define the structure of an application, and when you create your subclasses they fit effortlessly into the application structure and work seamlessly with other objects.

  You usually do not create an instance of an abstract class, since it really can't do anything, being dependent on its subclasses to implement the key functionality. It does, however, contain code that each of its subclasses normally has to create on its own. In this case, `Transaction` is an abstract class.

  Unlike some other languages, in Objective-C, there is no way to specify a class as abstract; therefore, making it possible to create an instance of an abstract class.

- **Reuse code.** Reusing code has traditionally been a poster child for inheritance use. There are three approaches:

  - Increasing specialization. If classes have some things in common, but also differ in key ways, the common functionality can be put in a superclass that all classes can inherit. `Transaction` is a good example of that.

  - Implementing generic functionality, which is often coupled with the protocol approach. In the `AppKit` and `UIKit`, user interface objects have been created for your using pleasure. They implement as much generic functionality as they can, but it is up to you to add the specific functionality to make it so they do something useful in your application. For example, a view can display itself on the screen, scroll, and so on, but you need to implement methods that display what you want displayed.

- Modifying a class that more or less does what you want it to do. There may be a class that does most of what you want it to, but you need to change some things about how it works. You can make the changes in a subclass.

In programming, as in life, however, not much is either/or. You use inheritance to do all those things, and often you create new subclasses to implement one or more than one of the approaches I just described.

Implementing Inheritance in a Program

Now it's time to put everything you know about inheritance and polymorphism together and add it to your program. You have to start by making some changes to the `Transaction` class.

Creating the Transaction superclass

If you have been following along with me, I extend what you do in Chapter 9. If you prefer to start with a clean copy of the project from where you left off, you can use the project found in the Chapter 10 Start Here folder which can be found in the Chapter 10 folder.

Go into the Xcode editor and click on Transaction.m to edit it. Then delete the code in Listings 10-1 and 10-2 with a strikethrough, and then add the code in bold .

Listing 10-1:   Transaction.m

```
#import "Transaction.h"
#import "Budget.h"
@implementation Transaction
//- (void) createTransaction: (double) theAmount ofType:
          (transactionType) aType{
- (void) createTransaction: (double) theAmount forBudget:
          (Budget*) aBudget {

  //type = aType;
```

```
  budget = aBudget;
  amount = theAmount;
}
- (void) spend {

// Fill in the method in subclasses
}

- (void) trackSpending: (double) theAmount {

  NSLog (@"You are about to spend another %.2f",
          theAmount);
}

//- (double) returnAmount{
//
//  return amount;
//}

//- (transactionType) returnType {
//
//  return type;
//};
@end
```

Listing 10-2:   Transaction.h

```
#import <Cocoa/Cocoa.h>
@class Budget;
//typedef enum {cash, charge} transactionType;

@interface Transaction : NSObject {

//transactionType type;
  Budget *budget;
  double  amount;
}

// - (void) createTransaction: (double) theAmount ofType:
//          (transactionType) aType;
- (void) createTransaction: (double) theAmount forBudget:
          (Budget*) aBudget;
- (void) spend;
- (void) trackSpending: (double) theAmount;
//- (double) returnAmount;
// - transactionType) returnType;
@end
```

Here are the steps you took to create the `Transaction` superclass:

1. Changed the arguments used in `createTransaction::` by deleting `aType`, and passing in `aBudget` instead.

   As I mentioned earlier, each transaction sends the right message to the `Budget` object, and it has to know what `Budget` it needs to spend against.

2. Created an empty `spend` method to be implemented in the subclasses.

3. Deleted `returnAmount` and `returnType` because you won't need them any more — that information was needed by the `switch` statement.

4. Added a new method, `trackSpending:`, which shows you how to send messages to inherited methods. (I do that in the `spend:` methods of `CashTransaction` and `CreditCardTransaction`.)

   ```
   - (void) trackSpending: (double) theAmount;
   ```

5. Made the necessary changes (in Listing 10-2) to the interface to support the implementation changes.

   You also included a `@class` statement. Earlier, I explained that the compiler needed to know certain things about classes that you were using, such as what methods you defined and so on, and the `#import` statement in the implementation (.m) file solved that problem. But when you get into objects that point at other objects, you also need to provide that information in the interface file, which can cause a problem if there are circular dependencies (sounds cool, but it is beyond the scope of this book). To solve that problem, Objective-C introduces the `@class` keyword as a way to tell the compiler that the instance variable `budget`, whose type `Budget` the compiler knows nothing about (yet), is a pointer to that class. Knowing that is enough for the compiler, at least in the interface files. You still have to do the `#import` in the implementation file when you refer to methods of that class, however.

If you examine what you have done so far, you realize that you have really created an abstract superclass, which creates a protocol for subsequent subclasses.

Adding the files for the new subclasses

ext, you take advantage of what you just did and create two subclasses of `Transaction`, `CashTransaction` and `CreditCardTransaction`. They inherit all of the methods and instance variables of the `Transaction` class, but each implements its own `spend:` method. I also have both methods send a message to their superclass's `trackSpending:` method, to show you how to send messages to your superclass.

Object-oriented programmers like to think of subclasses like `Cash Transaction` as having an "is-a" relationship to their superclasses. A cash transaction "is-a" transaction.

Now, look at how to create the two new subclasses.

First, you need to create four new files, as you do in Chapter 6.

1. **Select the Classes folder in the Groups & Files list.**

   This tells Xcode to place the new file in the Classes folder.

2. **Select File⇨New File from the main menu (or press ⌘+n) to get the New File dialog box.**

3. **In the leftmost column of the dialog box, first select Cocoa under Mac OS X; then select the Objective-C class template in the top-right pane. Make sure NSObject is selected in the Subclass of drop down menu.**

   You see a new dialog asking for some more information.

4. **Enter CashTransaction.m in the File Name field; then click Finish. You can see a bunch of other things in that window. There's a checkbox you can use to have Xcode create CashTransaction.h for you — make sure it is checked.**

5. **Select File⇨New again (or press ⌘+n) to get the New File dialog.**

6. **In the leftmost column of the dialog box, first select Cocoa under Mac OS X; then select the Objective-C class template in the top-right pane. Make sure NSObject is selected in the Subclass of drop down menu.**

   You see a new dialog asking for some more information.

7. **This time enter** CreditCardTransaction.m **in the File Name field; then click Finish.**

   You should now have four new files under the classes folder, CashTranaction.h and .m and CreditCardTransaction.h and .m.

Implementing the new subclasses

Now that you have the files for the new subclasses in place, it's time to get to work filling those files with code. You do that by adding and deleting the code in Listings 10-3 through 10-6 to the CashTransaction.h and .m and CreditCardTransaction.h and .m files.

Listing 10-3: CashTransaction.h

```
#import <Cocoa/Cocoa.h>
#import "Transaction.h"

//@interface CashTransaction : NSObject {
@interface CashTransaction : Transaction {
}

@end
```

Listing 10-4: CashTransaction.m

```
#import "CashTransaction.h"
#import "Budget.h"

@implementation CashTransaction
- (void) spend {

  [self trackSpending:amount];
  [budget spendDollars:amount];
}

@end
```

Listing 10-5: CreditCardTransaction.h

```
#import <Cocoa/Cocoa.h>
#import "Transaction.h"

//@interface CreditCardTransaction : NSObject {
@interface CreditCardTransaction : Transaction {
}

@end
```

Listing 10-6: CreditCardTransaction.m

```
#import "CreditCardTransaction.h"
#import "Budget.h"

@implementation CreditCardTransaction
- (void) spend {

  [super trackSpending:amount];
  [budget chargeForeignCurrency:amount];
}

@end
```

To add the two new subclasses, you only had to declare the unique behavior in each class.

1. You deleted the template-generated @interface statement and replaced it with one that specifies Transaction as the superclass.

```
@interface CreditCardTransaction : NSObject {
@interface CashTransaction : Transaction {
```

The deletions are necessary because when you add a new class to a project, Xcode doesn't know what its subclass is, so it uses NSObject. Up until now that has been fine, but as you define your own super- and subclasses it's up to you to change the NSObject default to the right superclass.

Your new subclasses inherit all of the methods and instance variables of the Transaction class, which includes all of the instance variables and methods it inherits from its superclass and so on up the inheritance hierarchy. (In this case, as you can see, the Transaction superclass is NSObject, so it ends there.) So you're cool when it comes to being able to behave like a good Objective-C object.

While you didn't do it here, you can also add instance variables to a subclass as well, and as many methods as you need.

2. You added the #imports for the Transaction and Budget interface files since both are used by the methods in the CashTransaction and CreditCardTransaction classes.

As I explain in Chapter 6, you need to import both interface files so the compiler can understand what Transaction and Budget are.

3. You had CashTransaction and CreditCardTransaction send a message to their superclass's method, trackSpending:.

trackSpending: displays that you are about to spend some money (a feature my wife, for one, thinks is a good idea to remind me that even though the money looks funny, ordering another bottle of wine does cost something). Notice, I had you do this in two different ways.

```
[self trackSpending:amount];
[super trackSpending:amount];
```

The first statement shows you how to send messages to methods that are part of your class, which includes those that you inherit. As you can see, even though trackSpending: is defined only in the superclass Transaction, you have inherited trackSpending: and the message to self works fine, although unless you have overridden it you should really use [super trackSpending: amount]. In this case self and super are interchangeable, but as you see in the Chapter 12 section called "Initializing objects," that isn't always the case.

Modifying main to use the new classes

Now that you have done all the spadework, you can take the final step in making your program much more extensible and enhanceable. You use that new inheritance–based `Transaction` class design in `main`..

To do that, add the code in bold and delete the code with a strikethrough in Listing 10-7 to `main` in the Budget Object.m file.

Listing 10- 7:   main in Budget Object.m

```
#import <Foundation/Foundation.h>
#import "Budget.h"

#import "Transaction.h"
#import "CashTransaction.h"
#import "CreditCardTransaction.h"

int main (int argc, const char * argv[]) {

//double numberPounds = 100;

  Budget   *europeBudget = [Budget new];
  [europeBudget createBudget:1000.00
                            withExchangeRate:1.2500];
  Budget   *englandBudget = [Budget new];
  [englandBudget createBudget:2000.00
                            withExchangeRate:1.5000];

  NSMutableArray *transactions = [[NSMutableArray alloc]
          initWithCapacity:10];
  Transaction *aTransaction ;
  for (int n = 1; n <  2; n++) {
//  aTransaction = [Transaction new];
      aTransaction = [CashTransaction new];
//  [aTransaction createTransaction:n*100 ofType:cash];
    [aTransaction createTransaction:n*100
                                forBudget:europeBudget];
    [transactions addObject:aTransaction];
    aTransaction = [CashTransaction new];
    [aTransaction createTransaction:n*100
                                forBudget:englandBudget];
    [transactions addObject:aTransaction];
  }

  int n =1;
  while (n < 4) { //** now 4
//  aTransaction = [Transaction new];

    aTransaction = [CreditCardTransaction new];
```

```
//    [aTransaction createTransaction:n*100 ofType:charge];
      [aTransaction createTransaction:n*100
                                    forBudget:europeBudget];
      [transactions addObject:aTransaction];
      aTransaction = [CreditCardTransaction new];
      [aTransaction createTransaction:n*100
                                    forBudget:englandBudget];
      [transactions addObject:aTransaction];
      n++;
  }


//do {
//    aTransaction = [Transaction new];
//    [aTransaction createTransaction:n*100 ofType:charge];
//    [transactions addObject:aTransaction];
//    n++;
//} while (n <= 3);


//Budget *europeBudget = [Budget new];
//[europeBudget  createBudget:1000.00
                                withExchangeRate:1.2500];

  for (Transaction*  aTransaction in transactions) {
//switch ((int)[aTransaction returnType]) {
//    case cash:
//       [europeBudget spendDollars:[aTransaction
//          returnAmount]];
//      break;

//    case charge:
//       [europeBudget chargeForeignCurrency:[aTransaction
//          returnAmount]];
//      break;
//    default:
//      break;
    [aTransaction spend];
  }

//Budget *englandBudget = [Budget new];
//[englandBudget createBudget:2000.00
                                withExchangeRate:1.5000];
//[englandBudget spendDollars:englandDollarTransaction];
//[englandBudget chargeForeignCurrency:numberPounds];

  return 0;
}
```

This is what you did in Listing 10-7:

1. You added the necessary #import statements so the compiler knows what to do with the new classes.

```
#import "Transaction.h"
#import "CashTransaction.h"
#import "CreditCardTransaction.h"
```

2. You moved up the code that created the Budget objects because you need use the Budget as an argument when you initialize the Transaction.

```
Budget *europeBudget = [Budget new];
[europeBudget createBudget:1000.00
                  withExchangeRate:1.2500];

Budget  *englandBudget = [Budget new];
[englandBudget createBudget:2000.00
                  withExchangeRate:1.5000];
```

3. You created cash and credit card transactions for both Europe *and* England in both the for and while loops (to which one more iteration is added — from n = 3 to n = 4).

```
aTransaction = [CreditCardTransaction new];
[aTransaction createTransaction:n*100
                              forBudget:europeBudget];
[transactions addObject:aTransaction];
aTransaction = [CreditCardTransaction new];
[aTransaction createTransaction:n*100
                              forBudget:englandBudget];
[transactions addObject:aTransaction];
```

4. You changed the enumerator to send the spend message to each Transaction object in the transactions array. You deleted

```
[europeBudget spend:aTransaction];
```

and replaced it with

```
[aTransaction spend];
```

This is something you find in many applications — a set of instructions that send the same message to a list of objects. *This is what polymorphism is all about* — a program architecture that makes your program easier to extend. This is because as long as it is a subclass of Transaction, any new transactions immediately can be used in your program without any changes to the rest of your program (except, of course, to create and implement the transaction itself)!

5. You deleted all the stuff no longer needed, including the gratuitous do while loop.

Once you are done with all that deleting and adding, main looks like Listing 10-8. You can see how much "cleaner" it looks. More important, you can see how easy it is to add a new kind of transaction to the mix. All you have to do is create the new transaction type and add it to the array, and it makes itself at home with the rest of the transactions.

Listing 10-8:   Budget Object.m

```
#import <Foundation/Foundation.h>
#import "Budget.h"

#import "Transaction.h"
#import "CashTransaction.h"
#import "CreditCardTransaction.h"

int main (int argc, const char * argv[]) {

  Budget *europeBudget = [Budget new];
  [europeBudget createBudget:1000.00
                               withExchangeRate:1.2500];
  Budget *englandBudget = [Budget new];
  [englandBudget createBudget:2000.00
                               withExchangeRate:1.5000];


  NSMutableArray *transactions = [[NSMutableArray alloc]
          initWithCapacity:10];
  Transaction *aTransaction ;
  for (int n = 1; n < 2; n++) {
    aTransaction = [CashTransaction new];
    [aTransaction createTransaction:n*100
                               forBudget:europeBudget];
    [transactions addObject:aTransaction];
    aTransaction = [CashTransaction new];
    [aTransaction createTransaction:n*100
                               forBudget:englandBudget];
    [transactions addObject:aTransaction];
  }

  int n =1;
  while (n < 4) {
    aTransaction = [CreditCardTransaction new];
    [aTransaction createTransaction:n*100
                               forBudget:europeBudget];
    [transactions addObject:aTransaction];
     aTransaction = [CreditCardTransaction new];
    [aTransaction createTransaction:n*100
                               forBudget:englandBudget];
    [transactions addObject:aTransaction];
```

(continued)

Listing 10-8 *(continued)*

```
    n++;
}

for (Transaction* aTransaction in transactions) {
    [aTransaction spend];
}

return 0;
}
```

Keep in mind that the `for` and `while` loops are there only to generate transactions — think of them as simulating a user interface.

Now select the Build and Run button in the Project Window toolbar to build and run the application.

You should see the following in the Debugger Console:

```
You are about to spend another 100.00
Converting 100.00 US dollars into foreign currency
        leaves $900.00
You are about to spend another 100.00
Converting 100.00 US dollars into foreign currency
        leaves $1900.00
You are about to spend another 100.00
Charging 100.00 in foreign currency leaves $775.00
You are about to spend another 100.00
Charging 100.00 in foreign currency leaves $1750.00
You are about to spend another 200.00
Charging 200.00 in foreign currency leaves $525.00
You are about to spend another 200.00
Charging 200.00 in foreign currency leaves $1450.00
You are about to spend another 300.00
Charging 300.00 in foreign currency leaves $150.00
You are about to spend another 300.00
Charging 300.00 in foreign currency leaves $1000.00
```

As expected, the output is the same, except for the additional transactions I added for the England part of my trip (shown in bold) as well as the output from `trackSpending:`.

You can find the completed project on the CD in the Example 10 folder, which can be found in the Chapter 10 folder.

Considering Polymorphism and Inheritance

You have just used one of the Objective-C extensions to C — inheritance, to implement polymorphism (or as I like to think of it, More-Of-The-Same). As you have seen, polymorphism is the ability of different object types to respond to the same message, each one in its own way. Since each object can have its own version of a method, a program becomes easier to extend and enhance because you don't have to change the message to add functionality. All you have to do is create a new subclass, and it responds to the same messages in its own way.

This allows you to isolate code in the methods of different objects rather than gathering them in a single function that has to know all the possible cases and in control structures such as `if` and `switch` statements. As you have seen, this makes the code you write more extensible and enhanceable, because when a new case comes along, you won't have to re-code all those `if` and `switch` statements — you need only add a new class with a new method, leaving well enough alone as far as the code that you've already written, tested, and debugged is concerned.

Using inheritance together with polymorphism is one of the extensions to C that is hard to implement without language support. For this to really work, the exact behavior can be determined only at runtime (this is called *late binding* or *dynamic binding*).

When a message is sent, the Objective-C runtime I talk about in Chapter 1 looks at the object you are sending the message to, finds the implementation of the method matching the name, and then invokes that method.

Chapter 11

Encapsulating Objects

· ·

In This Chapter

▶ Understanding the Model-View-Controller pattern

▶ The role of interfaces

▶ How composite objects work

▶ Factoring your code to implement Model-View-Controller

· ·

*U*sing encapsulation enables you to safely tuck data behind an object's walls. You can keep the data safe and reduce the dependencies of other parts of your program on what the data is and how it is structured.

Encapsulation is also useful when you apply it to application functionality. When you limit what your objects know about other objects in your application, changing objects or their functionality becomes much easier because it reduces the impact of those changes on the rest of your application.

In this chapter, I'll show you a way to design, or architect, your application that limits the knowledge that objects have of other objects.

Getting to Know the Model-View-Controller (MVC) Pattern

The Cocoa framework you'll use on the Mac is designed around certain programming paradigms, known as *design patterns* — a commonly used template that gives you a consistent way to get a particular task done.

While you'll need to be comfortable with several design patterns in Cocoa, there is one that implements the kind of object encapsulation that reduces the impact of changes to an application — the Model-View-Controller (MVC) design pattern. This design pattern is not unique to Cocoa — a version of it has been in use since the early days of Smalltalk (which the Objective-C extensions to the C language were based on). It goes a long way back, and the fact that it is still being used tells you something about its value.

MVC divides your application into three groups of objects and encourages you to limit the interaction between objects to others in its own group as much as possible. It creates, in effect, a world for the application, placing objects in one of three categories — *model*, *view*, and *controller*, described in the following list — and specifies roles and responsibilities for all three kinds of objects as well as the way they're supposed to interact with each other. The best example I have ever come up with, and one I used in *iPhone Application Development For Dummies,* is a 60-inch flat screen TV.

- **Model objects:** Model objects make up what I will call *the content engine* of your application. This is where all of the objects (as opposed to the code in the `main` function) you have been developing so far fit in. They process transactions and compute what you have left in your budget. If you were to add things such as hotel objects, train objects, and the like, this is where they belong. They are very generous with what they can do and are happy to share what they know with the rest of your application. But not only do they not care about what other objects use them, or what these other objects do with the information they provide; being good objects, they really don't want to know.

  You can think of the *model* (which may be one object or several objects that interact) as a particular television program. One that does not give a hoot about what TV set it is being shown on.

- **View objects:** These objects display things on the screen and respond to user actions. This is what is generally thought of as the user interface, and pretty much anything you see on the screen is part of the view group of objects. View objects are pros at formatting and displaying data, as well as handing user interactions, such as allowing the user to enter a credit card transaction, make a new hotel reservation, and add a destination or even create a new trip. But they don't care about where that data comes from and are unaware of the model.

  You can think of the *view* as a television screen that doesn't care about what program it is showing or what channel you just selected.

  If you create an ideal world where the view knows nothing about the model and the model knows nothing about the view, then you need to add one more set of objects. These objects connect the model and view — making requests for data from the model and sending that data back for the view to display. This is the collective responsibility of controller objects, described next.

- **Controller objects:** These objects connect the application's view objects to its model objects. They deliver to the view the data that needs to be displayed — getting it from the model. They deliver user requests for current data (how much money do I have left in my budget?) to the model, as well as new data (I just spent 300 euros) to the model as well.

  You can think of the *controller* as the circuitry that pulls the show off the cable and sends it to the screen or that can request a particular pay-per-view show.

One of the advantages of using this application model is that it allows you to separate these three parts to your application and work on them separately. You just need to make sure each group has a well-defined interface. When the time is right, you just connect the parts — and you have an application.

 A category of functionality that is not handled by the MVC pattern exists at the *application level,* or all the nuts and bolts and plumbing needed to run an application. These objects are responsible for startup, shut down, file management, event handling, and everything else that is not M, V, or C.

Implementing the MVC Pattern

Since you will eventually be providing user-interface functionality, it is time to make sure that you have only model functionality (managing data, for example) in the model objects, and similarly that all of the model functionality is in model objects and not scattered in main. That way, you can easily slide the model into place after you define the views and controllers necessary for your application.

Earlier, I said what made the separation between models, views, and controllers possible is a well-defined interface, which I'll show you how to develop in this chapter. You'll create an interface between the model and the sometime-in-the-future-to-be-developed controller by using a technique called *composition*, which is a useful way to create interfaces.

I'm a big fan of composition, because it's another way to hide what is really going on behind the curtains. It keeps the objects that use the composite object ignorant of the objects the composite object uses and actually makes the components ignorant of each other, allowing you to switch components in and out at will.

As it stands now, some user-interface type functionality is scattered throughout our model, and a lot of model knowledge is in main, so I'll start by having you take all of the user interface functionality and putting it in main. You'll also take model functionality out of main and create a new composite object — Destination — that will be the interface to main. You will use main as a surrogate for both the views and controllers that you will be adding in Chapters 17 and 18. Practically speaking, as you'll see, controllers need to be more intimate with views than with models, so I'm comfortable having you place all that functionality in main and then separate it when you develop the user interface.

> # Oh no, not factoring again!
>
> While it may appear to you that you have spent a lot of time writing code, only to discard it, that is in fact true.
>
> As I mentioned earlier, I need to show you both the mechanics of programming in Objective-C and how to use those mechanics to create an application. This means that as you learn more,
>
> you need to refine the application to use what you have learned.
>
> In this chapter especially, you will do a major factoring of your code, which you will find, when developing your own applications, is an integral part of the development process.

Get out of/into main

Now, take a look at the application so far and think about how functionality is currently distributed and what you would have to do to make it consistent with the MVC pattern.

Get out of main

In Listing 11-1, you can look at what goes on in main and begin to think about what needs to be moved into the new Destination object.

Listing 11-1:   The Current main Function

```
int main (int argc, const char * argv[]) {

  Budget *europeBudget = [Budget new];
  [europeBudget  createBudget:1000.00
                              withExchangeRate:1.2500];
  Budget *englandBudget = [Budget new];
  [englandBudget createBudget:2000.00
                              withExchangeRate:1.5000];

  NSMutableArray *transactions =
              [[NSMutableArray alloc] initWithCapacity:10];
  Transaction *aTransaction ;
  for (int n = 1; n <  2; n++) {
    aTransaction = [CashTransaction new];
    [aTransaction createTransaction:n*100
                              forBudget:europeBudget];
    [transactions addObject:aTransaction];
    aTransaction = [CashTransaction new];
```

```
        [aTransaction createTransaction:n*100
                                    forBudget:englandBudget];
        [transactions addObject:aTransaction];
    }

    int n =1;
    while (n < 4) {
        aTransaction = [CreditCardTransaction new];
        [aTransaction createTransaction:n*100
                                      forBudget:europeBudget];
        [transactions addObject:aTransaction];
        aTransaction = [CreditCardTransaction new];
        [aTransaction createTransaction:n*100
                                      forBudget:englandBudget];
        [transactions addObject:aTransaction];
        n++;
    }

    for (Transaction *aTransaction in transactions) {
        [aTransaction spend];
    }

    return 0;
}
```

What comes to my mind is the following:

1. Take the creation of the Budgets for each leg of my trip out of main. While the request for a budget for a new leg of my trip would come from the user interface — hey, I want to go someplace new — it shouldn't be the user interface or controller that creates those Budget objects. It's not in their respective job descriptions.

2. Similarly, take the creation and management of the Transactions for each part of my trip out of main. While a user interface is definitely responsible for delivering transactions to the model, managing the list of transaction objects is not something that should be in a controller or view.

3. If you do Steps 1 and 2, then you'll also need to take sending the message to each Transaction to apply itself to its Budget out of main.

Get into main

While you're at it, remember that views are responsible for supplying information to the user. Currently Budget has NSLog statements that will evolve into user interface functionality. That functionality should be moved into main and later into a view.

Creating a New Project

Now that you have some idea of what you need to move out of `main`, I want you to create a new object @md `Destination` — that acts as the interface to `main` and that becomes the composite object for each part of my trip.

Up to now, you've been experimenting with the various features of Objective-C as you've built this program. Now that you know quite a bit, it is time to take a more professional attitude toward this project. From this chapter on, you'll move away from learning about Objective-C as a *language* and toward how to use the language you've learned to build useful *applications*. I'll concentrate on architecture and the functionality you need to make your application commercial quality.

I'll show you how to design this as you would a "real" application and create a structure that will actually be the basis for an application of this type, in case you want to move forward with it.

You'll start by creating a new project that will be the basis for your commercial quality application (and also because the name Budget Object no longer describes what the application is about). I also want you to go through creating a new project so I can show you the mechanics for reusing the classes you've developed thus far in a new project — something you'll likely be doing regularly.

You will be creating a new project here. You can do that, or you can skip Steps 1 through 9 (I know it's tedious, but it's for your own good) and start with the Project in Example 11A , in the Chapter 11 folder on the CD.

If you have been following along with me, I'll be extending what you just did in Chapter 10. If you would like to start from a clean copy of the project from where you left off, you can use the project found in the Chapter 11 Start Here folder, which is in the Chapter 11 folder.

1. **Launch Xcode.**

2. **Start the New Project Assistant by Choosing File⇨New Project from the main menu to create a new project.**

3. **In the New Project window, click Application under the Mac OS X heading.**

4. **Select Command Line Tool from the choices displayed and then select Foundation from the Type drop-down menu. Click Choose.**

   Xcode will then display a standard save sheet.

5. **Enter the name** `Vacation` **in the Save As field, choose a Save location, and then click Save.**

After you click Save, Xcode creates the project and opens the project window.

6. **Go back to Xcode, open the previous version of the Budget Object project (or the project found in the Chapter 11 Start Here folder, which is in the Chapter 11 folder on the CD), and place it next to your new project, as shown in Figure 11-1.**

7. **Drag the classes folder from the current project to the new one, as shown in Figure 11-1.**

An alternative is to click the `Classes` folder in the new project and choose Project⇨Add to Project and then navigate to the files you want to add (I show you how to do that in more detail in Chapter 18).

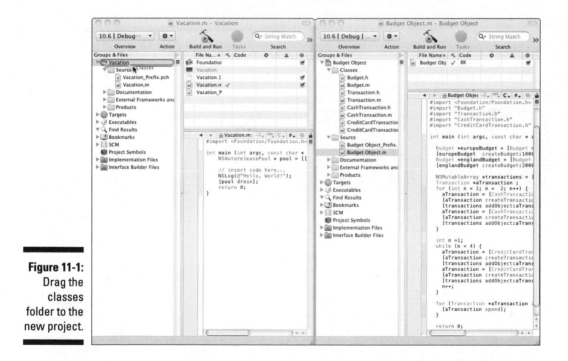

Figure 11-1:
Drag the classes folder to the new project.

The copy dialog shown in Figure 11-2 appears.

8. **Be sure to check the Copy (if needed), to copy items into the destination group's folder, as shown in Figure 11-2.**

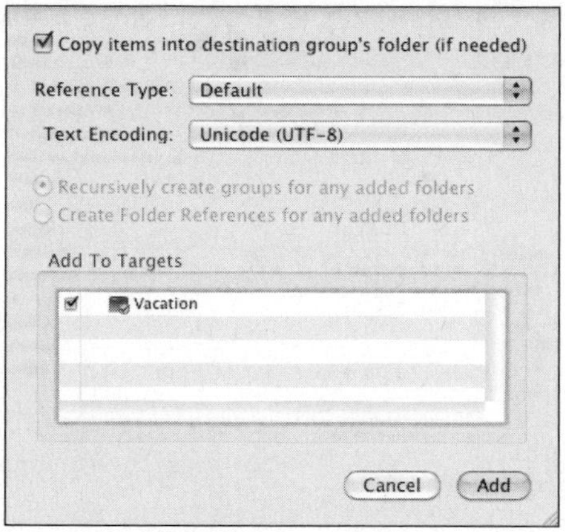

Figure 11-2:
Be sure to
check Copy.

9. **Select and copy all of the code in Budget Object.m in the original
   Xcode project and copy it. Then delete everything in Vacation.m
   in the new project and paste what was in Budget Object.m into
   Vacation.m (see Figure 11-3).**

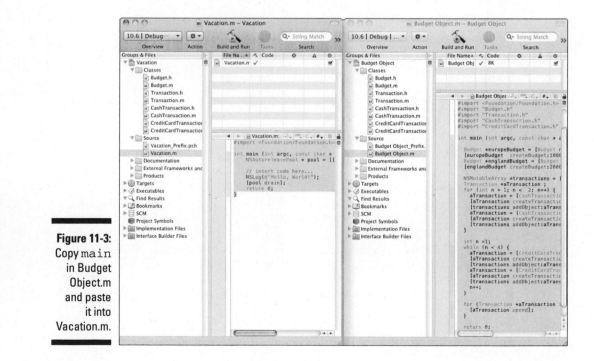

Figure 11-3:
Copy `main`
in Budget
Object.m
and paste
it into
Vacation.m.

10. **To make sure the preceding steps worked, select the Build and Run button in the Project Window toolbar to build and run the application.**

    You should see the following in the Debugger Console:

```
You are about to spend another 100.00
Converting 100.00 US dollars into foreign currency
        leaves $900.00
You are about to spend another 100.00
Converting 100.00 US dollars into foreign currency
        leaves $1900.00
You are about to spend another 100.00
Charging 100.00 in foreign currency leaves $775.00
You are about to spend another 100.00
Charging 100.00 in foreign currency leaves $1750.00
You are about to spend another 200.00
Charging 200.00 in foreign currency leaves $525.00
You are about to spend another 200.00
Charging 200.00 in foreign currency leaves $1450.00
You are about to spend another 300.00
Charging 300.00 in foreign currency leaves $150.00
You are about to spend another 300.00
Charging 300.00 in foreign currency leaves $1000.00
```

Nice to see that the application still works. Now, it's time to get down to work.

You can find the completed project on the CD in the Example 11A folder, which is in the Chapter 11 folder.

Creating the Destination Class

If you have been following along with me, I'll be extending what you just did in the first exercise. If you would like to start from a clean copy of the project from where you left off, you can use the project found in the Example 11A folder, which is in the Chapter 11 folder.

The next thing I want you to do is to add the new Destination object, as follows:

1. **Select the Classes folder in the Groups & Files list.**

   This tells Xcode to place the new file in the Classes folder.

2. **Select File⇨New File from the main menu (or press ⌘+N) to get the New File dialog.**

3. **In the leftmost column of the dialog, select Cocoa under Mac OS X and then select the Objective-C class template in the top-right pane. Make sure NSObject is selected in the Subclass of the drop-down menu.**

   You'll see a new screen asking for some more information.

4. **Enter Destination.m in the File Name field and make sure that the checkbox to have Xcode create Destination.h is checked; then click Finish.**

Now, take a look at designing and implementing this new Destination class. This "design" I have been referring to is really in the @interface for the new Destination.

To act as an interface to be used by a controller, the Destination class needs to declare methods that do the following:

✔ Create Transaction objects from the transaction amounts that will be sent from the user interface.

✔ Return the data the user interface needs to display.

In Listing 11-2, in the following section, you can see that the Destination class interface that accomplishes both of the preceding tasks.

Designing the destination

Enter Listing 11-2 into the Destination.h file.

Listing 11-2: Destination.h — the Destination Design

```
#import <Cocoa/Cocoa.h>
@class Budget;
@interface Destination : NSObject {

  NSString       *country;
  NSMutableArray *transactions;
  Budget         *theBudget;
}

- (void) createWithCountry: (NSString*) theCountry
          andBudget: (double) budgetAmount
          withExchangeRate: (double) theExchangeRate;
- (void) spendCash: (double) aTransaction;
- (void) chargeCreditCard: (double) aTransaction;
- (double) leftToSpend;

@end
```

The methods and instance variables you declared in this class will enable you to do the following:

1. `createWithCountry:::`'s arguments will allow you to initialize a new `Destination` with the country you are headed to (as you can see, as you factor the code, I'm having you add additional functionality that you can use), the amount you want to budget, and the current exchange rate.

2. Create the `Budget` object previously created in `main`. This was the first goal in the section "Get out of/into main."

3. Create and manage a `Transaction` array. This supports the second goal in the section "Get out of/into main."

4. Enable `main` (the controller surrogate) to send transaction amounts to the `Destination` object (by sending the `spendCash:` and `charge CreditCard:` messages). The `Destination` object can then, in turn, create and manage the appropriate `Transaction` objects and send them the `spend:` message. This was the balance of the second goal in the section "Get out of/into main."

5. Enable the `main` (by sending the `leftToSpend`) method to ask the model for the information it needs to deliver to the surrogate user interface. This displays how much money remains in the budget.

Notice the instance variables that reference other objects — the `transactions` array and `theBudget`. This is a model for what makes a composite object and how it gets its work done — using other objects to distribute the work.

Object-oriented programmers like to think of composite objects like `Destination` as having a "has-a" relationship to their parts. The destination has-a budget, for example.

Now, it's time to take a look at how to implement these methods.

Implementing the methods

Enter Listing 11-3 into the Destination.m file.

Listing 11-3:   Destination.m

```
#import "Destination.h"
#import "CashTransaction.h"
#import "CreditCardTransaction.h"
#import "Budget.h"
```

(continued)

Listing 11-3: *(continued)*

```objc
#import "Transaction.h"

@implementation Destination

- (void) createWithCountry: (NSString*) theCountry
          andBudget: (double) budgetAmount
          withExchangeRate: (double) theExchangeRate{

  transactions = [[NSMutableArray alloc]
                                    initWithCapacity:10];
  theBudget = [Budget new];
  [theBudget createBudget:budgetAmount
                    withExchangeRate:theExchangeRate];
  country = theCountry;
  NSLog (@"I'm off to %@", theCountry);
}


-(void) spendCash: (double) amount {

  Transaction *aTransaction = [CashTransaction new];
  [aTransaction createTransaction:amount
                            forBudget:theBudget];
  [transactions addObject:aTransaction];
  [aTransaction spend];
}

-(void) chargeCreditCard: (double) amount {

  Transaction *aTransaction = [CreditCardTransaction new];
  [aTransaction createTransaction:amount
                            forBudget:theBudget];
  [transactions addObject:aTransaction];
  [aTransaction spend];
}

- (double) leftToSpend {

  return [theBudget returnBalance];
}

@end
```

All of this is pretty straightforward. It is either what was being done in main before or new code to implement the new functionality.

This new functionality is as follows:

✔ A new method leftToSpend. It is there, as I said, to provide the user interface with the data it needs to display. (This will also require adding a new method to Budget, as you will see next.)

✔ A new NSLog statement:

```
NSLog (@"I'm off to %@", theCountry);
```

This statement in `Destination` is not intended to be part of the user interface — you are just including it to trace program execution (I also use it to illustrate some points about memory management in Chapter 13). It uses my newly minted `country` instance variable.

Modifying the Budget class

Finishing the implementation of the `Destination` object's functionality as the interface to the model requires that you make changes to the `Budget` class. Because the `Destination` object is responsible for reporting to the controller the amount left to spend, it will need to get the amount from the `Budget` object, requiring you to add a new method, `returnBalance`, to `Budget`. And in line with factoring all of your code to move all user interface functionality out of the model objects, you'll also need to remove the "user interface" from `Budget` — that is, the `NSLog` statements.

> 1. **Delete the code with the strikethrough in Listing 11-4 in the Budget.m file. Then add the code in bold.**

Listing 11-4:   Budget.m

```
#import "Budget.h"

@implementation Budget

- (void) createBudget: (double) aBudget
              withExchangeRate: (float) anExchangeRate {

  exchangeRate = anExchangeRate;
  budget = aBudget;
}

- (void) spendDollars: (double) dollars {

  budget -= dollars;
//NSLog(@"Converting %.2f US dollars into foreign
          currency leaves $%.2f", dollars, budget);
}

- (void) chargeForeignCurrency: (double) foreignCurrency {

  transaction = foreignCurrency*exchangeRate;
  budget -= transaction;
```

(continued)

Listing 11-4 *(continued)*

```
//NSLog(@"Charging %.2f in foreign currency leaves
        $%.2f", foreignCurrency, budget);
}

- (double) returnBalance {

  return budget;
}

@end
```

2. **Add the code in bold in Listing 11-5 to the Budget.h file.**

Listing 11-5:   Budget.h

```
#import <Cocoa/Cocoa.h>

@interface Budget : NSObject {

  float  exchangeRate;
  double budget;
  double transaction;
}

- (void) createBudget: (double) aBudget
               withExchangeRate: (float) anExchangeRate;

- (void) spendDollars: (double) dollars ;

- (void) chargeForeignCurrency: (double) euros;
- (double) returnBalance;
@end
```

Removing UI type functionality from the Transaction objects

Since you are moving all the user interface functionality out of the model, you can delete the Transaction's trackSpending message used by CashTransaction and CreditCardTransaction. You'll implement comparable functionality in main.

Delete the code with strikethrough in Listings 11-6 through 11-9.

Listing 11-6:   Transaction.h

```
#import <Cocoa/Cocoa.h>
@class Budget;
@interface Transaction : NSObject {

  Budget *budget;
  double amount;
}

- (void) createTransaction: (double) theAmount forBudget:
          (Budget*) aBudget;
- (void) spend;
//- (void) trackSpending: (double) theAmount;

@end
```

Listing 11-7:   Transaction.m

```
#import "Transaction.h"
#import "Budget.h"

@implementation Transaction

- (void) createTransaction: (double) theAmount forBudget:
          (Budget*) aBudget {

  budget = aBudget;
  amount = theAmount;
}

- (void) spend {

}

//- (void) trackSpending: (double) theAmount {
//    NSLog (@"You are about to spend another %.2f",
         theAmount);
//}

@end
```

Listing 11-8:   CashTransaction.m

```
#import "CashTransaction.h"
#import "Budget.h"

@implementation CashTransaction

- (void) spend {
```

(continued)

Listing 11-8 *(continued)*

```
//[self trackSpending:amount];
  [budget spendDollars:amount];
}

@end
```

Listing 11-9: CreditCardTransaction.m

```
#import "CreditCardTransaction.h"
#import "Budget.h"

@implementation CreditCardTransaction

- (void) spend {

//[super trackSpending:amount];
  [budget chargeForeignCurrency:amount];
}

@end
```

Coding the New main

That leaves only `main`. As I said, the functionality that remains there will act as a surrogate for the user interface and controller.

Since the changes you'll need to make to `main` are so significant, it's easier to delete everything in `main` and start from scratch. So in the Vacation.m file, replace `main` with Listing 11-10. (Notice that you no longer need that long list of `#import`s in `main` since now its sole interface to the model is through `Destination`.)

```
#import "Budget.h"
#import "Transaction.h"
#import "CashTransaction.h"
#import "CreditCardTransaction.h"
```

Listing 11-10: The New main Function in Vacation.m

```
#import <Foundation/Foundation.h>
#import "Destination.h"

int main (int argc, const char * argv[]) {

  Destination* europe = [Destination new] ;
```

```
NSString* europeText = [[NSString alloc]
                        initWithFormat:@"%@", @"Europe"];
[europe createWithCountry:europeText andBudget:1000.00
                             withExchangeRate:1.25];
Destination* england = [Destination new] ;
NSString* englandText = [[NSString alloc]
                   initWithFormat:@"%@", @"England"];
[england createWithCountry:englandText andBudget:2000.00
                             withExchangeRate:1.50];

for (int n = 1; n < 2; n++) {
  double transaction = n*100.00;
  NSLog(@"Sending a %.2f cash transaction",
                                        transaction);
  [europe spendCash:transaction];
  NSLog(@"Remaining budget %.2f", [europe leftToSpend]);
  NSLog(@"Sending a %.2f cash transaction",
                                        transaction);
  [england spendCash:transaction];
  NSLog(@"Remaining budget %.2f",
                              [england leftToSpend]);
}

int n = 1;
while (n < 4) {
  double transaction = n*100.00;
  NSLog(@"Sending a %.2f credit card transaction",
                                        transaction);
  [europe chargeCreditCard:transaction];
  NSLog(@"Remaining budget %.2f", [europe leftToSpend]);
  NSLog(@"Sending a %.2f credit card transaction",
                                        transaction);
  [england chargeCreditCard:transaction];
  NSLog(@"Remaining budget %.2f",
                              [england leftToSpend]);
  n++;
}

return 0;
}
```

I want to review exactly what you did when you added the new code to `main`.

1. You started by creating the destination objects.

```
Destination* europe = [Destination new];
```

One interesting thing is the way you created the `country` string to use as an argument.

```
NSString* europeText = [[NSString alloc]
                initWithFormat:@"%@", @"Europe"];
```

This initializes a new string as the result of a formatting operation, just like you've been doing within the `NSLog` statements, except here I'm creating an honest to goodness `NSString` object to use as the country argument in `createWithCountry:::`. There are alternative ways to create a string, but there are memory management issues to consider that I cover in Chapter 13.

2. You then initialized the `Destination` object for Europe and created and initialized the `Destination` object for England.

```
[europe createWithCountry:europeText
          andBudget:1000.00 withExchangeRate:1.25];
Destination* england = [Destination new];
NSString* englandText = [[NSString alloc]
                    initWithFormat:@"%@", @"England"];
[england createWithCountry:englandText
          andBudget:2000.00 withExchangeRate:1.50];
```

3. Then you sent some transaction *amounts* to the `Destination` objects. Notice that you are no longer creating `Transaction` objects, but simply sending transaction amounts.

```
[europe spendCash:transaction];
...
[england chargeCreditCard:transaction];
```

4. You added `NSLog` statements to "simulate" user interface behavior. The first `NSLog` lets you know that the user will be entering a transaction. The second `NSLog` acts as a surrogate for displaying the updated budget information to the user. It uses the new `leftToSpend` method. As you will see when you create your controllers, `spendCash:` and `chargeCreditCard:` will be the methods the controllers use to send data to the model, and the `leftToSpend` method will be used to request data from the model.

To make sure this worked, select the Build and Run button in the Project Window toolbar to build and run the application.

You should see the following in the Debugger Console:

```
I'm off to Europe
I'm off to England
Sending a 100.00 cash transaction
Remaining budget 900.00
Sending a 100.00 cash transaction
Remaining budget 1900.00
Sending a 100.00 credit card transaction
Remaining budget 775.00
Sending a 100.00 credit card transaction
Remaining budget 1750.00
```

```
Sending a 200.00 credit card transaction
Remaining budget 525.00
Sending a 200.00 credit card transaction
Remaining budget 1450.00
Sending a 300.00 credit card transaction
Remaining budget 150.00
Sending a 300.00 credit card transaction
Remaining budget 1000.00
```

You can find the completed project on the CD in the Example 11B folder, which is in the Chapter 11 folder.

If I were designing this application from scratch, rather than using as a way to teach you about how to program in Objective-C, I'd actually end up in the same place. The difference is that I would have started with this `Destination` object in the beginning; then I would have created the `Budget` and `Transaction` objects that the `Destination` needs, rather than take the `Budget` and `Transaction` objects that already exist and make them part of `Destination`.

Yes, Another Two Steps Forward and One Step Back

What you've accomplished in this chapter is significant. You have factored your code in a way that will make adding an iPhone user interface in Chapter 17 and a Mac user interface in Chapter 18 as easy as pie.

You have achieved this at a cost, however — the time and effort needed to factor your code.

As I mentioned earlier, I need to show you both the mechanics of programming in Objective-C and how to use those mechanics to create an application. This means that as you learn more, you need to refine the application to use what you have learned.

Although, to be fair, if I were talking only about application design, I would have started with a `Destination` object from the beginning — and I expect in the future, based on what you have learned in this chapter, you will, too.

Chapter 12

The Birth of an Object

In This Chapter

▶ How objects are created

▶ What it means to allocate an object

▶ The standard way to do initialization

▶ Initialization and superclasses and subclasses

*U*p until now, you have been doing initialization on an ad hoc basis, using initialization methods such as these:

```
- (void) createTransaction: (double) theAmount
                            forBudget: (Budget*) aBudget;
- (void) createBudget: (double) aBudget
               withExchangeRate: (float) anExchangeRate;
```

There is a standard way to do initialization, however — one designed to work in a class hierarchy that ensures all of the super- and subclasses are initialized properly.

In this chapter, I show you the how to implement these standard initialization methods. First, though, you must allocate memory for the new object, as described in the first section of this chapter.

Allocating Objects

To create an object in Objective-C, you must do the following:

1. **Allocate memory for the new object.**

2. **Initialize the newly allocated memory, as described in the next section.**

Allocation (`alloc`) starts the process of creating a new object by getting the amount of memory it needs from the operating system to hold all of the object's instance variables. The `alloc` message is sent to the `NSObject` class, from which all of the classes you are using are derived. But not only does the `alloc` method allocate the memory for the object; it also initializes all the memory it allocates to 0 — all the `int`s are 0; all the `float`s become 0.0; all the pointers are `nil`; and the object's `isa` instance variable points to the object's class (this tells an object of what class it is an instance).

Well, at least that was easy.

Initializing Objects

Initialization is not required. And if you can live with all of the instance variables initialized to 0 and `nil`, then there is nothing you need to do. But if your class (or your superclass) has instance variables that you need to initialize to anything other than 0 or `nil`, you are going to have to code some kind of initialization method.

The initialization method does not have to include an argument for every instance variable, since some will only become relevant during the course of your object's existence. You must make sure, however, that all the instance variables your object needs, including objects it needs to do its work, are in a state that enables your object to respond to the messages it is sent.

For example, right after

```
Destination *europe = [Destination new]
```

I had you code a method

```
- (void) createWithCountry: (NSString*) theCountry
            andBudget: (double) budgetAmount
            withExchangeRate: (double) theExchangeRate;
```

in which you created a budget, a transactions array, and set the exchange rate.

In fact, the `Destination` object you created was unusable until you did that.

You may think the main job in initialization is to, well, initialize your objects (hence, the name), but more is involved when there is a superclass and a subclass chain.

Start by looking at the new initializer that I'll have you code for the `CashTransaction` class in Listing 12-1.

Listing 12-1: CashTransaction initializer

```
- (id) initWithAmount: (double) theAmount forBudget:
         (Budget*) aBudget {

  if (self = [super initWithAmount:theAmount
                            forBudget:aBudget]) {

   name = @"Cash";
  }
  return self;
}
```

By convention, initialization methods begin with the abbreviation `init`.
(This is true, however, only for instance — as opposed to class — methods.)
If the method takes no arguments, the method name is just `init`. If it takes
arguments, labels for the arguments follow the "init" prefix. For example, you
have been initializing `NSMutableArrays` with the `initWithCapacity:`
method. As you can see, the initializer has to have a return type of `id`. You'll
discover the reason for that later in the section "Invoking the superclass's init
method."

```
  if (self = [super initWithAmount:theAmount
                            forBudget:aBudget]) {
```

I've named my new initializer `initWithAmount:` plus another argument
(`forBudget`) that completely describes what I am going to initialize. It
should be no surprise that both of these are initialized in the `create
Transaction::` method you have been using to initialize a transaction.

Initialization involves these three steps:

1. Invoke the superclass's `init` method.

2. Initialize instance variables.

3. Return `self`.

The following sections explain each step.

Invoking the superclass's init method

This is the general form you use:

```
(self = [super initWithAmount:theAmount
                              forBudget:aBudget])
```

If you are having a little problem figuring this out, you might like to know that it took me more than a few minutes to get my arms around this statement, so don't feel badly. Fortunately, I do understand it now, and I'll explain it to you very slowly (which is what I wish someone had done for me).

I'll start with the easy part of the compound statement, where all I'm doing is invoking the superclass's `init` method.

```
[super initWithAmount:theAmount forBudget:aBudget]
```

In Chapter 10, you see that this is how you send a message to your superclass.

In Chapter 10, you also see that you can use `self` to send a message to your superclass, and I also say that `self` and `super` are not always interchangeable. In this case, you need to be careful to use `super` because the method sending the message has the same name as the method you want to invoke in your superclass. If you were to use `self` here, you would just send a message to yourself, the `initWithAmount::` method in `CashTransaction`, which would turn around and send the same message to itself again, which then would then send the same message to itself again, which would then....You get the picture. Fortunately, the OS will put up with this for only a limited amount of time before it gets really annoyed and terminates the program.

Notice that the superclass's initialization method is always invoked before the subclass does any initialization. Your superclass is equally as respectful of its superclass and does the same thing; and up, up, and away you go from superclass to superclass until you reach `NSObject`'s `init` method. `NSObject`'s `init` method doesn't do anything; it just returns `self`. It's there to establish the naming convention described earlier, and all it does is return back to its invoker, which does its thing and then returns back to its invoker, until it gets back to you.

In this case, the `CashTransaction`'s superclass is `Transaction`, and you invoke its initialization method `initWithAmount::`. As you can see in Listing 12-2, `Transaction` invokes its superclass's `init` method as well. But in this case, it simply calls `init` (as per convention) since its superclass is `NSObject`.

Listing 12-2:   Transaction initializer

```
- (id) initWithAmount: (double) theAmount forBudget:
          (Budget*) aBudget {

  if (self = [super init]) {

    budget = aBudget;
```

```
        amount = theAmount;
    }
  return self;
}
```

Next, examine this unusual-looking statement:

```
if (self = [super initWithAmount:theAmount
           forBudget:aBudget]) {
```

Ignore the `if` for the moment (I promise I'll get back to it). What you are doing is assigning what you got back from your superclass's `init` method to `self`. As you remember, `self` is the "hidden" variable accessible to methods in an object that points to its instance variables (if you're unclear on this, refer to the discussion in Chapter 6). So it would seem that `self` should be whatever you got back from your allocation step. Well, yes and no. Most of the time, the answer is yes; but sometimes the answer is no, which may or may not be a big deal. So, examine the possibilities.

When you invoke a superclass's initialization method, one of three things can happen.

- ✔ **You get back the object you expect.** Most of the time, this is precisely what happens, and you go on your merry way. This will be true all the time for the classes you are working on in this part of the book — those where you have control over the entire hierarchy — such as the `Transaction` class you are working on now.

- ✔ **You get back a different object type.** Getting back a different object type is something that can happen with some of the framework classes, but it's not an issue here. Even when it happens, if you are playing by the rules (a good idea if you're not the one who gets to make them), you don't even care.

  Why, you might ask? Well, some of the framework classes such as `NSString` are really class clusters. When you create an object of one of these classes, its initialization method looks at the arguments you are passing and returns back the object it thinks you need (big brotherish to say the least, but effective nonetheless). Anything more about getting back different object types is way beyond the scope of this book.

  But as I said, if you follow the rules, not only will you not notice getting back a different object type, but you won't care. It is in these cases that the compound statement format I've been showing you is important.

```
SomeClass *aPointerToSomeClass =
                    [[SomeClass alloc] init];
```

If you had done the following

```
SomeClass *aPointerToSomeClass = [SomeClass alloc]
[aPointerToSomeClass init];
```

`init` could return a different pointer, which you haven't assigned to `aPointerToSomeClass`. If you then send that object a message, you are in for a big surprise. This is also why the return type for an initializer needs to be `id` (a pointer to an object) and not the specific class you are dealing with.

✔ **You get `nil` back.**

One possibility, of course, is that you simply run out of memory or some catastrophe befalls the system, in which case, you are in deep trouble. While there are some things you might be able to do, they aren't for the faint-hearted or beginners, so I'll skip them for now.

But there also may be times when returning `nil` is an acceptable response to an attempt to instantiate an object, and you should be prepared to deal with it. This, too, is beyond the scope of this book.

Getting back `nil` actually explains the statement that seems so puzzling.

```
if (self = [super initWithAmount:theAmount forBudget:
        aBudget]) {
```

When `nil` is retuned, two things happen here. `self` is *assigned* to `nil`, which as a side effect causes the `if` statement to be evaluated as `NO`. As a result, the code block that contains the statements you would have used to initialize your subclass are never executed.

Initializing instance variables

Initializing instance variables, including creating the objects you need, is what you probably thought initialization is about. Notice that you are initializing your instance variable after your superclass's initialization, which you can see in Listings 12-1 and 12-2. Waiting until after your superclass does its initialization gives you the opportunity to actually change something your superclass may have in initialization, but more importantly, it allows you to perform initialization knowing that what you have inherited is initialized and ready to be used.

In the `CashTransaction initWithAmount::` initializer, all that is done is the initialization of the `name` instance variable of the superclass (`Transaction`) with the kind of transaction it is.

```
name = @"Cash";
```

Returning back self

In the section, "Invoking the superclass's `init` variable," the `self` = statement ensures that `self` is set to whatever object I get back from the superclass initializer. After the code block that initializes the variables, you find

```
return self;
```

No matter what you get back from invoking the superclass initializer, in the initialization method, you need to set `self` to that value and then return it to the invoking method. That could be a method that wants to instantiate the object or a subclass of that invoked the `init` method (the `init` method being its superclass's `init` method).

When you are instantiating a new object, it behooves you to determine whether a return of `nil` is a nonfatal response to your request (and, if so, coding for it). In this book, the answer will always be no, and that will generally be the case with framework objects as well. In this example

```
theBudget = [[Budget alloc] initWithAmount:budgetAmount
            withExchangeRate:theExchangeRate];
```

getting `nil` back would be more than my poor app could handle and would signal that I am in very deep trouble.

Listings 12-3 through 12-13 show the modifications you need to make in order to finally implement initializers in the conventional way. You'll be deleting the initializers you had been using and creating the correct `init...` structure that will enable you to more easily initialize new instance variables you may add to existing classes, as well ensure that you can do initialization correctly when you add new superclasses or subclasses.

If you have been following along with me, I'll be extending what you do in Chapter 11. If you would like to start from a clean copy of the project from where you left off, you can use the project found in the Chapter 12 Start Here folder, which is in the Chapter 12 folder.

1. Since the changes you'll need to make are quite specific, I'll just indicate what needs to be deleted with strikethrough and what needs to be added in bold in each file in Listings 12-3 through 12-10. (Be sure to note the new **name** instance variable in Transaction.h.)

Listing 12-3:   Budget.h

```
//- (void) createBudget: (double) aBudget
              withExchangeRate: (float) anExchangeRate;
- (id) initWithAmount: (double) aBudget
            withExchangeRate: (double) anExchangeRate ;
```

Listing 12-4:   Budget.m

```
//- (void) createBudget: (double) aBudget
              withExchangeRate: (float) anExchangeRate{
//  exchangeRate = anExchangeRate;
//  budget = aBudget;
//}
- (id) initWithAmount: (double) aBudget
            withExchangeRate: (double) anExchangeRate {

  if (self = [super init]) {
    exchangeRate = anExchangeRate;
    budget = aBudget;
  }
  return self;
```

Listing 12-5:   Transaction.h

```
NSString *name;

//- void) createTransaction: (double) theAmount
                          forBudget: (Budget*) aBudget;
- (id) initWithAmount: (double) theAmount
                    forBudget: (Budget*) aBudget;
```

Listing 12-6:   Transaction.m

```
//- (void) createTransaction: (double) theAmount
          forBudget: (Budget*) aBudget {
//  budget = aBudget;
//  amount = theAmount;
//}

- (id) initWithAmount: (double) theAmount
                    forBudget: (Budget*) aBudget {

  if (self = [super init]) {

    budget = aBudget;
    amount = theAmount;
```

```
    }
    return self;
}
```

Listing 12-7: CashTransaction.h

```
- (id) initWithAmount: (double) theAmount
                      forBudget: (Budget*) aBudget;
```

Listing 12-8: CashTransaction.m

```
- (id) initWithAmount: (double) theAmount
                      forBudget: (Budget*) aBudget {

  if (self = [super initWithAmount:theAmount
                         forBudget:aBudget]) {
    name = @"Cash";
  }
  return self;
}
```

Listing 12-9: CreditCardTransaction.h

```
- (id) initWithAmount: (double) theAmount
                      forBudget: (Budget*) aBudget;
```

Listing 12-10: CreditCardTransaction.m

```
- (id) initWithAmount: (double) theAmount
                      forBudget: (Budget*) aBudget {

  if (self = [super initWithAmount:theAmount
                         forBudget:aBudget]) {
    name = @"Credit card";
  }
  return self;
}
```

2. Since the changes to the Destination class and main are a bit more involved, I've included all of the code in Listings 12-11 through 12-13.

Listing 12-11:   Destination.h

```
#import <Cocoa/Cocoa.h>
@class Budget;

@interface Destination : NSObject {

  NSString       *country;
  double          exchangeRate;
  NSMutableArray *transactions;
  Budget         *theBudget;

}
//(void) createWithCountry: (NSString*) theCountry
         andBudget: (double) budgetAmount
         withExchangeRate: (double) theExchangeRate;
- (id) initWithCountry: (NSString*) theCountry
         andBudget: (double) budgetAmount
         withExchangeRate:(double) theExchangeRate;
- (void) spendCash: (double) aTransaction;
- (void) chargeCreditCard:(double) aTransaction;
- (double) leftToSpend;

@end
```

Listing 12-12:   Destination.m

```
#import "Destination.h"
#import "CashTransaction.h"
#import "CreditCardTransaction.h"
#import "Budget.h"
#import "Transaction.h"
@implementation Destination

//- (void) createWithCountry: (NSString*) theCountry
         andBudget: (double) budgetAmount
         withExchangeRate: (double) theExchangeRate{

//  transactions = [[NSMutableArray alloc]
         initWithCapacity:10];
//  theBudget = [Budget new];
//  [theBudget  createBudget:budgetAmount withExchange
         Rate:theExchangeRate];
//  exchangeRate = theExchangeRate;
//  country = theCountry;
//  NSLog (@"I'm off to %@", theCountry);
```

```
//}

- (id) initWithCountry: (NSString*) theCountry andBudget:
           (double) budgetAmount withExchangeRate:
           (double) theExchangeRate{
  if (self = [super init]) {
    transactions = [[NSMutableArray alloc]
           initWithCapacity:10];
    theBudget = [[Budget alloc]
           initWithAmount:budgetAmount withExchangeRate:
           theExchangeRate];
    country = theCountry;
    NSLog (@"I'm off to %@", theCountry);
  }

  return self;
}


-(void) spendCash:(double)amount{

//Transaction *aTransaction = [CashTransaction new];
//aTransaction createTransaction:amount
                                  forBudget:theBudget];
  Transaction *aTransaction = [[CashTransaction alloc]
           initWithAmount:amount forBudget:theBudget];
  [transactions addObject:aTransaction];
  [aTransaction spend];
}

-(void) chargeCreditCard: (double) amount{

//Transaction *aTransaction = [CreditCardTransaction
           new];
//[aTransaction createTransaction:amount
                                  forBudget:theBudget];
  Transaction *aTransaction =
           [[CreditCardTransaction alloc]
           initWithAmount:amount forBudget:theBudget];
  [transactions addObject:aTransaction];
  [aTransaction spend];
}

- (double ) leftToSpend {

  return [theBudget returnBalance];
}

@end
```

Listing 12-13:   main in Vacation.m

```
#import <Foundation/Foundation.h>
#import "Destination.h"

int main (int argc, const char * argv[]) {

//Destination* europe = [Destination new] ;
  NSString* europeText = [[NSString alloc]
        initWithFormat:@"%@", @"Europe"];
//[europe createWithCountry:europeText andBudget:1000.00
        withExchangeRate:1.25];
  Destination* europe = [[Destination alloc]
        initWithCountry:europeText andBudget:1000.00
        withExchangeRate:1.25];
//Destination* england = [Destination new] ;
  NSString* englandText = [[NSString alloc]
                    initWithFormat:@"%@", @"England"];
//[england createWithCountry:englandText andBudget:2000.00
        withExchangeRate:1.50];
  Destination* england = [[Destination alloc]
        initWithCountry:englandText andBudget:2000.00
        withExchangeRate:1.50];

  for (int n = 1; n < 2; n++) {
    double transaction = n*100.00;
    NSLog (@"Sending a %.2f cash transaction",
        transaction);
    [europe spendCash:transaction];
    NSLog(@"Remaining budget %.2f", [europe leftToSpend]);
    NSLog (@"Sending a %.2f cash transaction",
        transaction);
    [england spendCash:transaction];
    NSLog(@"Remaining budget %.2f", [england
        leftToSpend]);
  }

  int n = 1;
  while (n < 4) {
    double transaction = n*100.00;
    NSLog(@"Sending a %.2f credit card transaction",
        transaction);
    [europe chargeCreditCard:transaction];
    NSLog(@"Remaining budget %.2f", [europe leftToSpend]);
    NSLog(@"Sending a %.2f credit card transaction",
        transaction);
    [england chargeCreditCard:transaction];
    NSLog(@"Remaining budget %.2f", [england
        leftToSpend]);
    n++;
  }
  return 0;
}
```

3. **To make sure this worked, select the Build and Run button in the Project Window toolbar to build and run the application.**

   You should see the following in the Debugger Console. This output should be identical to the output in the previous example:

```
I'm off to Europe
I'm off to England
Sending a 100.00 cash transaction
Remaining budget 900.00
Sending a 100.00 cash transaction
Remaining budget 1900.00
Sending a 100.00 credit card transaction
Remaining budget 775.00
Sending a 100.00 credit card transaction
Remaining budget 1750.00
Sending a 200.00 credit card transaction
Remaining budget 525.00
Sending a 200.00 credit card transaction
Remaining budget 1450.00
Sending a 300.00 credit card transaction
Remaining budget 150.00
Sending a 300.00 credit card transaction
Remaining budget 1000.00
```

The Designated Initializer

It is possible to have more than one initializer per class. Once you have more than one initializer in a class, according to Cocoa convention, you are expected to designate one as the *designated initializer*. This designated initializer is usually the one that does the most initialization, and it *is the one responsible for invoking the superclass's initializer*. Since this initializer is the one that does the most work, again by convention, the other initializers are expected to invoke it with appropriate default values as needed.

While at some point you will need to explore this topic further, it is really a framework and therefore beyond the scope of this book.

Chapter 13

Getting a Handle on Memory Management

*I*n Chapter 12, I explain about object allocation and initialization. You start with alloc and init. It is alloc, if you remember, that sets aside some memory for the object and returns back a *pointer* to that memory. This is important to keep in mind, because once you create these new objects, you become responsible for managing them.

Managing the memory allocated for your objects can be one of the few real hassles in programming with Objective-C. And although a new feature in Objective-C 2.0, *garbage collection*, makes Mac OS X programming easier, it isn't available on the iPhone. But a word to the wise: Even if you want to program the Mac using only Objective-C 2.0 and garbage collection, read through this chapter anyway because it really will help solidify your understanding of pointers and objects and what gets passed when you include objects as arguments in messages.

Memory management is not glamorous, but it trumps cool in an application. In fact, memory management is probably the single most vexing thing about iPhone and Mac programming. It has made countless programmers crazy, and I can't stress enough how important it is to build memory management into your code from the start. Take it from me, retrofitting can be a nightmare, and I still have dreams where "Hell" is having to go back through an infinite number of lines of code and retrofit memory management code.

Raising and Terminating Responsible Objects

What with everything else going on, managing memory can be a real challenge not only to someone new to programming, but also to those of us with many lines of code under our belts. Allocating memory when you need it isn't that hard. It is realizing you don't need an object anymore and then releasing the memory back to the operating system that can be a challenge. If you don't do that, and your program runs long enough, eventually you run out of memory (sooner on an iPhone than a Mac for a variety of reasons — see the upcoming sidebar, "The iPhone challenge") and your program will come crashing down. Long before that you may even notice system performance approaching "molasses in February — outdoors in Hibbing, Minnesota." Oh, and by the way, if you do free an object (memory) and that object is still being used, you have "London Bridge Is Falling Down" as well. Now, if you've created a giant application and run out of memory while all the objects you created are being used, that's one issue, and one I'm not going to deal with here. But if you run out of memory because you have all these objects floating around that no one is using, that's another thing, and it's known as a *memory leak*.

But memory management isn't really that hard, if you understand how it all works, which also isn't that hard if you pay attention to it. In addition, Xcode can help you track down memory problems. I show you how to use it in the section "Running the Static Analyzer," later in this chapter. The problem is that sometimes in the rush to develop an application and see things happen on the screen, programmers ignore memory management and plan to come back later to do it right. Trust me on this one (I speak from personal experience), this is not a strategy that leads to happy and healthy applications or application developers.

Understanding the object life cycle

In the previous chapter, you found out how to allocate and initialize objects using a combination of `alloc` and `init`. Many objects you allocate stay around for the duration of your program, and for those objects, all you have to do is, well, nothing really. When your program terminates, they are deallocated, and the memory is returned to the operating system.

But some objects you use for a while get your money's worth, and then you're done with them. When you are done with them, you should return the memory allocated to them back to the OS so it can allocate that memory for new objects. This is the scenario that can cause problems.

The iPhone challenge

While the iPhone OS and the Mac both use what is known as virtual memory, unlike the Mac, virtual memory in the iPhone is limited to the actual amount of physical memory. This is because when it begins to run low on memory, the iPhone OS frees up memory pages that contain read-only content (such as code), where all it has to do is load the "originals" back into memory when they're needed. It doesn't, like the Mac, temporarily store "changeable" memory (such as object data) to the disk to free up space and then read the data back later when it's needed. This state of affairs limits the amount of memory available.

Start by looking at how memory management works.

In Objective-C 2.0 (as opposed to earlier versions), you can manage memory two ways:

✔ **Reference counting:** You are the one responsible for doing your part in keeping the system up to date on whether an object is currently being used.

✔ **Garbage collection:** The operating system takes all the responsibility and does all the work.

First, turn your attention to reference counting.

Using reference counting

In many ways, Objective-C is like the coolest guy in your school, who now makes a seven-figure income bungee jumping and skateboarding during the summers, while snowboarding around the world in the winter.

In other ways, though, Objective-C is like the nerd in your class, who grew up to be an accountant and reads the *Financial Times* for fun. Memory management falls into this category.

In fact, memory management is simply an exercise in counting. To manage its memory, Objective-C (actually Cocoa) uses a technique known as *reference counting*. Every object has its own reference count, or *retain count*. When an object is created via `alloc` or `new` — or through a `copy` message, which creates a copy of an object, but has some subtleties beyond the scope of this book — the object's retain count is set to 1. As long as the retain count is greater than zero, the memory manager assumes that someone cares about that object and leaves it alone. It is your responsibility to maintain that reference count by directly or indirectly increasing the retain count when you are using an object, and then decreasing it when you are finished with it. When the retain count goes to zero, Cocoa assumes that no one needs it anymore. Cocoa automatically sends the object a `dealloc` message, and after that its memory is returned to the system to be reused. As part of your responsibility for memory management, you may need to override `dealloc` to release any related resources the object being deallocated might have allocated.

Never invoke `dealloc` directly — Cocoa sends the `dealloc` message to your object at the right time.

Take a look at an example now. In Vacation.m, you create a string object and then pass that as an argument into the `init` method when you create the `destination` object, as shown here:

```
NSString* englandText = [[NSString alloc]
                    initWithFormat:@"%@", @"England"];
Destination* england = [[Destination alloc]
        initWithCountry:englandText andBudget:2000.00
        withExchangeRate:1.50];
```

I explain why I need to create the `englandText` using `alloc` and `init` later in this section as I promise to do in Chapter 11.

The `Destination` object remains around until the program is terminated. At that point, everything gets deallocated, so there is really no problem and no real (although some potential) memory management issues.

But what happens if I decide sometime along the way on my trip not to go to England after all. I really have always wanted to go to Antarctica, and an opportunity to hitch a ride on a rock star's private jet presents itself, so bye-bye England, and hello Ushuaia, Tierra del Fuego, Argentina.

Before I take off, however, I want to do one thing, besides send for my long underwear, which I left safely packed away at a friend's house in Minneapolis. I need to delete England as a destination, freeing up that budget money, and create a new destination — Antarctica.

As I said earlier, when you are doing memory management, it is your responsibility to keep Cocoa informed about your use of objects, so if you don't need an object any longer, you send it a release message.

```
[england release];
```

`release` does not deallocate the object!

Let me say that again — `release` does not deallocate the object!

All `release` does is decrement the retain count by 1. This is very important to keep in mind because while one method or object in your application may no longer need an object, it still may be needed by another method or object in your program. That's why you don't `dealloc` it yourself, trusting Cocoa to manage the retain count for you. But it is your job (and I repeat myself a lot here to make sure you understand this) to keep Cocoa informed of your object by using the `release` message.

Well that's cool, and being a good citizen, the `england` object wants to release all of its objects in its `dealloc` method. No problem here, one would think. `Destination` has instance variables pointing to the objects it uses:

```
NSString* country;
double exchangeRate;
NSMutableArray *transactions;
Budget* theBudget;
```

So in the `dealloc` method that is invoked before the `Destination` object is deallocated by the OS, those other objects can be released.

```
- (void) dealloc {

  [transactions release];
  [country release];
  [theBudget release];
  [super dealloc];
}
```

While you don't have to release the `exchangeRate` because it is not an object, do you really want to release all those other objects? What if there are other objects in your program that still need to use those objects? Actually, taking that into account is very easy, as long as you follow the rules.

As I said earlier, when you create an object using `alloc` or `new`, or through a `copy` message, the object's retain count is set to 1. So you are cool. In fact, whenever you create an object like that, your solemn responsibility is to release it when you are done. There is a flip side to this coin, however; if you are using an object, a pointer to it is sent to you as an argument in a message, as is the case for the `NSString` object in the following:

```
Destination* england = [[Destination alloc]
          initWithCountry:englandText andBudget:2000.00
          withExchangeRate:1.50];
```

Then it is also your responsibility to increment the retain count by sending it the `retain` message, as you can see in the implementation of the `init WithCountry:::` method:

```
- (id) initWithCountry: (NSString*) theCountry andBudget:
            (double) budgetAmount withExchangeRate:
            (double) theExchangeRate{
  if (self = [super init]) {
    transactions = [[NSMutableArray alloc]
                                    initWithCapacity:10];
    theBudget = [[Budget alloc]
                      initWithAmount:budgetAmount
                      withExchangeRate:theExchangeRate];
    exchangeRate = theExchangeRate;
    country = theCountry;
    [country retain];
  }
  return self;
}
```

In this method, the `Destination` object creates two objects on its own, `theBudget` and `transactions`. As a result, the retain count for each is set to 1. It also gets passed a pointer to an `NSString` object that was created at another time and place. If `Destination` plans to use that object, it needs to send it the `retain` message. That way, the retain count is increased by 1. If the creator of that object decides it no longer needs the object and sends it the `release` message, the retain count is decremented by 1. But because the `Destination` object sent it a `retain` message, the release count is still greater than 0 — the object lives!

In fact, that is exactly what happens. In `main`, after the object is created and sent as an argument to the `Destination` objects, the good little code releases the object because it really has no need for the object. When you do release an object in your code, you are counting on the fact that other objects are playing according to the rules, and the receiving object increases the retain count if it needs to continue to use an object you created. This frees the creator of an object from the responsibility of having to know anything about who is using an object it has created and worrying about when it has to free it.

In the code in `main`, the string object sent in the `initWithCountry:::` message is released after the message is sent, since the code in `main` has no further use for the string object it created.

```
NSString* englandText = [[NSString alloc]
        initWithFormat:@"%@", @"England"];
Destination* england = [[Destination alloc]
        initWithCountry:englandText andBudget:2000.00
        withExchangeRate:1.50];
[englandText release];
```

`europeText` is released as well. All's right with the world.

What really does confuse some developers is the concept of `retain` and `release`. They worry that releasing an object will deallocate that object. (Note that all `release` does is tell the memory manager that you are no longer interested in it. The memory manager is the one that makes the life-and-death decision.) New developers sometimes worry that as a creator they have to be concerned about others using their objects. In reality, it is your job to simply follow the memory management rules.

Here's the fundamental rule of memory management:

> You are responsible for releasing any object that you create using a method whose name begins with `alloc` or `new` or contains `copy`, or if you send it a `retain` message. You can do that by sending it a `release` or `autorelease` message (which I explain shortly). In Applespeak, if you do any of these things, you are said to *own* the object (objects are allowed to have more than one owner — talk about how to use terminology to really make things confusing).

That's it, with corollaries of course.

> If you want to continue to use an object outside the method it was received in, save a pointer to it as an instance variable, as you just did with the `NSString` object. Then you must send the object the `retain` message. In Applespeak, that means you are now an owner of the object.

In general, somewhere in your code there should be a `release` for every statement that creates an object using `alloc` or `new`, or contains `copy` or sends a `retain` message.

I'd like to explain now why I have you create a string object in the Chapter 11 section "Coding the New main" when you initialize a `Destination` object. I could have had you code it this way:

```
Destination* england = [[Destination alloc]
        initWithCountry:@"England" andBudget:2000.00
        withExchangeRate:1.50];
```

If you had done so, the compiler would have created a string constant that existed for the life of the program. In this case, sending it a `retain` or `release` message has no impact (try it yourself). If there are only a couple of these string constants, the impact is insignificant, but a lot of them could have an impact on your memory footprint — although creating and then deallocating lots of small objects has its own cost in CPU use as well.

Running the Static Analyzer

Until the release of Xcode 3.2, you had to track down memory leaks by using the Instruments application (which I cover in the book, *iPhone Application Development For Dummies*).

But as I mention in Chapter 8, Xcode has a new Build and Analyze feature (the Static Analyzer) that analyzes your code. It is especially good at detecting certain kinds of memory leaks — especially ones where you create an object and then pass it to another object, and then forget to release it.

Now try running the Static Analyzer on your project as it's developed so far.

The results show up like warnings and errors, with explanations of where and what the issue is. You can also see the flow of control of the (potential) problem. I say *potential* because the Static Analyzer can give you false positives.

In this section, I extend what you do in Chapter 12. If you would like to start from a clean copy of the project from where you left off, you can use the project found in the Chapter 13 Start Here folder, which is in the Chapter 13 folder.

1. **Chose Build and Analyze from the Build menu (Build⇨Build and Analyze).**

   I'm also going to turn on line numbers in the text Editing section of Xcode preferences.

   You see four potential memory leaks in the Build Results window (see Figure 13-1), two in Vacation.m and two in Destination.m.

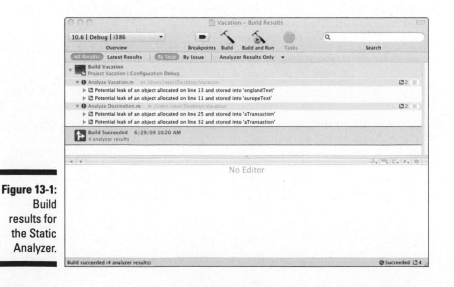

Figure 13-1: Build results for the Static Analyzer.

You can also see this in the Editor as well in Figure 13-2. You can work in either the Project Window, or the Build Results window, but I am going to work in the Project Window (see Figure 13-2).

Figure 13-2:
The Static Analyzer results in the Project Window.

2. **Click the first error message (right after Line 13), and in Figure 13-3 you see how you got into this predicament.**

   Figure 13-3 shows you that the object you created on Line 11, europe Text, is no longer referenced after Line 12, when you use it as an argument in initWithCountry::. It still has a retain count of 1, so even if all the other objects that use it do release it, it continues to take up precious memory, even though it isn't being used in main, because it hasn't been released.

3. **Open the Destination.m file.**

   When you look at Destination.m, you see the same sorry story. Figure 13-4 warns you of a potential leak.

4. **Click the error message on Line 28, and in Figure 13-5 you see the scenario.**

   Figure 13-5 shows you that the Transaction object you created on Line 25 is never referenced after you send it the spend: message and add it to the transactions array.

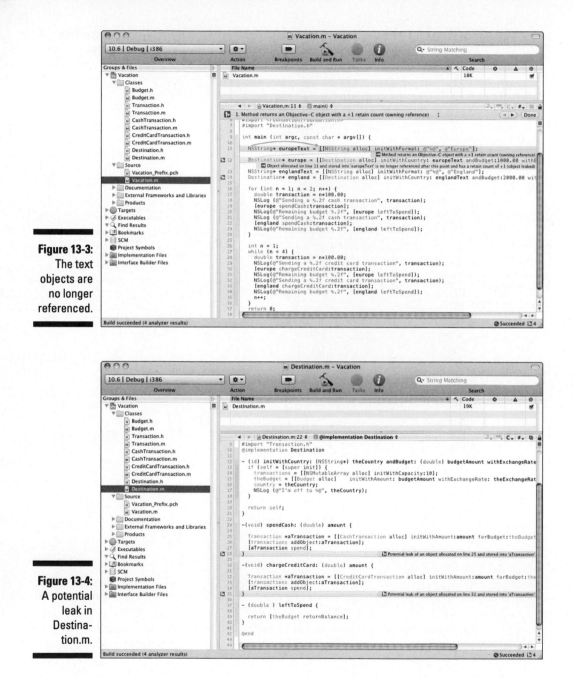

Figure 13-3:
The text objects are no longer referenced.

Figure 13-4:
A potential leak in Destina-tion.m.

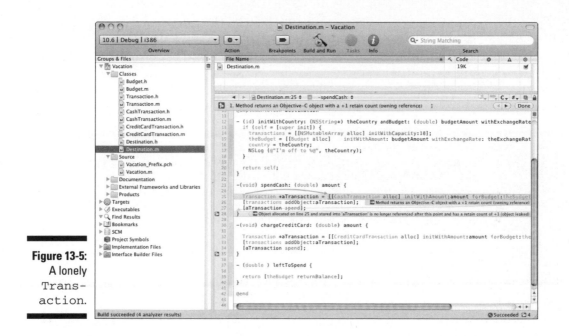

Figure 13-5:
A lonely
Trans-
action.

Plugging the Leaks

Now it's time to add responsible memory management to your program.

To fix the problems discovered by the Static Analyzer, you need to release `aTransaction` in the `spendCash:` and `chargeCreditCard:` methods in Destination.m (see Listing 13-5). You also need to release `europeText` and `englandText` in `main` (see Listing 13-6).

While the Static Analyzer is a giant step forward, it can't catch everything. You still need to be methodical about releasing objects on which you've increased the retain count in the `Transaction` and `Destination` objects' `dellaoc` methods.

Two comments about the `dealloc` methods. First, as you can see, you need to send your superclass a `dealloc` message after you release the objects that you need to release in the subclass. Remember, the object that creates an object or retains it needs to release the object, so you may find yourself releasing the same object in both a subclass's and a superclass's `dealloc` method. That's fine, as long as the object was created or retained by the class that releases it.

I also added `dealloc` methods for those classes that (presently) do not have any objects they need to release when they are deallocated. I do that to keep you focused on how important it is to release objects. In fact, in the file templates that you use for iPhone classes, when you create a new class file that's derived from anything other than `NSObject`, the template has a default `dealloc` method that just invokes its superclass's `dealloc` method.

One final point: If you have a `dealloc` method that does release objects, when its superclass is `NSObject`, you really don't need to invoke it from `dealloc`. It is, however, not a bad habit to always invoke your superclass's `dealloc` method. This keeps you from getting into trouble when you factor your code. You may find yourself creating a new superclass for a class that previously was based on `NSObject`, and always invoking its superclass's `dealloc` method keeps you from having to remember to add the code to invoke it in your (now) subclass's `dealloc` method.

In this section, I expand on Chapter 12. If you want to start from a clean copy of the project from where you left off, you can use the project found in the Chapter 13 Start Here folder, which is in the Chapter 13 folder.

Add the code shown in bold in Listings 13-1 through 13-6 to the appropriate files in your program.

Listing 13-1:   Budget.m

```
#import "Budget.h"

@implementation Budget

- (id) initWithAmount: (double) aBudget withExchangeRate:
        (double) anExchangeRate {

  if (self = [super init]) {
    exchangeRate = anExchangeRate;
    budget = aBudget;
  }
  return self;
}

- (void) spendDollars: (double) dollars {

  budget -= dollars;
}

- (void) chargeForeignCurrency: (double) foreignCurrency {
  transaction = foreignCurrency*exchangeRate;
```

```
   budget -= transaction;
}

- (double) returnBalance {

   return budget;
}

- (void) dealloc {

   [super dealloc];
}

@end
```

Listing 13-2:   Transaction.m

```
#import "Transaction.h"
#import "Budget.h"

@implementation Transaction

- (void) spend {

}

- (id) initWithAmount: (double) theAmount forBudget:
         (Budget*) aBudget {
  if (self = [super init]) {
    budget = aBudget;
    [budget retain];
    amount = theAmount;
  }
   return self;
}

- (void) dealloc {

   [budget release];
   [super dealloc];
}

@end
```

Listing 13-3:   CashTransaction.m

```objc
#import "CashTransaction.h"
#import "Budget.h"

@implementation CashTransaction

- (id) initWithAmount: (double) theAmount forBudget:
          (Budget*) aBudget  {

  if (self = [super initWithAmount:theAmount
          forBudget:aBudget]) {
    name = @"Cash";
  }
  return self;
}

- (void) spend {
  [budget spendDollars:amount];
}

- (void) dealloc {

  [super dealloc];
}

@end
```

Listing 13-4:   CreditCardTransaction.m

```objc
#import "CreditCardTransaction.h"
#import "Budget.h"

@implementation CreditCardTransaction

- (id) initWithAmount: (double) theAmount forBudget:
          (Budget*) aBudget {

  if (self = [super initWithAmount: theAmount forBudget:
          aBudget]) {
    name = @"Credit Card";
  }
    return self;
}

- (void) spend {

  [budget chargeForeignCurrency:amount];
```

```
}

- (void) dealloc {

  [super dealloc];
}

@end
```

Listing 13-5:   Destination.m

```
#import "Destination.h"
#import "CashTransaction.h"
#import "CreditCardTransaction.h"
#import "Budget.h"
#import "Transaction.h"

@implementation Destination

- (id) initWithCountry: (NSString*) theCountry andBudget:
          (double) budgetAmount withExchangeRate:
          (double) theExchangeRate{
  if (self = [super init]) {
    transactions = [[NSMutableArray alloc]
          initWithCapacity:10];
    theBudget = [[Budget alloc]
          initWithAmount:budgetAmount withExchangeRate:
          theExchangeRate];
    exchangeRate = theExchangeRate;
    country = theCountry;
    [country retain];
    NSLog(@"I'm off to %@", theCountry);
  }
  return self;
}

- (void) updateExchangeRate: (double) newExchangeRate {

exchangeRate = newExchangeRate;
}

- (void) spendCash: (double)amount {

Transaction *aTransaction = [[CashTransaction alloc]
          initWithAmount:amount forBudget:theBudget ];
[transactions addObject:aTransaction];
[aTransaction spend];
```

(continued)

Listing 13-5 *(continued)*

```
[aTransaction release];

}

- (void) chargeCreditCard: (double) amount {

Transaction *aTransaction = [[CreditCardTransaction alloc]
        initWithAmount:amount forBudget:theBudget ];
[transactions addObject:aTransaction];
[aTransaction spend];
[aTransaction release];
}


- (double ) leftToSpend {

return   [theBudget returnBalance];
}

- (void) dealloc {

[transactions release];
[theBudget release];
[country release];
[super dealloc];
}

@end
```

Listing 13-6: main in Vacation.m

```
#import <Foundation/Foundation.h>
#import "Destination.h"

int main (int argc, const char * argv[]) {

  NSString* europeText = [[NSString alloc]
        initWithFormat:@"%@", @"Europe"];
  Destination* europe = [[Destination alloc]
        initWithCountry:europeText andBudget:1000.00
        withExchangeRate:1.25];
  [europeText release];
  NSString* englandText = [[NSString alloc]
        initWithFormat:@"%@", @"England"];
  Destination* england = [[Destination alloc]
        initWithCountry:englandText andBudget:2000.00
        withExchangeRate:1.50];
```

```
[englandText release];

for (int n = 1; n <  2; n++) {
  double transaction = n*100.00;
  NSLog (@"Sending a %.2f cash transaction",
         transaction);
  [europe spendCash:transaction];

  NSLog(@"Remaining budget %.2f", [europe leftToSpend]);
  NSLog(@"Sending a %.2f cash transaction",
         transaction);
  [england spendCash:transaction];
  NSLog(@"Remaining budget %.2f", [england
         leftToSpend]);
}

int n = 1;
while (n < 4) {
  double transaction = n*100.00;
  NSLog (@"Sending a %.2f credit card transaction",
         transaction);
  [europe chargeCreditCard:transaction];
  NSLog(@"Remaining budget %.2f", [europe leftToSpend]);
  NSLog (@"Sending a %.2f credit card transaction",
         transaction);
  [england chargeCreditCard:transaction];
  NSLog(@"Remaining budget %.2f", [england
         leftToSpend]);
  n++;
}

[england release];

return 0;
}
```

Notice that in the Destination methods cashTransaction: and CreditCardTransaction:, you release the Transaction object when you're done with it. The upcoming section "Considering objects in arrays" explains why that is safe, even though you've added it to the array.

To make sure these changes worked, select the Build and Run button in the Project Window toolbar to build and run the application.

You should see the following in the Debugger Console:

```
I'm off to Europe
I'm off to England
Sending a 100.00 cash transaction
```

```
Remaining budget 900.00
Sending a 100.00 cash transaction
Remaining budget 1900.00
Sending a 100.00 credit card transaction
Remaining budget 775.00
Sending a 100.00 credit card transaction
Remaining budget 1750.00
Sending a 200.00 credit card transaction
Remaining budget 525.00
Sending a 200.00 credit card transaction
Remaining budget 1450.00
Sending a 300.00 credit card transaction
Remaining budget 150.00
Sending a 300.00 credit card transaction
Remaining budget 1000.00
```

The most important result of this example is that the program still functions in the same way as it did before you made the changes, which underlies why it's so easy to postpone doing memory management until you need it. But while it doesn't seem to add any (observable) functionality early on, correctly managing memory saves you many hours of anguish later when your program expands to the point where memory becomes an issue, which (too) often happens much sooner that you might expect.

If you want to trace the deallocation process, put an NSLog statement in your dealloc method to see when objects are being deallocated. You can also send an object the retainCount message to find out its current retain count (it returns an unsigned int).

Attending to Memory Management Subtleties — Arrays and Autorelease

While memory management is generally straightforward, there are a few subtleties that may not be so obvious — only a few mind you, but they are important.

✔ Objects in arrays

✔ Autorelease and the autorelease pool

Considering objects in arrays

Look at the `dealloc` method in `Destination.m`:

```
- (void) dealloc {

  [transactions release];
  [theBudget release];
  [country release];
  [super dealloc];
}
```

Notice you release the `transactions` array. What happens to all the objects you added to it? As you might expect, the rules are that if you want to use an object, you must send it a `retain` message, and if you do, then you must `release` it. The array follows those rules, and when you add an object to an array, the array object sends the object that was just added a retain `message`. When the array is deallocated, it sends `release` messages to all its objects. If you want to use the object after the array is deallocated, you need to send it (or have sent it) a `retain` message before the array is deallocated.

In addition, if you remove an object from a mutable array, which is the only kind that you can add and remove objects from (refer to Chapter 7 for more on this topic), the object that has been removed receives a `release` message. So, if an array is the only owner of an object, then (by standard rules of memory management) the object is deallocated when it is removed. If you want to use the object after its removal, you need to send it a `retain` message *before* you remove it from the array.

Understanding autorelease

In Chapter 2, when you initially create your first Foundation Command Line Tool, you find some generated code that you delete (highlighted in bold in the following code):

```
#import <Foundation/Foundation.h>

int main (int argc, const char * argv[]) {
  NSAutoreleasePool * pool = [[NSAutoreleasePool alloc]
            init];

  // insert code here...
  NSLog(@"Hello, World!");
  [pool drain];
  return 0;
}
```

This code created an autorelease pool that is a way to manage memory for objects when it is not possible for the object creator to easily release them. In this section, I explain why and when this autorelease pool is used.

As I just explained, the memory management rules require you to release objects when you are done with them, and often that is pretty easy, as shown in the following example:

```
NSString* englandText = [[NSString alloc]
        initWithFormat:@"%@", @"England"];

Destination* england = [[Destination alloc]
        initWithCountry:englandText andBudget:2000.00
        withExchangeRate:1.50];

  [englandText release];
```

In `main`, the string object is created and then used as an argument in the `Destination initWithCountry:::` method. Once control is returned to `main`, you can safely release that object because as far as you are concerned, you are done with it; and if `Destination` needs it, well, it's `Destination`'s responsibility to retain it. But what about those circumstances where the creator never gets control back? For example, what if I were to create a new method called `returnCountry` that created a copy of the `country` string and returned it back to the invoker?

```
- (NSString*) returnCountry {

  return [country copy];
}
```

I might want to do that if the receiver could possibly modify it. The problem here is that control is never returned back to `returnCountry`, so `return Country` never has a chance to release the copy it made.

To deal with the problem of control never being returned to a creator of an object so the creator can release it, Cocoa has the concept of an *autorelease pool,* and the statement

```
NSAutoreleasePool * pool =
                        [[NSAutoreleasePool alloc] init];
```

creates one of those pools to be used by `main`. The pool is nothing more than a collection of objects that will be released sometime in the future. When you send `autorelease` to an object, the object is added to an `NSAutoreleasePool`. When that pool is "cleared" (which happens on a regular basis), all the objects in the pool are sent a `release` message.

As glamorous as it sounds, the `autorelease` pool is just an array, and knowing what you know, you could write and manage one yourself, but why bother?

So, I can now write a `returnCountry` method that manages memory correctly.

```
- (NSString*) returnCountry {

  return [[country copy] autorelease];
}
```

Now, memory management works just right because the `returnCountry` method creates a new string, autoreleases it, and returns it to the object that requested it. If that object wants to continue to use the string, that object has to send a `retain` message to the string, since the string gets a `release` message in the future.

So when is that release message sent? If you're using an AppKit or UIKit application, the release message is sent in the main event loop that you return to after your program handles the current event, such as a mouse click or touch. (For more on the main event loop, see *iPhone Application Development For Dummies.*) With a Foundation Command Line Tool (which you're using now), the `release` message is sent when you destroy or drain the pool.

```
[pool drain];
```

That's as far as I'm going with how the autorelease pool works — it's beyond the scope of this book. Besides, I assume that you are using Cocoa for your application, which automatically takes care of managing the autorelease pool for you — both creating the pool and releasing it periodically.

Using the autorelease pool

You want to avoid using the autorelease pool on the iPhone when possible. The memory allocated for an autoreleased object remains allocated for some period of time after you're done with it and can be an issue in more memory-intensive applications. But `autorelease` could be used "behind your back" at times.

For example, Objective-C has a concept called *class* methods. This method belongs to the class object (as opposed to an instance object of the class), and class methods used to create new instances are called *factory* or *convenience methods*. The objects it creates are autoreleased. The ones you will probably be most concerned with are in the `NSString` class (although you'll find many more, even in the `NSMutableArray` class you have been using), such as the following:

```
stringWithContentsOfFile
stringWithContentsOfURL
stringWithCString
stringWithFormat:
stringWithString:
```

So, instead of using

```
NSString *newText = [NSString stringWithFormat:
@"Yo ", name];
```

you have been using

```
NSString *newText = [[NSString alloc] initWithFormat:
@"Yo ", name];
```

and doing the `release` yourself.

Notice these methods are of the form `stringWith`, as opposed to `init`.... this naming convention is a handy way to differentiate a class method that uses autorelease from the `init` methods shown in the last chapter that used `alloc`.

If you do need to continue to use an autoreleased object, just like with any other object you receive, you need to send it a `retain` message. In doing so, you become responsible for managing that object, and you must send a `release` message at some point, as I explained in the memory rules.

In iPhone programming, Apple recommends that you avoid using autorelease in your own code and that you also avoid class methods that return autoreleased objects. As I said, the memory allocated for an autoreleased object remains allocated for some period of time after you're done with it and can be an issue in more memory-intensive applications. This book does not cover these class methods, although you can find many examples of them being used.

These methods occur most commonly, as I said, when creating an object using a class methos, which saves you the trouble of doing an `alloc`, an `init`..., and then a `release` for the object. If you look in the documentation, as illustrated in Figure 13-6, these are under the heading Class Methods. They all have a + instead of a - before the return type, which designates them as a class method.

In Figure 13-6, you can see the NSString Class reference. In the Table of Contents I expanded the disclosure triangle next to Class Methods, and then clicked the stringWithFormat: class method, the counterpart to the initWithFormat: instance method that you've been using. You can see the + in front of the method declaration.

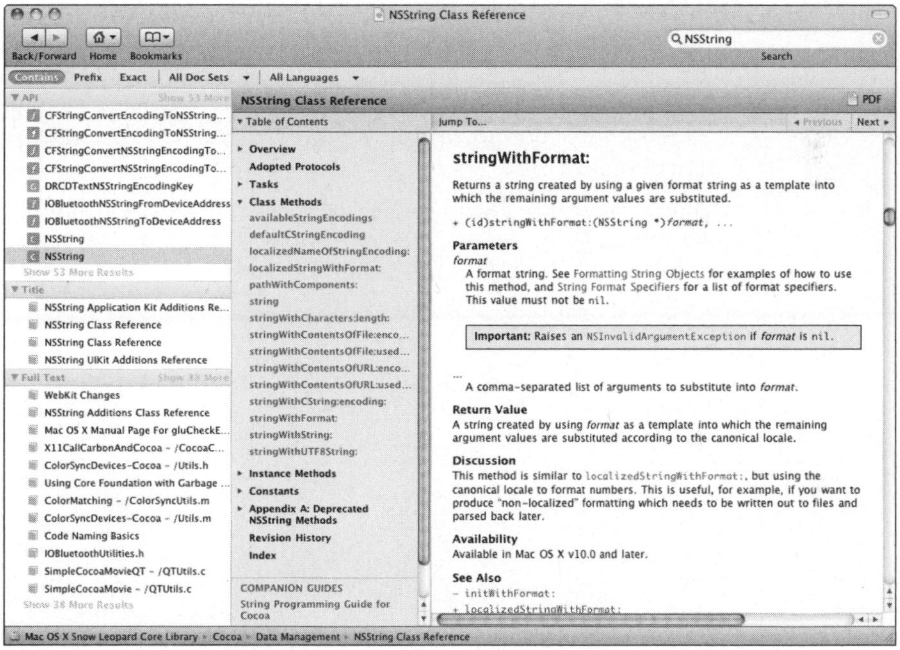

Figure 13-6:
Class
methods.

Notice that for class methods like these, instead of having their names start with init (for example, initWithFormat: for an NSString), they start with a reference to the class name (stringWithFormat:, for example).

Garbage Collection — Taking the Easy Way Out

Objective-C 2.0 introduces automatic memory management, also called *garbage collection*. It's quite common in other object-oriented languages. You just create the objects you need, and then when no one is using them any longer, the system automatically deallocates them.

1. **In the Xcode Project window, select the project — Vacation (the first line in the Groups & Files pane) — and click the blue info button on the toolbar.**

   You can also select Vacation and then right-click ➪ Get Info, or file➪Get Info, or you can even press ⌘+I.

   A window with project information appears.

2. **In the Project "Vacation" Info window that opens, click the Build tab and scroll down to GCC 4.2 - Code Generation (see Figure 13-7).**

3. **Using the pop-up menu next to Objective-C Garbage Collection, select Supported or Required (see Figure 13-7). (Currently Unsupported is checked.)**

   Supported gives you code that supports both garbage collection and your own memory management. You want to do that if you need to run, for example, on both the iPhone and Mac, or if you want to support earlier versions of the Mac OS.

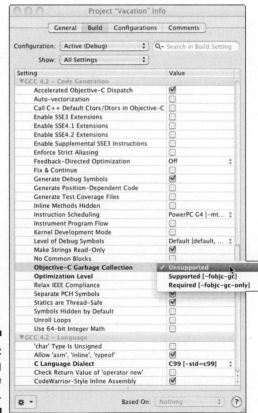

Figure 13-7:
Selecting
Garbage
Collection.

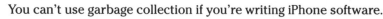

The garbage collector periodically looks at your variables and objects and follows the pointers between them. If it finds an object that has no pointers pointing to it, the object is collected. So, it's important to set the pointer to `nil` when you no longer need an object.

You can't use garbage collection if you're writing iPhone software.

Reference counting is a pretty simple concept. When you create the object, it is given a reference count of 1. As other objects use this object, they use methods to increase the reference count and decrease it when they are done. When the reference count reaches 0, the object is no longer needed, and the memory is deallocated.

Some Basic Memory Management Rules You Shouldn't Forget

Although I have spent a number of pages (but who's counting) on memory management, it really comes down to one simple rule:

> If you do anything to increase the retain count of an object, it is your responsibility to decrease the retain account by the same amount when you're no longer going to send messages to that object.

That's it. Of course, the goodness lies in knowing both when you've increased the retain count and when you need to decrease it.

- ✔ You automatically increase the retain count whenever you create an object using `alloc` or `new` or any method that contains `copy`.

- ✔ Assume that any object you receive whose creation you didn't personally witness dies as soon as you turn your back. It may have been passed as an argument, for example, or perhaps you're using one of those class convenience methods I spoke of earlier — you know, the ones you really shouldn't use on the iPhone.

- ✔ As you see in Chapter 14, when I explain declared properties, assigning an instance variable with a property attribute of `retain` is the moral equivalent of sending the object the `retain` message yourself.

You should decrease the retain count by sending an object a `release` message when you no longer need to send the object any messages. This is always true when you are being deallocated. So override the `dealloc` method to release all objects you haven't previously released and to which you've sent a `retain` message.

At the end of the day, the number of `alloc`, `new`, `copy`, and `retain` messages should equal (not be close to, equal) the number of `release` messages.

Do not make yourself crazy wondering about what is going on outside your little world. If you follow the rules in every object, things work out correctly. This is one of the few times when everyone acting in their best interest always works in the best interest of the whole.

Part IV
Moving from Language to Application

The 5th Wave
By Rich Tennant

"You can sure do a lot with an iPhone, but I never thought dressing one up in G.I. Joe clothes and calling it your little desk commander would be one of them."

In this part . . .

In this part, you begin to add more functionality to your program. I show you how to work with data as well as more advanced ways to extend your program.

Once you get all the application functionality up and running, you will probably be eager to make it available to the user. In this part, you fit your application into the user interface frameworks on the Mac and the iPhone that make developing applications for them so easy (well, okay, relatively easy). What will be really exciting (for me at least) is when you experience how easy it is to take the application you develop and just slide it into a user interface. Of course, you have to create the user interface, and I'll give you a crash course in Interface Builder, a tool that comes with Xcode. Once you do that, just add a few lines of code, and presto change-o, you're running iPhone and then Mac applications (the same application code, I might add, with some minor user interface differences).

The technical term for this accomplished feat is "way cool."

Chapter 14

Getting Data from Other Objects

• •

• •

*I*n Chapter 11, you factor your code to create a `Destination` object that manages the other objects you needed in your model. You see how the `Destination` object can use other objects by sending them messages. While most of those messages are to get an object to do something (`spendDollars:`, for example), as you see when you implement `returnBalance` in `Budget` and `leftToSpend` in `Destination`, some of these messages are about data.

That data returned by those methods is stored as instance variables, but as you know, one object can't and shouldn't access another object's instance variables directly (hence, the need for those two methods). In this chapter, I will show you another way to get data from an object — *declared properties* — and I'll also tell you about some things you need to handle with care.

Getting Data from Objects

As I refine the Vacation application, I need to start thinking more about the practical aspects of using this application, especially as I march down the road toward putting on a user interface.

One thing that strikes me is that this whole exchange rate thing is not very robust. After all, the exchange rate changes often during the day, so I do need a way to update it. Right now at least, `Budget` owns the exchange rate, but there is no way to communicate with the `Budget`, other than through a `Destination`. So, before deciding how I want to update the exchange rate, I really need to consider which object should own the exchange rate. Currently, both `Budget` and `Destination` have instance variables storing it.

Peering into my crystal ball, I see in the future an exchange rate object that will be able to get exchange rates in real time. When this happens, you'll create an exchange rate object that will be used by the `Destination` object. To prepare for the eventuality, it makes sense for the `Destination` object to own the exchange rate now. Then when you implement an exchange rate object, you will have to make only a few changes to the `Destination` object's code, and none to the other objects that need to know the exchange rate. They'll still use `Destination` to get it, and `Destination` will simply turn around and ask the exchange rate object to do its bidding (no pun intended). It makes sense then for `Destination` to own the exchange rate for now, keeping the exchange rate a `Destination` instance variable and creating a method that can be invoked from `main` to update the exchange rate (and later by a controller).

Having its exchange rate instance variable taken away creates a problem for `Budget`. How will `Budget` get the exchange rate it needs to compute the budget impact of a credit card transaction?

By now, you know of course that `Budget` can't, and shouldn't be able to, access the `exchangeRate` instance variable in `Destination`. In object-oriented programming, a class's instance variables are safely protected behind the object's walls and can't be accessed directly. The only way to access them is by creating *accessor methods*, which allow the specific instance variable of an object to be read and (if you want) updated. But even if you were tempted to access them directly, the compiler wouldn't let you because, as I discuss in Chapter 6, its scope is defined as `@protected` (the default) in the class. I dare you — go try it on your own.

I also want access to the country name of a `Destination`. When I delete a destination, as I did earlier in this chapter, I will give users a chance to change their minds — I want to be able to display, "Are you sure you want to delete *country* from your trip?" For now, however, I'll just display that the destination country was deleted.

Well, I could write methods to return the exchange rate and the country name as I have been doing with `returnBalance` in `Budget` and `leftToSpend`, or I could use a feature of Objective-C 2.0 called *declared properties*. When you use declared properties, the compiler can synthesize the accessor methods for you.

Working with Declared Properties

As you'll soon discover, you will use declared properties a lot (most people just call them *properties*). If you need to have an instance variable accessible by other objects in your program, you'll need to create accessor methods for that particular instance variable.

Accessor methods effectively get (using a *getter method*) and set (using a *setter method*) the values for an instance variable. For many years, programmers had to code these methods themselves or buy add-on tools that would do it for them (usually advertised late at night on the Programmers Channel). The nice folks in charge of Objective-C came to our collective rescue when they released Objective-C 2.0 with its *declared properties* feature. Now the compiler can write access methods for you, according to the direction you give it in the *property declaration*. Kind of like getting the smartest kid in your class to do your homework while you hang out with your friends at the malt shoppe.

Objective-C creates the getter and setter methods for you by using a @property declaration in the interface file, combined with the @synthesize declaration in the implementation file. The default names for the getter and setter methods associated with a property are *whateverThePropertyNameIs* for the getter (yes, the default getter method name is the same as the property's name) and set*WhateverThePropertyNameIs*: for the setter. (You replace what is in italics with the actual property name or identifier.) For example, the accessors that would be generated for the exchangeRate instance variable are exchangeRate as the getter and setExchangeRate: as the setter.

Adding properties

If you have been following along with me, I'll be extending what you do in Chapter 13. If you would like to start from a clean copy of the project from where you left off, you can use the project found in the Chapter 14 Start Here folder, which is in the Chapter 14 folder.

Follow these steps to declare some properties for the Destination class, and then I'll explain them in more detail.

1. **Add the code in bold in Listing 14-1 Destination.h.**

Listing 14-1: Adding properties to the Destination class

```
#import <Cocoa/Cocoa.h>
@class Budget;

@interface Destination : NSObject {

  NSString* country;
  double exchangeRate;
  NSMutableArray *transactions;
  Budget* theBudget;
}

- (id) initWithCountry: (NSString*) theCountry
          andBudget: (double) budgetAmount
          withExchangeRate: (double) theExchangeRate;
- (void) spendCash: (double) aTransaction;
- (void) chargeCreditCard: (double) aTransaction;
- (double) leftToSpend;

@property (nonatomic, retain) NSString* country;
@property (readwrite) double exchangeRate;
@end
```

That is what you just did — coded the corresponding @property declarations for country and exchangeRate. These specify how the accessor methods are to behave. I explain exactly what that means in the next section. For now, just know that you need to add them.

But while the @property statement tells the compiler that there are accessor methods, they still have to be created. In the good old days, you had to code these accessors methods yourself, which in a large program was very tedious. Fortunately, Objective-C will create these accessor methods whenever you include an @synthesize statement for a property.

2. **Add the line of code in bold in Listing 14-2 to the Destination.m file after @implementation Destination and before anything else.**

Listing 14-2: Adding synthesize to Destination.m

```
#import "Destination.h"
#import "CashTransaction.h"
#import "CreditCardTransaction.h"
#import "Budget.h"
#import "Transaction.h"
```

```
@implementation Destination

@synthesize exchangeRate, country;
```

What you just did by adding the `@synthesize` statement was direct the compiler to create two accessor methods — one for each `@property` declaration.

Implementing declared properties

At the end of the day, you need to do three things in your code in order for the compiler to create accessors:

1. **Declare an instance variable in the interface file.**
2. **Add a `@property` declaration of that instance variable in the same interface file.**
3. **Add a `@synthesize` statement in the implementation file so that Objective-C generates the accessors for you.**

Step 1 is straightforward, but Steps 2 and 3 take some explanation.

The declaration specifies the name and type of the property and some *attributes* that provide the compiler with information about exactly how you want the accessor methods to be implemented.

For example, the declaration

```
@property (readwrite) double exchangeRate;
```

declares a property named `exchangeRate`, which is a `double`. The property attribute (`readwrite`) tells the compiler that this property can be both read and updated outside the object.

You also could have specified `readonly`, in which case, only a getter method is required in the `@implementation`. If you use `@synthesize` in the implementation block, only the getter method is synthesized. Moreover, if you attempt to assign a value using the accessor (I explain how to do that later for variables you can update), you get a compiler error.

Now take a look at the following declaration:

```
@property (nonatomic, retain) NSString* country;
```

It declares a property named `country`, which is a pointer to a `NSString` object. Enclosed in parentheses are two attributes: `nonatomic` and `retain`.

`nonatomic` addresses an important technical consideration for multi-threaded systems, which is beyond the scope of this book. `nonatomic` works fine for applications like this one.

`retain` directs the compiler to create an access method that sends a `retain` message to any object that is assigned to this property. I mention in Chapter 13 that properties can have some memory management implications.

And, oh yes, `nonatomic` and `retain` apply only to pointers to objects.

The `@property` declaration (like the two you placed in the interface file in the previous section) only informs the compiler that there are accessors. As I said, it is the `@synthesize` statement that tells the compiler to create them for you. Using `@synthesize` results in four new methods.

```
exchangeRate
setexchangeRate:
country
setcountry:
```

If I didn't use `@synthesize` and I declared the properties, it would be up to me to implement the methods myself, according to the attributes in the `@property` statement. So, if I were to write my own accessors, I would be responsible for sending a `retain` message to the `exchangeRate` when it is assigned to the instance variables. You may have to do that under certain circumstances, which I'll discuss later in the section "Properly Using Properties."

Accessing the instance variables from within the class

Once you have declared the properties, you can access them from other objects or from `main`. But before I show you that, I want to show you about accessing them within the class.

If you want to take advantage of the `retain` message being sent automatically upon assignment, you'll have to access the instance variable through the accessor, even within the object walls.

```
[self setCountry:theCountry];
```

You also can use the dot notation (which refugees from other object-oriented languages will recognize).

```
self.country = theCountry;
```

When you use the setter accessor with a class to assign an object pointer, you don't need to send the object a `retain` message, like the one you had to send to the `country` object in the `Destination`'s `initWithCountry:::` method, since the setter accessor does the retain for you.

```
[country retain];
```

Releasing the object assigned to a property

As I said in the previous section, using an accessor will automatically send a `retain` message. But you still have to release it when you are done.

Normally you send an object a `release` message:

```
[country release];
```

But if you use an accessor, you have a new option:

```
self.country = nil;
```

That's because when you assign a new value to a property, the accessor sends a `release` message to the previous object. As you can see, accessors are good citizens here.

In your `dealloc` method, however, you should continue to send the object a `release` message as you have been doing.

Now, I'd like you to update Destination.m to use properties by deleting the code with a strikethrough in Listing 14-3 and adding the code in bold. (You've already added the `@synthesize` statement, but I kept it in bold.)

Listing 14-3: Using accessors within the Destination class

```
#import "Destination.h"
#import "CashTransaction.h"
#import "CreditCardTransaction.h"
#import "Budget.h"
#import "Transaction.h"


@implementation Destination
@synthesize exchangeRate, country;


- (id) initWithCountry: (NSString*) theCountry andBudget:
          (double) budgetAmount withExchangeRate:
          (double) theExchangeRate{
  if (self = [super init]) {
    transactions = [[NSMutableArray alloc]
          initWithCapacity:10];

    // theBudget = [[Budget alloc]  initWithAmount:
    // budgetAmount withExchangeRate: theExchangeRate];
    theBudget = [[Budget alloc]
          initWithAmount:budgetAmount forDestination:self];
    // exchangeRate = theExchangeRate;
    self.exchangeRate = theExchangeRate;
    // country = theCountry;
    [self setCountry: theCountry];
    // [country retain];
    NSLog (@"I'm off to %@", theCountry);
  }
  return self;
}


- (void) spendCash: (double)amount{

  Transaction *aTransaction = [[CashTransaction alloc]
          initWithAmount: amount forBudget: theBudget];
  [transactions addObject:aTransaction];
  [aTransaction spend];
  [aTransaction release];

}

- (void) chargeCreditCard: (double) amount{

  Transaction *aTransaction = [[CreditCardTransaction
          alloc] initWithAmount: amount forBudget:
          theBudget];
```

```
    [transactions addObject:aTransaction];
    [aTransaction spend];
    [aTransaction release];
}

- (double) leftToSpend {

    return [theBudget returnBalance];
}

- (void) dealloc {

    [transactions release];
    [theBudget release];
    [country release];
    [super dealloc];
}

@end
```

You did the following to `Destination`:

1. You changed the `Budget init` method, which is explained in the next section, "Using Accessors to Get Data from Objects."

   You had to change the `Budget init` method in order to pass in a refer-ence to the `Destination` object. `Budget` will need that to send a mes-sage in order to get the `exchangeRate`.

2. You used an accessor to assign the `theExchangeRate` argument in the `initWithAmount::` method to the `exchangeRate` instance variable using the dot notation.

   ```
   self.exchangeRate = theExchangeRate;
   ```

3. You used an accessor to assign the `theCountry` argument in the `initWith Amount:` method to the `country` instance variable using an Objective-C message.

   ```
   [self setCountry:theCountry];
   ```

4. You deleted the `retain` message you had sent the `country` because the assigning to the `country` property does that for you.

Using Accessors to Get Data from Objects

Now that you have created these accessors, you can use them. You will have to make some changes to Budget.m and Budget.h. These are shown in Listings 14-4 and 14-5.

1. **Start by deleting the code with a strikethrough in Listing 14-4 and adding the code in bold to Budget.m.**

Listing 14-4: Budget.m

```
#import "Budget.h"
#import "Destination.h"


@implementation Budget

//- (id) initWithAmount: (double) aBudget
//          withExchangeRate: (double) anExchangeRate {
//
//   if (self = [super init]) {
//      exchangeRate = anExchangeRate;
//      budget = aBudget;
//   }
//   return self;
//}

- (id) initWithAmount: (double) aBudget forDestination:
          (Destination*) aDestination {
  if (self = [super init]) {
    destination = aDestination;
    [destination retain];
    budget = aBudget;
  }
  return self;
}


- (void) spendDollars: (double) dollars {

  budget -= dollars;
}


- (void) chargeForeignCurrency: (double) foreignCurrency {
//transaction = foreignCurrency*exchangeRate;
```

```
    transaction = foreignCurrency*
                              [destination exchangeRate];
    budget -= transaction;
}

- (double) returnBalance {

    return budget;
}

- (void) dealloc {
    [destination release];
    [super dealloc];
}

@end
```

You added the #import "Destination.h" to make the compiler happy when it sees a message to the Destination object. You also did the following:

1. Modified the init method to add a pointer to the Destination object as an argument and removed the anExchangeRate argument. You also stored the pointer to the Destination object in a new instance variable destination — which you also added. You had to send it a retain message because you have not declared it as property, nor is there any need to.

2. You changed chargeForeignCurrency: to use the getter accessor exchangeRate to get the exchange rate from the Destination object.

What you also may have noticed is that you left the returnBalance, which you coded earlier, instead of replacing it with an accessor. Why didn't I have you make that a property as well?

I have (as you might expect) some definite opinions, and really mixed feelings about properties, which I explain in section "Properly Using Properties," later in this chapter. For now though, you'll finish the changes to Budget.h.

2. **Delete the code with a strikethrough in Listing 14-5 and add the code in bold to Budget.h.**

Listing 14-5: Budget.h

```
#import <Cocoa/Cocoa.h>
@class Destination;

@interface Budget : NSObject {
  float       exchangeRate;
  double      budget;
  double      transaction;
  Destination* destination;
}



//(id) initWithAmount: (double) aBudget withExchangeRate:
        (double) anExchangeRate ;
- (id) initWithAmount: (double) aBudget
            forDestination: (Destination*) aDestination;

- (void) spendDollars: (double) dollars ;
- (void) chargeForeignCurrency: (double) euros;
- (double) returnBalance;
@end
```

There are no surprises here. You added the `@class` statement to make the compiler happy, added the new instance variable, `destination`, and made the changes to the `init` method declaration that you did in the implementation.

Now, look at Listing 14-6, which shows the changes to Vacation.m that allow you to change the exchange rate as needed.

3. Delete the code with a strikethrough in Listing 14-6 and add the code in bold to main (in the file Vacation.m).

Listing 14-6: Modifying main in Vacation.m

```
#import <Foundation/Foundation.h>
#import "Destination.h"

int main (int argc, const char * argv[]) {

  NSAutoreleasePool * pool = [[NSAutoreleasePool alloc]
          init];

  NSString* europeText = [[NSString alloc]
                    initWithFormat:@"%@", @"Europe"];
  Destination* europe = [[Destination alloc]
          initWithCountry:europeText andBudget:1000.00
          withExchangeRate:1.25];
  [europeText release];
```

```
NSString* englandText = [[NSString alloc]
                        initWithFormat:@"%@", @"England"];
Destination* england = [[Destination alloc]
        initWithCountry:englandText andBudget:2000.00
        withExchangeRate:1.50];
[englandText release];

for (int n = 1; n < 2; n++) {
  double transaction = n*100.00;
  NSLog (@"Sending a %.2f cash transaction",
        transaction);
  [europe spendCash:transaction];

  NSLog(@"Remaining budget %.2f", [europe leftToSpend]);
  NSLog (@"Sending a %.2f cash transaction",
        transaction);
  [england spendCash:transaction];
  NSLog(@"Remaining budget %.2f",
                              [england leftToSpend]);
}

[europe setExchangeRate:1.30];
[england setExchangeRate:1.40];

int n = 1;
while (n < 4) {
  double transaction = n*100.00;
  NSLog(@"Sending a %.2f credit card transaction",
        transaction);
  [europe chargeCreditCard:transaction];
  NSLog(@"Remaining budget %.2f", [europe leftToSpend]);
  NSLog(@"Sending a %.2f credit card transaction",
        transaction);
  [england chargeCreditCard:transaction];
  NSLog(@"Remaining budget %.2f", [england
        leftToSpend]);
  n++;
}

NSString *returnedCountry = [england country];
NSLog (@"You have deleted the %@ part of your
        trip",returnedCountry);
[returnedCountry release];
[england release];

[pool drain];
return 0;
}
```

All you did in `main` was add the `autorelease pool` allocation and `drain` back, as I explained in the last chapter. You also added statements using the `Destination` object's `setExchangeRate:` and country accessors to update the exchange rate and access the country name and display it to the user before deleting a destination.

You also added sending a `setExchange:` rate message to both the `europe` and `england` objects, which updates the exchange rate for each, replacing the value for `exchangeRate` that you originally initialized them with.

Being a good citizen, you also released the string `returnedCountry`.

Notice how easy all this is.

4. **Select Build and Run button in the Project Window toolbar to build and run the application.**

You should see the following in the Debugger Console:

```
I'm off to Europe
I'm off to England
Sending a 100.00 cash transaction
Remaining budget 900.00
Sending a 100.00 cash transaction
Remaining budget 1900.00
Sending a 100.00 credit card transaction
Remaining budget 770.00
Sending a 100.00 credit card transaction
Remaining budget 1760.00
Sending a 200.00 credit card transaction
Remaining budget 510.00
Sending a 200.00 credit card transaction
Remaining budget 1480.00
Sending a 300.00 credit card transaction
Remaining budget 120.00
Sending a 300.00 credit card transaction
Remaining budget 1060.00
You have deleted the England part of your trip
```

You can find the completed project on the CD in the Example 14 folder, which is in the Chapter 14 folder.

Properly Using Properties

What you just did with the exchange rate and country data in the `Destination` object may seem, well, a bit pointless to you. If the point of object-oriented programming is to encapsulate data, what difference does it really make if you allow direct data access or if you force the user of the data to send a message and the supplier to code the @property and @synthesize statements? It really seems like gratuitous code, and that this whole data encapsulation thing is a sham.

For example, what happens when I change how I get the exchange rate from being set by the user, and store it in a Destination instance variable, to access it from another object — my plan as I mentioned in the beginning of this chapter? It would seem that would break the clients of Destination that use the exchangeRate property.

I actually agree with that criticism of properties to an extent, although as you will see, there are ways to deal with this issue.

Putting on my methodologist hat for a second (well, only a few seconds, I promise), let me explain this issue.

First, look at when accessing the object's data through accessors is really the way to do things:

- **Customizing user interface objects.** In a framework, the user interface object, a window or view, for example, really needs to have certain parameters set to make it function in the way the user needs. Instead of forcing the user to subclass it, properties allow it to be tailored to a particular user's (the developer's) needs. In this case, properties are being used to set parameters, like color, rather than to implement a class's responsibility to accept data.

- **Accessing instance variables.** Again, in a framework, the same argument applies to accessing the instance variables. The instance variables should become properties when they hold information about the state of the object — is the window opened or closed, where did the user just drag this object to on the screen, and so on.

It's my opinion, however, that except for those and similar circumstances in your own classes, you are much better off from an enhanceability perspective to avoid using properties to implement an object's responsibility to accept data from and supply data to other objects. You should define methods that accept or supply data and not use property that implies structural information about the data.

That being said, some features about properties also allow you to do some interesting things to mitigate the impact if you later decide to change an instance variable you have made available as a property. For example:

✔ **In order to deal with changes, you can implement the accessor (instead of having it generated by the complier) to access the property.** For example, if you moved the exchange rate to an exchange rate object, you could implement your own exchangeRate method currently synthesized by the compiler (it will only synthesize those methods if you have not implemented them in your implementation file). The method you implemented would send a message to the new exchange rate object to get, and then return back, the exchange rate (you probably wouldn't need a setter in this case). If you do that though, you will have to be sure to implement the accessor in a way that is consistent with the property's attributes. Creating your own accessors for properties is another topic that is beyond the scope of this book.

✔ **The accessor does not have to be named the same as the instance variable.** If you want to hide the name of the instance variable, you can use

```
@property (readwrite, getter=returnTheExchangeRate)
                                 double exchangeRate;
```

✔ **The property name must have the same name as an instance variable.** For example

```
@property (readwrite ) double er;
...
@synthesize country, er = exchangeRate;
```

directs the complier to synthesize getEr and setEr: to get and set the instance variable exchangeRate. If you try this for yourself, you'll find that

```
[europe setEr:1.30];
[england setEr:1.40];
```

works just as well as setExchangeRate: does.

Chapter 15

Show Me the Data

In This Chapter

▶ Creating and using property lists

▶ How dictionaries work

▶ Updating dictionaries and plists

▶ Having a property list object (array) write itself to a file

*I*n Chapter 1, I explain that a computer program is a set of instructions that perform operations on data. While this is what you have been steadily doing since Chapter 1 — coding statements that operate on data — all of the data you have been working with so far has been "hard coded" into the program.

Once you put on the user interface, of course, that will change. The user will be entering transactions, and you will be processing them, and probably storing both the transactions and the results as well. For example, you'll want to save all the credit card transactions to reconcile them against your statement when you get home, and you definitely want the ability to store what's left of your budget after a series of transactions so that every time you restart the program, you don't start with your original budget (well, it would be nice if you could do that, but I guess that's not realistic).

In this chapter, I will show you how to store what's left of your budget after a series of transactions to a file, and then read that file when the application starts up again. This will illustrate some of the ways you can save data. But before I show you that, I want to make you aware of another kind of data you need for your program, *application-based data*.

Understanding Application-Based Data

As I look at my program, I think it would be nice to be able to display the euro symbol (€) when I display a euro-based credit card transaction and the pound symbol (£) when I display a pound-based one.

While I could "hard code" those symbols in my program, doing so doesn't give me much flexibility. Either I have to build some kind of array into my program for the currency symbols of the places I might go (and "waste" the CPU cycles and memory to build it every time I run the program), or I can store all of the currency symbols in a file, and based on the country I am processing transactions for, look up the currency symbols in that file.

When that kind of data is in a file, I won't have to rebuild my program every time I add or change a country, currency, or currency symbol — all I will have to do is change the file, which as you'll see, is pretty easy.

Fortunately, Cocoa supports an easy-to-use mechanism called a *property list* to manage this kind of data. The next section covers property lists.

Defining property lists

Property lists are used extensively by applications and other system software on Mac OS X and iPhone OS. For example, the Mac OS X Finder stores file and directory attributes in a property list, and the iPhone OS uses them for user defaults. You also get a property list editor with Xcode, which makes property list files (or *plists* as they are referred to) easy to create and maintain in your own programs.

Figure 15-1 shows the property list I'll show you how to build, one that will enable you to add the euro and pound symbols to your application.

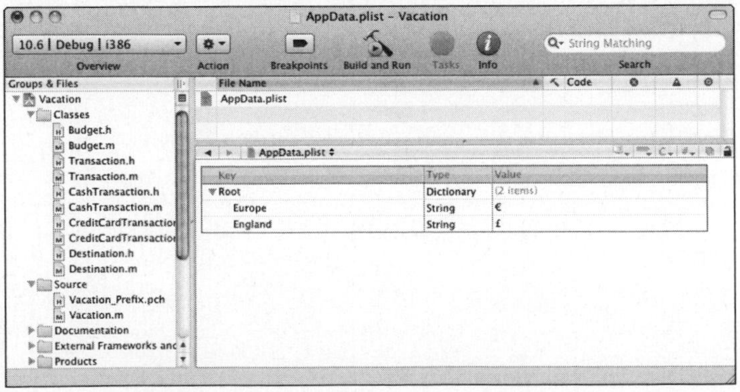

Figure 15-1:
AppData
property list.

Once you know how to work with property lists, it's actually easy, but like most things, getting there is half the fun.

Working with property lists

Property lists are perfect for storing small amounts of data that consist primarily of strings and numbers. What adds to their appeal is the ability to easily read them into your programs, use or even modify the data, and then write them back out again. That's because Cocoa provides a small set of objects that have that behavior built in.

 The technical term for these objects is *serializable.* A serializable object can convert itself into a stream of bytes so that it can be stored in a file and can then reconstitute itself into the object it once was when it is read back in — yes "beam me up, Scotty" does exist, at least on your computer.

These objects, called *property list objects,* that you have to work with are as follows:

- ✔ NSData and NSMutableData
- ✔ NSDate
- ✔ NSNumber
- ✔ NSString and NSMutableString
- ✔ NSArray and NSMutableArray
- ✔ NSDictionary and NSMutableDictionary

As you can see in the plist in Figure 15-1, the root is a dictionary and the Europe and England currency symbols are strings.

You'll notice a division in the preceding list. That is because there are two kinds of property list objects.

- ✔ **Primitives:** The term *primitives* is not a reflection on how civilized these property objects are, but it is a word used to describe the simplest kind of object. They are what they are.
- ✔ **Containers:** Containers can hold primitives as well as other containers.

One thing that differentiates property list object containers (NSArray, NSDictionary), besides their ability to hold other objects, is that they both have methods called writeToFile::, which write the property list to a file, and a corresponding initWithContentsOfFile:, which initializes the object with the content of a file. So, if I create an array or dictionary and fill it chock full of objects of the property list type, all I have to do to save it to a file is tell it to go save itself or create an array or dictionary and then tell it to initialize itself from a file.

You have already worked with arrays, and I'll introduce you to dictionaries in the next section. The containers can contain other containers as well as the primitive types. Thus, you might have an array of dictionaries, and each dictionary might contain other arrays and dictionaries, as well as the primitive types.

But before I tell you any more about property lists, let me explain one of the more important property list objects — the dictionary.

You haven't seen NSDate yet, and I won't be using it in the book, but for your information, it is a Cocoa class for date and time handling. NSData and NSMutableData are wrappers (an object that is there mostly to turn something into an object) in which you can dump any kind of data and then have that data act as an object. They are used extensively to store and manipulate blocks of data. (I won't be getting into them in this book, although I use them a lot in *iPhone Application Development For Dummies*.)

Using Dictionaries

Dictionaries are like the city cousins of arrays. They both pretty much do the same things, but dictionaries add a new level of sophistication.

I love dictionaries, now. But I have to admit that when I started programming with Objective-C and Cocoa, trying to get my head around the idea of dictionaries was a real challenge — not because dictionaries are hard, they really aren't. The "problem" was because of what you can do with them. Not only will you use them to hold property list objects, but also you'll use them to hold application objects — just as you did with the array that holds Transaction objects.

So, now, I'll take you go through them slowly and with lots of illustrations.

Understanding a dictionary's keys and values

As I said, in many ways, dictionaries are like the arrays you used earlier — they are a container for other objects. Dictionaries are made up of pairs of *keys* and *values*. A key-value pair within a dictionary is called an *entry*. Both the key and the value must be *objects*, so each entry consists of one *object* that is the key (usually an NSString) and a second object that is that key's value (which can be anything, but in a property list must be a property list object). Within a dictionary, the keys are unique.

You use a key to look up the corresponding value. This works like your real-world dictionary, where the word is the key, and its definition is the value. (Do you suppose that's why they are called dictionaries?)

So, for example, if you have an NSDictionary that stores the currency symbol for each currency, you can ask that dictionary for the currency symbol (value) for the euro (key).

Although you can use any kind of object as a key in an NSDictionary, keys in property list dictionaries have to be strings, and I'll stick to that here. You can also have any kind of object for a value, but again if you are using them in a property list, they all have to be property list objects as well.

The same rules hold for arrays. Now you are using one to hold Transaction objects, but if you want to write and read an array as a plist file (and you will), they can hold only property list objects.

NSDictionary has a couple of basic methods you will be using:

- ✔ count — The count method gives you the number of entries in the dictionary.
- ✔ objectForKey: — The objectForKey: method gives the value for a given key.

In addition, the methods writeToFile:atomically: and initWithContentsOfFile: cause a dictionary to write a representation of itself to a file and to read itself in from a file, respectively.

If an array or dictionary contains objects that are not property list objects, you can't save and then restore them using the built-in methods for doing so.

Just as with an array, a dictionary can be *static* (NSDictionary) or *mutable* (NSMutableDictionary). NSMutableDictionary adds a couple of additional basic methods — setObjectForKey: and removeObjectForKey:, which enable you to add and remove entries, respectively.

Creating a dictionary

Enough talk; it's time to code.

To create a dictionary in my program that will enable me to look up the currency symbol for a given country, I must add the following lines of code:

```
NSDictionary *appDictionary = [[NSDictionary alloc]
        initWithObjectsAndKeys:
            @"€", @"Europe", @"£", @"England", nil];
```

This creates a dictionary for me with two keys, Europe and England. (To get the currency symbols as I did, in Xcode select Edit⇨Special Characters or press ⌘+option+T.)

initWithObjectsAndKeys: takes an alternating sequence of *objects* and keys, terminated by a nil value (as you can probably guess, just as with an array, you can't store a nil value in an NSDictionary).

I want to point out that the order is *objects* and keys. I can't begin to tell you how often I get that backward.

This step creates the dictionary that you see in Figure 15-2.

appDictionary	
Key	**Value**
Europe	€
England	£

To look up the value for a key in a dictionary, you send the objectForKey: message.

```
NSLog(@"The currency symbol for the euro is %@",
        [appDictionary objectForKey:@"Europe"]);
```

In this case, I am using the key Europe to look up the currency symbol in the appDictionary. And lo and behold what I get is

```
The currency symbol for the euro is €
```

You can imagine using this quite a bit in applications like this one, as well as for other things. By the way, if there's no key, for Antarctica for example, objectForKey: returns nil, which gives me the opportunity to respond to the user or do whatever I might want to about it.

On Mac OS X v10.5 and later, NSDictionary supports fast enumeration just like its cousin NSArray. As I have been pointing out, a dictionary is very similar to an array with obviously some extra stuff. You can, for example, iterate through a dictionary by using the for in construct to go through the keys of a dictionary.

```
for (id key in appDictionary) {
  NSLog(@"key: %@, value: %@", key,
                          [appDictionary objectForKey:key]);
  }
```

These lines of code will go through every key in the dictionary, returning the key in the key variable, allowing you to look up that entry using the object ForKey: method.

```
key: Europe, value: €
key: England, value: £
```

Adding a plist to Your Project

While I'm sure you found that explanation of dictionaries fascinating, I still haven't shown you how to use a file instead of having to create the dictionary in your program. If you use a file, you can use Xcode's handy editor (which I'll show you in a moment) to add new currencies and countries as you develop your program.

If you have been following along with me, note that I'll be extending what you did in Chapter 14. If you want to start from a clean copy of the project, you can use the project found in the Chapter 15 Start Here folder on the CD.

1. **In the Groups & Files listing (at the left in the Xcode project window), select Vacation (at the top of the Groups & Files pane) and then choose File⇨New File from the main menu, or press ⌘+n.**

   The New File dialog appears.

2. **Choose Resource under the Mac OS X heading in the left pane, and then select Property List, as shown in Figure 15-3.**

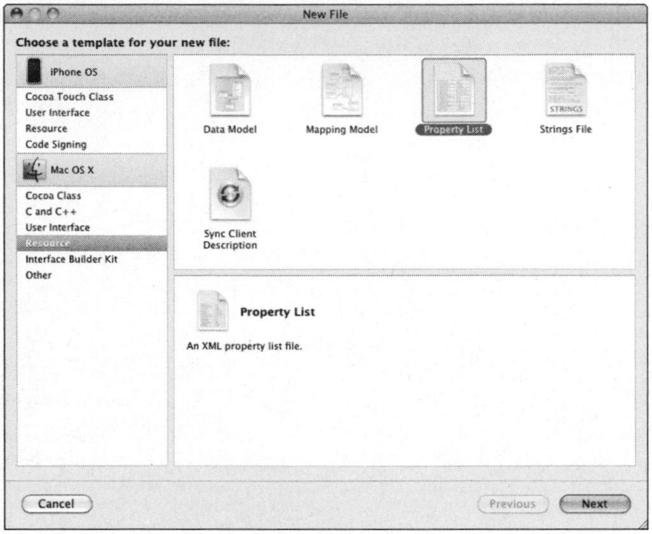

Figure 15-3:
Creating the plist.

3. **Click the Next button.**

4. **Enter the filename** `AppData.plist`; **then press Return (Enter) or click Finish.**

   You should now see a new item called `AppData.plist` under Vacation, in the Groups & Files list shown in Figure 15-4.

   In the editor pane, you can see Xcode's property list editor with the root entry selected. (In this case, it has defaulted to a Dictionary; the other option is Array.)

5. **Click the icon at the end of the entry, as shown in Figure 15-4.**

   A new entry appears, as you can see in Figure 15-5.

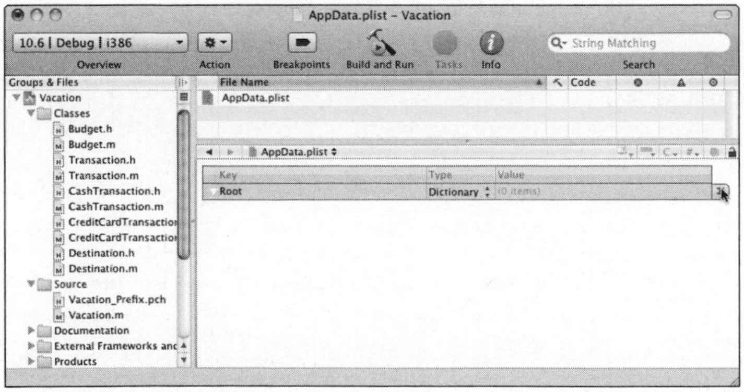

Figure 15-4:
New plist file.

6. **Click the pop-up menu arrows to choose the Type of entry, and select String.**

   It can be any of the property list objects I talked about at the beginning of this chapter, but String, which will already be selected, is the one you want here.

Figure 15-5:
Select
String.

7. **In the Key field, enter** Europe, **and then double-click (or tab to) the Value field and enter €, as shown in Figure 15-6.**

   To get the currency symbols, select Edit⇨Special Characters or press ⌘+option+T.

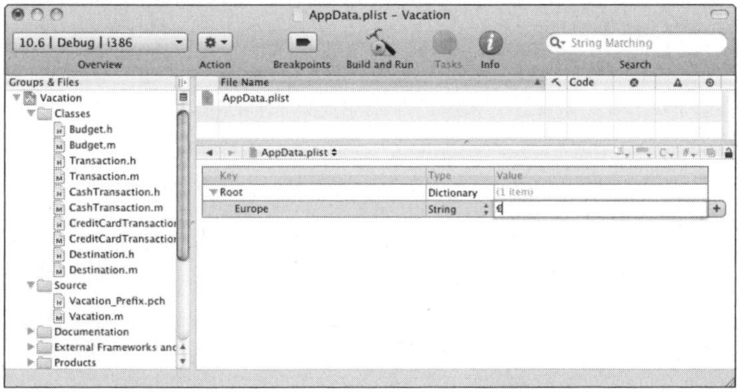

Figure 15-6:
Enter
Europe
and €.

8. **Click the + icon at the end of the entry (row) you just added, and you will get a new entry. This time enter** England **and** £.

   When you are done, your plist should look like the one I showed you earlier in Figure 15-1.

Using plists

The only file you work with in this chapter is Vacation.m. So start by
making the following changes in order to use the plist.

In main in Vacation.m, add the code to main in bold and delete the code
with the strikethrough in Listing 15-1.

Listing 15-1: Using plists

```
#import <Foundation/Foundation.h>
#import "Destination.h"

int main (int argc, const char * argv[]) {

  NSAutoreleasePool * pool = [[NSAutoreleasePool alloc]
        init];
  NSString* appDataPath =
        @"/Users/neal/Desktop/Example 15A/AppData.plist";
  NSMutableDictionary *appDictionary =
        [[NSMutableDictionary alloc] initWithContentsOf
        File:appDataPath];
  NSString* europeSymbol = [[NSString alloc]
        initWithFormat:@"%@",
        [appDictionary valueForKey:@"Europe"]];
  NSString* englandSymbol = [[NSString alloc]
        initWithFormat:@"%@",
        [appDictionary valueForKey:@"England"]];

  NSString* europeText = [[NSString alloc]
                    initWithFormat:@"%@", @"Europe"];
  Destination* europe = [[Destination alloc]
        initWithCountry:europeText andBudget:1000.00
        withExchangeRate:1.25];
  [europeText release];
  NSString* englandText = [[NSString alloc]
        initWithFormat:@"%@", @"England"];
  Destination* england = [[Destination alloc]
        initWithCountry:englandText andBudget:2000.00
        withExchangeRate:1.50];
  [englandText release];


  for (int n = 1; n < 2; n++) {
    double transaction = n*100.00;
// NSLog (@"Sending a %.2f cash transaction",
        transaction);
    NSLog (@"Sending a $%.2f cash transaction",
        transaction);
    [europe spendCash:transaction];
```

```
//   NSLog(@"Remaining budget %.2f", [europe leftToSpend]);
     NSLog(@"Remaining budget $%.2f", [europe
            leftToSpend]);
//   NSLog (@"Sending a %.2f cash transaction",
            transaction);
     NSLog (@"Sending a $%.2f cash transaction",
            transaction);
     [england spendCash:transaction];
//   NSLog(@"Remaining budget %.2f", [england
            leftToSpend]);
     NSLog(@"Remaining budget $%.2f", [england
            leftToSpend]);
   }

  [europe setExchangeRate:1.30];
  [england setExchangeRate:1.40];

  int n =1;
  while (n < 4) {
     double transaction = n*100.00;
//   NSLog (@"Sending a %.2f credit card transaction",
            transaction);
     NSLog (@"Sending a %@%.2f credit card transaction",
            europeSymbol, transaction);
     [europe chargeCreditCard:transaction];
//   NSLog(@"Remaining budget %.2f", [europe leftToSpend]);
     NSLog(@"Remaining budget $%.2f", [europe
            leftToSpend]);
//   NSLog (@"Sending a %.2f credit card transaction",
            transaction);
     NSLog (@"Sending a %@%.2f credit card transaction",
            englandSymbol , transaction);
     [england chargeCreditCard:transaction];
//   NSLog(@"Remaining budget %.2f", [england
            leftToSpend]);
     NSLog(@"Remaining budget $%.2f", [england
            leftToSpend]);

     n++;
  }

  NSString *returnedCountry = [england country];
  NSLog (@"You have deleted the %@ part of your trip",
          returnedCountry);
  [returnedCountry release];
  [england release];

  [pool drain];
  return 0;
}
```

The first thing you did here was tell the file system where the `AppData` file is.

```
NSString* appDataPath =
    @"/Users/neal/Desktop/Example 15A/AppData.plist";
```

As you can see, mine is on the desktop (`/Users/neal/Desktop`) in a folder called Example 15A (`/Example 15A`), and the name of the file is AppData. plist (`/AppData.plist`), which is what I named it in Step 4. This is known as a *path*. A path is a string that contains the location and name of a file.

Yours will be in the folder in which your project is located. You will have to change that (unless your name is neal) to reflect your unique configuration.

You will be changing the path every time you change the location or name of a folder your project is in.

When you start programming with either the `AppKit` (for the Mac) or the `UIKit` (for the iPhone), you won't have to specify the path so precisely. You will generally have your plist files in either what's called a *bundle* or in your home directory. An application bundle contains the application executable and any resources used by the application. It includes, for example, the application icon, other images, localized content, *and plist files*. You could also will be storing your files in your home directory, or some other place where you will be able to find it using Cocoa functionality available in your program — you won't have to "hard code" it as I have here. In the case of a Foundation Command Line Tool, however, you need to specify exactly where the plist file is.

This is a great opportunity to introduce bugs, as you move this code from project to project. So, if something doesn't seem to be working right, the location of the plist file is one of the first places to check to see if it's the cause of the problem.

Creating a mutable dictionary

Next you create a mutable dictionary and read the file into it using the `init WithContentsOfFile:` method (it needs to be mutable because I'll be showing you how to modify in the section "Updating the dictionary."

```
NSMutableDictionary *appDictionary =
        [[NSMutableDictionary alloc]    initWithContentsO
        fFile:appDataPath];
```

You specified where the file was located (`appDataPath`) and then sent a message to the `NSMutableDictionary` to initialize itself with that file.

NSDictionary, NSMutableDictionary, NSArray, and NSMutableArray all have the methods initWithContentsOfFile: and writeToFile:: that read themselves in from a file and write themselves out to a file, respectively. This is one of the things that makes property list objects so useful.

As I mentioned earlier, property list containers, and only property list containers, can read themselves in from and write themselves out to a file. The other property list objects can only store themselves, without any effort on your part, as part of a file.

Creating, initializing, and using the symbol string

The next thing you do is access the key Europe and create and initialize a string europeSymbol with its value. I do the same thing for England and englandSymbol.

```
NSString* europeSymbol = [[NSString alloc] initWithFormat:
         @"%@", [appDictionary valueForKey:@"Europe"]];
NSString* englandSymbol = [[NSString alloc]
         initWithFormat:@"%@",
         [appDictionary valueForKey:@"England"]];
```

The valueForKey: method looks for the key you give it (@"England"). If it finds the key, the corresponding value is returned (in this case £), if it can't find the key, it returns nil.

The rest of the changes just add the right currency symbol to the NSLog statements for the currency you are using — $ for your dollar-based transactions and the amount of your budget remaining, and europeSymbol (€) and englandSymbol (£) for credit card transaction in euros and pounds, respectively.

Now that you have updated the file, select the Build and Run button in the Project Window toolbar to build and run the application.

You should see the following in the Debugger Console.

```
I'm off to Europe
I'm off to England
Sending a $100.00 cash transaction
Remaining budget $900.00
Sending a $100.00 cash transaction
Remaining budget $1900.00
```

```
Sending a €100.00 credit card transaction
Remaining budget $770.00

Sending a £100.00 credit card transaction
Remaining budget $1760.00

Sending a €200.00 credit card transaction
Remaining budget $510.00

Sending a £200.00 credit card transaction
Remaining budget $1480.00

a €300.00 credit card transaction
Remaining budget $120.00

Sending a £300.00 credit card transaction
Remaining budget $1060.00
You have deleted the England part of your trip
```

You can find the completed project on the CD in the Example 15A folder, which is in the Chapter 15 folder.

Dictionaries of Dictionaries

While using a plist and dictionary this way is very clever (at least I think so), it just barely shows what you can do with dictionaries — especially considering what you will see as you look at some of the code in the frameworks. In that spirit, let's make things a little more interesting.

Creating a more complex plist

Follow these steps to delete all the entries in the plist and create a more interesting plist.

You can continue working based on what you have done or use the project in the Example 15A folder, which is in the Chapter 15 folder on the CD, as your base.

1. **Delete the Europe and England entries from your plist.**

    That will take you back to what was shown earlier in Figure 15-4. You'll have no entries.

2. **In the editor window, the root entry will be selected. Click the icon at the end of the entry, as you did in Step 5 in the earlier section "Adding a plist to Your Project" (refer to Figure 15-4).**

A new entry appears.

3. **Click the pop-up menu arrows to select Dictionary for the Type of entry you want instead of String, again, as you did in Step 5 in the section "Adding a plist to Your Project."**

4. **Type** Europe **as the key.**

5. **Click the triangle next to Europe and make sure it is pointing down, as shown in Figure 15-7. Then select the plus icon (make sure the triangle is pointing down; if not, you won't see the +).**

These disclosure triangles work the same way as those in the Finder and the Xcode editor. The property list editor interprets what you want to add based on the triangle. So, if the items are revealed (that is, the triangle is pointing down), it assumes you want to add a sub item. If the sub items are not revealed (that is, the triangle is pointing sideways), it assumes you want to add an item at that level. In this case, with the arrow pointing down, you will be adding a new entry to the Europe dictionary. If the triangle were pointing sideways, you would be entering a new entry under the root. The icon at the end of the row also helps. If it is three lines, as you see in Figure 15-7, you are going to be creating a new sub item of the entry in that row. A + tells you that you are going to be creating a new item at the root level.

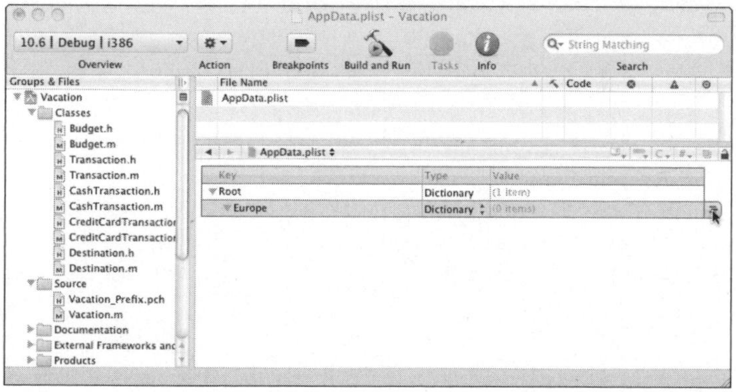

Figure 15-7:
Click to
add a new
entry to the
Europe
dictionary.

6. **Enter a String, with a Key of** `Currency` **and a Value of** `euro`**, as shown in Figure 15-8.**

   This dictionary will have two entries. One will be the name of the currency, in this case `euro`, with the key of `Currency`, and the other will be the currency symbol with the key of `Symbol`. (You won't need the currency name until you add more functionality — on your own — but you will have it here for future use.)

7. **Add the second entry to the Europe dictionary, this time with the Key of** `Symbol` **and the value of €, as shown in Figure 15-9.**

8. **Click the disclosure triangle to hide the Europe dictionary entries, as shown in Figure 15-10.**

9. **Click the + icon next to the Europe dictionary and add the England dictionary, as shown in Figure 15-11.**

   As I mentioned, since the Europe dictionary sub items are hidden, clicking the + icon adds a new entry to the root.

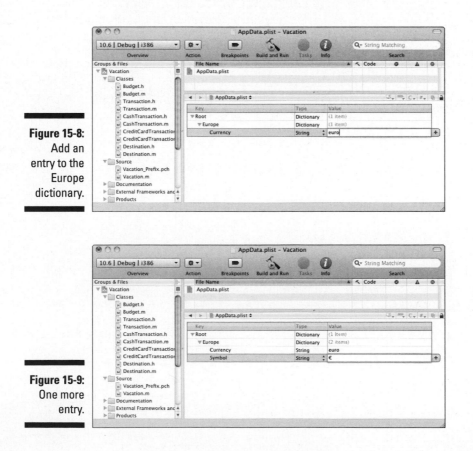

Figure 15-8:
Add an entry to the Europe dictionary.

Figure 15-9:
One more entry.

10. **Redo Steps 6 and 7 for the England dictionary. This time use the Key** `Currency` **and the Value** pound**, and the Key** `Symbol` **and the Value** £**.**

When you are done, it should look like Figure 15-12. (Make sure you click all the disclosure triangles to expand it all so you can see it all.)

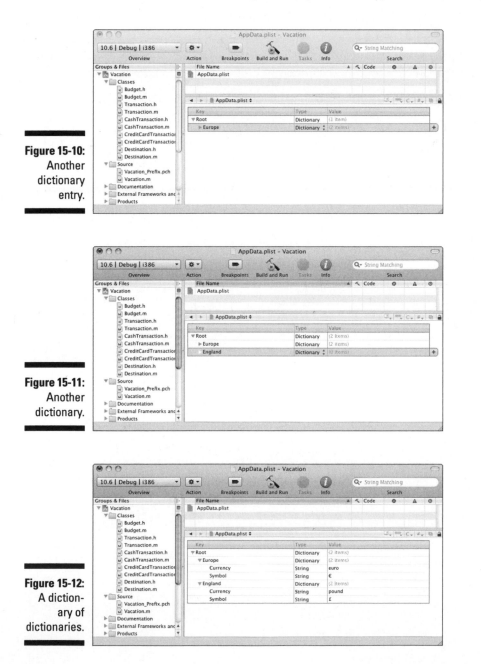

Figure 15-10:
Another
dictionary
entry.

Figure 15-11:
Another
dictionary.

Figure 15-12:
A diction-
ary of
dictionaries.

Earlier I said the entries in a dictionary can be any property list object. What you have just done is create a dictionary of dictionaries. You have a dictionary for each country that enables you to find the currency (`Currency`) for each country you are visiting and its associated currency symbol (`Symbol`). Again, although you won't be using the currency name, you will need in it the future as you turn this into a "real" application.

The first time I saw the use of a dictionary of dictionaries in code, I had trouble figuring it out, but you will see things like this, as well as arrays of dictionaries, and dictionaries of arrays, and so on throughout Cocoa and sample apps.

And since a picture is worth many hours of contemplation, Figure 15-13 shows how everything fits together.

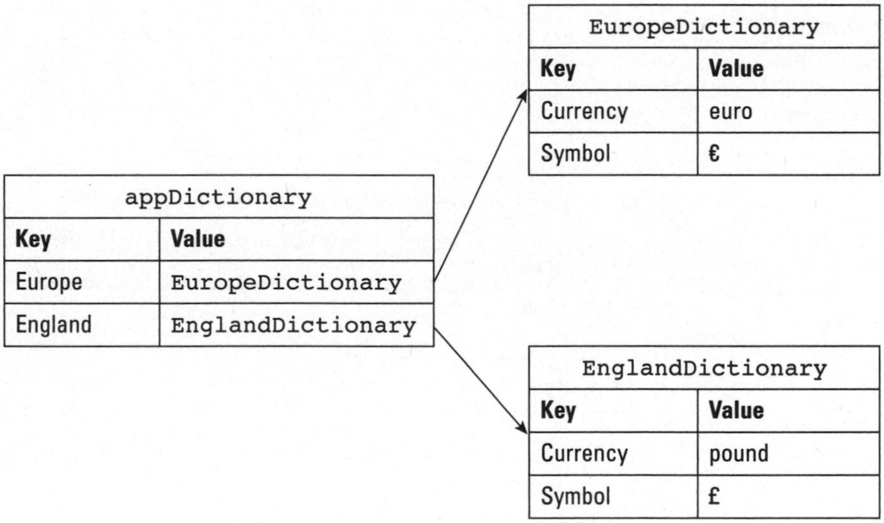

Figure 15-13: A dictionary of dictionaries.

EuropeDictionary	
Key	**Value**
Currency	euro
Symbol	€

appDictionary	
Key	**Value**
Europe	EuropeDictionary
England	EnglandDictionary

EnglandDictionary	
Key	**Value**
Currency	pound
Symbol	£

Using this new "dictionary of a dictionary" is a little more complex than before, but not much, as you will see when you write the code.

Managing a dictionary of dictionaries

Just as you did with the simple dictionary in the last version, you read in the plist and create a dictionary.

```
NSMutableDictionary* appDataDictionary=[[NSMutableDictionary alloc] initWithContentsOfFile:appDataPath];
```

This time, however, the Europe and England keys have a value of another dictionary instead of a currency symbol. So what you'll need to do is treat them as NSDictionary objects. The following code takes the value for both the Europe and England keys and assigns it to pointers to those dictionaries.

```
NSDictionary* europeDictionary = [appDataDictionary
        valueForKey:@"Europe"];
NSDictionary* englandDictionary = [appDataDictionary
        valueForKey:@"England"];
```

Now, you can access the dictionary just as you did before using the key Symbol to get the currency symbol and store it in the variables europe Symbol and englandSymbol.

```
NSString* europeSymbol = [[NSString alloc]
        initWithFormat:@"%@",
        [europeDictionary valueForKey:@"Symbol"]];
NSString* englandSymbol = [[NSString alloc]
        initWithFormat:@"%@",
        [englandDictionary valueForKey:@"Symbol"]];
```

The methods that add entries to dictionaries (as well as arrays) make *copies* of each key argument and add the copy to the dictionary. The value object, on the other hand, receives a retain message to ensure that it won't be deallocated before the dictionary is finished with it.

To create a dictionary of dictionaries in main, you need to do the following:

1. **In main in Vacation.m, shown in Figure 15-2, delete the code with the strikethrough and add the code in bold.**

    I didn't put in the whole listing for main because I made changes only to the first few lines of code.

2. **Be sure to change the** appDataPath **to whatever your folder name is for this project. I duplicated my project and gave the folder a new name Example 15B, but use your own project folder name here.**

Listing 15-2: New improved plist

```
//NSString* appDataPath = @"/Users/neal/Desktop/Example
        15A/AppData.plist";
NSString* appDataPath = @"/Users/neal/Desktop/Example 15
        B/AppData.plist";
NSMutableDictionary* appDataDictionary=[[NSMutableDictiona
        ry alloc]initWithContentsOfFile:appDataPath];
NSDictionary* europeDictionary = [appDataDictionary
        valueForKey:@"Europe"];
```

(continued)

Listing 15-2 *(continued)*

```
NSDictionary* englandDictionary = [appDataDictionary
        valueForKey:@"England"];
//NSString* europeSymbol = [[NSString alloc]
        initWithFormat:@"%@",
        [appDictionary valueForKey:@"Europe"]];
NSString* europeSymbol = [[NSString alloc]
        initWithFormat: @"%@", [europeDictionary
        valueForKey:@"Symbol"]];
//NSString* englandSymbol = [[NSString alloc]
        initWithFormat: @"%@",
        [appDictionary valueForKey:@"England"]];
NSString* englandSymbol = [[NSString alloc]
        initWithFormat: @"%@",
        [englandDictionary valueForKey:@"Symbol"]];
```

3. **Select the Build and Go icon in the Project Window toolbar to build and run the application.**

   You should see the following in the Debugger Console.

```
I'm off to Europe
I'm off to England
Sending a $100.00 cash transaction
Remaining budget $900.00
Sending a $100.00 cash transaction
Remaining budget $1900.00

Sending a €100.00 credit card transaction
Remaining budget $770.00

Sending a £100.00 credit card transaction
Remaining budget $1760.00

Sending a €200.00 credit card transaction
Remaining budget $510.00

Sending a £200.00 credit card transaction
Remaining budget $1480.00

a €300.00 credit card transaction
Remaining budget $120.00

Sending a £300.00 credit card transaction
Remaining budget $1060.00
You have deleted the England part of your trip
```

You can find the completed project on the CD in the Example 15B folder, which is in the Chapter 15 folder.

Modifying the plist

One thing about plists is that they can be modified. Although you don't want to directly modify the system-level files that you will be using (like preferences — you should use the API provided instead), it's open season on your own files.

As I said, one of the limitations of this application is that each time you run it, you start with a clean budget. While this is fun from a fantasy viewpoint, it doesn't help you manage your money. So, as all good things must come to an end, you will start keeping track of the remaining budget. Each time you run the program, you'll start where you left off the last time.

You can do this a couple of ways. You can add a new entry to the existing container you created earlier (`AppData`), or you can create a new file to store what remains in your budget. I'll show you both ways.

You'll start by adding a new entry to the `AppData` plist list, a `Budgets` dictionary. This dictionary will have keys for Europe and England. The value for each key will be the amount of the remaining budget.

Of course, you could have used Xcode's property list editor to add the new entry, but I want to show you how to do this kind of thing in your program.

Adding a new entry to the plist

To save the `budget` data, you'll start by declaring two variables to hold the budget balances for `Europe` and `England`.

```
float europeBudget = 1000;
float englandBudget = 2000;
```

Checking to see if the dictionary is there

You have to initialize these variables because the first time you run the program, there will be no `Budgets` key and corresponding dictionary in the `AppData` plist. This gives you a place to start.

Just as I did with the value for the `Europe` and `England` keys, I'll take the value of the `Budgets` key and assign it to a pointer to that dictionary.

```
NSMutableDictionary* budgetsDictionary =
        [appDataDictionary valueForKey:@"Budgets"];
```

This dictionary has to be mutable since I'll be updating the values later with the new balances.

Since the `Budgets` dictionary isn't in the plist the first time you run the application, you'll need to create it. You can determine if it's already there by checking whether `valueForKey:` returns `nil` when you look up the `Budgets` key value.

```
if (budgetsDictionary) {
   ...
}
  else {
```

Creating the new entry if it's not there

If `valueForKey:` returns `nil`, you create the new dictionary with the default values and add it to the plist.

```
NSNumber* europeBalance = [[NSNumber alloc]
                       initWithFloat: europeBudget];
NSNumber* englandBalance = [[NSNumber alloc]
                       initWithFloat: englandBudget];
budgetsDictionary = [[NSMutableDictionary alloc] initW
        ithObjectsAndKeys:europeBalance, @"Europe",
        englandBalance, @"England", nil];
```

If you remember, this is exactly what you did earlier in this chapter when I first showed you how to create a dictionary programmatically. In this case, you create a `budgetsDictionary` and initialize it with the `europeBalance` object (our old friend `NSNumber`) and the `Europe` key, and the `england Balance` objects and the `England` key.

Since dictionaries require each entry to be an object, you are going to create `NSNumber` objects for each of those balances — this is covered in Chapter 7. (Yes, sometimes programming has a strong resemblance to the movie *Groundhog Day*.)

Getting the data stored in the dictionary if it's there

If the dictionary is there, however, you look up the remaining balances for Europe and England using those keys, and assign those values to the two variables you declared earlier.

```
if (budgetsDictionary) {
  europeBudget = [[budgetsDictionary
          valueForKey:@"Europe"] floatValue];
  englandBudget = [[budgetsDictionary
          valueForKey:@"England"] floatValue];
  }
```

Then to keep everyone informed, you display the amount left to spend.

```
NSLog(@"You have $%.2f to spend in Europe",
        europeBudget);
NSLog(@"You have $%.2f to spend in England",
        englandBudget);
```

You'll also now use these balances when you create the destination objects.

```
Destination* europe = [[Destination alloc]
        initWithCountry: europeText
        andBudget:europeBudget withExchangeRate:1.25];
Destination* england = [[Destination alloc]
        initWithCountry:englandText
        andBudget:englandBudget withExchangeRate:1.50];
```

Updating the dictionary

Every time you run your program, you'll save what's left of your budget by using setObject:forKey:. If you use setObject:forKey: on a key that's already there, it replaces the old value with the new one. (If you want to take a key out of a mutable dictionary, use the removeObjectForKey: method.) Remember, these methods work only for NSMutableDictionary objects.

First you create the europeBalance and englandBalance as objects.

```
NSNumber* europeBalance = [[NSNumber alloc]
        initWithFloat:[europe leftToSpend]];
NSNumber* englandBalance = [[NSNumber alloc]
        initWithFloat:[england leftToSpend]];
```

Now that you have europeBalance and englandBalance as objects, you update the dictionary you created earlier when you read in the plist.

```
[budgetsDictionary setObject:europeBalance
                            forKey:@"Europe"];
[budgetsDictionary setObject:englandBalance
                            forKey:@"England"];
```

Now for the exciting part. Once you update the Budgets dictionary, you write the whole file back to the plist file using the path you defined earlier (appDataPath).

```
[appDataDictionary writeToFile:appDataPath
                                    atomically:YES];
```

Well, actually you don't write it; in fact, you don't do any work at all.
`writeToFile::` is an `NSDictionary` method and does what it implies. You
are actually directing the dictionary to write itself to a file. The `atomically`
parameter tells it to first write the data to an auxiliary file and once that is
successful, rename it to the path you specified. This guarantees that the file
won't be corrupted even if the system crashes during the write operation.

Now that I have written it out, I will be using the new updated dictionary
when I read it back in.

You can continue working based on what you have done or use the project
in the Example 15B folder, which is in the Chapter 15 folder on the CD, as
your base.

To add the code that keeps a running balance and saves it in a new dictionary in the plist, make the following changes in Listing 15-3 to `main` in the
`Vacation.m` file:

1. **In Listing 15-3, delete the code in** `main` **in `Vacation.m` with the
   strikethrough and add the code in bold.**

2. **Be sure to change the** `appDataPath` **to whatever your folder name
   is for this project. I duplicated my project and put it in a new folder,
   Example 15C, but use your own project folder name here.**

Listing 15-3: Modifying the Dictionary and plist

```
#import <Foundation/Foundation.h>
#import "Destination.h"

int main (int argc, const char * argv[]) {

  NSAutoreleasePool * pool = [[NSAutoreleasePool alloc]
          init];

  //NSString* appDataPath  = @"/Users/neal/Desktop/Example
          14 B/AppData.plist";
  NSString* appDataPath  = @"/Users/neal/Desktop/Example
          15 C/AppData.plist";
  NSMutableDictionary* appDataDictionary=[[NSMutableDictio
          nary alloc]initWithContentsOfFile:appDataPath];
  NSDictionary* europeDictionary = [appDataDictionary
          valueForKey:@"Europe"];
  NSDictionary* englandDictionary = [appDataDictionary
          valueForKey:@"England"];
  NSString* europeSymbol = [[NSString alloc]
          initWithFormat:@"%@", [europeDictionary
          valueForKey:@"Symbol"]];
  NSString* englandSymbol = [[NSString alloc]
          initWithFormat:@"%@", [englandDictionary
          valueForKey:@"Symbol"]];
```

```
float europeBudget = 1000;
float englandBudget = 2000;
NSMutableDictionary* budgetsDictionary =
        [appDataDictionary valueForKey:@"Budgets"] ;
if (budgetsDictionary) {
  europeBudget = [[budgetsDictionary
        valueForKey:@"Europe"] floatValue];
  englandBudget = [[budgetsDictionary
        valueForKey:@"England"] floatValue];
}
else {
  NSNumber* europeBalance = [[NSNumber alloc]
        initWithFloat:  europeBudget];
  NSNumber* englandBalance = [[NSNumber alloc]
        initWithFloat:  englandBudget];

  budgetsDictionary = [[NSMutableDictionary alloc]
        initWithObjectsAndKeys:
        europeBalance,@"Europe",
        englandBalance,@"England", nil];
  [appDataDictionary setObject: budgetsDictionary
        forKey: @"Budgets"];
}
  NSLog(@"You have $%.2f to spend in Europe",
        europeBudget );
  NSLog(@"You have $%.2f to spend in England",
        englandBudget );


NSString* europeText = [[NSString alloc] initWithFormat:
        @"%@", @"Europe"];
//Destination* europe = [[Destination alloc]
        initWithCountry: europeText andBudget:1000.00
        withExchangeRate: 1.25];
Destination* europe = [[Destination
        alloc] initWithCountry:europeText
        andBudget:europeBudget withExchangeRate:1.25];
[europeText release];
NSString* englandText = [[NSString alloc]
        initWithFormat:@"%@", @"England"];
//Destination* england = [[Destination alloc]
        initWithCountry:englandText andBudget:2000.00
        withExchangeRate:1.50];
Destination* england = [[Destination alloc]
        initWithCountry:englandText
        andBudget:englandBudget withExchangeRate: 1.50];
[englandText release];

for (int n = 1; n <  2; n++) {
  double transaction = n*100.00;
  NSLog (@"Sending a $%.2f cash transaction",
        transaction);
```

(continued)

Listing 15-3 *(continued)*

```
  [europe spendCash:transaction];
  NSLog(@"Remaining budget $%.2f", [europe
        leftToSpend]);
  NSLog(@"Sending a $%.2f cash transaction",
        transaction);
  [england spendCash:transaction];
  NSLog(@"Remaining budget $%.2f", [england
        leftToSpend]);
}


[europe setExchangeRate:1.30];
[england setExchangeRate:1.40];

int n =1;
while (n < 4) {
double transaction = n*100.00;
NSLog (@"Sending a %@%.2f credit card transaction",
        europeSymbol, transaction);
[europe chargeCreditCard:transaction];
NSLog(@"Remaining budget $%.2f", [europe leftToSpend]);
NSLog (@"Sending a %@%.2f credit card transaction",
        englandSymbol, transaction);
[england chargeCreditCard:transaction];
NSLog(@"Remaining budget $%.2f", [england leftToSpend]);
n++;
}

NSNumber* europeBalance = [[NSNumber alloc]
        initWithFloat:[europe leftToSpend]];
NSNumber* englandBalance = [[NSNumber alloc]
        initWithFloat:[england leftToSpend]];
[budgetsDictionary setObject: europeBalance
        forKey:@"Europe"];
[budgetsDictionary setObject: englandBalance
        forKey:@"England"];
[appDataDictionary writeToFile:appDataPath
        atomically:YES];


NSString *returnedCountry = [england country];
NSLog (@"You have deleted the %@ part of your trip",
        returnedCountry);
[returnedCountry release];
[england release];
[pool drain];
return 0;
}
```

3. Select the Build and Run button in the Project Window toolbar to build and run the application.

You should see the following in the Debugger Console:

```
You have $1000.00 to spend in Europe
You have $2000.00 to spend in England
I'm off to Europe
I'm off to England
Sending a $100.00 cash transaction
Remaining budget $900.00
Sending a $100.00 cash transaction
Remaining budget $1900.00

Sending a €100.00 credit card transaction
Remaining budget $770.00

Sending a £100.00 credit card transaction
Remaining budget $1760.00

Sending a €200.00 credit card transaction
Remaining budget $510.00

Sending a £200.00 credit card transaction
Remaining budget $1480.00

Sending a €300.00 credit card transaction
Remaining budget $120.00

Sending a £300.00 credit card transaction
Remaining budget $1060.00
You have deleted the England part of your trip
```

You'll need to run this again to appreciate your handiwork. Before you do, notice the amounts in the last two "Remaining budget" statements — $120.00 and $1060.00, respectively (they are shown in bold).

4. Select the Build and Run button in the Project Window toolbar to build and run the application.

As you can see, the starting budgets (in bold) are the same as the ending ones I had you notice in Step 3 (as you would expect).

```
You have $120.00 to spend in Europe
You have $1060.00 to spend in England
I'm off to Europe
I'm off to England
Sending a $100.00 cash transaction
Remaining budget $20.00
Sending a $100.00 cash transaction
Remaining budget $960.00
```

```
Sending a €100.00 credit card transaction
Remaining budget $-110.00
```

```
Sending a £100.00 credit card transaction
Remaining budget $820.00
```

```
Sending a €200.00 credit card transaction
Remaining budget $-370.00
```

```
a £200.00 credit card transaction
Remaining budget $540.00
```

```
Sending a €300.00 credit card transaction
Remaining budget $-760.00
```

```
Sending a £300.00 credit card transaction
Remaining budget $120.00
You have deleted the England part of your trip
```

Of course, after you run this a few times, you find yourself deeply in debt. If you close and then reopen the project, you will actually see the new entry in the AppData plist. Delete it in the dictionary using the Xcode plist editor by selecting the Budgets dictionary entry and pressing Delete, and then selecting File⇨Save or press ⌘+S.

If you don't see the Budgets dictionary in the plist, and you don't want to go to the trouble of closing and then opening the project, click in any Key or Value field in the AppData plist and add and then delete a space (I know you really haven't changed anything, but that's the point). Then select File⇨Save or press ⌘+S. You get a message saying, "This document's file has been changed by another application since you opened or saved it"; click Save and you'll go back to your original budget.

You can find the completed project on the CD in the Example 15C folder, which is in the Chapter 15 folder.

Saving Data in a Separate File

Of course, a dictionary is just another property list object, and so is an array. So instead of adding the new Budgets dictionary to the AppData plist, I'll show you how to save the budget data in an array.

You declare the array you are going to save and initialize it to nil.

NSArray* tripBalance = nil;

You'll be adding a new file here, so you need to create a new path for the file you want to save.

```
NSString* balancePath =@î/Users/neal/Desktop/Example 15 D/
        BalanceData.txt";
```

Notice the filename will be `BalanceData.txt`, and it will be in the Example 15D folder. As with `appData`, you will be changing the path every time you change the location or the name of the folder your project is in.

You'll start again by reading in the data. Reading in the array you saved is similar to reading in the plist.

```
if ([[NSFileManager defaultManager] fileExistsAtPath:
        balancePath]) {
```

First, you ask the file manager (`[NSFileManager defaultManager]`) to check whether the file is there. Previously, you knew the plist was there; you just weren't sure the Budgets entry had been added. If this is the first time you are running the program, the file won't be there. Alternatively, you could have just read in the file and checked for `nil`.

If the file is there, you read in the array using its `initWithContentsOf File:` (just as I did with the plist) and copy the values in the array to the `europeBudget` and `englandBudget` variables as you did before.

```
tripBalance = [[NSArray alloc]
                        initWithContentsOfFile:balancePath];
europeBudget = [[tripBalance objectAtIndex:0] floatValue];
englandBudget = [[tripBalance objectAtIndex:1]
                                            floatValue];
    }
```

If the file isn't there, you'll just continue to use the default values you initialized `europeBudget` and `englandBudget` with earlier.

The following is an alternative method for reading in files:

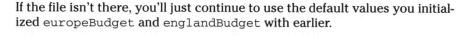

```
initWithContentsOfFile:options:error:
```

The `options:` argument gives you control over file system caching and is way, way beyond the scope of this book. The `error:` argument returns a pointer to an NSError object. I'll leave the exploration of this topic to you as a "personal" exercise.

Again, after sleeping, eating, and drinking your way through Europe and England, you'll need to save what little you have left.

```
if (tripBalance) [tripBalance release];
tripBalance= [[NSArray alloc] initWithObjects:
           europeBalance, englandBalance, nil];
[tripBalance writeToFile:balancePath atomically:YES];
```

You check to see if there is an array that you created when you read in the data — that is why you have to be sure to initialize it to nil when you declare it. If there is, you release it and create a new one. This is an alternative to replacing each object in the array and means that you don't need a mutable array. Then, just as you did with the dictionary, you tell the array to write itself as a file.

You can continue working based on what you have done or use the project in the Example 15C folder, which is in the Chapter 15 folder on the CD, as your base.

1. **In Listing 15-4, delete the code in main in Vacation.m with the strikethrough and add the code in bold.**

   I didn't include the whole listing for main because you will delete only the code you added in the previous section, "Modifying the plist."

   Instead of doing the delete and add thing, you could start again with the Example 15B project on the CD and add the new code in the same places you added the code in the previous section.

2. **Be sure to change the appDataPath to whatever your folder name is for this project. I duplicated my project and put it in a new folder, Example 15D, but use your own project folder name here.**

3. **Notice that there is a new file balancePath. Be sure to change the balancePath to whatever your folder name is for this project.**

Listing 15-4: Saving Balance Data to an Array

```
//NSString* appDataPath = @"/Users/neal/Desktop/Example
           15 C/AppData.plist";
  NSString* appDataPath = @"/Users/neal/Desktop/Example
           15 D/AppData.plist";
...
  float europeBudget = 1000;
  float englandBudget =2000;;
```

```
//NSMutableDictionary* budgetsDictionary =
        [appDataDictionary valueForKey:@"Budgets"] ;
//if (budgetsDictionary) {
//   europeBudget = [[budgetsDictionary
        valueForKey:@"Europe"] floatValue];
//   englandBudget = [[budgetsDictionary
        valueForKey:@"England"] floatValue];
//}
//}
//else {
//   NSNumber* europeBalance = [[NSNumber alloc]
        initWithFloat: europeBudget];
//   NSNumber* englandBalance = [[NSNumber alloc]
        initWithFloat: englandBudget];

//   budgetsDictionary = [[NSMutableDictionary alloc] ini
        tWithObjectsAndKeys:europeBalance, @"Europe",
        englandBalance, @"England", nil];
//   [appDataDictionary setObject:budgetsDictionary
                                forKey: @"Budgets"];
//}

  NSArray* tripBalance = nil;
  NSString* balancePath =@"/Users/neal/Desktop/Example 15
        D/BalanceData.txt";

  if ([[NSFileManager defaultManager]
                  fileExistsAtPath: balancePath]) {
    tripBalance = [[NSArray alloc]
                  initWithContentsOfFile:balancePath];
    europeBudget = [[tripBalance objectAtIndex:0]
                                        floatValue];
    englandBudget = [[tripBalance objectAtIndex:1]
                                        floatValue];
  }
  NSLog(@"You have $%.2f to spend in Europe",
                                  europeBudget );
  NSLog(@"You have $%.2f to spend in England",
                                  englandBudget );
...

  NSNumber* europeBalance = [[NSNumber alloc]
        initWithFloat:[europe leftToSpend]];
  NSNumber* englandBalance = [[NSNumber alloc]
        initWithFloat:[england leftToSpend]];
```

(continued)

Listing 15-4 *(continued)*

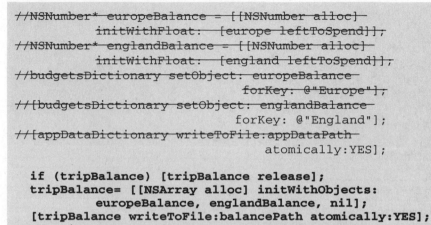

```
//NSNumber* europeBalance = [[NSNumber alloc]
        initWithFloat:  [europe leftToSpend]];
//NSNumber* englandBalance = [[NSNumber alloc]
        initWithFloat:  [england leftToSpend]];
//budgetsDictionary setObject: europeBalance
                            forKey: @"Europe"];
//[budgetsDictionary setObject: englandBalance
                            forKey: @"England"];
//[appDataDictionary writeToFile:appDataPath
                            atomically:YES];

if (tripBalance) [tripBalance release];
tripBalance= [[NSArray alloc] initWithObjects:
        europeBalance, englandBalance, nil];
[tripBalance writeToFile:balancePath atomically:YES];
NSString *returnedCountry = [england country];
```

4. **Select the Build and Run button in the Project Window toolbar to build and run the application.**

   You should see the same result that you saw previously.

This time to start over, you will need to delete the new file you created — `BalanceData.txt`, which you will find in your project folder.

You can find the completed project on the CD in the Example 15D folder, which is in the Chapter 15 folder.

Saving Objects as Objects

This chapter shows you a great way to start saving your data, but there are other ways as well.

As you develop applications, you will find that not all of your objects are made up of property list objects. Even in this simple application, your `Destination` object has an array of `Transaction` objects.

While most objects can eventually be deconstructed into property list objects, this can take a lot of work and requires changing the logic you use if you add or remove something from an object — not very extensible is it?

Cocoa does, however, provide several ways to save objects as objects. I'll leave this, too, as an exercise for the reader.

Chapter 16

Extending the Behavior of Objects

● ●

In This Chapter

▶ Using delegation to implement a new transaction

▶ Defining formal and informal protocols

▶ Using categories to extend a class

● ●

*I*n your application so far, you have two kinds of transaction objects, a
`CashTransaction` and a `CreditCardTransaction`. As I was field testing the application, sitting in a bar (bars in Italy serve coffee, so don't get too
excited) on the Grand Canal in Venice, I needed some euros, so I went to the
ATM machine.

It dawned on me that since this was not my own bank's ATM, I had to pay a
$2.00 transaction fee. I realized I need to add a new type of transaction — ATM.

In Chapter 11, you learn to use inheritance to create subclasses such as
`CashTransaction` and `CreditCardTransaction` to *implement generic
functionality* that was defined as a superclass, such as the spend functionality
in the `Transaction` class. I also mentioned that you could also use inheritance to add new functionality, new methods, and new instance variables to a
subclass.

So it would make sense to use inheritance to create a new subclass. If I did
that it would also mean, thanks to polymorphism, the only changes I would
have to make to my program, besides defining the new class, would be to
add a new method to `Destination` (in addition to the existing `spendCash:`
and `chargeCreditCard:` methods) — `useATM:` to create the new ATM
transaction.

As you start to work with the UIKit and AppKit frameworks, you will be using
inheritance to extend the behavior of framework classes and to add your own
unique application behavior. But sometimes, for some technical and architec-
tural reason beyond the scope of this book, inheritance will not be an option.
But all is not lost. Objective-C allows you to accomplish virtually the same

thing using *delegation*, which enables you to implement methods defined by other classes, and *categories*, which enable you to extend a behavior of a class without subclassing.

While you are probably not going to use delegation and categories in your programs (yet), they are used a lot in the frameworks. So, in order to make using the frameworks as transparent as possible, I will explain them before you stumble across them on you own. As I've mentioned, frameworks provide a good model for how to create extensible and enhanceable applications, and in this chapter, you'll see an example of that in action.

To show you how to do that, instead of using inheritance and modifying the code in `Destination` (or creating a `Destination` subclass) to implement `useATM:`, I'll show you how to accomplish the same thing using delegation and categories.

I am not suggesting you implement a new `Transaction` type this way. On the contrary, creating a new `Transaction` subclass is the best way to do that. I am only showing you how to use delegation and categories in this way to illustrate how delegation and categories work since it is often one of the more difficult concepts for programmers new to Cocoa and Objective-C to understand.

Understanding Delegation

I'll start by showing you how to use delegation to create a class that implements the `spend` method of the `Transaction` (the *delegator*) class, one that will behave in the same way as subclass.

Delegation is a pattern (I explain patterns in Chapter 11) used extensively in the UIKit and AppKit frameworks to customize the behavior of an object without subclassing. Instead, one object (a framework object) delegates the task of implementing one of its methods to another object.

To implement a delegated method, you will put the code for your application-specific behavior in a separate (*delegate*) object. When a request is made of the delegator, the delegate's method that implements the application-specific behavior is invoked by the delegator.

The methods a class delegates are defined in a *protocol* — similar to the "spend: protocol" you define in the `Transaction` class in Chapter 10. Protocols can be *formal* or *informal*. I'm going to start with formal protocols and then work my way into informal ones.

Using Protocols

The Objective-C language provides a way to formally declare a list of methods (including declared properties) as a protocol. Formal protocols are supported by the language and the runtime system. For example, the compiler can check for types based on protocols, and objects can report whether they conform to a protocol.

Declaring a protocol

You declare formal protocols with the @protocol directive. If you wanted to create a Transaction Delegate protocol that required that its delegates implement a spend message (like its subclasses), you would code the following:

```
@protocol TransactionDelegate
@required

- (void) spend: (Transaction *) aTransaction;

@optional

- (void) transaction: (Transaction *) transaction spend:
        (double) amount;

@end
```

Methods can be optional or required. If you do not mark a method as optional, it is assumed to be required; but you can make that designation specific via the use of the @required keyword.

I have declared the TransactionDelegate protocol with a required method — spend: — and an optional method transaction: spend:.

The more formal representation is

```
@protocol ProtocolName

   method declarations
@end
```

The method transaction: (Transaction*) transaction spend: (double) amount may look a little weird. The method name is transaction:spend:, and you'll see examples of this in some of the framework protocols where a pointer to the delegating object is the first argument in the method.

In Chapter 17, you see that you can use Interface Builder to connect objects to their delegates; or you can set the connection programmatically through the delegating object's `setDelegate:` method or `delegate` property. In this chapter, I'll show you how to set the connection programmatically.

Generally, protocol declarations are in the file of the class that defines it. In this case, you will add the `TransactionDelegate` protocol declaration to the Transaction.h file.

Adopting a protocol

Adopting a protocol is similar in some ways to declaring a superclass. In both cases, you are adding methods to your class. When you use a superclass, you are adding inherited methods; when you use a protocol, you are adding methods declared in the protocol list. A class adopts a formal protocol by listing the protocol within angle brackets after the superclass name.

```
@interface ClassName : ItsSuperclass < protocol list >
```

A class can adopt more than one protocol, and if so, names in the protocol list are separated by commas.

```
@interface Translator : NSObject < English, Italian >
```

Just as with any other class, you can add instance variables, properties, and even nonprotocol methods to a class that adopts a protocol.

In this case, you will be creating a new class, `ATMTransactionDelegate` that will adopt the `TransactionDelegate` protocol.

If you have been following along with me, I'll now be extending what you do in Chapter 15. If you want to start from a clean copy, you can use the project found in the Chapter 16 Start Here folder on the CD.

1. **Select the Classes folder in the Groups & Files list and then select File⇨New File from the main menu (or press ⌘+N) to get the New File dialog.**

   This tells Xcode to place the new file in the Classes folder.

2. **In the leftmost column of the dialog, first select Cocoa under Mac OS X; then select the Objective-C class template in the top-right pane. Make sure NSObject is selected in the Subclass of the drop-down menu.**

   You'll see a new screen asking for some more information.

3. **Enter ATMTransactionDelegate.m in the File Name field and make sure the checkbox to have Xcode create ATMTransactionDelegate.h. is checked; then click Finish.**

   This is the new class that will process the ATM transactions.

4. **Add the code in bold to the ATMTransactionDelegate.h file.**

```
#import <Cocoa/Cocoa.h>
#import "Transaction.h"

@interface ATMTransactionDelegate : NSObject
        <TransactionDelegate> {

}

@end
```

   You will need to import the header file where the protocol is declared since the methods declared in the protocol you adopted are not declared elsewhere — in this case, as I said, you will be declaring the protocol in the Transaction.h file.

5. **Add the** spend: **and** dealloc **methods to the ATMTransactionDelegate.m file.**

```
#import "ATMTransactionDelegate.h"
#import "Budget.h"

@implementation ATMTransactionDelegate

- (void) spend: (Transaction *) aTransaction {

  [aTransaction.budget spendDollars:
                       aTransaction.amount + 2.00];
}

- (void) dealloc {

  [super dealloc];
}

@end
```

   When you adopt a protocol, you must implement all the required methods the protocol declares; otherwise, the compiler issues a warning. As you can see, the ATMTransactionDelegate class does define all the required methods declared in the TransactionDelegate protocol. As I said, you can add instance variables, properties, and even nonprotocol methods to a class that adopts a protocol, although your ATMTransactionDelegate is a class that simply implements the required protocol methods.

As you can see, this new transaction is at heart a dollar transaction that adds the $2.00 "convenience" fee charged by the ATM.

Even though `ATMTransactionDelegate` implements a protocol that is used by the `Transaction` object, it does not automatically have access to the instance variables of the `Transaction` object. This means that you will have to make `amount` and `budget` `Transaction` class properties and pass a pointer the `Transaction` object so `ATMTransactionDelegate` can access those instance variables.

I am not going to implement the optional method; I just wanted to show you how to declare one.

Adding delegation to Transaction

So far you have defined protocol based on the `Transaction` class that requires `Transaction` class delegates to implement the `spend:` method. It now becomes the responsibility of the delegator, `Transaction`, to invoke the `spend:` method in its delegate. Here's how you'll do that in `Transactions`.

1. **Add the code in bold to the Transaction.h file.**

```
#import <Cocoa/Cocoa.h>
@class Budget;

@interface Transaction : NSObject {

  Budget *budget;
  double amount;
  NSString* name;
  id delegate;
}

- (id) initWithAmount: (double) theAmount forBudget:
        (Budget*) aBudget;
- (void) spend;
@property (nonatomic, retain) Budget *budget;
@property (nonatomic, retain) id delegate;
@property (readwrite) double amount;

@end


@protocol TransactionDelegate
@required

- (void) spend: (Transaction *) aTransaction;

@optional
```

```
- (void) transaction: (Transaction*) transaction
        spend: (double) amount;

@end
```

You did several things here:

    a. Added the instance variable `delegate`. This is the object that will implement the behavior you specified in the protocol. These are generally declared to be a generic object (`id`) since the point here is that you won't know what class is implementing the delegate behavior (although you do here).

    b. Added three properties, one to be able to set the delegate, and two others to allow the delegate access to the `amount` and `budget` instance variable.

    c. Declared the `TransactionDelegate` protocol.

2. Add the code in bold to the Transaction.m file.

```
#import "Transaction.h"
#import "Budget.h"

@implementation Transaction
@synthesize budget, delegate , amount;

- (void) spend {
  if ([delegate respondsToSelector:
                       @selector(spend:)])
    [delegate spend:self];
}

- (id) initWithAmount: (double) theAmount forBudget:
        (Budget*) aBudget {
  if (self = [super init]) {
      self. budget = aBudget;
    amount = theAmount;
  }
   return self;
}

- (void) dealloc {

  [budget release];
  [super dealloc];
}

@end
```

You added the @synthesize statement for delegate, amount, and budget to have the compiler generate the getters and setters for you.

Thus far, Destination has never created a Transaction object, and its spend: method has never been invoked. Using delegation, however, requires creating Transaction objects that invoke the delegate's spend: method in Transaction object's spend: method.

Because this is a formal protocol, I can assume that since spend: is @required, the delegate object will have implemented it. If this were an informal protocol, I would need to determine if spend is implemented. I can send the delegate the message.

```
if ([delegate respondsToSelector:
                    @selector(spend:)])
```

respondsToSelector: is an NSObject method that tells you whether a method has been implemented. As I said, since I am making this method @required, I don't have do determine that. However, I wanted to show you how much information is available at runtime in Objective-C, and how to implement delegation for the optional methods of formal protocols and for all methods of informal protocols.

If the method has been implemented, I then send it the spend: message.

Categories

In order to complete the implementation of the ATM transaction, you'll need to add a method like destination to process an ATM transaction just as it does cash and credit cards. The preferred approach is to add the new method to the Destination class or add a new method to a subclass (you'd have to add a subclass if you did have the source code, as is the case with a framework), but instead I want to show another Objective-C feature.

One of the features of the dynamic runtime dispatch mechanism employed by Objective-C is that you can add methods to existing classes without sub-classing. The Objective-C term for these new methods is *categories*. A *category* allows you to add methods to an existing class — even to one to which you do not have the source. This is a powerful feature that allows you to extend the functionality of existing classes.

Using categories, you can also split the implementation of your own classes between several files.

How would I use categories to add the `useATM:` method to my `Destination` class? I would start by creating a new category — `ATM`.

```
@interface Destination (ATM)
```

This looks a lot like class interface declaration — except the category name is listed within parentheses after the class name, and there is no superclass (or colon for that matter). Unlike protocols, categories *do* have access to all the instance variables and methods of a class. And I do mean all, even ones declared `@private`, but you'll need to import the interface file for the class it extends. You can also add as many categories as you want.

You can add methods to a class by declaring them in an interface file under a category name and defining them in an implementation file under the same name. What you can't do is add additional instance variables.

The methods the category adds become honestly and truly part of the class type; they aren't treated as "step methods." The methods you will add to `Destination` using the `ATM` category become part of the `Destination` class and are inherited by all the class's subclasses, just like other methods. The category methods can do anything that methods defined in the class proper can do. At runtime, there's no difference.

So, to add this new method, `useATM:`, to `Destination`, you create a category, as follows:

1. **Select the Classes folder in the Groups & Files list and then select File⇨New File from the main menu (or press ⌘+N) to get the New File dialog.**

   This tells Xcode to place the new file in the Classes folder.

2. **In the leftmost column of the dialog, first select Cocoa under Mac OS X; then select the Objective-C class template in the top-right pane. Make sure NSObject is selected in the Subclass of the drop-down menu.**

   You'll see a new screen asking for some more information.

3. **Enter DestinationCategory.m in the File Name field and make sure the checkbox to have Xcode create DestinationCategory.h. is checked; then click Finish.**

4. **Be sure to change the `appDataPath` and `balanceDataPath` in main in Vacation.m to whatever your folder name is for this project.**

   I duplicated my project and gave it a new name, Example 16, but use your own project name here.

```
//NSString* appDataPath =@"/Users/neal/Desktop/Example
      15 D/AppData.plist";
NSString* appDataPath = @"/Users/neal/Desktop/Example
      16/AppData.plist";
//NSString* balancePath =@"/Users/neal/Desktop/Example
      15 D/BalanceData.txt";
NSString* balancePath = @"/Users/neal/Desktop/Example
      16/BalanceData.txt";
```

5. **Delete the code with the strikethrough and add the code in bold to the DestinationCategory.h file.**

```
#import <Cocoa/Cocoa.h>
#import "Destination.h"


//@interface DestinationCategory : NSObject {
  @interface Destination (ATM)

  -(void) useATM: (double)amount;

//}

@end
```

6. **Delete the commented-out code with the strikethrough and add the code in bold to the DestinationCategory.m file.**

```
#import "DestinationCategory.h"
#import "Transaction.h"
#import "ATMTransactionDelegate.h"

// @implementation DestinationCategory

@implementation Destination (ATM)

-(void) useATM: (double)amount {

  ATMTransactionDelegate *aTransactionDelegate =
        [[ATMTransactionDelegate alloc] init];

  Transaction *aTransaction = [[Transaction alloc]
        initWithAmount: amount forBudget: theBudget];
  aTransaction.delegate = aTransactionDelegate;
  [transactions addObject:aTransaction];
  [aTransaction spend];
  [aTransaction release];
}

@end
```

The new `useATM:` method is almost the same as the previous destination methods; you even added the transaction to the `transactions` array. The only difference here is that you are creating both a `Transaction` object and a delegate that will implement the `spend:` message and updating the transaction object with its delegate in the `useATM:` method.

Figure 16-1 shows the relationship between the `DestinationCategory`'s `useATM:`, the `Transaction`'s `spend:`, and the `ATMTransactionDelegate`'s `spend:` methods.

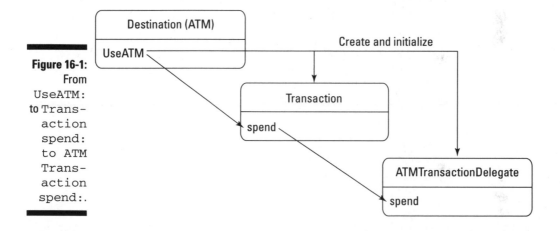

Figure 16-1:
From
`UseATM:`
to `Trans-`
`action`
`spend:`
to ATM
`Trans-`
`action`
`spend:`.

It would have been a lot easier not to create all these new files and just stuff the implementations and interfaces in existing files. I chose to do it the "hard way" because I want you to understand how to structure a real application. You'll thank me later.

7. **Somewhere in the group of** `#imports` **in** main **in Vacation.m, add**

```
#import "DestinationCategory.h"
```

8. **Scroll down and after the** while **loop in** main **in Vacation.m, add the following line of code — this will be your only ATM transaction.**

```
NSLog (@"Sending a $50.00 ATM transaction");
[europe useATM: 50];
NSLog(@"Remaining budget $%.2f",
                      [europe leftToSpend]);
```

9. **Delete the previous `balanceData.txt` file — which makes it easier to see that your updated application works correctly.**

10. **Select the Build and Run button in the Project Window toolbar to build and run the application.**

    You should see the following in the Debugger Console. I've highlighted the new transaction in bold.

```
You have $1000.00 to spend in Europe
You have $2000.00 to spend in England
I'm off to Europe
I'm off to England
Sending a $100.00 cash transaction
Remaining budget $900.00
Sending a $100.00 cash transaction
Remaining budget $1900.00
Sending a €100.00 credit card transaction
Remaining budget $770.00
Sending a £100.00 credit card transaction
Remaining budget $1760.00
Sending a €200.00 credit card transaction
Remaining budget $510.00
Sending a £200.00 credit card transaction
Remaining budget $1480.00
Sending a €300.00 credit card transaction
Remaining budget $120.00
Sending a £300.00 credit card transaction
Remaining budget $1060.00
Sending a $50.00 ATM transaction
Remaining budget $68.00
You have deleted the England part of your trip
```

You can find the completed project on the CD in the Chapter 16 folder.

Using categories

You can use categories several ways:

- ✔ To extend classes defined by other implementers (instead of subclassing — this is what you just did for `Destination`).

- ✔ To declare informal protocols — I told you I'd get back to this; you have come full circle here, so let's examine informal protocols.

Defining informal protocols

In addition to formal protocols, you can also define an informal protocol by grouping the methods in a category declaration:

```
@interface Transaction (TransactionDelegate)

- (void) spend;

@end
```

In fact, if you added the preceding code to the Transaction.h file and changed the ATMTransactionDelegate.h as follows:

```
@interface ATMTransactionDelegate : NSObject/*
           <TransactionDelegate> */
```

your program would work the same way.

Being informal, protocols declared in categories don't receive much language support. There's no type checking at compile time, for example.

An informal protocol may be useful when all the methods are optional, such as for a delegate, but it is typically better to use a formal protocol with optional methods.

I've included informal protocols here because they are used by Cocoa, especially in the AppKit on the Mac.

Chapter 17

Adding an iPhone User Interface

● ●

In This Chapter

▶ Painlessly putting a user interface on the model

▶ Using Interface Builder to create a user interface

▶ Adding controls to the view

▶ Creating a view controller

▶ Launching the application in the iPhone Simulator

● ●

I've been promising you all along, at least since Chapter 11, that if you create the right class structure, putting on a user interface will be easy. As you'll see, I wasn't exaggerating when I said that. The only challenge will be actually learning to create a user interface on the iPhone in this chapter and the Mac in Chapter 18. To do that, you'll need to know the basics of a program called Interface Builder (part of the SDK), which you will use to build the user interface.

Along the way, I will also tie together a number of the concepts I've talked about that relate to creating enhanceable and extensible applications. Frameworks, as I've said again and again, are the poster children for enhanceability and extensibility, and now you will finally get to see why. They are created to be reused, which as I said earlier, is the same thing as being extensible, and you can integrate techniques that the framework builders use into your own programs.

When you are done with this chapter and Chapter 18, though you will have learned some about developing iPhone and Mac OS X applications, you'll need to learn more about both. So, I suggest you get yourself copies of *iPhone Application Development For Dummies* by yours truly and *Cocoa Programming for Mac OS X For Dummies* by Erick Tejkowski.

I will start with the iPhone and then move on to the Mac in the next chapter. Even if you are interested in only one of these platforms, I encourage you to read both chapters because I'll be discussing different aspects of extensibility in each.

Creating Your Project

To develop an iPhone application, you work in an Xcode project — just as you have done so far. The only difference is that this time you will be creating an iPhone project.

1. **Launch Xcode if it is not already running.**

2. **Choose File⇨New Project to create a new project, or press Shift+⌘+N.**

3. **In the New Project window (see Figure 17-1), click Application under the iPhone OS heading.**

   Just as before, when you select a template, a brief description of the template is displayed underneath the main pane. As you know, each of these choices is actually a template that generates some code. In the past, when you were using the Foundation Command Line Tool, that code was minimal. Now, however, you are going to see a lot more.

Figure 17-1:
The New
Project
Assistant.

4. **Select View-based Application from the choices displayed and then click Choose.**

   Xcode will then display a standard save sheet.

5. **Enter the name** `iVacation` **in the Save As field, choose a Save location, and then click Save.**

After you click Save, Xcode creates the project and opens the project window.

If you explore the project at this point, you will see code generated for you that does many of the things you need to do to initialize an application. You'll also see some code commented out. I'll get to what's relevant to this application later.

Note that the Overview menu in the Project Window toolbar shows Simulator - 3.0 | Debug (or whatever the latest release of the iPhone OS is). If not, select it from the drop-down menu.

With your project set up, you are now ready to use Interface Builder — an application is included in the SDK that you'll use to design and build the user interface. Interface Builder uses .xib files, which Xcode conveniently created for you when you chose the View-based Application template.

Using Interface Builder to Create a User Interface

Here's how to use Interface Builder to create a user interface:

1. **In the Groups & Files list (on the left side of the project window), click the triangles next to the Classes and Resources folders to expand them, as shown in Figure 17-2.**

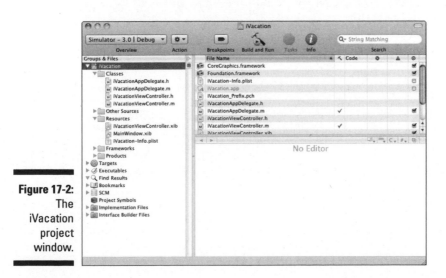

Figure 17-2: The iVacation project window.

2. **In the Resources folder, double-click the**
   IVacationViewController.xib file.

   Doing so launches Interface Builder. If you've never run this program
   before, you'll end up with something that looks like Figure 17-3. (If
   you've already been using Interface Builder, you'll see the windows as
   you last left them.)

   Interface Builder is not merely a program that builds graphical user
   interfaces. As you'll see, it works with Objective-C to let you build (and
   automatically create at runtime) both objects for the user interface and
   the objects that provide the infrastructure for your application.

3. **Check to see whether the Library window (at the right in Figure**
   17-3) is open. If it isn't, open it by choosing Tools⇨Library or press
   ⌘⇨+Shift+L. Make sure Objects is selected in the mode selector at the
   top of the Library window and Library is selected in the drop-down
   menu below the mode selector.

   The Library has all the components you can use to build a user interface. These include the things you see on the iPhone screen — such
   as labels, buttons, and text fields — and those you need to create the
   "plumbing" to support the views (and your model), such as the controller I explain in Chapter 11. You won't need to add any objects in this
   chapter, but you do in Chapter 18.

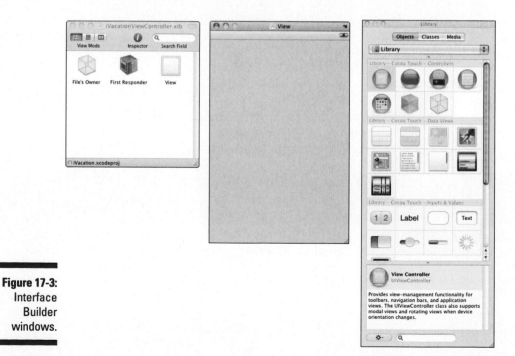

Figure 17-3:
Interface
Builder
windows.

As you saw, `iVacationViewController.xib` was created by Xcode when you created the project from the template. In the iVacationView-Controller window, as you can see in Figure 17-3, a *view* is already here, which is what you will see on the iPhone screen. Now you add some text fields, buttons, and labels so that you can enter a transaction and have the remaining budget displayed. When your application is launched, those items will be created for you and displayed on the screen.

4. **Drag a Text Field item from the Library into the View window to add a text entry field, as shown in Figure 17-4.**

Notice the blue lines (at the border) displayed by Interface Builder. They're there to help you conform to the Apple User Interface Guidelines. (You can see the lines best onscreen.)

A Text Field allows you to enter data, and this is where you will be able to enter a transaction amount (yes, no more automatically generated transactions in `for` and `while` loops — I bet you thought that would never end).

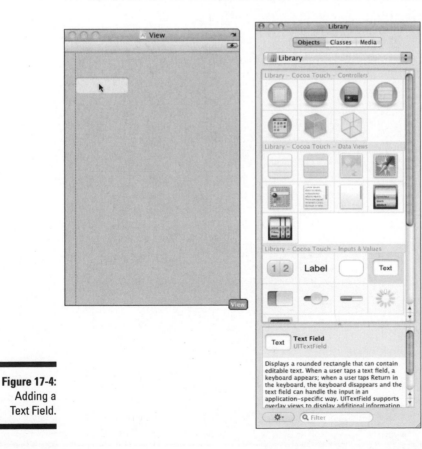

Figure 17-4:
Adding a Text Field.

5. **Drag a Label item from Library window over to the View window, as shown in Figure 17-5.**

   You'll see the blue lines again to help you align the items.

   Labels display static text in the view (*static text* can't be edited by the user).

6. **Double-click in the Label to enter** 10,000.00 **(my default budget — don't I wish) as I did in Figure 17-6.**

   This will display momentarily when the application launches and before the application has a chance to fill in the real budget. I did that to provide enough room in the label to display the budget.

Alternatively, you can widen the label by selecting it and using the selection points you'll see. Then you'll want to double-click the Label text and delete the text, "Label" — that way nothing will be displayed in the Label when you launch the application.

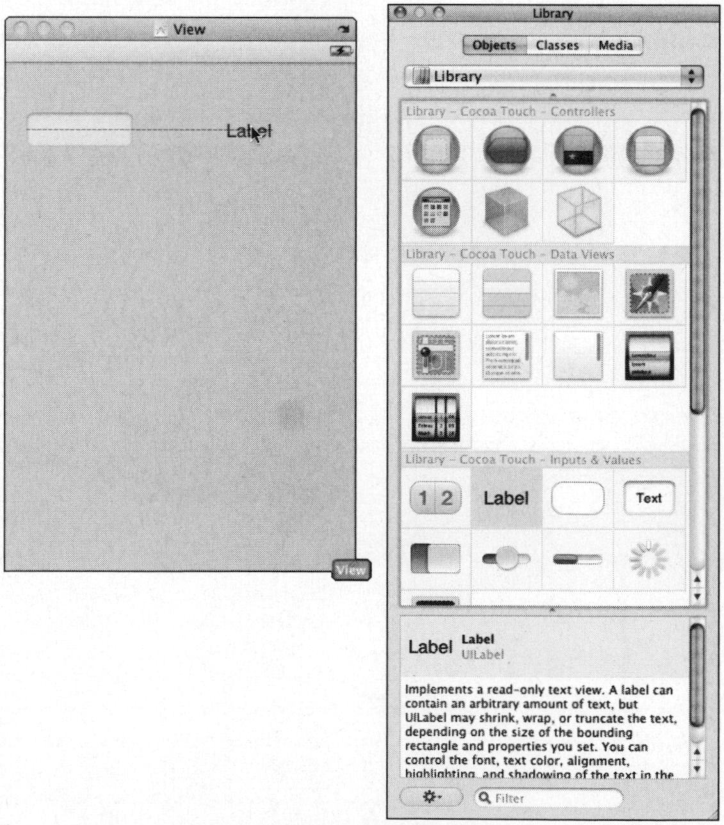

Figure 17-5:
Adding a
Label.

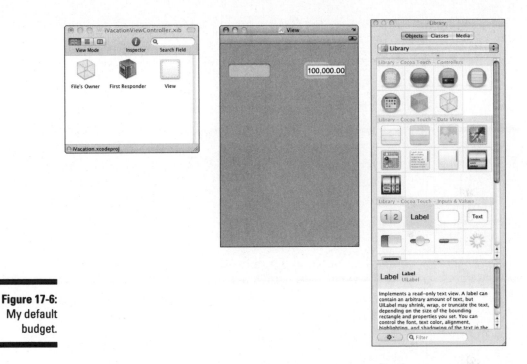

Figure 17-6:
My default
budget.

7. **Drag in two more Labels. Double-click each and enter** `Transaction`
and `Balance`, **respectively.**

8. **Drag in two Round Rect buttons (located between the Label and Text**
items); double-click each; and enter `Cash` **and** `Charge`, **respectively.**

When you are done, your window should look like Figure 17-7.

This is pretty ugly, but it shows you a lot. While I know I said this is a
crash course, I think you ought to do something about the window color.

9. **Click to select the View itself (rather than any of the Labels or the Text**
Field) in the View window and choose Tools⇨Attributes Inspector, or
press ⌘+1.

The Attributes Inspector appears onscreen, as shown in Figure 17-7.

Note the four icons across the top of the Attributes Inspector window.
They correspond to the Attributes, Connections, Size, and Identity
Inspectors, respectively, in the Tools menu.

10. **Click the Background field in the Attributes Inspector.**

A color picker appears. If it is not the crayon box, select the crayon box
button at the top of the Colors window, as shown in Figure 17-7.

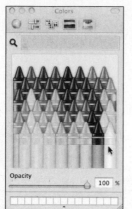

Figure 17-7:
Changing
the back-
ground
color.

11. **Choose the white crayon in the Color Picker to change the View background from gray to white.**

    I chose white because the book's screenshots are in black and white. Feel free to let your imagination soar at this point.

    You can see the results of your color selection in Figure 17-8.

    Now, I want to show you how to do a couple more things to make the user interface a little more iPhone–like.

12. **Click the Label that is displaying 100,000.00.**

    Note that selecting the view rather than the label changes what you see in the Attributes Inspector.

13. **Next to Layout in the Inspector window, select center in the Alignment control, as shown in Figure 17-8.**

    This will keep the amount left in your budget centered over the Balance Label.

    Finally, if you touch in a Text Field on an iPhone or click in one using the simulator, a keyboard is automatically displayed. The default keyboard has both text and numbers, but you can customize the keyboard using the Inspector.

14. **Click Text Field in the View window, click the Keyboard drop-down menu, and select Numbers & Punctuation, as shown in Figure 17-9.**

15. **To see what your user interface will look like on the iPhone, choose File➪Simulate Interface or press ⌘+R. Figure 17-10 shows the final result.**

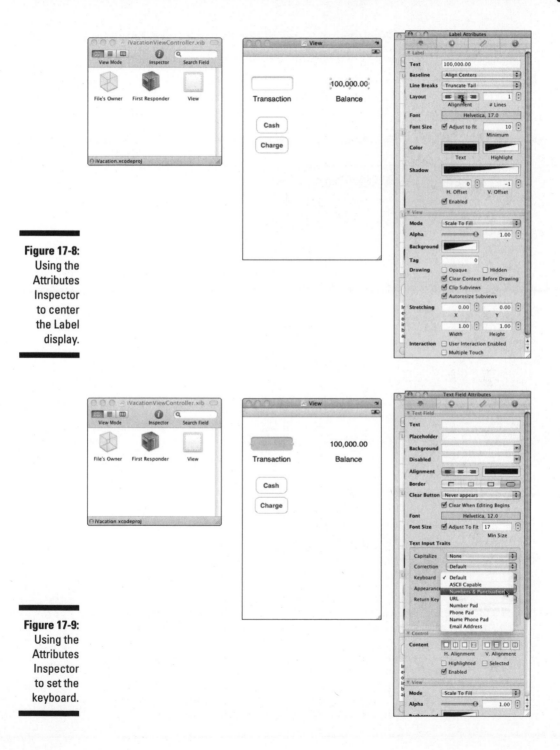

Figure 17-8:
Using the
Attributes
Inspector
to center
the Label
display.

Figure 17-9:
Using the
Attributes
Inspector
to set the
keyboard.

16. Choose File➪Save or press ⌘+S to save what you have done.

17. Make your Xcode window the active window again.

If you can't find it or you minimized it, just click the Xcode icon in the Dock. The iVacation project should still be the active project. (You can always tell the active project by looking at the project name at the top of the Groups & Files pane.)

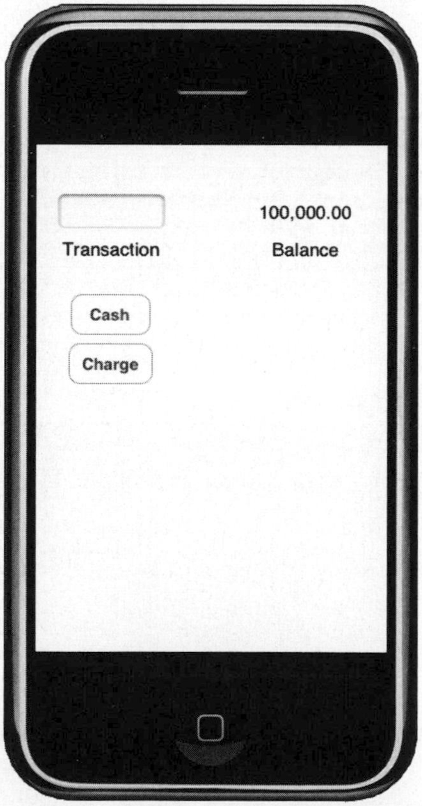

Figure 17-10:
The user interface in all its glory.

At this point, even though you haven't put any of your code into the project, you could build and run the project. Xcode will install it on the iPhone Simulator and launch the Simulator, displaying the user interface.

The simulator allows you to debug your application and do some other testing on your Mac by simulating the iPhone. Instead of touches, though, you'll need to use your mouse. You can also use the keyboard you see on the iPhone, clicking one key at a time using your mouse, or the "real" keyboard on the Mac you're running the simulator on.

This is only a fraction, and a small one at that, of what you can do with Interface Builder. Now it's time to go back to Xcode and do what little coding you need to run your application on the iPhone. Then you'll come back to Interface Builder, and I'll show you how to hook everything up so that when the application is launched, you're ready to go.

Implementing the User Interface in Code

As I promised earlier, the coding you will have to do is minimal to hook up the user interface.

In this section, I extend what you do in Chapter 16. If you want to start from a clean copy of the project from where you left off, you can use the project found in the Chapter 17 Start Here folder, which is in the Chapter 17 folder.

The first thing you'll have to do is copy all of the classes in the Class folder in the Groups & Files list in the Vacation project (from Chapter 16 into the iVacation project). I show you how to do that in Chapter 11 — you can see how to do that in Figure 17-11.

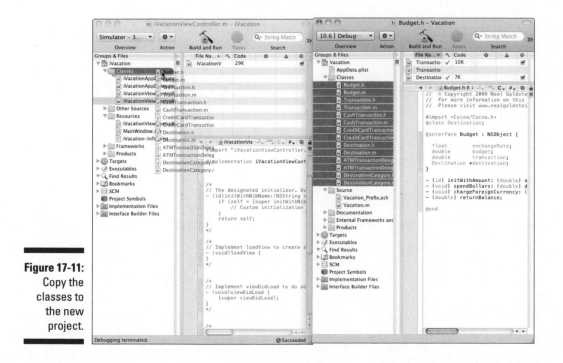

Figure 17-11: Copy the classes to the new project.

Be sure to check Copy when the Copy dialog pops up.

I also could have selected Project⇨Add To Project or pressed ⌘+Option+A, navigated to the Vacation project folder, and selected the classes I wanted to add.

While developing for the iPhone and Mac OS are amazingly similar, there are a few differences.

So far, you have used Cocoa headers. But for iPhone development, you will have to change that. You will need to replace `#import <Cocoa/Cocoa.h>` in the .h files of your classes with `#import <UIKit/UIKit.h>`. You can do that one of two ways.

You can go through all of your .h files and replace the statements one by one. Or you can do a global search and replace. Since I am basically lazy, I'll pick the latter.

1. **Press ⌘+Shift+F, which will bring up the Project Find window that you see in Figure 17-12.**

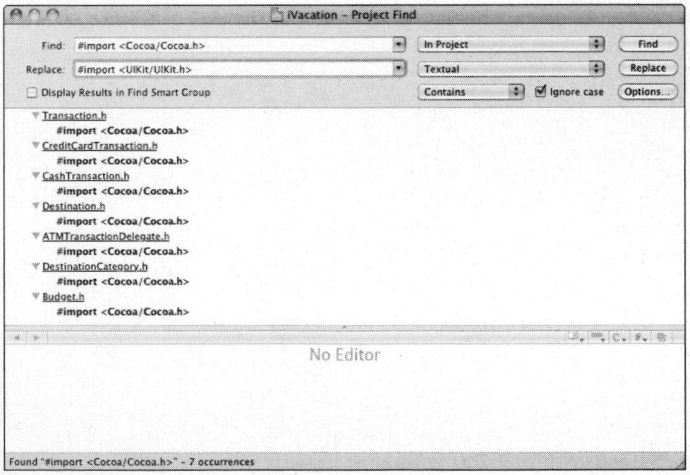

Figure 17-12:
Find and
Replace.

2. **Enter** `#import <Cocoa/Cocoa.h>` **in the Find field (if it's not already there) and click Find. This gives you a list of all the occurrences. There should be seven.**

3. **Enter** `#import <UIKit/UIKit.h>` **and click Replace (see Figure 17-12). You'll see a dialog asking you if you really want to do that. Click Replace, and you'll be ready to go.**

When you create the project, Xcode gives you two classes to start with. The first is the `iVacationAppDelegate` class. This is a *delegate* that is implemented using a formal protocol of the kind I talk about in Chapter 16. If you click the iVacationAppDelegate.h file, you can see the following:

```
@interface iVacationAppDelegate :
                      NSObject <UIApplicationDelegate>
```

If you look in the iVacationAppDelegate.m file, you'll see that `application DidFinishLaunching:` was implemented automatically by the template. Adding code here gives you an opportunity to do application-level initialization. You might want to restore the balance data you have been saving here, for example. You can see that the code here does some fancy footwork with the `viewController` and `window`. In addition, you'll see `dealloc` implemented. You'll also often implement `applicationWillTerminate:`, which will give you an opportunity to do what is necessary before your application shuts down. It is here that you will likely save the balance data. I'll not get into that in this book, but you are welcome to play around with it yourself.

This is a great example of how to create extensible applications using the Objective-C features I explain in Chapter 16. The framework knows how to do everything to create and run a "generic" iPhone application, but it can't know what you need to do for your particular application. To solve that problem, the framework designers created a (formal) UIApplicationDelegate Protocol for you to adopt, with a number of methods you can implement to give you a say in the application running process. As I explain in Chapter 16, this is a situation where the framework has to count on your code because it doesn't know what you want to do to initialize or shut down an application. Subclassing is not an option here (the application object is created at startup, before your individual application is even a glimmer in anyone's eye).

But enough of the interesting stuff; you have to explore that on your own or by reading my book, *iPhone Application Development For Dummies*. What you now will be focusing on is the `iVacationViewController`. In Chapter 11, I explain the Model-View-Controller (MVC) pattern. Understanding it is critical if you are going to develop iPhone apps, so if you are a little foggy on that topic, please refer to Chapter 11. The `iVacationViewController` plays the role of the controller in the MVC pattern. In fact, the view you created in Interface Builder is the view part of the pattern, and all those classes you just added are the model, with the `Destination` object acting as the interface for the controller to the model. See, it does all finally fit together.

The `iVacationViewController` is responsible for getting data from the model to the view (which you created in Interface Builder) to display (that `Balance` label, for example) and for sending messages to the model to update itself with new information (transactions, for example). `iVacation ViewController` is also responsible for view control actions (Text Field input and the Cash and Charge buttons).

You'll start by entering the code necessary to implement these view controller responsibilities.

I'll start with some things you need to add to the iVacationViewController.h file.

1. **Go to the Xcode project window and in the Groups & Files pane, click the triangle next to Classes to expand the folder.**

2. **From the Classes folder, select iVacationViewController.h — the header file for** `iVacationViewController`.

3. **Look for the following lines of code in the header:**

```
#import <UIKit/UIKit.h>

@interface iVacationViewController : UIViewController{


}
@end
```

4. **Type the following six lines of code, indicated in bold, into the iVacationViewController.h file:**

```
#import <UIKit/UIKit.h>
@class Destination;

@interface iVacationViewController : UIViewController
        {

   Destination           *europe;
   IBOutlet UITextField  *transactionField;
   IBOutlet UILabel      *balanceField;

}

- (IBAction)spendDollars:(id)sender;
- (IBAction)chargeCreditCard:(id)sender;

@end
```

`@class Destination` declares the `Destination` class, just as before. The `iVacationViewController` creates the `Destination` object, and `Destination *Europe` is an instance variable the `iVacationView Controller` uses to send messages to `Destination` (the model interface). I'll show you how to implement only a single destination in this example. In a real application, you would probably have an array of destinations instead.

Adding outlets

Next, look at the two IBOutlets:

```
IBOutlet UITextField  *transactionField;
IBOutlet UILabel      *balanceField;
```

As I said, the view controller connects the view to the model. In the view, the user will be entering the amount of a transaction in the UITextField (the object that implements a Text Field) you just added to the view, and you'll be displaying the balance in the UILabel (the object that implements the Label). But in order to get information from the Text Field and update the Label text, you need to know where those objects are. Fortunately, the framework is designed to allow you to do this easily and gracefully. The view controller can refer to objects in the nib (as the .xib file is called) by using a special kind of instance variable referred to as an *outlet*. To access the UITextField and UILabel objects in your iVacation application, you need to do two things:

1. Declare an outlet in your code.

2. Use Interface Builder to point the outlet to the text field in the view you just created.

Then, when your application is initialized, the text field and label outlets are automatically initialized with a pointer to the UITextField and UILabel objects, respectively. You can then use those outlets from within your code to get the text the user entered in the text field and display the balance in the label field. Pretty cool, isn't it?

The first two lines of code here declare the outlets, which will automatically be initialized with a pointer to the text field (transactionField) and label (balanceField) objects when the application is launched. But, while this will happen automatically, it won't *automatically* happen automatically. You have to help a bit, and I'll show you how when you go back to Interface Builder. First, though, you need to examine the IBAction statements.

Implementing Target-Action

If you have a button in your interface, you need to add a method to your code to handle those times when somebody decides to actually tap the button. This involves declaring the action methods for each button in the interface, actually just as you do any other method.

```
- (IBAction)spendDollars:(id)sender;
- (IBAction)chargeCreditCard:(id)sender;
```

Here, I declared two new methods — spendDollars: and chargeCredit Card:. While declaring methods is not new, what is new is the keyword — IBAction.

IBAction is one of those cool little techniques, like IBOutlet, that does nothing in the code but provide a way to inform Interface Builder (hence, the IB in both of them) that this method can be used as an action for Target-Action connections. All IBAction does is act as a tag for Interface Builder — identifying this method (action) as one you can connect to an object (namely the button) in an .nib file. In this respect, the IBAction mechanism is similar to the IBOutlet mechanism I discussed earlier. In that case, however, you were tagging instance variables; while in this case, you are tagging methods. Same difference.

You will see how the IBAction and IBOutlet keywords work later when you launch Interface Builder and connect a button to its iVacationView Controller method. IBAction is actually defined as a void, so if you think about it, all you've done is declare a new method with a return type of void.

```
(IBAction) buttonPressed: (id) sender;
```

is functionally equivalent to

```
(void) buttonPressed: (id) sender;
```

The actual name you give the method can be anything you want, but it must have a return type of IBAction. Usually, the action method takes one argument — typically defined as id, a pointer to the instance variables of an object — which is given the name sender. The control that triggers your action will use the sender argument to pass a reference to itself. So, for example, if your action method is called as the result of a button tap, the argument sender will contain a reference to the specific button that was tapped.

The Target-Action mechanism enables you to create a control object and tell it not only what object you want to handle the event, but also the message to send. For example, if the user touches the Cash button onscreen, you want to send a "spendDollars" message to the view controller. But if the Charge button on the screen is touched, you want to be able to send the same view controller the "chargeCreditCard" message. If you couldn't do that and every button had to send the same message, the coding would be more complex. You would have to determine which button had sent the message and then what to do in response (likely using a switch statement). That would make changing the user interface more work and more error prone.

Having the `sender` argument contain a reference to the specific button that was tapped is a very handy mechanism, even if you're not going to take advantage of that in this application. With a reference to the specific button that was tapped, you can access the variables of the control that was tapped.

What you are doing here is implementing the third of the three major design patterns for applications. The first was *Model-View-Controller*, the second was *Delegation*, and this third one is *Target-Action*.

The Target-Action pattern is used to let your application know that a user has done something. For example, he or she may have tapped a button or entered some text. The control — a button, say — sends a message (the action message) that you specify to the target you have selected to handle that particular action. The receiving object, or the target, is usually a view controller object.

You can also change the target and action dynamically by sending the control `setTarget:` and `setAction:` messages.

Adding the methods

Now that you are finished with the interface specifications, it is time to implement the code.

Okay, you've declared the method; the next thing for you to do is actually add the `spendDollars:` and `chargeCreditCard:` methods to the implementation file, iViewController.m.

1. **Go back to the Classes folder in the Groups & Files list and select iVacationViewController.m — the implementation file for** `iVacation ViewController`.

2. **Look for the following lines of code in the implementation file:**

   ```
   #import "iVacationViewController.h"

   @implementation iVacationViewController
   ```

3. **Add this after** `#import "iVacationViewController.h"`:

   ```
   #import "Destination.h"
   ```

4. **Add the following lines after the** `@implementation iVacation ViewController` **statement:**

```
- (IBAction)spendDollars:(id)sender{

  NSLog (@"Sending a %.2f cash transaction",
                    [transactionField.text floatValue]);
  [europe spendCash:[transactionField.text floatValue]];
  balanceField.text = [[NSString alloc]initWithFormat:
                    @"%.2f",[europe leftToSpend]];
}

- (IBAction)chargeCreditCard:(id)sender {
  NSLog (@"Sending a %.2f credit card transaction",
          [transactionField.text floatValue]);
  [europe chargeCreditCard:[transactionField.text
          floatValue]];
  balanceField.text = [[NSString alloc]initWithFormat:
                    @"%.2f",[europe leftToSpend]];
}
```

Notice that I am still tracking what my program is doing in the Debugger Console.

balanceField.text is a property in the Label object that points to the text the label is supposed to display. What you are having it display, in this case, is a string you created to display the balance.

```
[[NSString alloc]initWithFormat:
                    @"%.2f",[europe leftToSpend]];
```

I want to remind you that when you assign to a property in this way (using the dot syntax), you are actually calling the setter method. You could have coded that statement as

```
[balanceField setText:[[NSString alloc]initWithFormat:
                    @"%.2f", [europe leftToSpend]]];
```

The same thing is also true of transactionField.text. This could have been coded as

```
[europe spendCash:[[transactionField text] floatValue]];
```

This code should look familiar, since it is basically what you have been using for the last several chapters to send transactions to the Destination object. The only difference here is the transaction amount. Instead of the fixed values you have been using, now you are getting the transaction amount the user has entered. You get that by sending a message to the transactionField object in your view, using the outlet you declared in the interface file to retrieve the text the user enters. (Notice how easy it is to turn a string into a float using an NSString method.)

Similarly, instead of the NSLog statement you used to use to display the remaining balance, you are sending a message to the Label through the balanceField outlet to update its text and display it in the view.

This is all the logic you need to connect the model and user interface — of course, there is some plumbing left to do — and to hook up the connections in Interface Builder.

1. **Scroll down the code for iVacationViewController.m until you reach the following lines:**

```
/*
// Implement viewDidLoad to do additional setup after
       loading the view, typically from a nib.
- (void)viewDidLoad
{
    [super viewDidLoad];
}
/*
```

2. **Delete the /* and the */ and add the lines of code in bold:**

```
// Implement viewDidLoad to do additional setup after
       loading the view, typically from a nib.
- (void)viewDidLoad {

    [super viewDidLoad];
    NSString* europeText = [[NSString alloc]
                    initWithFormat: @"%@", @"Europe"];
    europe = [[Destination alloc]
        initWithCountry:europeText andBudget:10000.00
                            withExchangeRate:1.25];
    [europeText release];
    NSString* balanceFieldText = [[NSString alloc]
        initWithFormat:@"%.2f", [europe leftToSpend]];
    balanceField.text = balanceFieldText;
    [balanceFieldText release];
}
```

viewDidLoad is a view controller method that you are *overriding*. Again, there are no surprises here in the code. The only difference is that I added a message to the balanceField to initialize it with the starting budget, which you may have noticed, I bumped up to $10,000. Of course, in a "real" application, you would provide a way for the user to enter the starting budget in a view.

3. **Scroll down the code in iVacationViewController until you reach the following lines:**

```
- (void)dealloc {

    [super dealloc];
}
```

You can press ⌘+F to find something in a single file, as opposed to shift+⌘+F, which finds it in all the project files.

4. **Enter the following lines of code between the** (void)dealloc { **and** [super dealloc]; **lines:**

```
[europe release];
```

5. **Choose File⇨Save or press ⌘+S to save what you have done.**

Connecting Everything Up in Interface Builder and Running iVacation in the Simulator

Now it is time to go back to Interface Builder and hook up the IBOutlets to the text and label fields and the IBActions to the buttons.

1. **In the Groups & Files listing on the left, double-click the iVacation ViewController.xib file.**

2. **Right-click the File's Owner icon in the iVacationViewController. xib window to display a list of connections (see Figure 17-13).**

Figure 17-13:
Connect the outlet to the text field.

There you see the IBOutlets you declared, balanceField and TransactionField under Outlets (ignore the others; you won't be using them) and chargeCreditCard and spendDollars under Received Actions.

Cool isn't it — kind of like getting to the end of a jigsaw puzzle and finally seeing the whole picture.

3. **Click the little circle next to transactionField and drag the blue line to the Text Field, as shown in Figure 17-13, and then let go. Do the same thing for the balanceField, clicking the circle next to it and dragging the blue line to the Label (the 100,000.00 one).**

The buttons work similarly, but there is another step involved.

4. **Click the little circle next to spendDollars and drag the blue line to the Cash button and let go. This time, as you see in Figure 17-14, another list of connections will pop up. Select Touch Up Inside for the connection. Do the same thing for chargeCreditCard and the Charge button.**

The Touch Up Inside is the event that is generated when inside the button is the last place the user touched before lifting his or her finger. This setting is more or less the standard for an iPhone button control like this.

Figure 17-14:
Connecting
the button.

5. **Choose File➪Save or press ⌘+S to save what you have done.**

6. **Go back to the Xcode project window and select the Build and Run button in the Project Window toolbar.**

   This launches the iPhone simulator. Figure 17-15 shows what happens if you click in the Text Field, enter 100 (either clicking on the simulator keyboard or using your Mac keyboard), and then click the Cash button.

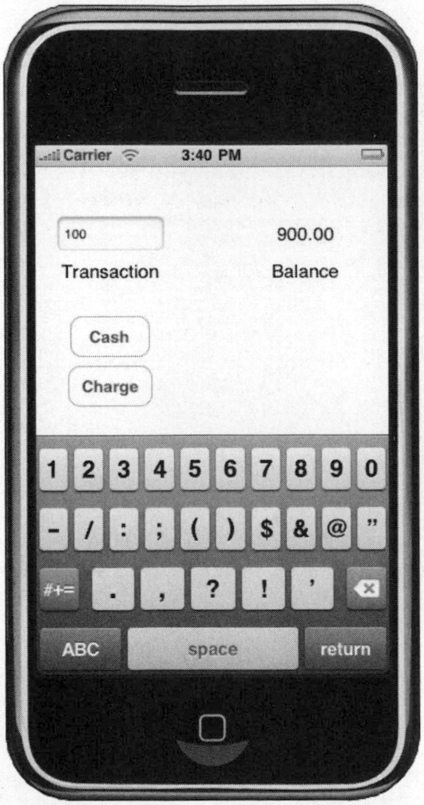

Figure 17-15:
Click in the text field to enter a transaction.

You can find the completed project on the CD in the Example 17 folder, which is in the Chapter 17 folder.

Frankly, I could have done a lot better job with the aesthetics of this user interface, and before showing it to a user I would. If you come up with anything you are proud of, send it to me at http://nealgoldstein.com. I'd love to see it.

A Final Note

This is it! For those of you who haven't programmed before, you may be thinking that just as you expected (and I promised), the programming described in this book is pretty easy. But for those of you with programming experience, the ease with which you can accomplish things using object-oriented programming can be truly breathtaking. I still feel like a kid in candy store when I code this way.

While there is a lot more you'll need to do to turn iVacation into a useful application, including saving data, you now have the knowledge and skill to explore extending this application on your own — so go for it!

Chapter 18

Adding a Mac User Interface

• •

In This Chapter

▶ Painlessly putting a user interface on the model

▶ Using Interface Builder to create a user interface

▶ Adding controls to the view

▶ Creating a view controller

▶ Running the application on the Mac

• •

*I*n this chapter, I keep the second part of the promise I've been talking about since Chapter 11 — if you create the right class structure, putting on a user interface will be easy.

Now that you have seen how easy it is to take your "model" and add an iPhone user interface, I'll show you how to do the same thing for the Mac OS. While the basic idea is the same, there are a few differences in detail that I'll explain.

Creating Your Project

As with the iPhone you will be working in an Xcode project.

1. **Launch Xcode if it is not already running.**

2. **Choose File⇨New Project to create a new project. You can also press Shift+⌘+N.**

3. **In the New Project window (see Figure 18-1), click Application under the iPhone OS heading.**

   Just as before, when you select a template, a brief description of the template is displayed underneath the main pane. As you know, each of these choices is actually a template that generates some code. In the past, when you were using the Foundation Command Line Tool, that code was minimal. Now, however, you are going to see a lot more.

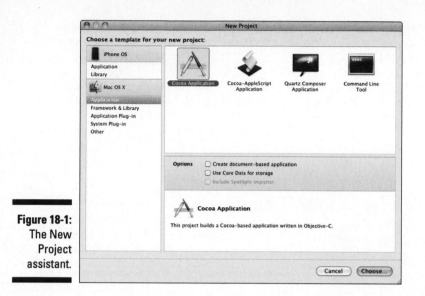

Figure 18-1:
The New
Project
assistant.

4. **Select View-Based Application from the choices displayed and then click Choose.**

   Xcode then displays a standard save sheet.

5. **Enter the name** `mVacation` **in the Save As field, choose a Save location, and click Save.**

   After you click Save, Xcode creates the project and opens the Project window (see Figure 18-2).

Figure 18-2:
The Project
window.

6. **In the Groups & Files list (on the left side of the Project window), click the triangles next to the Classes and Resources folders to expand them.**

You'll notice there is only an `mVacationAppDelegate` class, but nothing corresponding to the `iVacationViewController`. That's one difference between the iPhone and Mac OS X templates. You'll create a class to accomplish the same things that `iVacationViewController` did in the last chapter, but for now go on to Interface Builder.

Using Interface Builder to Create a User Interface

Just as you do in Chapter 17, you use Interface Builder to create your user interface.

1. **In the Resources folder, double-click the MainMenu.xib file.**

You will also see a disclosure triangle next to the MainMenu.xib file. This is part of the localization mechanism (this enables foreign speakers to use your application in their native language), and I won't get into that here (your Xcode configuration may not show this).

Interface Builder launches.

2. **Check to see whether the Library window (at the right in Figure 18-3) is open. If it isn't, open it by choosing Tools⇨Library or ⌘+Shift+L. Make sure Objects is selected in the mode selector at the top of the Library window and select View & Cells in the drop-down menu below the mode selector.**

As you see in Chapter 17, the Library has all the components you can use to build a user interface. This one looks a little different than the one in iPhone though.

MainMenu.xib was created by Xcode when you created the project from the template. In Figure 18-3, as you can see, a *window* is already there, and that's what you will see on the Mac when you launch the application. A menu window is also there, but I won't be getting into that, and you can close it if you like.

Next, you need to add the Mac version of the text field, buttons, and labels that you can use to enter a transaction and have the remaining budget displayed. When your application is launched, those items will be created for you automatically, just as they were on the iPhone.

TIP

Also notice that a warning (the yellow triangle with the exclamation point inside) is in the bottom-right corner of the MainMenu.xib-English window. You probably won't see it on your desktop. It has to do with the resolution I need on one of the multiple monitors on my Mac to capture screen shots.

3. **Scroll down in the Views & Cells view to the Views & Cells - Inputs and Values subheader. Drag a Text Field item from the Library into the View window to add a text entry field (see Figure 18-3).**

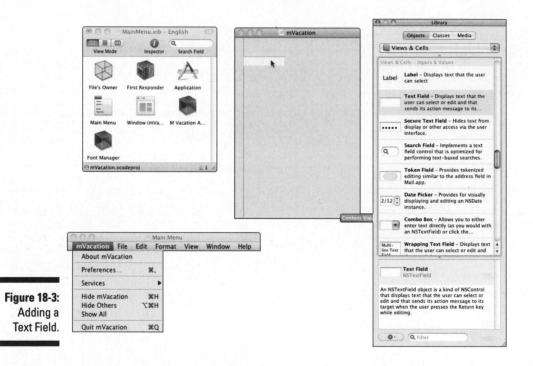

Figure 18-3:
Adding a
Text Field.

A **Text Field item** is just like the text field for the iPhone, although a different class.

4. **Drag a Label item from the Library window over to the View window, as you do in the Chapter 17.**

5. **Double-click the Label to enter** 100,000.00 **(still my default budget, talk about wishful thinking).**

As I explain in Chapter 17, "Using Interface Builder to Create a User Interface" Step 6, this will make the label wide enough to display the budget.

6. **Drag in two more Labels; double-click each one; and enter** `Transaction` **and** `Balance`, **respectively.**

7. **Scroll back up to the top of the Views & Cells view and drag in two Push Buttons.**

8. **Double-click the first button and type** `Cash`. **Do the same thing for the second button, but this time type** `Charge`.

    When you are done, your window should look like Figure 18-4.

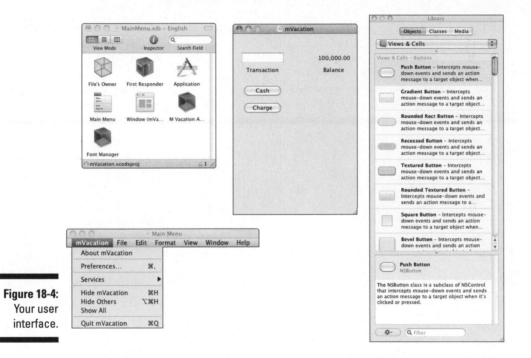

9. **Select the 100,000.00 Label and open the Inspector Window as you do in Chapter 17 by choosing Tools⇨Attributes Inspector or by pressing ⌘+1.**

10. **Select center alignment in Alignment control. This time I left the color the same.**

11. **Choose File⇨Save to save what you have done.**

12. **Make your Xcode window the active window again.**

    If you can't find it, or you minimized it, just click the Xcode icon in the Dock. The mVacation project should still be the active one. (You can always tell the active project by looking at the project name at the top of the Groups & Files pane.)

Implementing the User Interface in Code

Just as on the iPhone, the coding required to hook the user interface to the model is minimal.

If you have been following along with me, I'll be extending what you did in Chapter 16. If you would like to start from a clean copy of the project from where you left off, you can use the project found in the Chapter 18 Start Here folder, which can be found in the Chapter 18 folder.

As with the iPhone application, you will have to copy all of the classes from Chapter 16 into your new project. In Chapter 17, I have you drag them in. You can do it that way or you can use Project⇨Add To Project.

1. **Select the classes folder in the Project window, and select Project⇨Add To Project or press ⌘+Option+A. Navigate to the Vacation Project from Chapter 16 (or whichever project you are using) as I did in Figure 18-5.**

	Name	▲	Date Modified
	Vacation		
▼ **DEVICES**			
Neal Gol...	h ATMTransactionDelegate.h		5/19/09
Test	m ATMTransactionDelegate.m		5/19/09
Macinto...	BalanceData.txt		4:41 PM
iDisk	h Budget.h		6/24/09
	m Budget.m		6/25/09
▼ **SHARED**	build		6/14/09
Neal Gol...	h CashTransaction.h		5/20/09
	m CashTransaction.m		6/25/09
▼ **PLACES**	h CreditCardTransaction.h		5/20/09
Desktop	m CreditCardTransaction.m		6/25/09
neal	h Destination.h		5/20/09
Applicati...	m Destination.m		5/18/09
Documents	h DestinationCategory.h		5/19/09
Applicati...	m DestinationCategory.m		5/20/09
Desktop	h Transaction.h		5/20/09
	m Transaction.m		5/20/09
▼ **SEARCH FOR**	h Vacation_Prefix.pch		4/16/09
Today	Vacation.1		4/16/09
Yesterday	m Vacation.m		4:41 PM
Past Week	Vacation.xcodeproj		4:39 PM
All Images			

Figure 18-5: Adding files to the project.

2. **Again, be sure to check "Copy items into the destination group's folder (if needed)..." when the dialog pops up.**

While developing for the iPhone and Mac OS are amazingly similar, there are a few differences.

In your iPhone project, you deleted `#import <Cocoa/Cocoa.h>` in header files. This time you'll leave them unchanged.

While the iPhone Xcode template you used added a view controller class to your project, in the case of the Mac, you'll have to do that yourself. Here's how:

1. **Select the Classes folder in the Groups & Files list.**

   This tells Xcode to place the new file in the Classes folder.

2. **Select File⇨New File from the main menu (or press ⌘+N) to get the New File dialog.**

3. **In the leftmost column of the dialog, first select Cocoa under Mac OS X; then select the Objective-C class template in the top-right pane. Make sure NSObject is selected in the Subclass of the drop-down menu.**

   You see a new screen asking for some more information.

4. **Enter** mVacationController.m **in the File Name field and make sure the checkbox "Also create mVacationController.m" is checked and then click Finish.**

I start with some things you need to add to the mVacationController.h file.

1. **Go to the Xcode Project window and, in the Groups & Files pane, click the triangle next to Classes to expand the folder.**

2. **From the Classes folder, select mVacationController.h — the header file for mVacationController.**

3. **Look for the following lines of code in the header:**

```
#import <Cocoa/Cocoa.h>
@interface mVacationController : NSObject{


}
@end
```

4. **Add the following six lines of code, indicated in bold, to the mVacation Controller .h file:**

```
#import <Cocoa/Cocoa.h>
@class Destination;


@interface mVacationController : NSObject {
  Destination            *europe;
  IBOutlet NSTextField   *transactionField;
  IBOutlet NSTextField   *balanceField;


}
- (IBAction)spendDollars:(id)sender;
- (IBAction)chargeCreditCard:(id)sender;

@end
```

The first line (@class Destination) declares the Destination class, just as you have been doing so far. The mVacationController will create the Destination object and Destination *Europe; is an instance variable the mVacationController uses to send messages to Destination (the model interface).

Adding outlets, Target-Action, and the methods

The only differences between what you have to do here and what you do in Chapter 17 are that the classes of the Label and the Text Field have changed in the IBOutlet declarations. On the iPhone, you use a UITextField and UILabel; on the Mac OS, you use NSTextField for both.

The two IBAction method declarations — spendDollars: and chargeCreditCard: are the same.

Okay, you've declared the methods; the next thing you need to do is add the spendDollars: and chargeCreditCard: methods to the implementation file, mVacationController.m.

1. **Go back to the Classes folder in the Groups & Files listing and select mVacationController.m — the implementation file for mVacationController.**

2. **Look for the following lines of code in the implementation file:**

   ```
   #import "mVacationController.h"

   @implementation mVacationController
   ```

3. **Add this after** #import "iVacationViewController .h":

   ```
   #import "Destination.h"
   ```

4. **Add the following code after** @implementation mVacation Controller:

   ```
   - (IBAction)spendDollars:(id)sender{

     NSLog (@"Sending a %.2f cash transaction",
             [transactionField.stringValue floatValue]);
     [europe spendCash:
             [transactionField.stringValue floatValue]];
     [balanceField setStringValue:
             [[[NSString alloc]initWithFormat:@"%.2f",
             [europe leftToSpend]]autorelease]];
   }
   ```

```
- (IBAction)chargeCreditCard:(id)sender {

    NSLog (@"Sending a %.2f credit card transaction",
            [transactionField.stringValue floatValue]);
    [europe chargeCreditCard:
            [transactionField.stringValue floatValue]];
    [balanceField setStringValue:
            [[[NSString alloc]initWithFormat:@"%.2f",
            [europe leftToSpend]] autorelease]];
}
```

This is essentially the same thing you do for the iPhone implementation
in Chapter 17 (you can refer to it if you are a little hazy on the topic). The
differences are that instead of `balanceField.text` and `transaction`
`Field.text` that you used on the iPhone, you are using `balanceField.`
`stringValue` and `transactionField.stringValue`. You'll also notice
that this time instead of the dot notation, you are sending a message to the
getters and setters in the "conventional way," and you are using `auto`
`Release` to release the text values you created.

This is all the logic you need to connect the model and user interface. Of
course, just as with the iPhone, there is some plumbing left to do here.

1. **Now you add the following code:**

```
- (void)awakeFromNib {

    [super awakeFromNib];
    NSString* europeText = [[NSString alloc]
                    initWithFormat:@"%@", @"Europe"];
    europe = [[Destination alloc]
            initWithCountry:europeText andBudget:10000.00
            withExchangeRate:1.25];
    [europeText release];
    [balanceField setStringValue:[[[NSString alloc]
            initWithFormat:@"%.2f",
            [europe leftToSpend]] autorelease]];
}
```

This is virtually the same code you add to the `viewDidLoad:` method in
Chapter 17. Instead of `viewDidLoad`, which you *override*, you are going
to use `awakeFromNib`. This is actually an *informal* protocol method, and
classes implement this method to initialize application information after
objects have been loaded from the Interface Builder nib file. An `awake`
`FromNib` message is sent to each object loaded from the nib file after all
the objects in the archive have been loaded and initialized. This is one of
the reasons I explain informal protocols in Chapter 16. This also means
that in order for this method to be invoked, you must have this object
created by the nib loading code. I'll show you how to do that shortly.

2. **You can also add the `dealloc` method while you're at it.**

```
- (void)dealloc {

    [europe release];
    [super dealloc];
}
```

3. **Choose File➪Save to save what you have done.**

Connecting Everything in Interface Builder and Running mVacation on the Mac

Now it is time to go back to Interface Builder and hook up the IBOutlets to the text and label fields and the IBActions to the buttons.

1. **In the Groups & Files listing on the left, double-click the MainMenu. xib file.**

2. **The Library window should still be open, if not open it.**

3. **This time, in the mode selector at the top of the Library window, select Object & Controllers. Then drag an Object icon to the MainMenu.xib - English window, as shown in Figure 18-6.**

4. **Open the Identity Inspector by choosing Tools➪Identity Inspector or press ⌘+6. Make sure the Object icon MainMenu.xib window is still selected and click the Class pop-up menu. Scroll down and select mVacationController as I did in Figure 18-7.**

You do this because when your application is launched, the runtime will go out and load and create the objects in your nib file (there's actually more to it, but this is more or less what happens). Adding an mVacationController object here means that in addition to the window and menu you see on the screen, your mVacationController object will be created automatically as well. That also means the awakeFromNib message will be automatically sent to the method that you just implemented (since it is sent to all objects created from the nib) — all's right with the world.

The next thing you'll do is make the same connections you made to the view controller object (which was already in a nib file thanks to the template), which will initialize the IBOutlets and connect the buttons to the action methods you declared earlier in the IBAction statements.

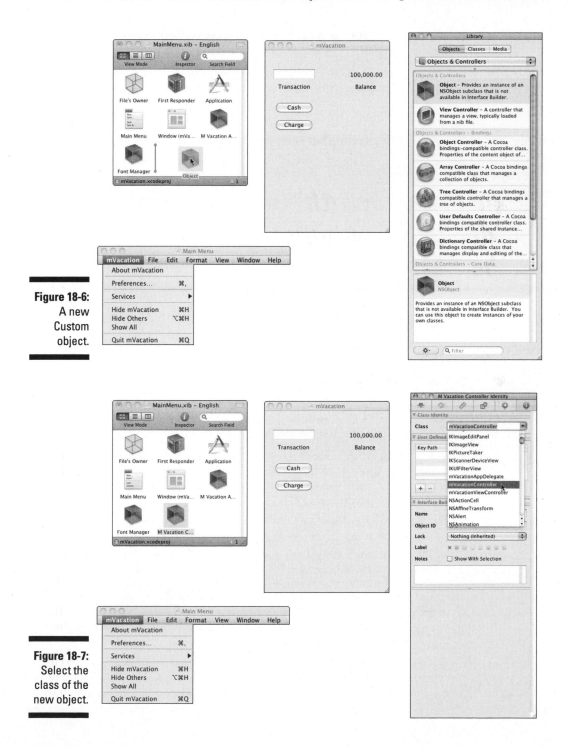

Figure 18-6:
A new
Custom
object.

Figure 18-7:
Select the
class of the
new object.

5. **Right-click the File's Owner icon in the MainMenu.xib window to display a list of connections, just as you do in Chapter 16.**

6. **Click the little circle next to balanceField and drag the blue line to the Label (where it shows 100,000.00), as I did in Figure 18-8, and then let go.**

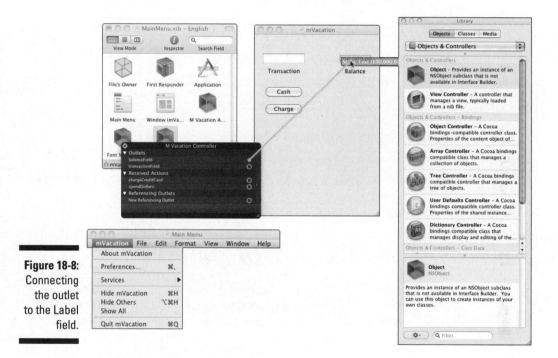

Figure 18-8:
Connecting
the outlet
to the Label
field.

7. **Do the same thing for the transactionField — click the circle next to it and drag the blue line to the Text Field.**

8. **Drag the blue line from the circle next to spendDollars in the Received Actions section to the Cash button and let go. This time you won't have to choose anything when you connect the buttons. Do the same thing for chargeCreditCard and the Charge button.**

When you are done, the result should look like Figure 18-9.

9. **Go back to the Xcode Project window and click the Build and Run button to compile and build the application.**

You can click in the Transaction field to enter a transaction, and then click one of the buttons. In Figure 18-9, you can see that I entered 100 and then clicked the Cash button — and lo and behold, the math works.

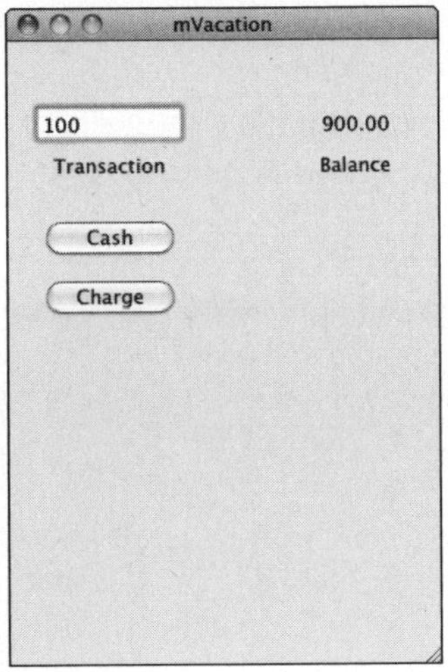

Figure 18-9:
The Mac
version
of the
application.

You can find the completed project on the CD in the Example 17 folder, which is in the Chapter 17 folder.

Knowing What's Left to Do

Just like the iPhone application, you have a little more to do. Besides the cosmetics and additional application functionality — for example, the menu and other user interface functionality expected by the user of a Mac application.

The End of the Beginning

Now that you've finished *Objective-C For Dummies,* your adventure really starts.

Go out there and write programs, and let me know how you are doing. You'll find information and ideas about programming and design on my Web site, www.nealgoldstein.com.

Until then — happy programming until we meet again.

Part V
The Part of Tens

The 5th Wave   By Rich Tennant

In this part . . .

Along the way, I have been sprinkling words of wisdom based on not just my own but also other developers' collective experience. In this part, I codify some of them.

First, I talk a bit about debugging and give you some tips on both avoiding bugs and where and how to look for them. Bugs are inevitable, so it's better to take a Zen-like approach and "be at one" with the debugging process.

Finally, I close by giving you some ideas about how to avoid the kinds of problems most new developers encounter in their first few applications. Think of this as a map of places to avoid when you are alone at night, around 3:00 a.m. in a strange city.

Chapter 19

Ten Debugging Tips

*W*hen you're developing an application, there are always a few things that initially don't work out quite the way you planned. That means you will have to go through your code and determine what happened, and more importantly, what to do about it.

Check for Semicolons

Semicolons are the heart and soul of Objective-C statements, and leaving one out can cause incredible havoc. For some reason, forgetting to end a statement with one is something I'm pretty good at. So when I see a lot of errors and warnings, especially if I've just added a few lines of code, semicolons are one of the first things I check.

"Right" Is Not Always "right"

Remember, Objective-C is case-sensitive and `For` is not the same thing as `for`. Using the wrong case can send the complier into a tizzy, and while you will get warnings and errors, what you have done may not always be obvious.

When You've Blown It, You've Blown It

It's generally better to ignore the subsequent errors after the first syntax error because they may be the result of that first error. This is especially true when you leave out `#import` statements (or spell them wrong) or forget a semicolon or comma, or colon, or anything else the complier uses to make sense of your statements.

Compiler Warnings Are for Your Own Good

You may get only one chance to pay attention to a compiler warning. If you don't make any changes to the file that generated the warning, you won't see the warning the next time you build your program, although if you keep the Build Results window open and you have All Results Selected, you will still see them.

You can also select Build⇨Clean All Targets to rebuild everything, and you probably should on a regular basis.

Don't Forget about Memory Errors

Look for memory errors. Remember, only you (and your best friend, the Static Analyzer) can prevent memory leaks.

While it's bad enough when you don't release something and you cause a memory leak, it's just as bad (and maybe even worse) when you do release something that you end up sending a message to later. Your program will crash, and tell you why (EXC_BAD_ACCESS) but you won't have a clue where to start. Be sure to retain objects you don't create yourself (sent as a method argument, for example) if you want to continue to use them.

Get Friendly with Your Debugger

The debugger has a lot of features that can really help you. Breakpoints are especially helpful. Take the compiler out for a date some time and really get to know it.

While intuitively obvious (although in the heat of the moment after a program crash, you may forget), try reading what the Debugger Console says. For example

```
2009-06-30 09:33:07.148 Vacation[2048:a0f] *** Terminating
app due to uncaught exception NSInvalidArgumentException',
reason: '-[NSCFNumber doublValue]: unrecognized selector
sent to instance 0x102a10'
```

makes things pretty obvious. Although not covered here, you should also get to know the commands that you can type into the Debugger Console.

Messages to nil

In Objective-C, you can send messages to a `nil` object. While this enables lots of features, in some cases it will make you crazy trying to figure out why something doesn't work the way it should.

Dialing a Wrong Number

One of the great features of Objective-C is its implementation of polymorphism. As long as the object has implemented the method you are sending the message to, Objective-C will let you send the object that message. Sometimes, however, that object may not be the one you wanted to send the message to, so be careful of that concern.

Create a "Paper" Trail

I am a big fan of NSLog. Sure, the debugger gives you a stack trace, and you can use breakpoints, but NSLog can create a narrative of what is going on. Use it to display where you are in your code and the value of variables. Using all of the tools available gives you the best chance of fixing that bug before the next SDK and all those new devices are released.

Just be careful, though, because NSLog can also be a source of bugs — ironic but true. If you try to use a C String like ("I'm here"), you will get complier warnings. If you try to display a non-object using the %@ string formatter, you may cause a program crash. What is more insidious, though, is when you use the wrong formatter, and you don't get what you expect, and you spend hours tracking it down, only to find you were trying to display an int as a float.

Incrementally Test

Most software developers quickly figure out that incremental development is the way to go. Write a method and try to test it immediately if you can, even if it means just putting in NSLog statements to examine the output. It is a lot easier to debug 15 lines of code than to try to figure out why the 200 lines of code you've been working on for two days don't work the way you expect.

Use Your Brain

I do use all the tools and tips I just gave you to track down bugs, but for logic errors, which are by far the hardest, I actually find thinking about it first is the fastest way to a solution. I find two approaches useful. First, start by trying to figure out what would have to be true for this to happen, and then see if that's the fact. A second way is to ask, "How could I have made this happen if I'd wanted it to." And then go look to see if that's what you did.

Chapter 20

Ten Ways to Be a Happy Developer

In This Chapter

▶ Limiting dependencies to what objects do, not how they do it

▶ Creating code that is easy to understand

▶ Following memory management rules

▶ Initializing the right way

▶ Using the documentation

▶ Practicing your coding

▶ Understanding the development process

▶ Trying to get it right the first time

▶ Knowing what's important — that the software works

▶ Planning ahead to extend your code

▶ Keeping it fun

I really like writing software. When I first started I couldn't believe that they would actually pay me to do something that was so much fun (believe me, I quickly got over that). Along the way I've learned a few ways make my life as a developer easier.

Keep Everyone in the Dark

One of the things that can really cause you problems as you develop your application is building into your code "detailed" knowledge about how things in your program work. This ranges from data structures, to instance variable visibility (to other objects), to how methods work, to the basic structure of the program. As I spoke about more than once, you want to make sure you keep your objects as ignorant as you can about their environment. While there will always be some dependency whenever one object uses another, limit those dependencies to what other objects do rather than to how they do it, and limit the number of objects each one uses.

Similarly, avoid the compulsion to create switch statement–like control structures that determine the order in which objects get called and that dole out instructions to them. The best object-oriented programs have their objects work like a team, with everyone playing their roles and doing their part rather than the traditional hierarchical command and control structure where someone is in charge and tells everyone else what to do.

Sergeant Schultz of *Hogan's Heroes* captured the spirit of object-oriented programming with his trademark line:

"I hear nothing, I see nothing, I know nothing!"

Make Your Code Easy to Understand

Often developers think comments are for other people who are reading your code. In reality, think about them as being for yourself when you are picking up some code you wrote six months ago. It will amaze you how foreign it can appear. I suggest the following:

✔ Use comments often, but especially when you are doing something clever — especially if it took you a while to figure out how to do something in the first place.

✔ Name your classes with descriptive names.

✔ Do the same thing with method names.

✔ Do the same thing with both local and instance variables.

✔ Take advantage of argument names in method declarations to let you know what each argument is for.

Remember Memory

While Mac OS X 10.56 does have an opt-in garbage collection function, the iPhone does not, so if you are developing for the iPhone or an earlier version of the Mac OS without garbage collection, this is something you need to pay attention to early on in your program. Follow the memory management rules in Chapter 13.

✔ Memory management is really about creating pairs of messages. Balance every `alloc`, `new`, and `retain` with a `release`.

✔ When you assign an instance variable using an accessor with a `retain` property attribute, you now own the object. When you're done with it, you'll need to release it (or set it to `nil`).

Start by Initializing the Right Way

Even though it is just about as unglamorous as things get, initialization is extremely important. Don't try and back-fit later in your development cycle, do it correctly from the start. Always use the form

```
- (id) init…: {

  if (self = [super …]) {
    your initialization goes here
  }
  return self;
}
```

Take Advantage of the Documentation

This may sound silly, but it's a good idea to actually read the documentation if you want to know how something works. What I find myself doing when I am learning something new, control right-click on a symbol and then select Find Text in Documentation — I use this all the time.

There is of course search in the Help menu, and Option double-click on a symbol to bring up Quick Help. Also, these two Apple Dev Center sites have a plethora of reference material:

```
http://developer.apple.com/iphone/
http://developer.apple.com/mac/
```

Code Code Code

Every book I write has a few themes running through it, and one of those in this book is code code code. My experience, both personally and in teaching, is that the more you type — that is, the more code you actually write — the more you learn, and the faster you learn it.

You should try things out to see how they work. For example, experiment with similar methods to see how they work differently. Try everything out to make sure that when you invoke a method, you can predict what the result will be. Let your curiosity run free, and if something intrigues you, go explore it. And don't worry, there's nothing you can do in an Xcode application that will break anything in Xcode, much less take down your entire system. This isn't Windows, after all.

Understand that Development Is Not Linear

Development is not linear. In this book, I talked about showing you how to do something, and then having you delete the code and try it a different or better way. If I'm trying something new, I'll often just code a rough version of it to make sure I understand the basics before things get complicated.

You'll find yourself creating a rough application structure, implementing a few classes, seeing if the idea works, and then going back and refining it, especially when it comes to using inheritance and polymorphism. Personally, even if I know I will have class hierarchy, like I did with `Transaction`, I'll build out one concrete example of it — say `CashTransaction` — and make sure it works. Then I create the superclass and the first subclass and make sure I get the same results, and then go on to create other subclasses. This is known as *factoring* your code, and it's all in a day's work.

Do It Right from the Start if You Need to Do It Right from the Start

I just talked about the nonlinear approach to development: building something to see how it works and then doing it the right way. While that works for some things, it doesn't work for a few other things over a long term. There are things you have to start doing the right way from day one of development, including the following:

- ✔ Building your application using the Model-View-Controller pattern
- ✔ Initialization
- ✔ Memory management
- ✔ Localization (I haven't covered this but there's lots of information available on it, including an introduction in *iPhone Application Development For Dummies*)
- ✔ Error handling

While you might not always do them exactly right from the get-go, you better go back and do them before you get very far — it becomes an enormously error-prone task to back-fit these. I still have nightmares about going back and retrofitting my first iPhone program to correctly manage memory.

Avoid the Code Slinger Mentality

Some programmers get so carried away with the purity of the language and programming that they'll spend days arguing about a point that, in the long run, makes no difference to how well your program actually works.

Also avoid cleverness as much as you can, as well as excessive nesting of statements. If clarity requires a few more lines of code, you are always better off in the long run.

This is a good time to point out that your main interest should be in developing great applications, while quickly working through differences (often style issues) that make no difference. Usually, if there is equal passion on both sides, each side has its pros and cons, and no one is really "right."

I like to keep in mind a quotation from Voltaire:

> *The perfect is the enemy of the good.*

The Software Isn't Finished until the Last User Is Dead

If there is one thing I can guarantee about app development, it's that Nobody Gets It Right the First Time. The design for all applications evolves over time, as you learn the capabilities and intricacies of the platform; as user behavior changes in response to your application; and as the users, based on usage, get a better idea of what they can do with technology.

Object orientation makes extending your application (not to mention fixing bugs) easier, so pay attention to the principles.

Keep It Fun

This is another one of those ongoing themes in this and my other books (and personally in my life as well). Programming is inherently fun (at least once you get going), and the point is to keep it that way.

It's important to remember this when you have spent hours trying to debug your program, and you think all is lost. Don't worry; you'll eventually figure it out. You wrote it, after all.

Take a break, play a game, go for a walk, or e-mail me ruing the day you started programming. Whatever works — then go back, and (perhaps) miraculously what you need to do will become obvious.

Appendix

About the CD

This appendix shows you what's on the CD and how to access it. I also give you some tips for troubleshooting, just in case you run into problems.

On the CD

The CD that accompanies this book has a folder for each chapter starting with Chapter 4 (except for Chapter 10). These are located in the Author directory on the CD. In each of these chapter folders, you will find a folder that contains the Xcode project that provides the starting point for each chapter. The folders are labeled by chapter. So for Chapter 4, for example, you see a folder labeled Chapter 4 Start Here.

In that same chapter folder, you'll find a folder that contains the final version of the project for each chapter (except for Chapter 4 where it isn't applicable). Some chapters will also have intermediate versions that will labeled (using Chapter 5 as an example) Chapter 5 A, Chapter 5 B, and so on. I'll explain what is in each.in the corresponding chapter.

System Requirements

Make sure that your computer meets the minimum system requirements shown in the following list. If your computer doesn't match up to most of these requirements, you may have problems using the software and files on the CD. For the latest and greatest information, please refer to the ReadMe file located at the root of the CD-ROM.

- A Macintosh running Apple OS X 10.5 or later
- An Internet connection
- A CD-ROM or DVD-ROM drive

If you need more information on the basics, check out *Macs For Dummies* by Edward C. Baig (Wiley).

Using the CD

To install the items from the CD to your hard drive, follow these steps.

1. **Insert the CD into your computer's CD-ROM drive.**

   The license agreement appears.

   When the CD icon appears on your desktop, double-click the icon to open the CD and double-click the Start icon.

2. **Read through the license agreement and then click the Accept button if you want to use the CD.**

   The CD interface appears. The interface allows you to browse the contents and install the programs with just a click of a button (or two).

What You'll Find on the CD

All the examples provided in this book are located in the Author directory on the CD and work with Macintosh computers. These files contain much of the sample code from the book. The structure of the Author directory is

```
Author/Chapter 1
Author/Chapter x
```

Troubleshooting

I tried my best to create examples that work on most computers with the minimum system requirements. Alas, your computer may differ, and some examples may not work properly for some reason.

The likeliest problem is that you don't have enough memory (RAM). You can have your local computer store add more RAM to your computer. Adding more memory can really help the speed of your computer and allow more programs to run at the same time.

Customer Care

If you have trouble with the CD-ROM, please call Wiley Product Technical Support at 800-762-2974. Outside the United States, call 317-572-3993. You can also contact Wiley Product Technical Support at `http://support.wiley.com`. Wiley Publishing will provide technical support only for installation and other general quality control items. For technical support on the applications themselves, consult the program's vendor or author.

To place additional orders or to request information about other Wiley products, please call 877-762-2974.

Index

Wiley Publishing, Inc.
End-User License Agreement

READ THIS. You should carefully read these terms and conditions before opening the software packet(s) included with this book "Book". This is a license agreement "Agreement" between you and Wiley Publishing, Inc. "WPI". By opening the accompanying software packet(s), you acknowledge that you have read and accept the following terms and conditions. If you do not agree and do not want to be bound by such terms and conditions, promptly return the Book and the unopened software packet(s) to the place you obtained them for a full refund.

1. **License Grant.** WPI grants to you (either an individual or entity) a nonexclusive license to use one copy of the enclosed software program(s) (collectively, the "Software") solely for your own personal or business purposes on a single computer (whether a standard computer or a workstation component of a multi-user network). The Software is in use on a computer when it is loaded into temporary memory (RAM) or installed into permanent memory (hard disk, CD-ROM, or other storage device). WPI reserves all rights not expressly granted herein.

2. **Ownership.** WPI is the owner of all right, title, and interest, including copyright, in and to the compilation of the Software recorded on the physical packet included with this Book "Software Media". Copyright to the individual programs recorded on the Software Media is owned by the author or other authorized copyright owner of each program. Ownership of the Software and all proprietary rights relating thereto remain with WPI and its licensers.

3. **Restrictions on Use and Transfer.**

   (a) You may only (i) make one copy of the Software for backup or archival purposes, or (ii) transfer the Software to a single hard disk, provided that you keep the original for backup or archival purposes. You may not (i) rent or lease the Software, (ii) copy or reproduce the Software through a LAN or other network system or through any computer subscriber system or bulletin-board system, or (iii) modify, adapt, or create derivative works based on the Software.

   (b) You may not reverse engineer, decompile, or disassemble the Software. You may transfer the Software and user documentation on a permanent basis, provided that the transferee agrees to accept the terms and conditions of this Agreement and you retain no copies. If the Software is an update or has been updated, any transfer must include the most recent update and all prior versions.

4. **Restrictions on Use of Individual Programs.** You must follow the individual requirements and restrictions detailed for each individual program in the "About the CD" appendix of this Book or on the Software Media. These limitations are also contained in the individual license agreements recorded on the Software Media. These limitations may include a requirement that after using the program for a specified period of time, the user must pay a registration fee or discontinue use. By opening the Software packet(s), you agree to abide by the licenses and restrictions for these individual programs that are detailed in the "About the CD" appendix and/or on the Software Media. None of the material on this Software Media or listed in this Book may ever be redistributed, in original or modified form, for commercial purposes.